Poetry Does Theology

CHAUCER, GROSSETESTE, AND THE *PEARL*-POET

Jim Rhodes

University of Notre Dame Press

NOTRE DAME, INDIANA

Manufactured in the United States of America

Library of Congress Cataloging-in-Publication Data

Rhodes, James Francis, 1940–
     Poetry does theology: Chaucer, Grosseteste, and the Pearl-Poet / Jim
Rhodes.
          p. cm.
Includes bibliographical references and index.
     ISBN 0-268-03869-4 (alk. paper)—ISBN 0-268-03870-8 (pbk.: alk. paper)
     1. Christian poetry, English (Middle)—History and criticism. 2. Theology in
literature. 3. English poetry—Middle English, 1100–1500—History and
criticism. 4. Grosseteste, Robert, 1175?–1253—criticism and interpretation.
5. Langland, William, 1330?–1400. Piers the Plowman. 6. Chaucer, Geoffrey,
d. 1400. Canterbury tales. 7. Theology—History—Middle Ages, 600–1500.
8. Patience (Middle English poem). 9. Purity (Middle English Poem). 10. Pearl
(Middle English poem). I. Title.
     PR317.T53 R48 2001
     821'.109382—dc21   2001002735

∞ This book was manufactured using acid-free paper.

For Meg, in love and friendship

Contents

Contents

Preface

When, in the epilogue to the Man of Law's tale, Chaucer's Host invites
the Parson to entertain the group by delivering a sermon, the Shipman
or, more plausibly, the Wife of Bath, vehemently protests: "Nay, by my
fader soule, that schal he nat! / ... Heer schal he nat preche; / He schal
no gospel glosen here ne teche."[1] The Shipman, who is worried that the
Parson will compromise the spirit of the tale-telling game, suggests that
he, or his "joly body," will tell a tale instead, one that "schal waken al
this compaignye." It is not that the Shipman or any other pilgrim is op-
posed to religious instruction ("We leven alle in the grete God," he says),
because many of the pilgrims speak freely and at great length on theo-
logical or biblical topics. Rather, the pilgrims prefer to debate and dis-
cuss the theological issues that concern them through the medium of a
poem or fiction. The game in which the pilgrims are engaged on the
road to Canterbury has its own rules, which permits a Miller to disagree
with a Knight, or a Shipman or Wife to supplant a Parson with his or her
own moral outlook. That is, the game enables the pilgrims to address
the moral and ethical issues of their day by transforming the discourse
of the theologians or of the pulpit into fictions. The stories they tell are
equally capable of sowing difficulty or sprinkling cockle in someone's
"clene corn," but, as fictions, they have less authority than a sermon and
pose no immediate threat to one's personal beliefs. The Wife of Bath
certainly knows the difference because she is free to deliver one but not
the other. It is this special mixture of play and seriousness that distin-
guishes the tale from a sermon. For, as Theodor Adorno says, "Art, which,
like knowledge, takes all its material and ultimately its forms from re-
ality, indeed from social reality, in order to transform them, thereby be-
comes entangled in reality's irreconcilable contradictions.... As some-
thing that has escaped from reality and is nevertheless permeated with it,
art vibrates between this seriousness and light heartedness. It is this ten-
sion which constitutes art."[2]

In keeping with Adorno, this study will insist that poetry can and should be treated as a separate discourse which works according to rules quite different from those operative in other modes of didactic writing. As one reader of this manuscript remarked, "this book could be called old-fashioned in its refusal of the kinds of historicism currently dominant in Middle English studies, with their emphasis on culture and politics, not aesthetics, and their refusal to isolate 'literature' as a special realm of inquiry and interest." And so it is. I have never wavered in my teaching and in my writing from the view that poetry is an inventive and utterly serious mode of exploration of issues that matter and in that endeavor it is neither transparent nor able to be ignored. Obviously, not everyone agrees with this approach. For the skeptical reader I can only suggest that he or she "Taketh the fruyt, and lat the chaf be stille."

In the course of writing this book I have incurred a heavy debt to friends and colleagues who have been unstinting both in their support and in helping me to separate the fruit from the chaff in my own thinking and writing. With deep gratitude I now acknowledge their generosity. First, I want to thank Barbara Hanrahan at the University of Notre Dame Press for her confidence in me and in my manuscript, for her judicious selection of readers who proved an immense help in the revision of the original text, and for her guidance through the entire process. One could not ask for a more knowing or congenial editor. I also want to thank Jeannette Morgenroth and her staff at JM Book Packaging for the highly professional fashion in which they proofed and prepared the manuscript, and I want to thank Jea in particular for her good counsel, her sense of humor, and her readiness to address any and all questions and concerns that I had along the way. For their encouragement and many helpful suggestions, I owe many thanks to David Aers, Malcolm Andrew, Sarah Beckwith, Joan Bernstein, Andrew Galloway, Anabel Patterson, Lee Patterson, Al Shoaf, and Peter Travis. I single out three individuals for the special help that I received from them. The first is Pete Wetherbee, that beacon of integrity and encouragement, who read early versions of some chapters and offered very solid advice to improve them. He prevented me from doubting myself and contributed in intangible ways to the completion of the work. Now, if there were only some way that I could make it possible for the Red Sox to win the World Series. Nicholas Watson read the manuscript as thoroughly and as critically as anyone could ever ask or imagine. His comments and suggestions were constructive and directed toward improving the quality and clarity of my arguments, particularly in places where we had serious disagreement. I especially want to thank Richard Neuse for introducing me to the world of medieval studies. Richard has been a mentor, advisor, and, above all, a friend. He taught me to see and to see better. Thanks, Rich. Finally, I want to thank Erin and Byron for being the wonderful children that they are. Special thanks go to Meg Bellinger, whose loving support makes all struggles worth enduring.

Earlier versions of parts of chapter 3 were published previously as "Vision and History in *Patience*," *Journal of Medieval and Renaissance Studies* 19 (1989): 1–13; and "The Dreamer Redeemed: Exile and the Kingdom in the Middle English *Pearl*," *Studies in the Age of Chaucer* 16 (1994): 119–42.

ONE

Poetry and Theology

Literature is always unrealistic, but its very unreality permits it to question the world—though these questions can never be direct: starting from a theocratic explanation of the world, Balzac finally does nothing but interrogate. Thus the author existentially forbids himself two kinds of language, whatever the intelligence or the sincerity of his enterprise: first, *doctrine,* since he converts despite himself, by his very project, every explanation into a spectacle: he is always an inductor of ambiguity; second, *evidence, . . .* by identifying himself with language, the author loses all claim to truth, for language is precisely that structure whose very goal (at least historically, since the Sophists), once it is no longer rigorously transitive, is to neutralize the true and the false. But what he obviously gains is the power to disturb the world, to afford it the dizzying spectacle of *praxis* without sanction.

Roland Barthes[1]

1.

Transforming Theological Discourse:
A Theoretical and Practical Approach

One of the distinctive contributions of the work in medieval studies during the last two decades of the twentieth century has been the effort to show the impact theology, specifically vernacular theology (in the form of sermons, pamphlets, conversations, treatises, hymns, and works of art), has had on social, political, and moral developments in the period from the twelfth to the fourteenth century.[2] This is a welcome change from past practice, which tended to treat theology as if it were an obstacle to change. While viewing theology as an integral part—the cornerstone even—of fourteenth-century English culture, the present study will

1

resist the postmodern tendency to treat a theologically inspired poetry as simply another form of vernacular theology. The intention here is not to privilege poetry but to offset the growing tendency to reduce poetry to the status of a document and to show that poetry is a significant discourse unto itself and that it has its own interests.[3]

What happens, then, when poetry deals explicitly with a serious theological issue? The purpose of this study is to provide an answer to that question through a detailed analysis of the symbiotic relationship that existed between poetry and theology in the fourteenth century in England, with special attention to the narrative poems of Geoffrey Chaucer, Robert Grosseteste, the *Pearl*-poet, the author of *Saint Erkenwald,* and, in a lesser role here, William Langland. *Symbiosis* may be defined as a relationship that is mutually beneficial or supportive, or it may be a close, prolonged association of two or more different organisms of different species that may but does not necessarily benefit each member. Both definitions characterize the relationship between poetry and theology in the fourteenth century because the relationship underwent radical transformation as the century progressed. At the beginning of the century, poetry is dependent on theology. As poetry begins to discover its own voice and poets become more conscious of themselves as poets, the relationship becomes increasingly complex and problematical. By the end of the century we have, in the works of Chaucer and his contemporaries, a body of poetry that still draws on theology, sometimes heavily, but is no longer continuous with it.

These poets, I shall argue, epitomize what is most English about English poetry in the fourteenth century and their poetry reflects what is distinctive about English theology in the era. They differ, often dramatically, in the way they approach and represent theological problems in their poetry, but they share an interest in one issue common to all of their poetry, the matter of human dignity. For, these poets are writing at the tail end of a linguistic and theological revolution, when revisionary perspectives on the creation and the incarnation gave birth to a new humanistic spirit that helped to transform late medieval theological culture and also helped to spur the development of both vernacular theology and vernacular poetry. It is my contention that these poets were not only familiar with the theological developments of their day; they also apprehended the deeper impulse behind them—the drive for human autonomy and the search for historical goals that were temporal and humanly realizable—and they produced a poetry that was socially oriented and consciously designed either "to support a contemporary ethic or incite to change."[4] Accordingly, the theological focus for this study is an English religious culture characterized by a semi-Pelagian, anthropocentric theology, which culminates in the fourteenth century under the aegis, roughly speaking, of Ockhamist theology. That is, this study will focus primarily on a theology that is incarnational, one that affirms human dignity and the sanctity of the human body.[5]

Taken as a whole, the aim of this study is to show that what previously had been the exclusive prerogative of a Latinate and clerical elite became in the later Middle Ages matters for widespread concern within vernacular culture, and specifically within the emerging category of "literature." This newly defined and self-conscious literature, moreover, provided not simply an arena within which theological questions could be raised but also privileged a secularist or humanist outlook that granted to earthly life its own legitimacy and dignity. In short, I am suggesting that one of the distinctive qualities of modernity—its secularist and this-worldly orientation—is a phenomenon that takes root in England in the fourteenth century and finds its primary site of development not in theological or philosophical circles per se but in a literature that opens for inquiry the theological and philosophical questions that dominated the era.[6]

I will attempt to ground the preceding assertions in three stages of argument. In the first stage I will outline both the historical and theoretical framework for my discussion of the relationship between poetry and theology in the fourteenth century, showing where the two discourses converge and where they diverge. The historical discussion is complemented by a theoretical framework, largely Wolfgang Iser's, and capped by an example from Dante, whose *Comedy* enacts a union of poetry and theology emulated by poets for generations to come. The second phase connects the poetry of Chaucer and his contemporaries with the rise of humanism[7] and with the *metamorphosis of scholastic discourse*, the crisis in language (and truth) that deepened during the period from the twelfth to the fourteenth century.[8] The third stage treats Chaucer's *Nun's Priest's Tale* as a particular instance of the metamorphosis of theological discourse. Monica McAlpine has shown that this tale is the one where

Chaucer "deploys, in place of the theologian's logical analysis and scriptural exegesis, the resources of art to explore the implications of a major concept about the human condition."[9] The Nun's Priest is a priest and a poet, torn between his priestly desire for the truth—epitomized in his frustration and impatience with the discourse of the clerks who cannot arrive at any unanimity of opinion on free will and predestination—and his poetic distrust of all modes of discourse or rhetoric, evidenced most humorously in Chauntecleer's free translation / interpretation of the *In principio* (as vivid an example of what poetry does to theology as one could ask for). The Nun's Priest is, in short, a master ironist in Richard Rorty's sense of the term. Rorty's ironist is a nominalist and historicist, always aware of the contingency and fragility of his *final vocabulary* and thus of himself.[10] Accordingly, the Nun's Priest's poetic narrative does not manage to bring the debate to its conclusion; it offers only a *redescription* or new description of events.[11] If the priest tells us to take the fruit and let the chaff be still, the poet has taught us that meaning is in the story and not in a moral tacked onto the text.

Subsequent chapters open with a consideration of the kind of theological problems and questions that are either presupposed or structured in the particular poem under review, including such issues as why God became man, the fate of the virtuous pagans, the role of the church in the world, the meaning of the beatitudes, and the nature of pilgrimage. (This is not a random list but follows the thematic structure outlined earlier.) Chapter 2, accordingly, begins in the thirteenth century with Robert Grosseteste and his Anglo-Norman poem *Le chateau d'amour*, better known, perhaps, by its English title and redaction as *The Castle of Love*. While this study is engaged in exploring what happens when poets appropriate and transform theological discourse, Grosseteste affords us the unusual opportunity to observe a professional theologian distilling his own theology into a poem.[12] Grosseteste wrote the poem to reach an audience that was unable to read his formal theological treatises. The poem fulfills its didactic function but has the added benefit of freeing him (from authority) to delineate some of his more innovative and idiosyncratic ideas on the creation and the incarnation—the focal points of his major theology. As a poem, *Le chateau d'amour* has limited artistic value, but Grosseteste does pay attention to the particulars of his story so that the fiction is able to speak for itself and is not always in the service of the moral instruction. The poetic medium also allows Grosseteste to feudalize Adam and Christ, giving the moral content of the poem an immediate and contemporary application.

The chapter concludes with a brief discussion of Langland's treatment of the redemption and the devil's rights in passus 18 of the B text of *Piers Plowman* to illustrate how it complements and augments Grosseteste's version. Langland's poem has its obvious didactic impulses but, as John Burrow has argued, Langland does not abandon fiction for history or for biblical paraphrase; even Christ "becomes, for the purposes of the poem, subject to the laws of fiction and the exigencies of art."[13] Langland's fictions, his allegorization of the redemption and his retelling of Grosseteste's story of the Four Daughters of God, broaden rather than limit the field of association with these themes. Passus 18 is only a small sample of Langland's "vision," but adequate to show his ability to transform an existing text into something substantially new. For example, where Grosseteste only hints at universal salvation in his version of the Four Daughters of God, Langland makes it explicit.

In the third chapter I will focus on the *Pearl*-poet, and on a close reading of *Cleanness, Patience,* and *Pearl.* This poet is obviously well schooled in theological matters, and he appears to move comfortably and easily between a theologian's grasp of the arguments current in his day and a poet's intuition of how these issues impinge upon lived experience. As Richard Newhauser has observed, the *Pearl*-poet knew the moral and homiletic literature of the church and was equally adept in his understanding and use of biblical material.[14] Second only to Chaucer in his craft, the *Pearl*-poet makes his own use of ambiguity and multivalence and is determined to articulate some specific theological positions, such as just reward in *Pearl* or God's forgiveness in *Patience.* Although his poems have been routinely read as theologically conservative or as unfailingly orthodox in their outlook, I will argue for a more questioning and unorthodox intelligence at work in the way this poet chooses to fictionalize biblical stories or parables, in the way he has his narrators struggle with the lessons or themes implicit in the stories they recite, and in the way he enmeshes his readers in the same ambiguities that apparently provoke him. Discussion of a related poem, *Saint Erkenwald,* rounds off this chapter. This poem, no longer believed to be the work of the *Pearl*-poet, adds to our appreciation of how a poem can deal

5

decisively with a serious theological problem—in this case the fate of the virtuous pagans—and shares with the *Pearl*-poems an interest in redefining God's relationship to a human world.

The fourth and final chapter is devoted to Chaucer, whose poetry is the most overtly secular and anthropocentric of the major poets. Chaucer sets his stories in the *Canterbury Tales* within the larger frame of a pilgrimage. The pilgrimage combines with the tale-telling game to release unsuspected depths in the pilgrims, to re-create (by "recreation") the flawed individuals introduced to us in their *General Prologue* portraits. That is, through the individual pilgrims and their tales, Chaucer shows how theological discourse has been absorbed or internalized by his creations and then dramatized or worked out through their individual performances.

I have selected four of Chaucer's tales for illustration, those of the Prioress, the Second Nun, the Reeve, and the Pardoner. Each one conveys that individual teller's understanding or experience of what the church in the fourteenth century is or should be. I begin with an analysis of the tales of the Prioress and the Second Nun, whose tales, because they come from the same convent and share a devotion to the Virgin, invite comparison. Inasmuch as all of the tales deal to one degree or another with versions and perversions of love, the tales of the Prioress and the Second Nun offer two contrasting views on *caritas* and on chastity, and on the relationship between the two. Next, I focus on the tales of the Reeve and the Pardoner, who share an ambivalent attitude toward *compaignye* and *communitas*. The Reeve rides hindmost of the company and the Pardoner is introduced last in the cast of pilgrims and looks upon himself as an outsider. Both are preachers of a sort, both are obsessed with age and death, and both are concerned with the place of the church in the world. Both are frustrated in their experience of sexual love. Their tales provide us with two additional facets of human love. The Reeve, speaking from his life's experience, tries in his tale to reconcile the church's ideal discourse on marital love with the "nayl" that "stiketh evere" in the human will; his tale seeks to redefine *caritas* itself. The Pardoner, who makes *cupiditas* the announced subject of his tale and his life's experience, poses the most serious challenge to the mimesis of a theological discourse as a whole, its power to incarnate the Word.

These poets, to paraphrase Giorgio Agamben on Arthur Rimbaud, ask poetry neither to produce beautiful works nor to respond to a disinterested aesthetic ideal, but to change man's life and to reopen the gates of Eden for him.[15] Accordingly, the task of poetry for Chaucer and his fellow poets is not to affirm a truth already determined by theology but to open up a space, a play world, where values are tested, new modes of thought and perception are tried out, and established ideas are transformed. For a clearer understanding of this play world, and the various ways it is realized in these poems, let us turn now to a historical and theoretical consideration of what happens when poetry does theology.

Historically, poetry always has been asked to serve interests other than its own. In the classical period, for example, Lucretius defended his use of poetry on the ground that it enabled rather than inhibited the presentation of meaning in a philosophical text. In book 4 of *The Nature of Things,* he likens poetry to the coat of honey on the lip of a cup that physicians use to cover the bitter wormwood. The honey helps the patient swallow or ingest the medicine that will improve his health. Poetry, in turn, makes what might be an abstruse argument accessible and intelligible to an audience that may lack technical knowledge.[16] It also makes the transmission of such knowledge a pleasant experience and may enable an audience to have the distance to look closely at an emotionally charged event or at a matter of personal faith and to see it afresh.

In the Middle Ages, theology made a similar gesture, choosing to dress some of its doctrine in the pleasing apparel of poetry. This is especially evident in the early stages of the fourteenth century when poetry and theology were coming into their own as discourses in the vernacular and their interests—and audiences—frequently intersected and overlapped.[17] Much of the poetry we encounter, ranging from lengthy, didactic narratives to the simple but effective—and affecting—devotional and meditative verse, is scarcely distinguishable from theology. Marcia Colish has suggested that the sheer volume of religious poetry produced in the thirteenth and fourteenth centuries "attests to the view that these poets believed poetry was capable of communicating moral truths and moving the hearer toward God."[18] Similarly, Miri Rubin has shown how much of this very accomplished verse worked as a medium of popular

7

instruction, citing "Of the Sacrament of the Altar" as an example of a pastoral poem being used to explain the doctrine of transubstantiation. Guidebooks of various kinds in the vernacular had tales interspersed with instruction and created what Rubin terms a "horizon of images" or "vocabulary of associations" that were widely recognized and understood by the laity.[19]

As far as the major narrative poetry of the latter half of the fourteenth century is concerned, there are (at least) two critical approaches we can take toward it: the direct approach, which continues the symbiotic relationship of mutual dependence of the two discourses, and the oblique approach, which treats the two discourses as divergent or asymbiotic. The direct approach regards all of the poetry of the period, including the sophisticated narratives of Chaucer, the *Pearl*-poet, and Langland, as an integral part of the great diversity of religious writing that was appearing in the vernacular at this time. Nicholas Watson, among others, has shown how this poetry can be read profitably as a form of theology or, better, as explorations of what theology might be.[20] Speaking explicitly of the *Gawain*-poet and implicitly of the others, Watson says that this poetry represents a broad initiative to "catechise the laity" and to provide an alternative means, not only to convey already formulated teachings, but also to explore "Christian truths from the often distinct perspective of the 'mother tongue.'"[21] Monica Brzezenski Potkay's recent article on *Cleanness* illustrates this point.

Cleanness, Potkay contends, is constructed as a sermon in order to exploit that genre's traditional power to effect the purification of its audience: "the poem thus claims for itself the same efficaciousness, which it attributes to the language of its pure characters. More specifically, it claims the same power to effect moral change that it attributes to Daniel."[22] *Cleanness,* Potkay concludes, "hopes not only to define cleanness, not only to urge its readers to be pure, but also actually to render them clean."[23] The appeal of this approach is that it links the poetry unequivocally to the theological and cultural issues that were emerging in the fourteenth century and it shows the poetry speaking directly to a lay audience about their moral and spiritual needs. This audience may be preponderantly male and aristocratic, but the *Pearl*-poet, no less than Langland and Chaucer, anticipates a more heterogeneous one.[24]

Given the rich theological content of many of these poems, it would be foolhardy to deny that many, perhaps most, of the readers of Langland

and the *Pearl*-poet valued these poems for their theological content, treating the poetry proper as if it were a coat of honey masking the spiritual instruction. But, as Lucretius was well aware, honey has a taste of its own and may compete with the medicine for the attention of the patient; it may constitute its own appeal or set of values to contemplate, and it can change the way the theological material is received. A poem like *Cleanness* certainly can accomplish what a sermon does or strives to do, but the question remains, how does the poem do it? And what happens when the poem does it?

Unlike the sermon, a poem does not rely on an explicit rhetoric for its (moral) effect. The poem's fiction and verse rhythm enact implicitly what, for the most part, the sermon states flatly. Peter Haidu has powerfully challenged the belief that the fundamental message contained in religious conventions or *topoi* or in a biblical story will remain intact despite variations in emphasis and detail when they appear in or as a fiction. A fiction, he says, is "a turning away of language from its extralinguistic reference, and substitutes for that normative referential function a production of meaning which may take mimetic form, or which may turn into a simulacrum of the world, but which is essentially unbound and unpredictable."[25] Haidu goes on to say that even when intentionally established in subordination to an ideological superstructure, fiction still "is inherently subversive of such vehiculation, and betrays that externally imposed purpose by its very nature."[26] In poems like *Pearl* and *Patience,* which also have a strong biblical foundation, the reception of the text is modified by the powerful presence of an inscribed narrator who plays a pivotal role in the presentation of the text and who, in this capacity, qualifies and mediates whatever truth claims are being advanced. This figure may assume the role of an enabler, as Lucretius's narrator does, or he may interfere with the narrative by foregrounding his own judgments and responses, a gesture which invites the reader, in turn, to make her own subjective response.[27] Another way in which the literary text acts subversively is through the autonomy of the characters who people the poem, such as we find in Chaucer's poetry, where his diverse and multidimensional creations enjoy an unprecedented level of self-expression. No one of his characters can be singled out to represent or speak for the author and the diversity of opinion and points of view in his poems prevent any particular set of theological or philosophical ideas from dominating the discourse. What M. M. Bakhtin calls *polyphony* or

9

heteroglossia achieves similar effects, such as the multiple voices we hear at work in *Cleanness* or the opposing voices of the bishop and the lawyer in *Saint Erkenwald*.[28] In the major poetry the theological material is characteristically lifted out of the realm of concepts and put to work as one component among many (though often the crucial one) that coalesce to produce meaning.

Reading the poems as fictions and not as an armature for theology empowers the audience to act as its own authority and empowers the poetry to speak of concerns beyond its purely religious or heuristic function. As Nicholas Watson has pointed out, poets in the fourteenth century had to "invent" their own authority because the church had established itself as the sole authority and arrogated to itself the power to determine boundaries of thought and to distinguish between a realm of orthodoxy and one of heterodoxy.[29] If, in its own domain, theological discourse is adequate to the task of glossing the Bible, seeking truth, and spelling out doctrine, it characteristically ignores the complex experience of the individual who tries to live out or to comprehend in existential terms the principle that is concealed in abstract theological ideals and language, such as cleanness of heart or any one of the other beatitudes. Once placed in a story or a poem, then, theological discourse becomes another text, one that no longer can claim its privileged status. It no longer can claim access to secret knowledge or to the hidden order and it becomes subject to criticism and revision. The more hypothetical or play-oriented realm of a fiction, however, grants the poet the freedom to offer his own unique, possibly unorthodox, perspective on the subject.

What I am proposing, without denying or suppressing the theological matter and didactic intent, is that there is a readerly involvement and level of fictionality in all of poetry, especially the major poetry. What the guidebooks and stories prepared for the laity cannot tell us are how the various audiences responded, individually and collectively, to the "horizon of images" inscribed in the texts. Seeing or hearing familiar religious material in a setting different from a church or a formal religious service, such as we have in the drama and in much of the sophisticated poetry, makes it likely that the reader received the text dialogically.

Dialogism is a term popularized by Bakhtin that stresses the connections between differences, and privileges context over text. Unlike monological or authoritative discourse, dialogism permits the "play of language" and "assumes that at any given time, in any given place, there is a set of powerful but highly unstable conditions at work that will give a word uttered then and there a meaning that is different from what it would be at other times and in other places."[30] In respect to the devotional and didactic poetry of the Middle Ages, this activity may not be as open ended or as inconclusive as Bakhtin imagines it; but the poetry under discussion does readily expand rather than limit the range of meanings a word or work may take on and it allows for much greater flexibility in the area of presentation. The same "vocabulary of associations" that grounds the reader or listener in a familiar context permits the poet to play with that language and thereby heighten the "semantic potential of the literary text."[31]

In the Miller's tale, for example, Nicholas and Alison climb down from the rafters to make love in the bed until the bell of "laudes gan to rynge, / And freres in the chauncel gonne synge" (1.3655–56).[32] At first glance, the juxtaposition of the friars and the lovers suggests activity that is mutually exclusive or antithetical. The musical allusions that abound in the *Canterbury Tales,* starting in the *General Prologue* with the "smale foweles" that "maken melodye" to the lovers here in the Miller's tale ("ther was the revel and melodye"), suggest harmony or continuity. Here we might include Nicholas making "a-nyghtes melodye" while singing the "Angelus ad virginem" (1.3214–16). Rather than contrasting night music and morning prayer, the language of the poem seeks a relationship with the sacred as a provocation.

A similar effect is produced in the tale of Rustico and Alibech from Boccaccio's *Decameron* (third day, tenth story), a story that is shot through with theological allusions. The story centers on a charmingly naive young woman (Alibech) from Capsa who goes into the desert to learn from the hermits how to serve God properly. She is turned away by several hermits who fear her beauty, but she is invited in by Rustico, who seizes the occasion as an opportunity to test his will-power—an experiment that fails almost before it starts. Rustico succeeds in "putting the devil in hell," in a rite he concocts to initiate Alibech into the mysteries of faith. When Rustico beholds Alibech kneeling in prayer, per his instructions, Boccaccio audaciously describes the presentation of the devil as the "resurrection of the flesh" *(resurrezion della carne).*

Here again, the reciprocal influence of the poetic and theological discourses encourages the reader to go beyond the humor and clever use of language to grasp an important moral point, namely, that the boundary of theological tradition can be stretched to make room for the erotic in the discourse of the redemption and the resurrection. One of the aims of Boccaccio's stories is to imitate and then to problematize or complexify other literary forms. The story of Alibech is a good example of how he appropriates the sermon *exemplum* as a model of instruction to illustrate his own moral truth: Alibech learns how to serve God, and her passion for putting the devil in hell turns into a popular proverb that uplifts the spirits of the city. As the narrator (Dioneo) says, putting the devil in hell "is not only pleasing in the sight of God but also to the parties concerned. And much good may rise and come from it."[33]

The fluidity of the discourse in these two examples illustrates one of the dominant characteristics of fictionality, namely, its play element. If we blur or eliminate altogether the distinction between poetic and theological discourse, we disable the text as a "space for play." For Iser, play is an umbrella concept that covers all the ongoing operations of the textual process, and the literary text itself is first and foremost a playground where authors play games with readers. I want to explain in some detail Iser's understanding of these operations, particularly the fictionalizing act and the play of the literary text because his model for the way that an author generates a literary text and a reader receives it is one that will be followed throughout this study.[34]

In the generation of the text, the author "intervenes" in an existing world; he aims at something that is not yet accessible to consciousness—a world yet to be identified but one that will be interpretable by a reader. The double action of imagining and interpreting engages the reader in the task of visualizing the many possible shapes of the identifiable world, so that inevitably "the world repeated in the text begins to undergo change."[35] The world referred to here is purely a fictional world or a "world enacted"; what happens within it is relieved of the consequences inherent in the world referred to. Fictionality signals that everything is to be taken "as if," or as play.

Because a work of fiction "devoid of any connection with known reality would be incomprehensible," Iser elects to discard the old oppositional frame of fiction / reality and replaces it with the triad of the real, the fictive, and the imaginary.[36] In this triad, the imaginary, the most complex of his terms, manifests itself in a diffuse manner, in fleeting impressions, defying our attempts to pin it down:

> By opening up spaces of play, the fictive compels the imaginary to take on a form at the same time that it acts as a medium for its manifestation. What the fictive targets is as yet empty and thus requires filling; and what is characteristic of the imaginary is its featurelessness, which thus requires form for its unfolding. Consequently, play arises out of the co-existence of the fictive and the imaginary.[37]

The play of the literary text is neither winning nor losing but a process of transforming positions; that is, fictionalizing is a "negating act" which brings about a *transformation* of the realities incorporated in or posited by the text by "overstepping" them.[38] Iser identifies this act of overstepping as "boundary crossing," a transgressive act which enables the text to disrupt and thereby double its referential world. This act of fictionalizing determines to what extent "the given world is to be transcoded, a non given world is to be conceived, and the reshuffled worlds to be made accessible to the reader's experience."[39]

Every literary text crosses boundaries, Iser says, because each contains a selection from a variety of social, historical, theological, cultural, and literary systems that exist as referential fields outside of the text. This very selection is a step outside of the boundary because these elements are lifted out of their respective systems in which they fulfill their specific function. That is, the literary text fills the play space with other discourses and it allows these discourses to speak through the fiction at the same time that it deprives them of their customary context and authority. Hence, in each literary text the reader encounters first a "repertoire of allusions" which open up familiar territory to the reader: they "quote" earlier answers to problems—answers that may no longer constitute a valid meaning for the present work but offer an orientation by which the new may be located. These fictions hold together within a single space a variety of languages, levels of focus, and points of view that would be incompatible in other kinds of discourse. This process is most evident in narrative literature (such as we have in the *Canterbury Tales*), Iser says, where the characters represent different norms "whose value is disclosed by the relating process only in order that their inevitable limitations should serve as the starting-point for their being transgressed."[40] The multiplicity of discourses undercuts the ability of any one of these systems to construct a stable consistency, and the reader, through this destabilization, glimpses a recodification of familiar norms. Deprived of his customary way of organizing the world the reader is moved to cross boundaries. In this way, "literature becomes a panorama of what is possible because it is not hedged in either by the limitations or by the considerations that determine the institutionalized organizations within which human life otherwise takes its course."[41] The special character of literature thus resides in the interplay or oscillation between a world represented as real and an imaginary one.

Iser's approach to literary discourse is especially valuable when it comes to the body of poetry under discussion in this study because it supports the premise that the poetry of the late fourteenth century played an instrumental role in the transition from a closed to an open system. In a closed system, like the traditional medieval world picture, "representation as mimesis" is privileged; that is, mimesis entails reference to a pregiven "reality" that is meant to be represented. Where there is openendedness, the mimetic component of representation declines and a "performative" one comes to the fore. In the performative model, the author-text-reader relationship (conceived of by Iser as a dynamic interrelationship that moves toward a final result) produces something that had not existed before. Iser also attributes a vital anthropological function to the literary text: fictions give presence to what would otherwise remain unavailable to us. The impossibility of being present to ourselves becomes our possibility to play ourselves out to a fullness that knows no bounds.[42]

Iser's—and Bakhtin's—defense of the reader's role in the construction of the world of the text is consistent with medieval defenses of poetry and invention. Rita Copeland has shown how Augustine gave *inventio* a new application when he changed the field of its operations to written discourse. The text itself became the *topos*—the region of argument—from which what had to be said was extracted. "The most important implication of this shift for later historical norms of invention is that Augustine transforms the *modus inveniendi* into the *modus interpretandi*."[43] His program confers on the reader the power of invention. It gives reading and interpretation new status "as textual power shifts from authorial intention to 'affective stylistics,' to what the reader can do with the text. In practice it transfers responsibility for making meaning from the writer to the reader."[44]

What a literary text achieves, then, is not something pregiven but a *transformation* of the pregiven material that it incorporates. "In the performative aspect of the author-text-reader relationship, the pregiven no longer is viewed as an object of representation reaching behind appearances in order to grasp an intelligible world in the Platonic sense, but turns into a 'way of world-making.'"[45] The pregiven becomes the material from which something new is fashioned.

Another way of approaching the operations of a literary text comes to us from Boccaccio. In his defense of poetry, Boccaccio speaks admiringly of the way Dante unties "with amazingly skillful demonstration the hard knots of holy theology."[46] Boccaccio's word for "unties" is *solventem,* meaning to "unyoke," "to release a thing from what holds it together," or "to free something from restrictions," all of which suggest some of the same activity ascribed by Iser to the play element of poetry.[47] There are two assumptions implicit in Boccaccio's statement that are germane to this study as well as to Dante's poetry. The first is that theological discourse in the late Middle Ages, no matter how much it shaped doctrine and practice, was often abstract and difficult to penetrate even by educated or literate individuals, but that Dante was adept at transforming that discourse into a vocabulary and experience that made it available to a wider audience whose understanding was enhanced by the poetic examples or "demonstrations" he created. The second follows from the first, namely, that poetry is the site where theological developments and changes are often most vivid and discernible. This does not mean that poetry in the Middle Ages, including Dante's, is not itself sometimes obscure. Boccaccio defends this obscurity on the same ground that Augustine stood to defend the obscurity of scripture: it provokes discussion about the truth.[48]

Boccaccio's appropriation of Dante as an example of what poetry does with theology speaks directly to the underlying thesis of this study. Dante's poetry accomplishes what Iser says poetry does best: it transforms the pregiven material it incorporates and gives presence to what would otherwise remain unavailable to us. Thematically, his poetry takes us to the other world in order to return us body and soul to the visible world. Dante's belief that the practice of moral virtue was the proper end or purpose of human beings in this world was his way of retying the theological knots that he had first unloosed. To this end, he engrafted onto Christianity Aristotle's notion of human dignity, which affirmed the human capacity for moral action independent of grace.[49] Dante's poetry focused attention on human beings in a new way: first, by incorporating into his poem all of the strivings of human beings for earthly autonomy and second, by letting earthly destinies and earthly passions with all of their tragic conflicts live on within the divine order.[50] This theme is amply demonstrated throughout the *Purgatorio,* the canticle in which Dante stages so many memorable encounters with teacher-poets like Sordello, Statius, and Guido Guinizelli.[51]

Statius represents a particularly interesting theological knot. Statius was a convert to Christianity but he was converted by a poem, specifically a pagan poem, which attests to the moral and ethical excellence of the pre-Christian poets. Statius never wavers in his gratitude toward Virgil, even after his stay in purgatory. I am thinking in particular of the six lines in canto 21.97–102 in which Statius first speaks of the *Aeneid* as having been mother and nurse to him, then confesses that he would gladly spend another year in purgatory for the opportunity to have lived in Virgil's time and to have been able to converse with him:

> I speak of the *Aeneid*; when I wrote
> verse, it was mother to me, it was nurse;
> my work, without it, would not weigh an ounce.
>   And to have lived on earth when Virgil lived—
> for that I would extend by one more year
> the time I owe before my exile's end.
>   (*Purgatorio* 21.97–102)

In these extraordinary lines, Statius's earthly circumstance is likened to Dante's present one and the immediate cause of his spiritual *renovatio* is earthly and poetic rather than heavenly and theological. As mother and nurse, the *Aeneid* is given attributes normally associated with the church, and Virgil's poetry is extolled both as a valid source of knowledge and as a means of (spiritual) self-discovery. In the canto, Statius confesses that during his earthly existence he lacked certainty in his knowledge of the transcendent realm, but that poetic language redeemed

16

him. It allowed him to feel and envision a harmony, to have an intellectual intuition of a larger whole. The importance Virgil attached to the founding of Rome, the city of this world, inspired Statius to write the history of Thebes. Like Camus's Sisyphus, Dante's Statius is now ready to return to this world, having retained his love and admiration for the *Aeneid* even after his purgation and penance, and even after he has set forth on his journey to the heavenly city. His desire to return to the *Aeneid* and to continue his own work shows that theology or theological enlightenment does not render poetic work or poetic vision obsolete or superfluous. Rather, from Dante through to the end of the fourteenth century, poetry and theology move in tandem toward an enlightened view of *this* world, one in which truth is an elusive and ambiguous proposition—one that is less a formal, abstract matter and more a moral, existential one.[52]

Statius's desire to return to this world underscores Dante's belief that human existence and human history have an end and purpose in themselves, separate and apart from salvation history, and that poetry plays a significant role in its realization. As Ernst Kantorowicz has shown, Dante's determination to give the "human" a value in its own right impelled him to separate *humanitas* from *Christianitas*. He set Adam apart from Christ in order to make "the return to man's original image on earth independent of man's transcendental perfection in Christ by grace."[53] His ultimate goal was to absolve human beings of original sin in a nonsacramental way—through poetry and through the purifying and regenerative power of moral virtue. Dante's poetry thus assumes the theological project; it retells salvation history from the side of this world and restores human beings to their original dignity.

The example of Italian poetry helped to shape the course and vision of English poetry during the latter half of the fourteenth century.[54] The legacy of Dante, Boccaccio, and Petrarch taught the English poets how powerful the voice of poetry could be in social, political, and moral matters. However much English poets learned from the Italians, they quickly discovered they had their own theological knots to untie. Anne Middleton has shown how public poetry in England in the late fourteenth century reflects both a self-consciousness on the part of its poets over the place their poetry was to occupy in their society and a determination to make their poetry an integral part of the foundation of a secular and civic piety. The poetic voice she detects in this poetry sounds very much like that of Dante: "vernacular, practical, worldly, plain, public-spirited, and peace-loving—in a word, 'common,' rather than courtly or clerical, in its professed values and social allegiances."[55] The poetry of this period is thus highly conscious of speaking to an English audience about English concerns and is intent upon shaping its own response to the crisis in language and the problem of truth current in medieval theological circles.[56] The outcome of this crisis, the breakdown of the traditional medieval synthesis, accelerated the growth of a characteristically English theology in the late fourteenth century, the particulars of which I now want to examine in closer detail.

2.
Theology and Humanism in the Fourteenth Century

The specifically English theology that had begun to crystallize in the fourteenth century, with its characteristic concern for freedom of the will in God and man, its recurrent Pelagianism, and its stress on God's friendship, provided the most congenial soil for the cultivation of a humanistic anthropology.[57] Yet, critical discussion of fourteenth-century English poetry has failed to connect the anthropocentrism implicit in the design of the poetry of Chaucer, Langland, and the *Pearl*-poet to its parallel developments in late medieval English theology. Even those critics who have been actively engaged in rewriting the social, political, and intellectual history of the late Middle Ages have underestimated the role played by theology as one of the more dynamic evolutionary forces promoting change in the period. Like the old, the new historicists tend to view theology in the period between Grosseteste and John Wyclif as monological, dominated by a single procession of ideas that come to an abrupt halt with the Renaissance.[58]

Late medieval theology was not as quiescent or as monological as we have been led to believe, however; judging from the sometimes violent nature of the debates, medieval theology was less about determining truths than about exploring the grounds on which such determinations might or might not be possible to make. The fourteenth century witnesses the emergence of a new critical attitude toward the church as well as "an increasing heterogeneity in both religious theory and practice."[59] Alongside the dominant Augustinian or Neoplatonic view, which focused upon the supernatural origins and destiny of human beings and their fallen status on earth, there arose an alternative vision that fixed its beam on their creatureliness, their inalienable dignity, and their capacity for active partnership with God in the completion of the creation. In this analysis, the humanism that springs to life in the twelfth century does not die out with the ascent of scholasticism, as commonly is held. Instead, in its determination to assess things from a human-centered or this-worldly perspective, humanism steered scholasticism toward a discourse more concerned with the individual living in the here and now.[60] The impulse to humanize both God and this world gathers momentum throughout the thirteenth century, in both popular and institutional forms, and culminates in the fourteenth century in what Heiko Oberman calls the nominalist anthropology of the *via moderna,* whereby human beings act "as the appointed representatives of God, responsible for their own life, society, and world, within the limits of the covenant stipulated by God."[61]

The covenant Oberman refers to is primarily English in its origin and nature, and it is closely connected to the debates over the contingency of language and the contingency of the world that dominated the late thirteenth and early fourteenth centuries. The period from 1270–1340 is best approached through its focus on language. Humanism and Ockham's "metamorphosis of scholastic discourse" had brought about a fundamental change in the "community of assumptions" that had obtained in theological circles and in the philosophy of language. Ockham's dismantling of the medieval synthesis, the preordained harmony between faith and reason, was not the destructive development Etienne Gilson and others previously had imagined it to be. His reliance on language analysis as a method changed what had been an intractable theological problem, the nature of being, into a problem of language, thereby effecting "a change from the diversity of being to the diversity of the terms describing it."[62] As Gordon Leff has argued, Ockham's preoccupation with language reversed the direction of scholasticism: "from having been predominantly metaphysical in attempting to extend the area of speculation beyond natural experience, it now came to be focused upon natural experience and the limits upon knowledge which it imposed."[63] Eventually, it led to an effort to explain the natural world in natural terms.

What was being restaged in the scholastic debates over language, Nancy Struever has shown, was the old tension between the rhetors, or sophists, and the philosophers.[64] The rhetors were those who thought sophistically about discourse and who placed aesthetic ends above truth questions. They were humanistic in their orientation and insisted on analyzing things from a human-centered as opposed to a God-centered perspective. The incorporation of Aristotelian thought into their discourse placed pressure on the schoolmen to concern themselves not only with the relationship between God and human beings but also with the relationship between human beings and this world. The ascendancy of Aristotle's "authority," especially in the aftermath of the commentaries of St. Thomas, gave birth to a new kind of theologian who invoked reason as the ground of his philosophic authority: "The interpreter, having abandoned the notion of truth possessed for the notion of truth to be sought, could approach the text of the Philosopher in a critical questioning way."[65]

The elevation of reason to an autonomous discipline meant that it now could challenge theology.[66] And it did. As William Courtenay has shown, scholastic thinking, especially in England, abandoned Sentences commentary, which had been the chief activity of the schoolmen prior to the fourteenth century, in favor of pursuing questions that were of interest to the author and his contemporaries, resulting in a greater focus on the created world.[67] Salvation no longer had to be the only legitimate goal for human beings; instead there was a vast broadening of the horizon of possibilities for human beings in the temporal world. Christian Aristotelianism, for example, saw the state or secular society, as outlined in the *Politics,* as a natural order that satisfied human needs and did not come into being solely as a consequence of sin.[68] As Walter Ullmann has shown, by the fourteenth century the secular world had its own autonomy, as did the work and activity human beings conducted in it.[69]

Limiting the human mind or reason to the realm of human experience had a positive outcome because it intensified the effort to rethink the bases of philosophical and theological truth. Things could still be known but they could not be known with certainty. This horizontal aspect of late medieval thinking dramatically affected the conveyance of meaning: "Whereas previously meaning had been established in the very act of creation by a wise God, it now fell upon the human mind to interpret a cosmos, the structure of which had ceased to be given as intelligible."[70] As Erwin Panofsky puts it, all that is real, such as the world of physical objects and psychological processes, can never be rational and all that is rational, such as the concepts distilled from these two worlds, can never be real, meaning that all metaphysical and theological problems— including the existence of God and the immortality of the soul—can be discussed only in terms of probability.[71]

To be sure, Ockham's motive for asserting that human beings could not know what was in the mind of God was intended to ensure God's freedom. But it had a liberating effect on human beings as well, opening them to an awareness of their existence as historical beings free to master the reality surrounding them and to reassess the possibilities open to them in this world.[72] The Ockhamist idea of salvation through merit restored the full meaning of the covenant because it shifted the responsibility for personal salvation and salvation of the world from God's providential design to human actions in time. By dint of his absolute power God could refuse to save the meritorious individual, but God, by the terms of the covenant or his ordained power, is a reliable God and he would not punish the just individual.[73]

By the end of the fourteenth century, in Hans Blumenberg's view, these theological developments had pushed the Middle Ages to the brink of the modern or secular age. Blumenberg is one of the few intellectual historians who has a genuine sensitivity to how the ever-changing history of theology forms the backbone of a secular history. He insists that the fierce theological debates of the fourteenth century waged over the omnipotence of God and the contingency of the world served as an indispensable preliminary stage to the scientific breakthroughs of the fifteenth and sixteenth centuries, such as the Copernican revolution, at the same time that they raised serious questions at all levels of society about the freedom of human beings and their historical purpose in the scheme of salvation.[74] Loss is gain. If human beings in the fourteenth century were deprived of immediate knowledge of the will of God, if they found themselves condemned to a rhetorical situation in which they were compelled to act without sufficient evidence, then the new value placed on action and individual merit helped to compensate for their indeterminateness, and rhetoric became the means to construct a counterworld wherein they could realize the possibilities of their nature and improve their world.[75]

What should now be clear is that theology in the fourteenth century did not confine itself exclusively to religious matters but extended itself into the secular realm. Theology itself underwent a kind of secularization in the era and, as the gap between the secular and the sacred worlds began to widen, and the secular world and its institutions increasingly turned to practical solutions to purely earthly problems, the church became more and more lay-oriented.[76] The rise of lay piety also induced the church to develop specific areas of theology and devotion, such as devotion to Mary, as a response to the demands made by the laity and the pastoral clergy.[77] Moral and ethical problems of everyday life were raised to a level formerly reserved for epistemological and metaphysical questions, and theological discourse on doctrinal matters, such as the creation and incarnation, was made more relevant and accessible to a nonprofessional audience. The historic turn toward the people in the wake of the Fourth Lateran Council (convened in 1215), coupled with the gradual separation of theology from philosophy—to the benefit of both—made the particular concern of theology more existential and pragmatic. Where the church hierarchy hesitated to adapt or expand its doctrine and teaching to satisfy their everyday concerns, the laity often initiated its own practices to satisfy their spiritual needs.[78] Prior to this lay revolution the church program had been almost exclusively descending in its power and authority, and the laity was expected to imitate clerical practices and to emulate clerical spirituality. But, as Sarah Beckwith has shown, late medieval piety was both a product and a symptom of vernacularity, which resulted in a fracturing both of authority and of the technique of authorization.[79] Writing in the vernacular, moreover, triggered a burst of humanistic energy that looked anew at human beings in their natural existence in this world, a view inhospitable to traditional attitudes of contempt for human existence and for this world.

The rapid growth and dissemination of vernacular writings in the late fourteenth century, ranging from primers like *The Lay Folks' Mass Book* and *The Lay Folks' Catechism,* to sermon literature and penitential manuals like the extremely popular *Pricke of Conscience,* and more sophisticated literary works such as the drama and the poetry of complaint, had the salutary effect of opening previously closed fields, the Bible and history, to new audiences and new avenues of inquiry. Information or instruction was also available through a "continuing flow of treatises on letter-writing and sermon-making, manuals laying down practical codes of behaviour, instructions for communicants and penitents, guides for priests, confessors, and rulers both secular and ecclesiastical."[80] In the aftermath of major treatises there was always a demand for popularizations. By the second half of the fourteenth century, vernacular writings had begun to reproduce stories and scenes from the Bible, giving the laity for the first time direct access to the word of God and personal knowledge of the law of Christ, what Wyclif had declared was the fundamental right of every Christian.[81] In a related development, the need of the lower clergy for training to meet the spiritual demands of the laity resulted in a greater proximity or more frequent encounter between the laity and professional clergy, "precipitating an exchange between popular and learned tradition."[82] The vernacularization of theology thus did not simply mediate the formal theology of the theologians downward to the people; it reflected the religious or spiritual interests of the people upward as well.[83]

One of these interests was Christology or a new appreciation for the human person and nature of Christ. Interest in the incarnation and in the question of why God became man *(cur deus homo)* had been gathering momentum in theological circles since the twelfth century, as theology developed a new understanding of Christ's humanity and humankind's capacity for deification. The artists and poets of the period contributed to this development in a significant way, rediscovering the concrete world beneath the world of symbols:

> The development in the arts might be said to be "From the future life to the present," or "From deity to humanity." Or, as has rightly been said, men now tried to bring God down to earth and to see and to touch him.... This direct approach—evidenced also by the contemporaneous Bible translations—powerfully stimulated the pictorial representation of gospel stories, with the result that they came to be set in natural surroundings which actually meant the environs with which the artist himself was familiar; their setting was contemporaneous.... As might be expected, every artist perceived a gospel

23

story in a different light, and in this way his product represented the subjective impact which biblical events and situations had made upon him.[84]

Ullmann refers to this development as incarnational, a change in perspective that led the artists and poets to reconfigure this world as redeemed rather than fallen. English poets and theologians, particularly Grosseteste and Langland, whose work will be discussed in the next chapter, took the lead in detailing the transforming effect Christ's *humanitas* had on the way human nature was approached and discussed. Renewed discussion of the incarnation accelerated the pace of anthropocentrism by interpreting the event as the rebirth or recovery of natural man.[85]

Not surprisingly, vernacular use of biblical materials generated alarm on the part of the clerks, who were genuinely concerned that lay access to the word of God, without a trained teacher to mediate the experience, might lead to heterodox beliefs and a multiplicity of private responses. Clerical efforts to restrict authority to Latin writings only widened the gap between beliefs and doctrines, between the religious conscience of the laity and the institutional representations of their faith. The popularity of sermon literature further complicated the problem. The growing sophistication and incorporation of the *exemplum* cultivated a literary sensibility that encouraged readers to be interpreters and shifted attention to the *exemplum* itself as the place where the message or meaning resided. Moreover, because vernacular writings lacked the formal authority the church had reserved for Latin works,[86] the vernacular texts could be more bold and innovative in their hermeneutics and in the way that they sought to apply the lessons of the gospels to everyday life.[87] The Lollards took the greatest advantage of this new openness toward scripture to point up discrepancies between the biblical ideal of justice conveyed in Christ's teachings and the failed state of social and ecclesiastical justice in the present world.[88] But, as Janet Coleman has observed, all that literary Lollardy did in this case was to articulate the trends already set in motion in fourteenth-century lay discussions.[89]

If vernacular theology transformed fourteenth-century English society, bringing to the fore new art forms and new intellectual movements as well as new spiritual currents, some of which were heresies that challenged and eventually altered orthodox belief, vernacular poetry was the instrument that gave shape and voice to the longings and the most deep-seated preoccupations of the people.[90] The unprecedented development of narrative poetry in the fourteenth century attests to how predisposed English poets were to create—and English audiences to inhabit—fictional worlds in which they could use their reason or natural faculties to remake themselves and their world. The *Canterbury Tales* is the most probing and varied example of a medieval poem that explores the myriad ways in which people in the Middle Ages were reimagining themselves and the world they inhabited. Chaucer obviously has immediate and important theological concerns in the *Canterbury Tales*, which vary in depth and seriousness from problems of an abstract and philosophical kind pertaining to free will and predestination, divine providence, and the authority of the Bible, to practical and doctrinal questions pertaining to marriage, sexual practices, the role of women in the church and society, and the teachings of Christ. The persistence of theological problems in the *Canterbury Tales* attests to the importance these issues had on the lives of the audience involved, both inside and outside the poem. In this poem, Chaucer successfully selects and combines a wide variety of discursive systems—chivalric, monastic, clerical, mercantile, and pastoral—while allowing no one of them to establish a stable consistency. His fictions, to borrow the vocabulary of Iser, allow human beings to become present to themselves as no other discourse can. Given their "extraordinary plasticity," his fictional creations, because they do not have a determinate nature, expand into an "almost unlimited range of culture-bound patternings." As a medium, his fiction resists essentialization and shows all determinacy to be illusory.[91] If we take the *Nun's Priest's Tale* as an example of how Chaucer transforms theological discourse, we will see how human beings can construct through a poem a new image of themselves in the absence of God's truth.

3.

The Nun's Priest's Metamorphosis of Scholastic Discourse

In his tale, the Nun's Priest suspends his narrative in order to address a specific theological problem that arises within it. In the familiar and oft-cited passage on free will and predestination (7.3215–50), theological and literary interests converge on the meaning of philosophical truth. The passage opens with the Nun's Priest wondering if Chauntecleer is destined to perish in the jaws of the fox because whatever God foresees "moot nedes bee," a view he immediately qualifies by adding the comment, "After the opinioun of certein clerkis." The earlier debate between Chauntecleer and Pertelote over the meaning of dreams nicely anticipates and parodies these clerkly debates in their inflexibility and their self-canceling appeals to authority and precedent. Through the parody, the Nun's Priest puts the reader on the alert to his own artful manipulation of language and intellectual distance from the emotions of this debate. When he turns to the aforementioned clerks for an authoritative resolution to the question of Chauntecleer's freedom, he encounters a bewildering welter of opinion:

> Witnesse on hym that any parfit clerk is,
> That in scole is greet altercacioun
> In this mateere, and greet disputisoun,
> And hath been of an hundred thousand men.
>
> (7.3236–39)

The multiplicity of opinion, only slightly exaggerated, not only attests to the instability of authoritative discourse, it also points to the level of disagreement over the technical vocabulary shared by the clerks. The "mateere" alluded to by the Nun's Priest is justification, which has been described as the single most important issue in the fourteenth century, particuarly as it pertains to a theology of reconciliation between God and this world.[92] It had both political and pastoral consequences and it appealed to all levels of fourteenth-century society, from the learned to the "lewed," so much so that we find it debated even among chickens! This is not to make light of the subject or the disputants; rather, in having Chauntecleer and Pertelote discuss fortune, the prophetic power of dreams, and God's justice, the Nun's Priest acknowledges how meaningful these issues are to ordinary individuals. The topic of free will attracted so many lay disputants that Ockham is said to have remarked that "laymen and old women" were poised to challenge theologians in open debate.[93]

To avoid further confusion and for the sake of convenience, I have divided the dominant fourteenth-century views on justification, future contingents, and God's foreknowledge into two main camps, with the understanding that there were innumerable divisions within them. On one side were the traditionalists, like Bradwardine, who followed Augustinian teaching to the effect that God's foreknowledge was his predestination and that human beings could not earn their own salvation or acquire moral virtue prior to grace. In the other camp were the "moderns," sometimes called semi-Pelagians, who argued against philosophical necessitarianism and emphasized instead the moral autonomy of human beings and their capacity to be virtuous *ex puris naturalibus*.[94] The moderns stressed a human being's capacity "'to do what is in him' *(facere quod in se est)* in order to live well and earn salvation."[95] To offset Augustine's view of predestination and his emphasis on human weakness, the moderns held that individuals were responsible for their salvation, making the event human-centered as well as God-centered. In Ockham's words, human freedom of the will, or liberty, is the basis of human dignity and is the font of moral goodness. Being held responsible for his acts is what makes him deserving of salvation.[96]

The Nun's Priest, who talks himself into as well as out of all kinds of philosophical and theological difficulties, declares his frustration with the utterly intractable nature of this problem: "But I ne kan nat bulte it to the bren, / As kan the holy doctour Augustyn, / Or Boece, or the Bisshop Bradwardyn" (7.3240–42). The passage may mean that the Nun's Priest defers to the authority of the learned doctors and the bishop, or it may mean that he is unable to rise to the level of their discourse in his effort to arrive at some conclusion. The collective authority of Boethius, Augustine, and Bradwardine, while still substantial and dominant, was undergoing revision in the fourteenth century, particularly in the area of justification, and what the Nun's Priest may be saying has more to do with his impatience with formal theological discourse than with personal incompetence or an inability to penetrate the scholastic language that frames the debate.[97] He seems poised in fact to offer his own critique of scholastic discourse.

For one thing, the Nun's Priest proves he is well-versed in the terms of the debate—his summation of Boethius's idea of conditional necessity is as lucid as it is succinct—so when he tells us that he "kan nat bulte it to the bren," he is saying that the problem with language and theological discourse in the fourteenth century makes the whole project of separating fruit from chaff problematical. What theology formerly was able to do, to get at a final or absolute truth, it no longer may be able to do with certainty. He is not denying the existence of truth; rather, like his creator, Chaucer, he is reluctant to make any authoritative claims about the nature of truth.[98] In the absence of metaphysical certainty there may be no essential "bran" to unhusk. The passage underscores the indeterminate nature of all discourse and the authority of none, including the theological, as it is reflected in the proliferation of schools and the increasing heterogeneity of religious theory.

Exasperated, the Nun's Priest breaks off his philosophical meditation, protesting that he will have nothing further to do with "swich mateere"; his tale is of a cock and nothing more. His cock, of course, has everything to do with "swich mateere" and helps us to understand it better. Bradwardine and Augustine, while on the same side in the debate over justification, do not view human nature in identical ways. Augustine considers human dependence on God's grace to be a consequence of the fall.[99] Bradwardine attributes it to creatureliness; that is, he finds a fundamental flaw in human nature that has always been there.[100] Returning to his beast fable, to creatureliness, the Nun's Priest manages to keep the debate on nature and freedom open, only now he takes up the issue in the context of a fiction. A literary solution should not be imagined as something that only has consequences or significance within the frame of its fiction. As McAlpine points out, the Nun's Priest's tale "demonstrates the capacity of fiction to project a vision of human reality however remote a fictional world may be in its particulars from human activity."[101] As a moral tale, the beast fable enables the Nun's Priest to move the debate out of the schools and into the arena of everyday life. In a simple barnyard, which doubles as the garden of Eden, a royal court, the site of Christ's betrayal, the fall of Troy, and the locus of the Peasants' Revolt, among a host of other human catastrophes reminiscent of the Monk's tale, the Nun's Priest reimagines the broad sweep of history from a bird's eye view.

Ironically, the Nun's Priest is not "free" to select the topic for his own tale; he is bound by a conditional necessity arising from the Host's disappointment with the Monk's performance:

> this Monk he clappeth lowde.
> He spak how Fortune covered with a clowde

28

I noot nevere what; and als of a tragedie
Right now ye herde, and, pardee, no remedie
It is for to biwaille ne compleyne
That that is doon, and als it is a peyne,
As ye han seyd, to heere of hevynesse.
(7.2781–87)

For all of his lack of finesse and sophistication, the Host displays an intuitive grasp of the suppressed subject of the Monk's tale: God's hiddenness and the absence of a "remedie" for human fallenness. He expects the Nun's Priest to provide that remedy, if only in the form of comic relief ("Telle us swich thyng as may oure hertes glade") from the Monk's lugubrious narrative. The discussion of free will and destiny in the middle of the Nun's Priest's tale is no digression or personal indulgence, then; it is an integral part of his answer to the Monk who has created the impression of a remote and retributive will at work in the universe whose lessons in justice are uneven and imperfect. I am not suggesting that the Nun's Priest's tale depends in any way on the Monk's tale for its meaning or content, only that the Monk's tale makes clear some of the negative consequences of the dissolution of the medieval synthesis, which adds impetus and urgency to the Nun's Priest's performance, to which I will return shortly.

The argument against the Monk's tale, aside from its being too repetitive, has been that his vision is too dark and unrelenting. His stories, Donald Howard says, "present a hopeless world in which man is powerless and the way he tells them reveals his own moral chaos."[102] The Monk's celebrated pessimism may be less a flawed personal vision and more an instance of the theological crisis that coincided with a decline in monastic idealism. As one who "heeld after the newe world the space," the Monk may be experimenting with the theological approach of the "moderns" and entertaining the consequences that ensue from a *deus absconditus,* a God whose acts or motives are hidden from or obscure to human understanding. The more one posits an omnipotent God whose Being is unknown, as the moderns did, the more one runs the risk of envisioning a world made exclusively for God in which human beings are in exile and cannot feel at home. Chaucer's Monk is, in several respects, himself homeless. Technically, he remains inside the narrow world of the cloister while habitually journeying outside, unwilling—or no longer able—to abandon the world or the curiosity the world arouses in him. Gerhart B. Ladner informs us that the word *monk,* derived though it is from the Greek word for "sole," does not refer to a monk's solitary life as much as it does to his rejection of all divisiveness and to the perfect single-mindedness of his devotion to God. Chaucer's Monk lacks this unity, making him a kind of *alienus,* a term Ladner associates with "confusion," or the sterile mind of someone not disposed to the order of the right life.[103] Chaucer's Monk appears not to have abandoned altogether his pursuit of holiness ("He yaf nat of that text a pulled hen / That seith that hunters ben nat hooly men") or of truth. He simply no longer expects to find it exclusively in withdrawal from this world. David Wallace has suggested that the Monk commits a grave error by telling the kind of tale that he does in the vernacular and to a mixed and socially heterogeneous audience.[104] To his credit, the Monk displays none of the hauteur of the Friar and none of the Friar's intellectual disdain toward the likes of the Wife of Bath or the Summoner. However unsuccessful his tale, the Monk's willingness to discuss a philosophical problem in the vernacular does indicate a desire both to break out of the circularity of his argument and to enter the play space of the pilgrimage more wholeheartedly.

In the person of the Monk, Chaucer has given us a large and expansive figure who has an insatiable appetite for this life and for earthly and physical activity, reflected in the pride he takes in the care of his horses, in sumptuously feeding and clothing himself, and in hunting for game. With the exception of the Wife of Bath, no pilgrim evinces as much enthusiasm as he, at least initially, for telling stories: "I will doon al my diligence, / As fer as sowneth into honestee, / To telle yow a tale, or two, or three" (7.1966–68). One of the puzzles and disappointments of the Monk's tale, which stands in the way of his rehabilitation as a narrator, is the absence in his tale of the enthusiasm for literature that he evinces in the *General Prologue* and in the prologue to his tale. To tell or to teach appears to be his dilemma. His fondness for the *exemplum* or the moral lesson that can be extracted from it undercuts the impulse of his fictionalizing—evident in the Sampson, Zenobia, and Ugolino episodes—to break out into extended narrative. The Monk's lack of "commitment" to the fictional openness of his tale is emblematic of his unwillingness to declare himself in or out of the monastery or his vocation. He will assert no "remedie" to the human condition until he finds an answer to the question "How shal the world be served?" His tale might best be approached, then, as a kind of intellectual experiment in which he chooses to look at human beings in the light of eschatological disappointment, in their distance from God, and in relationship to whatever consequences obtain from the fact of God's hiddenness or unknowability. Erich Auerbach has pointed out that there was a disposition in the fourteenth century "to free the human emotions from the religious frame, to consider the human tragedy as an absolute, independent of Christ's passion," and this may be what the Monk is doing in his tale.[105] The story of Adam ably illustrates the limits of the Monk's style and vision.

Adam is the paradigmatic "hero" of the Monk's tale, the figure who brings out all the ambivalence in the Monk and in his tale. First he affirms the uniqueness of Adam's creation in the image of God: "in the feeld of Damyssene, / With Goddes owene fynger wroght was he" (7.2007–8). Adam enjoyed the highest degree of dignity of any worldly man in part because he was not "bigetin of mannes sperme unclene," a direct reference to Augustine's idea of how original sin is transmitted from generation to generation and which accounts for the weakened nature of Adam's descendants. Adam's fall or sin appears intellectual rather than sexual (Eve is conspicuously absent from the account), because he attributes Adam's fall to his "mysgovernaunce," which could suggest an inability to control one's sexual appetites but has a stronger sense of Adam's failure to manage his estate properly. The Monk, who takes pride in his management of the monastic property, takes the idea of human responsibility for the created world seriously, a view consistent with the covenantal theology of the moderns. This is intimately connected to the idea of a "remedy" for the fall, a theme central to Grosseteste's view of the redemption and to the widow's management of her farm in the Nun's Priest's tale. Adam's fall "out of [his] hye prosperitee / To labour, and to helle, and to meschaunce" shows the loss of status and dignity suffered by humankind. For the Monk, what now obtains in place of order is mischance, or misfortune, and his gallery of portraits in its disorder brings attention to our plight as contingent beings in a contingent world. Fallenness makes it difficult for the Monk to affirm that human beings have been redeemed or brought back to their original state of dignity. But the Monk does not choose silence or despair as his final response, at least not yet.

The Monk's Adam is like Dante's Adam; his *humanitas* has been separated from his *Christianitas* and the Monk endeavors to absolve him of his sin in a nonsacramental way, that is, to search for a way for human beings to take possession of their own (historical) nature. The Monk doggedly calls up the past to work it through further, mixing together as he goes along, biblical, classical, and mythological figures whose past example may cast new light on present experience. In the course of his narrative the Monk comes across as a kind of pragmatic humanist trapped within a theological vocabulary that has tried to reduce all of human experience to a single central meaning that begins with Adam and repeats itself endlessly. To escape, the Monk tries to narrate himself out of a closed system. He shifts from history to story, a medium more open to alternative readings. He does not push his point to a nihilistic end, as Howard fears; he eludes that abyss by adopting a rigidly monological form that forestalls closure by making repetition its hidden subject.

Although the Monk's narrative does not openly show the continuity between the creation and the incarnation or the recovery of a christological dignity inherent in human nature, Richard Neuse recently has shown that this Monk has read, and internalized, Dante, which means that he knows the redemption is always implicit because each of the examples he provides represents another Adam—or another Christ— who undergoes his or her agonal struggle to be. Without denying the horrors of this life or the absence of God from human affairs, the Monk affirms, specifically in the Ugolino and Croesus episodes, that the human capacity for suffering does bring out in human nature the image of Christ or that which is regenerative.[106]

Neuse's efforts to rehabilitate the Monk and his theological outlook are persuasive and long overdue. It is time we viewed the Monk as a more sympathetic figure who is saying in his own way that he too cannot "bulte it to the bren." It is with that in mind that we should receive his last words, "I have no lust to pleye." The Monk has not lost interest in theology nor in tale telling; he simply has not found through his recitation a way to combine the two discourses or to reconcile their differences, any more than he can decide where he belongs, in the monastery or in this world, so his chapel bells accompany him wherever he goes.

If the Monk does not complete the movement from Adam to Christ in his narrative, the Nun's Priest finishes the story by showing exactly what the incarnation has meant to human nature and human history. In contrast to the vast world of the Monk's tale, the Nun's Priest places us in the enclosed, present-day world of an English dairy farm, as if to say that the drama of life occurs in the most humble of circumstances as well as in the exalted. Adam's "feeld of Damyssene" has been turned into an ordinary barnyard and his labor into the domestic economy of a humble widow who has learned how to make herself at home in this world:

> This wydwe, of which I telle yow my tale,
> Syn thilke day that she was last a wyf,
> In pacience ladde a ful symple lyf,
> For litel was hir catel and hir rente.
> By housbondrie of swich as God hire sente
> She foond hirself and eek hir doghtren two.
>   (7.2824–28)

If the widow is the subject of his tale, then the dominant theme is one of self-sufficiency, of her ability to provide for herself and her daughters from what is available to her in her own yard. The catchword in this passage is "housbondrie," which signifies both the widow's judicious use of her resources—her "governance"—and her marriage to God, with the sly suggestion, in the wake of the Wife of Bath, that Christ is the model for all husbands (see her appeal to Christ at tale's end, "and Jhesu Crist us sende / Housbondes meeke, yonge, and fressh abedde, / And grace t'overbyde hem that we wedde"). Husbandry functions in the tale as a practical application of the nominalist idea of "doing what is in one." If the widow functions as a metaphor for the church in the fourteenth century, as critics have claimed, then the Nun's Priest gives priority to its pastoral role and apostolic simplicity over its episcopal hierarchy and scholastic learning. Both she and the church serve God by serving this world. As the church in the world, the widow need not get entangled in debates over human freedom and God's powers. Those squabbles are consigned to the rhetors in her hen house!

Although the widow herself may lead something of a monastic existence, once we leave her black and white world and enter the technicolor world of the chickens, we are treated to the vibrancy and eroticism of this little world of hers. Chickens prove to be an excellent choice for the Nun's Priest's fable because they cannot fly very high—although Chauntecleer manages to fly just high enough—thus keeping the theological discourse well grounded. If traditional Christian theology is Platonist insofar as it seeks to transpose the essence of human beings out of daily life, Chauntecleer and Pertelote call us back to our origins in nature. Gregory of Nyssa believed Adam, not God, was the inventor of language.[107] Before the fall from grace, Adam was the name giver and by giving names to things he elevated their status, gave dignity to them, and redeemed them from mute anonymity.[108] By giving his chickens names, a voice, and subjectivity ("For thilke tyme, as I have understonde, / Beestes and briddes koude speke and synge")—the sheep named Malle sets off the anonymity of the widow—the Nun's Priest "humanizes" or anthropomorphizes them to remind us of what we are capable of *ex puris naturalibus.*

Chauntecleer's understanding of time, for example, "Wel siker was his crowyng in his logge / Than is a clokke or any abbey orlogge," places him squarely in the natural rhythm of life on earth. The analogy between his inner faculty and the abbey clock is one of a series of gestures (another is "His voys was murier than the murie orgon / On masse-dayes that in the chirche gon") that conflate the natural with the spiritual; that is, it collapses the presumed hierarchy that separates the two and infuses the natural order with spirit. Through such analogies, the Nun's Priest restores dignity to natural faculties that orient us to this world; he makes the instincts or animal nature a fundamental component of that which is in us.

The most distinguishing of these faculties is the power of language, which originally bound the whole of nature together and which, in this story, is the cause of Chauntecleer's fall. When he succumbs to the flattery of the fox we see the triumph of language over instinct. Language is also the means to his rise or redemption. Because human beings are not deprived of the power of language—or tale telling—the fall is not the disaster that leaves us victims to "meschaunce." Human beings once were knowers in the same language that God is the Creator.[109] After the fall this immediate link is lost and diffused into a multitude of tongues, although the connection can be dimly perceived: "The pure language of names is the 'origin' that has become the 'goal,' inasmuch as its affinity to the divine language of creation lends it the greatest proximity to a state of redemption."[110]

In making Chauntecleer and Pertelote stand-ins for Adam and Eve, the Nun's Priest brings us back to the Garden of Eden not to re-enact the fall, but to resee it or to reinterpret it through the lens of the incarnation, that is, to present us with an image of *animalitas* striving for union with *rationalitas*. He begins his work of redemption with what appears to be Chauntecleer's outrageous translation of *"In principio / Mulier est hominis confusio,"* as "Womman is mannes joye and al his blis." If this is intended as a joke, it is not at all clear on whom or for whom the joke is made, women or clerks.[111] Most likely it is a comment on the way clerks interpret texts as they apply to women. The "truth" lies in the interpretation, in the fundamental difference that exists between the authoritative, "clerkly" language of Latin and the English or vernacular version which is always an interpretation as well as a translation and which asserts its own truth or version of reality. Theologically, the translation possesses its own logic, in part because the phrase *in principio,* a medieval commonplace, links the story of Adam's creation in Genesis with the story of Christ's birth in the Gospel of John. The transition is also from Eve to Mary: humankind must experience the fall and pass through "confusion" in order to know what was true *in principio,* that Adam's creation and fall contain the seeds of Christ's birth, a point conspicuously absent from the Monk's narrative, but one the Nun's Priest says cannot be omitted from human history or human dignity.

The Nun's Priest's manipulation of the language of this passage provides us with an object lesson that goes to the heart of the language crisis. Shortly after Chauntecleer's "mistranslation," the Nun's Priest stages another of his narrative asides. In what may be his most effective defense of the "chaff," or story in itself, the narrator halts his narrative to isolate the "fruit" or truth of Chauntecleer's ordeal. He shows us Chauntecleer in the full flower of spring, feeling at one with nature and with Madame Pertelote, his "worldes blis." Suddenly, he is struck by the realization that "For evere the latter ende of joye is wo" (7.3205). The narrator repeats the point, "God woot that worldly joye is soone ago," then drains it of its meaning by exposing it for the cliche that it had become:

And if a rethor koude faire endite,
He in a cronycle saufly myghte it write
As for a sovereyn notabilitee.
(7.3207–9)

A "rethor," while friendly to poetry, is someone who is adept at sepa-
rating the fruit from the chaff, although it is possible the Nun's Priest
has the Monk in mind here who sometimes appears to be unsure of the
difference between the fruit and the chaff. Technically, a rhetor was
someone who wrote in accordance with the school treatises on rhetoric
and, as Robert O. Payne reports, the textbooks that were written by the
leading teachers of rhetoric "were usually analyses of the art of writing
poetry, and in their titles *rhetorica* and *poetica* were more or less inter-
changeable words."[112] To the Nun's Priest's "rethor," Chauntecleer's
adventure—his flight from the beam and his encounter with Pertelote
and with the fox—is all so much chaff to be discarded in favor of a pre-
established truth. In this context *saufly* probably means "without risk of
error" or "with certainty." Not all human experience is the same, how-
ever, or reducible to a theorem that can be copied into one's journal.
Chauntecleer does not suffer the same fate as his father; he is able to
thwart fate and deliver himself from the jaws of the fox, thus turning his
woe to high bliss.

For the rhetor's maxim to stand up, it necessarily has to suppress any
number of details, the importance of which can never be determined in
a single reading. This would seem to be the Nun's Priest's point when
he goes on to say, his tongue firmly lodged in his cheek, that "this storie,"
his fable, is as "true" as is the book of "Launcelot de Lake, / That
wommen hold in ful greet reverence" (7.3212–13). The allusion to
Dante's story of Paolo and Francesca is another example of a joy that is
short lived. The comparison with Dante's story problematizes rather than
clarifies the tension between Chauntecleer and Pertelote and makes
the rhetor's task of extracting a single truth all the more difficult.[113]
As a kind of literary joke in a tale of literary jokes, the Nun's Priest
treats Dante the way Dante was received, as someone who was writing
theology and not poetry. The real point here is that any number of
examples can be adduced to illustrate a maxim or truth, but in applying
any category one necessarily substitutes it for the individual or exis-

tential experience delineated in the narrative, including materials that might subvert the very lesson deduced by the rhetor. The fable or fiction, conversely, aims to generate an unlimited number of possible meanings, especially those that may have been suppressed by tradition or authority.

One of those truths has to do with Eve or women. The Nun's Priest seems determined to show that woman *is* man's worldly bliss even if she was his confusion. First he shows us that Chauntecleer's wound is self-inflicted. The mermaid's song, a sign of self-destruction, is sung by Chauntecleer and not by Pertelote. Nor is she reducible to the source of his temptation or to mere animal pride. Pertelote makes it clear she is no polysemous text for Chauntecleer or any clerk to read or misread as he sees fit. She evinces her own autonomy, and she too can do that which is in her. She is at once Eve, Mary, Venus, and the widow. She also has the practical intelligence of the Wife of Bath and uses it to provoke Chauntecleer to question authority, especially theological truth. Like the Wife of Bath's Hag, she tries to awaken her husband from his solipsism and to teach him to see her as more than a source of physical or sexual bliss.

If, at first glance, Chauntecleer's generous translation of the Latin passage appears to be a case of willed blindness or the inversion of the proper goods that leads to the fall, in this tale the fall is shown to be but a fall into this world. In the theological tradition, Chauntecleer has the choice of heeding his higher nature and resisting the "scarlet reed" about Pertelote's eye, or he can fly from the beams and succumb to his animal appetites, as if these dual aspects are separate natures independent of one another. The Nun's Priest takes into account the inescapability of nature, giving us a Chauntecleer who is free within the limits of that nature. Consequently, Chauntecleer's, if not Adam's, fall is inevitable. He cannot remain on his perch where he can only dream of adventures in this world and where he is beset by desire for Madame Pertelote but is prevented from acting because their "perche is maad so narwe, allas!" No, Chauntecleer must descend into the phenomenal world in order to act out his nature.

Once he flies from the beams, Chauntecleer struggles with the burdens of the past under the guise of fate and destiny and in his struggle discovers his freedom. He awakens from his "dream" in the realization that he is an autonomous being who determines his own fate. When he spies the fox lying in the "wortes," his first impulse is to flee, "For natureelly a beest desireth fle / Fro his contrarie, if he may it see, / Though he never erst hadde seyn it with his ye" (7.3279–81). Once in the jaws of the fox, Chauntecleer does that which is in him: he transforms himself from Adam to Christ (see the way Chauntecleer is identified with Christ in the closing lines of the poem), he brings from potency to actuality what has been present from the beginning, uniting *animalitas* to *rationalitas,* flesh to word. Chauntecleer's dream, while a necessary aspect of his nature and his link with the divine, was unnecessary for his protection. He did not require any forewarning from God, either to identify his enemy or to flee from him and, to balance this off, he did not need any divine intervention to escape from the fox, however subtle this beast of the field. As he remarks once safely in the tree, "For he that wynketh, whan he sholde see, / Al wilfully, God lat him nevere thee!" (7.3431–32). Now we can see the debate with Pertelote for what it is— an intellectual exercise, like a scholastic disputation, that without lived experience has only limited value or transferability for us.

Against those theologians in the fourteenth century who placed severe limits on the individual's moral autonomy and his capacity to be virtuous out of his own nature, the Nun's Priest shows that the redeemed body can work in harmony with the will and reason, not just against it. The authentic historical subject, as Martin Heidegger would have it, is the one who is capable of resolutely choosing his past. In anticipation of death this subject is afforded a glimpse of the connected life which reveals to him that the past is a part of one's life and not simply exterior to it.[114] Through his self-recovery Chauntecleer restores natural man, *homo animalis,* to his original goodness and dignity. Again, the body, along with the soul and reason, manifests the image and likeness of God.

To redeem time, to deliver his promise to the Host for a "remedy" to the Monk's narrative, the Nun's Priest's tale shows that there is an experience available to human beings on which a new concept of time can be founded, an experience which Agamben describes as "so essential to human beings that an ancient myth makes it humankind's original home: it is pleasure":

Adam's seven hours in Paradise are the primary core of all authentic historical experience. For history is not, as the dominant ideology would have it, man's servitude to continuous linear time, but man's liberation from it: the time of history and the *cairos* in which man, by his initiative, grasps favorable opportunity and chooses his own free-dom in the moment.... True historical materialism does not pursue an empty mirage of continuous progress along infinite linear time, but is ready at any moment to stop time, because it holds the memory that man's original home is pleasure.[115]

Agamben goes on to say that the person who has remembered history as he would remember his original home is the true revolutionary and the true seer.

Seated on his perch of his "jade," the Nun's Priest sounds like Agamben's theological revolutionary and visionary. In his tale he has looked back to human origins and fashioned, through language, an image of humanity as redeemed.[116] At the close of his tale he instructs his listeners to take the fruit and let the chaff be still. As we've seen, for the Nun's Priest, the chaff of history does not disappear with the fruit of interpretation. In his economy of play or "jouissance,"[117] *fruit* may derive from a late medieval application of *fruitio*, which was part of a widescale and much discussed "psychology of enjoyment," as de-veloped by Ockham and others.[118] According to A. S. McGrade, Ockham identifies that enjoyment or pleasure not with *delectatio*, but with a sort of volition he calls *dilectio*, which serves as a first cause in his account of human behavior. *Dilectio* can also be translated as "love." The Latin word for enjoyment is *fruitio*, derived from *fructus*, which, McGrade says, connotes a flourishing of the human spirit or the ultimate fruition of a thing's nature. In the operations of the will and reason, which Ockham holds as our highest and noblest powers, we flourish or fulfill our nature and recover our true home, our dignity.[119]

Acting out our nature brings us to "his heighe blisse," Christ's or Chauntecleer's, whichever one prefers.[120] The Nun's Priest has made Chauntecleer in the tree synonymous with Christ on the cross,[121] and he has made the sexual joy experienced by Chauntecleer, "Hym deigned nat to sette his foote to grounde" (7.3181), interchangeable with the perfect happiness and joy of heaven. Forging a link of identity between Chauntecleer and Christ through his fiction, the Nun's Priest makes bliss predicable of a this-worldly joy and shows that the erotic can be consti-tutive of the redemptive.

Finally, many readers regard the *Nun's Priest's Tale* as Chaucer's *ars poetica*, a tale about the act and art of storytelling itself. As such it stands up to the Parson's critique at the end of the *Canterbury Tales* on the limits of fiction as a medium of truth. In his prologue the Parson invokes the authority of Saint Paul to support his rejection not only of fable but also of "all personal speaking that does not confront, in the sacramental language of penance, the sinfulness of the human condition":[122]

> Thou getest fable noon ytoold for me;
> For Paul, that writeth unto Thymothee,
> Repreveth hem that weyven soothfastnesse,
> And tellen fables and swich wrecchednesse.
> Why sholde I sowen draf out of my fest,
> When I may sowen whete, if that me lest?
>
> (10.31–36)

As if to avoid the moral ambiguity of the Nun's Priest's tale, the Parson refuses to tell any fable at all. He issues his admonition to the pilgrims at the outset of his tale as his way of warning them not to mistake the pleasure and amusement of the tale-telling game for the spiritual values of the pilgrimage itself. For the Parson the distinction between poetry and theology is fixed; truth or "soothefastnesse" does not abide in fables—it resides in scripture as the only sure path to salvation. The Nun's Priest counters the Parson's invocation of St. Paul with his own citation from Paul "al that writen is, / To oure doctrine it is ywrite, ywis" (7.3441–42).[123]

As usual, the Host keeps us grounded in the world of the poem, and he sorts through the fruit and chaff of this debate. After giving the Parson the consent of the company to "enden in som vertuous sentence," he cautions the Parson "Beth fructuous, and that in litel space," which is an echo of the Nun's Priest's "fruit" or *fruitio*. Chaucer's poem accommodates the pleasure or enjoyment each pilgrim-teller may derive from his or her text, regardless of its form or content. For the Parson, the Christian or pilgrim flourishes or gains the celestial Jerusalem by the terms of his tale: confession, penance, and satisfaction. The Parson can say unselfconsciously that he will tell a "merry" tale, one that promises "pleasaunce leeful." But what is appropriate and desirable to the pilgrim near the goal may not meet the needs of the *viator* in the middle of his journey, who may have a need for narratives that orient him towards this world, such as the Nun's Priest's fable.

The *Canterbury Tales* survives the solemnizing judgment by the Parson of its fiction, just as the Nun's Priest's tale overcomes any attempt by a "rethor" to reduce its meaning to a moral function. The integration of the purely fictional world of the animals with the presumed "real" world of the widow and her daughters serves as an emblem of Chaucer's poetic vision. With the flight of the fox and its daring analogy to the Peasants' Revolt we are abruptly transported back into the black and white world of the widow, a peasant herself, who enlists the aid of all the animals as well as the workers on her farm to rout the fox and rescue Chauntecleer. It's as if the whole of nature rises up to offset the depredations of the fox. The "hideous noise" (7.3393) of the peasants as "they skriked and they howped" threatens to bring the very heavens down. Here we have a perfect example of the chaff of history refusing to be "still"; they demand to be heard, however dissonant or jarring their voices. And the heavens will not fall if Chaucer opens the vast middle of the *Canterbury Tales* to the peasant consciousness of churls like the Miller and Reeve, or to a wide variety of social discourses which might be suppressed by the authoritative discourse which opens and closes the poem in the epic consciousness of the Knight and the absolutism of the Parson's theological discourse.

If the *Nun's Priest's Tale* is Chaucer's *ars poetica* and if the language he uses is redemptive, it indicates that in his poetry he is prepared to transform theological discourse, and along with it epic consciousness and tragic consciousness, into the language and experience of everyday life. Because he no longer can "bulte it to the bren," the Nun's Priest's story of Chauntecleer and Pertelote does not arrive at any final resolution to the ambiguities and paradoxes of our experience of time. Nevertheless, in choosing a fiction as his medium, the Nun's Priest's narrative helps us to see that while we were created for this world and this world was created for us, we must live in it in untruth as well as in truth.

Chaucer, of course, both is and is not representative of what poetry was doing with theology at this time. What is impressive about English poetry in the fourteenth century is its variety, along with the distinctiveness of the voices and the individuality of the respective visions of the *Pearl*-poet, Langland, the author of *Saint Erkenwald,* and Chaucer. The chapters that follow will honor the individuality of these voices and show as well how they coalesce to make for a distinctively English consciousness, beginning first with Robert Grosseteste and his *Castle of Love*.

TWO

Grosseteste and Langland

1.

Robert Grosseteste's Le chateau d'amour *and
Late Medieval Anthropocentrism*

"And al þat man haþ mysdo I man wole amende."[1]
William Langland, Piers Plowman
B text, passus 18.341

In the epilogue to the Nun's Priest's tale, the Host, in obvious delight, turns to the Nun's Priest and exclaims: "I-blessed be thy breche, and every stoon!" Apparently the Host has heard from the Nun's Priest the sort of tale he originally had expected from the Monk because he attributes to the Nun's Priest those physical qualities he had previously predicated of the Monk, a fully eroticized and fleshly nature. In effect, the Host "incarnates" the Nun's Priest who heretofore has been to us only a disembodied voice. Comparing him as he does to a "tredefowl aright," that is to Chauntecleer himself, the Host repeats the basic premise of the Nun's Priest's tale, that human nature is one and that man and nature are one. The theological basis for this assertion rests on the doctrine of the incarnation and the discussion surrounding the question of why God became a human being—*cur deus homo?*— and what answering that question meant for a new understanding of human nature.

Why God became a human being was a matter of intense theological inquiry in the period from the twelfth to the fourteenth century. The first attempt to address the matter occurred in the fifth century at the Council of Chalcedon (451), where the question before them was *could* God become human, or how was it possible for God to have two natures— which the council concluded he did have. The entire nature of the debate had far-reaching consequences because of the ancillary questions it raised, such as, What makes for a human being? Did Christ have to have a human body in order to have a human nature? Did Christ simply inhabit a human body or did he assume a complete human nature? Did Christ retain his omnipotence and omniscience or was he more like ordinary human beings in his doubts and desires, and in his susceptibility to cold, hunger, and fatigue?[2]

The issue re-emerged in the twelfth century as a new Christology was evolving that approached the redemption as the work of a human being, as the work of Christ's human nature, rather than his divine nature. The question of why God became a human being provoked new thinking on justification and served as the nexus for any discussion of human dignity. For some time, in the absence of eschatological fulfillment, theology was under pressure to explain what was expected of human beings in time and to define the role human beings were to play in the work of their own salvation. Patristic thinking on the redemption had concerned itself with two broad questions, the defeat of the devil and the reconciliation of humanity to God and God to humanity.[3] In the twelfth century, the discussion of salvation shifted from the mythological plane, or from the notion of a cosmic battle between God and the devil, to what Alister McGrath describes as "theories of redemption in which emphasis was laid upon the moral or legal propriety of both the redemption of mankind in the first place, and the means subsequently employed by God in this redemption."[4] The key to this new understanding was the humanity of Christ.

Anselm (1033–1109) took up the question of why God became a human being because he was dissatisfied with previous accounts, which explained how, but not *why* God had become a human being. The full title of Anselm's treatise, *Why God became man in order to save mankind by his death, when it appears he could have done this in another way,* reveals the method of his inquiry.[5] He will first explore some of the options God might have exercised to bring about the redemption then explain why the sacrifice of Christ is the only way human beings could pay back what they owed.[6] In Anselm's economy, human beings were created in a state of harmony with God; that harmony was ruptured by humankind's transgression of the moral order and could not be restored by human actions alone. Anselm asks the question "By what rationale does God forgive the sins of men?"[7] Although he was not obligated to do so, God had to become a human being in order to provide the means to salvation that were lacking in human beings. For Anselm, the redemption of humankind was necessary as a matter of justice; the moral rectitude of the created order had to be restored because God, having created a world in his own image, could not, by his nature, permit a "disfigured" moral order to continue.[8] The incarnation is thus an act of justice on the part of God: God is good and always does what is appropriate to him as the highest good. In the process, Anselm hoped to do away with the notion of *devil's rights,* the idea that the devil had a legal right over sinners. In his argument for justice, Anselm showed that because the devil violated the moral order himself in his seduction of Adam, he never had a just claim over humankind and through his act he forfeited any claim to justice over humankind.[9] The devil's rights argument did not disappear in the aftermath of Anselm's treatise, however; it remained as popular as ever in various accounts of the redemption. Two of its liveliest revivals will be discussed in this chapter; first, in the debate between Christ and the devil in the Four Daughters of God section of Grosseteste's poem, and second, in Langland's staging of the confrontation between Christ and the devil outside the gates of hell as part of his version of the harrowing.[10]

Other theologians who addressed the question approached the incarnation in a fundamentally different light. They made it an integral part of the creation and viewed the redemption as a secondary event to Christ's humanization. Peter Abelard (c. 1079–c. 1142), citing the evidence of Christ's works and his preaching, insisted that Christ assumed flesh to provide a new motive for human action. The redemption of humankind was enacted to promote a change of heart and to infuse human beings with a motive for charity. For Abelard, the incarnation was less an instance of Christ's meeting the demands of God's justice and more a case of his fulfilling the demands of his own love. In his commentary on St. Paul's Epistle to the Romans Abelard argued that any good person would be given the opportunity by God to come to know him, asserting that love was the essential ingredient, not the sacraments of the church:

> Let this be sufficient for us concerning our justification, and the justification of everyone else as well, that it consists in love being interposed among us—and that is before the sacraments are taken up. This is why the prophet declares: "In whatever hour a sinner grieves, he shall be saved."[11]

Abelard was more interested in the kerygma of Christ and in the example of Christ as a figure of charity than he was in emphasizing Christ's suffering for sin. In his view it is the personal response to the example of Christ's love that leads human beings away from sin and initiates the reconciliation with God.[12] Like Abelard, John Duns Scotus (c. 1265–c. 1308) argued that the incarnation did not occur primarily for the redemption but for the glorification of human nature. God predestined Christ to human nature and preordained human nature to glory prior to grace and merit. Not even Christ's suffering was proof that he was incarnated for purposes of the redemption. The passion of Christ, Scotus says, "was envisioned as medicine against the fall, just as a physician first willed the health of a man before choosing the medicine for curing him."[13]

For some theologians, notably Scotus and Gabriel Biel (d. 1495), the incarnation was adequate cause in itself for the redemption. This is consistent with an anthropocentric theology that values the life of Christ over the death of Christ, and which assigns a purpose to human life other than the gaining of salvation. In this arrangement Christ undergoes the passion only to fulfill the law in its totality.[14] Thomas Aquinas (c. 1225–c. 1274) arrived at a similar conclusion: Christ assumes flesh for the benefit of human beings; he becomes a human being in order to make humankind divine. In his *Articles of Faith,* Thomas, who speaks of Christ as our brother, notes that after the incarnation the angel would not allow John to adore him, and Thomas speaks of this event as a sign of the great dignity the incarnation bestowed upon human nature.[15] Thomas makes the boldest statements aimed at restoring the soul to the body. In his *Commentary on the Gospel of John* he makes it clear that the Word became flesh to exclude the possibility of the Manichaean view that the body was evil.[16] In his most spirited defense of human dignity, Aquinas says, "the soul is more like God when united to the body than when separated from it because its nature is then more perfect."[17]

No one better understood, or explained, this phenomenon than Robert Grosseteste, who occupied a pivotal position in the transmission of ideas from the twelfth to the fourteenth century. In the first half of the thirteenth century (his professional career spans 1200–1253), Grosseteste easily was England's most learned and innovative theologian, producing enormously influential translations of Aristotle's *Ethics* and *Physics* and reviving interest in the Greek fathers, whose views on nature and the creation were more compatible with his rationalist and scientific temperament than those of the dominant Latin fathers. Yet, until recently, his contribution to late medieval thought was confined mainly to his scientific and technical writings. What has obscured his reputation as a theologian is the mistaken belief that his body of thought represents no significant advance over the often-revolutionary discoveries of his twelfth-century predecessors, such as Anselm and Hugh of St. Victor. This view fails to account for the evolution of Grosseteste's theology, the decisive turn it takes away from the dualistic language of the Neoplatonists in the formulation of his own theology of humanity and nature. Fresh approaches to his theology have dispelled some of the lingering misconceptions pertaining to his originality and independence as a thinker, and they have gone a long way toward restoring his prestige as a theologian, first by making available new editions of his major theological writings and second by bringing his anthropology to the forefront as the dominant strain of his mature period.

At the center of Grosseteste's theology lies a bold and dynamic concept of the incarnation whose primary function he conceived of as being the deification of human nature.[18] His starting point is the absolute predestination of Christ. Grosseteste determined that the incarnation and the church were part of the original creation and that Christ would have assumed human nature even if Adam had never sinned. Arguing from the Aristotelian premise that an effect cannot be greater than its cause, Grosseteste concluded that the incarnation plays too significant a role in human history to be either a contingent event or the consequence of sin. He concedes that humankind's fall conferred on Christ the additional role of savior, but his primary purpose remained his original one, that of making clear that spirit and matter are not opposed principles but one, in the same way that his divine and human natures are one, though distinct, and that the three persons of the Trinity form a single godhead. Unity, not transcendence, James McEvoy says, was always the goal of Grosseteste's theology, and it is in the totality of human nature, not just the soul or reason, that the fullest creaturely likeness to God is realized.[19] The fact that God could have brought about the redemption in other ways attests to a prior purpose for the incarnation. This is what gives the incarnation its special dignifying status: it has meaning separate and apart from sin and the work of the redemption.

The incarnation had to be an integral part of the creation, Grosseteste reasoned, because it most clearly announces the purpose of the creation: the condescension of the son as prelude to human participation in the divine being. Christ's human nature becomes the theme the Creator carries out in the rest of creation.[20] Extrapolating from Genesis 1.1, with its thematic link *(In principio)* to the opening of John's Gospel, Grosseteste imagines that the incarnate Word, or the image and likeness of God, was implanted in human nature at the creation in the form of hidden seeds—an idea prominent in Pauline theology—and time, and the world followed simultaneously to allow these seeds to germinate.[21] In his gloss of Genesis 1.26, Grosseteste places the same value on the pronoun "us" of *faciamus,* in the familiar opening line, "Let us make …," as traditionally is placed on the verb "make," in order to ensure that the whole of creation and human nature are imprinted with the image and likeness of all three figures in the Trinity. Grosseteste says:

> Let us make man to our image and likeness. This expression is very brief, but it is also extremely profound, and extremely fertile of extremely broad senses.… It includes the most secret thing of God and the most sacred thing of the human being. It shows the trinity of the one God and the supreme dignity of the creation of human beings: for it says that human beings were made in the image of the supreme Trinity.[22]

With an eye on medieval debates about the eternity of matter, Grosseteste insists on the necessity of creation *ex nihilo,* because creation by God means that humankind and nature itself, the whole realm of matter, originate in God and something of God's divinity is imparted to all in the act of creation. As a gift from God and as part of the original making of human beings, the image may become deformed (as it does through the fall) but the original similitude cannot be lost altogether.[23] What was lost in the fall, he avers, has been restored through divine revelation and through the incarnation. Individually and collectively, human beings are charged with the responsibility of cultivating these seeds in nature and in their own nature until they have realized all that God has willed for them in the creation. In this way Grosseteste successfully minimizes the traditional duality of body and soul in favor of the connaturality of their union.

The idea of the absolute predestination of Christ does not originate with Grosseteste, but he is the first one to base a theology of human dignity upon it. His companion idea of the *minor mundus* enhanced his thinking on dignity by resolving what had been a nagging philosophical problem: How could a human being, composed of an immortal spiritual substance and a mortal corporeal substance, constitute a true unity?[24] The incarnation, he reasoned, reveals that among all creatures, including the angels, human beings most closely approximate the image of the Godhead.[25] Because human beings are preeminently the creatures that combine in their being both "free intelligence and the dust of the earth," they must occupy the pivotal position in the continuity of the creation. As the *minor mundus,* or natural image of God, it is the special prerogative of each human being to reproduce within himself or herself the cosmic order that is revealed by the incarnation. Only Christ, however, as the hypostasis that unites all levels of being within him, can serve as the final unifying principle that links God with the created order. Human beings thus have a need for Christ that precedes and supersedes his role as redeemer.

Grosseteste's notion of the gradual perfection of human nature through time and through human instrumentality came to him, oddly enough, from alchemy. Apparently the pseudoscience gave him the basis for his belief in the ultimate unity of matter and its continuity throughout nature. The way in which the alchemical *opus* represents the creation and the incarnation as an ontogeny lent him the vocabulary he needed to articulate the process of deification as an earthly or natural phenomenon. As he envisions it, the earth was salted with metals, like the seeds implanted in human nature, at the time of the creation and they began ripening over time beneath the earth.[26] Just as the alchemist imagines the material world as alive and sacred, and uses the philosopher's stone to "marry" these metals or to unite contrary elements in the hope of giving birth to the true substance concealed beneath their base cover, so too Grosseteste insists on the sacred dimension of matter and makes Christ the catalyst or indispensable ingredient that empowers human beings to enact a profound change in their nature.[27] Through the incarnation Christ reproduces in his being the first light or *prima materia* out of which human beings were formed in the divine image, a kind of revelation of Being to and within each human being, to borrow Heidegger's language.

In several of his early scientific writings, moreover, Grosseteste draws upon the technical language and operations of alchemy to explain how the dispersion of light at the creation informs every natural object. In *De luce* he shows that every natural body on earth has something of celestial light and luminous fire in it, a divine spark which contains the human potential for deification. This view is strengthened by his appropriation of Aristotle's notion of the humiliation of the quintessence;[28] he speculates that its reverse, the eventual sublimation of elemental matter into a heavenly state of incorruptibility, was equally possible, making deification possible, and again lending scientific or rational support to theological faith. For Grosseteste the importance of this point is that the physics of the creation conform to the theology of the creation. In this way knowledge and the love of God can be attained through a study of the created world.

Grosseteste's most sustained treatment of the creation and the incarnation appears in several of his mature writings, foremost among them his *Hexaemeron,* his *De cessatione legalium,* and his sermon *Exiit edictum.* During the same period, roughly 1233–42, he composed the Anglo-Norman poem *Le chateau d'amour,* in which he compressed his main theological ideas (R. W. Southern refers to it as Grosseteste's *Summa theologiae*). Grosseteste was characteristically modest about the value of his own theological discoveries, even when he believed in them fervently, as he did in the absolute predestination of Christ:

> I confess I do not know if I am right, and I am afflicted by my ignorance on this matter. As I have said above, I do not remember that any authority has come to this conclusion, and I do not wish or dare to pronounce conclusively on so hard a question without express authority, knowing how easily a plausible argument may mislead my poor skill and learning. But if it is true that God would have become Man even if mankind had never sinned, this entails the subjection of all creatures to that Man-God who is head of the Church of men and angels alike.[29]

The word that stands out in this passage is *authority.*[30] Even though Grosseteste believes he is correct, he will not and dares not pronounce conclusively on this question without formal authority. But where he is tentative in his formal theology he is bold in his poem, finding the latter a medium in which he could dare to experiment freely with his original insights.

Although *Le chateau d'amour* is little known and rarely read today, it was enormously popular throughout the late Middle Ages, undergoing translation well into the fifteenth century and making Grosseteste's theology available to the very lay audience for which it was intended. It first appeared in English around 1300, but the most complete and reliable version was produced in 1390.[31] One indication of its importance is that three of the four known portraits of the bishop that appear in manuscripts are attached to the poem, suggesting the special place of authority the poem held among his writings.[32] Though heavily didactic in form and content, its fictionality, that is, its use of poetic analogies and devices, encourages readers to interpret and evaluate events in their own way. The poem may not have influenced Chaucer and his contemporaries in any direct way, but it gives us a clear idea of what kind of theological ideas enjoyed a broad circulation, and the poem gave medieval audiences a greater purchase on the christological and incarnational elements apparent in the poetry of Chaucer, Langland, and the *Pearl*-poet.

The poem comprises some 1,800 lines and is no mean accomplishment. Written in octosyllabic couplets, it was intended to be performed with musical accompaniment. The poem is best described as a modified *hexaemeron,* or modification of his own *Hexaemeron*, a genre which had begun to proliferate in the thirteenth century as interest in the creation came to the fore. The main body of the English text is remarkably faithful to Grosseteste's original, although there are some noteworthy additions and deletions. Grosseteste never named his version; it is the English text that gave the poem its title— *The Castle of Love*—after its central section depicting the incarnation. My discussion will concentrate primarily on Grosseteste's Anglo-Norman text but, given the popularity of the English version and the fact that fourteenth-century England was a multilingual society, I will cite the English version in conjunction with the French text whenever it meaningfully adds to, eliminates, or reacts to a part of Grosseteste's thinking.[33] Inasmuch as both texts appealed to large audiences, not necessarily the same ones, it can be said that both texts

illuminate one another. When they are taken together we get a clear picture of the durability and popularity of Grosseteste's ideas.

Both versions of the poem start with prologues that defend the use of the vernacular as a medium for instruction. Grosseteste begins with the announcement that he will speak in the vulgar tongue because not everyone in his audience is schooled in letters, as are the clergy: "Pur ceus ki ne sevent mie / Ne lettreüre ne clergie" (26–28).[34] The second reason he offers is that everybody should be able to sing a song of praise and thanksgiving to God in the language that is appropriate to them, whether it be Hebrew, Greek, or Latin, because God gives us his love and defends us from what is contrary to our well-being. He concludes with a brief outline of the biblical events and lessons he intends to treat, starting with the birth of Adam, "nostre premer pere." Our sonship in Adam is stressed at the outset to prepare for our rebirth as sons in Christ, who is also our father.

The poem orders events so that the Christian tradition conforms first to the anthropocentrism of the creation and incarnation and only secondarily with the theology of the fall and the crucifixion, a Christ-centered rather than a sin-centered vision. The poem omits altogether any dramatization of the temptation of Eve or the disobedience of Adam, suggesting that they are not the definitive events in the formation of the human spirit. The poem allows the reader to focus on what human beings are, not on what they have lost, so that their lapsed condition reflects more on their unrealized capacity for divinization than on the wound to their being.

The English text states its didactic intention in the opening lines: "Her byginnet a tretys... / For lewede mennes byhoue." The narrator both embellishes and suppresses aspects of Grosseteste's original while remaining faithful to its basic theme and structure. In the process he shows himself to be an astute reader as well as writer, one who draws on the authority of Grosseteste to validate some of his own theological intuitions, all the while adapting his material to a new, if socially and educationally identical, community.

The English redactor makes some of the same gestures of assurance to his audience that Grosseteste made, but he is decidedly more aggressive in defending his use of the vernacular. Prologues in the vernacular,

Ruth Evans has shown, did more than announce the scope and intention
of a work; they fulfilled a political function or made Latin traditions
"function in another register."[35] In his prologue Grosseteste makes little
fuss about his use of the vernacular, adhering closely to the Latin con-
ceits and conventions, whereas the English redactor seems eager to call
attention to the alleged deficiencies of English in order to disprove that
claim through the quality of the discourse that will follow. He repeats
Grosseteste's point that not everyone in this world was born in the same
land or is versed in the theological languages of Hebrew, Latin, Greek,
or French. Then, with visible pride, he advances his reasons for voicing
his song of praise to God in his native tongue:

> Þauh hit on Englisch be dim and derk
> Ne nabbe no sauur bifore [a] clerk,
> For lewed men þat luitel connen
> On Englisch hit is þus bigonnen.
> Ac whose is witer and wys of wit
> And ȝerne biholdeþ þis ilke writ
> And con þat muchel of luitel vnlouken
> And hony of þe harde ston souken,
> Alle poyntes he fynde may
> Of vre beleeue and Godes [fay]
> Þat bifalleþ to Godes godhede
> As wel as to his monhede.
>   (71–82)[36]

There are several points of interest here, and a touch of irony. While the
redactor readily acknowledges the unsophisticated nature of English, he
attributes the attitude of contempt rather exclusively to the clerks. He
understands clearly that textual authority resides with them and their
Latin discourse, but his use of the metaphor "hony of þe hard ston souken"
is striking and displays his own learning and ingenuity as he turns the
clerkly prejudice back on itself. The metaphor comes from Deuteronomy
32.13, and refers to the way God instructed his people, giving them
honey to suck from rocks in a barren land. However barren English may
be as a discourse for theology, however distasteful the clerks may
find it, and however unwilling they are to share their special knowledge
with the laity in a language or discourse the laity can understand, the

redactor is confident that English is an excellent medium for poetry and adequate for him to be able to communicate what is essential for an understanding of the Christian faith: God's manhood as well as his godhead. Singling out God's "manhode" equates it thematically with his divinity and enunciates the christological emphasis of the poem.

For the narrator, reading this poem becomes another form of sucking honey from a stone. The attention and the cooperation of the reader will reward those who are "wys of wit" to derive an understanding of things through their imagination as well as through their reason. Poetry will compensate for the limitations of language and learning that besets the "lewede" man. The poem will not distort the meaning of doctrine or of biblical episodes that will be retold; rather, it will bring out meaning in a nuanced way.

Both Grosseteste and the redactor, for example, make liberal use of a doctrinally discredited thesis like the devil's rights because it enables them to bring the kind of attention desired to the human dimension of Christ. Grosseteste sensed that the devil's rights idea still held appeal to the popular imagination (and quite possibly to that of the learned) because it had legal ramifications they could relate to and it depicted Christ as an advocate who could outsmart the devil and defeat him at his own game.[37] The situation holds dramatic appeal and at the same time conveys the personal love and concern Christ has for his fellow human beings. Grosseteste takes full advantage of the greater latitude with doctrine afforded by the poetic medium to communicate the spirit of what he has determined Christ means to the world and to human nature. The poetic medium and its projected audience allow Grosseteste to concentrate on the moral content without the need to engage in formal exegesis.

In the creation scene, for instance, one of the more lyrical sections of the poem, God creates the universe *ex nihilo* so that the whole created order, from the smallest speck of dust ascending upward, expresses the unity and diversity of the Trinity. Adam and Eve, though first in the order of intention, are created last because their nature presupposes all other creatures,[38] and the work of the preceding six days is required to constitute human nature in the divine image and likeness:

Tud au derrain Adam criad
El val de Hebron sanz dutance

Le fist de terre a sa semblance,
Après le seinte Trinité
Crea sa alme in verité.
Amur plus ne lipout mustrer
Ke après se meimes former.
(74–80)

He com to þe valeye of Ebron. / Þer he made Adam [alast] so riche /
Of eorþe after hymself iliche, / And aftur [þe] holy þrillihod / He
schop his soule feir and good. / How miȝte he him more loue
schowen / Þen his oune liknesse habben and owen? (126–32)

The salient point about Adam's creation is that his body as well as his
soul is fashioned in the likeness of God. The implication is that the soul
belongs to the body and is not in exile here. In his theology, Grosseteste
did not advocate the soul's increasing separation or freedom from the
body. Rather, as Richard Dales has shown, Grosseteste always focused
on the body-soul relationship and not on the soul as a separate sub-
stance: "The soul's overriding natural desire is to be united to its body,
to nurture and care for it, to give it life."[39] The poem makes this more
emphatic: the nobility of human nature (and of nature itself) is not limi-
ted to the interior person but includes perfection of the body and what
pertains to the material order as well. As a result, *Le chateau d'amour*
emerges as Grosseteste's most explicit statement on what it means to be
a human being and what it means to be a Christian in the world. The
main argument of the poem, the goodness of the creation and the cen-
trality of human beings in it, epitomizes what is most English about
English theology.

Like the visual artists, Grosseteste's poem existentializes the biblical
episodes and humanizes his characters, placing them in a familiar set-
ting surrounded by familiar concerns. God and Adam are feudalized;
God is depicted as a benevolent landowner and Adam as his vassal who
has been given permission to cultivate the estate of the world as his
seisine. Anselm had used the lord-vassal analogy in his treatise but
Grosseteste's poem improves upon it in its elaborate realism. The poem
sets up the entire proceeding so that the thrall's (Adam's) situation is
consistent with late medieval property laws, and he develops the case
within the language and confines of the legal and moral order in place in

the thirteenth century.[40] What we see is the way the laws bind human beings to God and God to his creation. Adam's dual heritage from the earth and from God grants him autonomy in his own domain. In return the lord has the right to exact allegiance from his vassal, in this instance in the form of two laws. The first is natural law or "conscience," by which Adam and Eve are to do everything that is expected of them according to their nature. The second is positive law or "law set," which forbids them to eat from the tree and which is enacted to strengthen their bond of obedience to the covenant. In a covenant both sides are said to enter the pact voluntarily and for their mutual benefit, making the partnership itself as important as the articles contained in the agreement. Thus, although the laws impose a restraint upon human freedom, they come to serve as the basis for human rights. Vassalage was the tie that bound a warrior to his lord; it was a mutual arrangement and marked the beginning of horizontal relationships in the social and political arena. The bond of vassalage, Susan Reynolds points out, eclipsed all other ties and "the word *fidelis,* like the word man *(homo),* became a synonym for vassal."[41]

The legal analogy has another benefit that exceeds its strictly theological function, namely, the way that it displaces the burden of sin, especially the idea of original sin. In the feudal analogy the thrall forfeits only his legal rights and privileges; he suffers nothing in the way of a permanent impairment to his inborn goodness. Legally, Adam or the thrall fails only to live up to his *seisine.* His trespass is characterized as a "defaute," a lack or absence. The stress falls on Adam's failure to do good rather than on his having an evil disposition or will. The most important consequence of Grosseteste's analogy is the primacy it gives to the effort to restore the thrall to his *seisine* or land tenure, making Adam's reconciliation with this world an integral part of his reconciliation with God.

This theme is played out in the central and most poetically accomplished section of the poem: the allegory of the King and His Four Daughters, which Grosseteste adapts and seamlessly weaves into his feudal pattern. The story, based on a psalm, centers on four daughters of a king—Mercy, Truth, Justice, and Peace—who have assembled to debate the fate of humankind. The story was quite popular in medieval literature as well as in illuminated manuscripts, and Grosseteste was doubtless familiar with pre-existing versions from Hugh of St. Victor and St. Bernard.[42] Originally, the allegory was a creation story and had become associated in the later Middle Ages with the justification and redemption of humankind. Grosseteste's version has dramatic power even if the speeches of the daughters, who address the king rather than one another, are static. The poem departs from tradition by making Mercy rather than Justice the older sister, and hence the first attribute of the Father, a view consistent with the creation sequence in which God is shown as benign and friendly toward human beings.

In Grosseteste's version Truth and Justice are first given their due; Truth convinces the Father that the thrall should suffer imprisonment and death, in accordance with the law, because he had been forewarned of the consequences should he break any law. The king agrees and the thrall is placed in a dungeon to await death. At this point Grosseteste's poem adds an unusual wrinkle. In protest, Mercy and Peace withdraw from the world, leaving it wracked by war and envy. To show what the world might be like bereft of Mercy and Peace, Grosseteste interpolates the story of the Flood, presented here as a terrible disaster rather than as a just punishment because it represents a perversion of the original creation:

> Ne Pès ne poet demurer
> De le païs l'estuet turner,
> Kar Pès ne demure mie
> En guerre ne en atie.
> Ne Misericorde n'est numee,
> Tuz unt le pais exillé.
> Ni ad rien ki seit remis
> Ke a destruction ne unt mis.
> Tuz unt les undes neiez;…
> Hidur est de penser ent,
> De si tres cruël jugement;
> E tut est Dreit e Verité
> Mes sanz Pès e sanz Pité.
>
> (353–70)

Ne Pees mot not mid hem be, / Out of londe heo mot fle, / For Pees bileueþ in no londe / Wher [þat] is were, nuþ, and onde, / Ne Merci

mot not among hem liue, / Ac boþe heo beþ of londe idriue. / Nis
þer nout in world bileued, / Þat nis destrued and to-dreued, / And
dreynt, forloren, and fordemed,... / Careful herte him ouȝte come /
Þat þencheþ vppon þe dredful dome, / And al hit is þorw Riht and
Soþ, / Þat withouten Pees and Merci doþ. (439–56)

Grosseteste strikes an especially strong note of poignancy, not unlike
the author of *Cleanness,* by succinctly envisioning the emptiness of the
world in which all have perished under the waves except for eight souls,
Noah, his wife, their three sons and their wives. No others existed in the
whole world ("Of al þe world nas beleued more"). All are under the
sway of Justice and Truth without Mercy and Peace.

The Son is so disturbed by the division among the sisters, and over
the plight of the thrall, that he volunteers to initiate a new covenant and
to bring the sisters together again. The remedy or "respit" for the thrall's
suffering must come in the form of a surrogate, someone who has been
born free, has not eaten from the tree, and has not violated the law of
Moses, which has been in force since the breach of the first covenant.
Above all, he must be fully human ("verrais home") and of the same
lineage as the thrall. The Son readily agrees to put on the habiliments of
the thrall, a sign of his complete humanity, if it will cause Peace and
Justice to kiss and restore the thrall to his land. The Son's willingness to
put on human nature and unite wholly with mankind is conveyed as an
act of fellowship. The shift from the king to the Son in Grosseteste's
conclusion to the allegory, in effect a shift from the traditional theme of
the king's mercy—Anselm's argument—to the regenerative will of the
Son, nicely conveys Grosseteste's abiding concern for the incarnation
as a human event keyed to the restoration of the original inheritance of
human beings and their need to resume their original responsibility.

The Four Daughters sequence also sustains and advances the legal
analogy. Mercy begins the work of reconciliation by pointing out to the
king the trickery used by the devil in his seduction of the thrall. She
petitions the king to ransom the thrall from the devil, another aspect of
the devil's rights motif. Anselm's opposition to the idea of the devil's
rights was based on the point that satisfaction must be made to God not
the devil, and that God delivered humankind from bondage because he
is just and thus does what is appropriate to him as the highest good.[43] In

the poem, God and the devil are constrained by a legal contract in the same way as the vassal and his lord are depicted. The devil presumably has won power of life and death over the thrall, but by exercising this power over the Son (even the devil is fooled by the authenticity of the Son's human nature), he is forced to forfeit the *seisine* he had won from the thrall. He loses both the prisoner in his charge and the Son too. By bringing close attention to the Son's shared lineage and brotherhood with the thrall, the poem initiates Anselm's switch from justification as God's righteousness to a righteousness that needs to be claimed by human beings.

Peace, who has Grosseteste's voice, brings Mercy's appeal to its logical conclusion. She credits Truth for showing that human beings brought their doom upon themselves, then argues that the true function of justice is to restore peace, to recover the original harmony that existed between God and his creation. No king whose name is Peace should tolerate a kingdom in disharmony or disunity, she says, in a statement freighted with social and political signification. By urging the king to release the vassal on the grounds that the magnificence of the land is being despoiled while the thrall languishes in prison, Peace reinforces the theme that human beings need to be free to do that which is in them, that it is their share of the covenant that obligates them to bring the kingdom to its perfection.

The legal terms of the covenant that had justified the thrall's imprisonment now speak in his defense. Peace avers that no final doom or "record" *(recordum habere)* can be fixed against a subject if his judges cannot agree on the nature of his punishment. In situations where the accused cannot appear in court, a substitute may appear in his stead. The Son's voluntary agreement to represent the thrall in court restores the terms of the original covenant: Mercy and Peace return to earth, Peace and Justice kiss, and the thrall recovers his *seisine*. As a poem with pastoral ambitions, *Le chateau d'amour* shows that a sublime imitation of Christ means that Mercy and Peace have to be made active in the world again if human beings are to attain a likeness to Christ.

The incarnation itself is depicted in the long middle section of the poem in which the Virgin Mary is compared in elaborate detail to a castle whose walls, barbicans, ditches, gates, and towers are invested with symbolic value. The mainspring of this interlude is the theme of descent. First Mary is compared to a ladder down which Christ descends to enter her body ("Ce est le cors e le pucele") and to clothe himself in flesh. The actual moment of the incarnation is described as a shaft of light—the brightest flash of light ever—that penetrates Mary and diffuses itself through the prism of her body so that she, as Mother and as physical embodiment of the church, becomes the medium through whom God's fructifying grace nourishes the whole world. Christ's descent as light reverses the Neoplatonic *topos* in which (sinful) humanity ascends to the light, leaving the realm of gross matter below. Mary, as the earthly vessel that houses and engenders the incarnate Christ, is shown to have the power to generate or "multiply" the light of God ("Sa beauté tant multiplie"). *Multiplie,* another of those alchemical terms of which Grosseteste was so fond, refers to the process of refinement and transmutation that the *sympathetic* substances undergo in the *magnum opus,* another term that doubles for the alchemical work and for the incarnation itself. The engendering and quickening of Christ in Mary's womb is likened to the shaping of a sword through the fusion of fire and steel (1228–32); the respective elements do not lose their individual properties when the sword is formed but are preserved in an existence more sublime. Thus, in the union of human and divine elements in Mary's womb, the human dimension is not obliterated or transfigured by the divine but reformed and preserved as deified human existence.

Another example of the anthropocentrism of the poem shows Christ descending the ladder, not to remove human beings from the earth, but to re-root them in their earthly origins. In conceiving Christ, Mary experiences instantaneously the "fin amur" (1384), or purifying love, set in motion at the creation and still laboring to produce the *prima materia* or image and likeness of Christ through the alembic of history. The alchemical analogy secures an active role for Mary and prevents us from regarding her body as merely a passive receptacle through which Christ passes to enter the world. Of this dramatization of the incarnation, one might say Christ does not bring dignity to human beings so much as he assumes human nature because it already possesses dignity.

Christ's transformation in the womb of Mary radiates throughout the whole of nature. In the most daring and imaginative passage in the entire poem, the one excluded from the English version, we learn how the incarnation augments nature, revivifying the animal and vegetative spirit lodged within it:

> Mult est nature enbelie,
> Kant nature naturante
> A nature est ignorante;   [ioygnante]
> Ke nature naturee.   [Ke nature est naturee]
> Lorcs est nature puree
> Cent tant plus ke einz ne esteit
> Einz ke Adam forfet aveit.   [Avant que]
>   (866–72)

Nature was much embellished when God, "natura naturans," was joined to Nature, "natura naturata." Then was Nature purified a hundred times more than it was before Adam paid the forfeit of sin.[44]

Southern nominates these as the single most important lines in the poem, granting us an insight into thirteenth-century views of nature. The distinction Grosseteste makes between "nature naturante" *(natura naturans)* and "nature naturee" *(natura naturata),* Southern says, was a new and highly controversial one, and may account for their omission from the English text. The former term generally refers to God as the source of all nature and the latter to the created universe, or the ordinary course of nature: "The description of God as *natura naturans,* seems to have made its way into Latin through Aristotle's *Physics* which drew a distinction between Nature as a first cause and Nature as that which was caused; and the phrase *natura naturata* may have come from the Latin translation of Averroes's commentary."[45] The deployment of these terms is calculated to elevate natural science over symbolism in respect to the creation and incarnation: God's presence is revealed through the very laws of nature he puts in motion.

What Grosseteste, who wrote an extensive commentary on the *Physics,* may have derived from Aristotle's text and employed here is his idea of nature as the genesis of growing things, as the principle of all motion and rest. For Aristotle, and Grosseteste after him, the search for the nature of things was a search for the active principle or source out of which things were formed and had the potentiality to change. In

James Weisheipl's words, "It was not simply a search for the one and the many, but a search for the ultimate explanation of the cosmos in terms of nature, an *active* principle of movement and becoming," making nature or the natural play of the elements, not the divine soul, the primary concept in the evolution of the physical world.[46] Hence Christ, when taken as the active principle behind the created universe—"the force that through the green fuse drives the flower"—is synonymous with nature *(natura naturans)*. Grosseteste conflates God with nature to show that nature is like God in its drive to wed spirit and matter and to suggest that the incarnation is the appointed goal of nature's growth.

What should not be lost amid this scientific language is Grosseteste's very simple and obvious truth: that Christ adds something to human nature, which makes deification possible. As *natura naturans,* the cosmic principle or vitalizing agent that keeps the universe in motion, Christ heals the split in nature and inspires the soul to love the body again. In the climax of the poem Christ becomes the new Father who engenders in human beings his image and who, by washing humankind in his blood, repurchases our freedom ("Il est dreir Nostre Pere; / Il nus engendra en manere / Ke de sun sanc nus lava / E nostre franchise rechata" [1379–82]). The baptismal image of blood from the crucified Christ foreshadows the resurrection of the body. For Christ's soul so loved its body, the poem says, that it could not suffer to be separated from it ("Kar tant eime l'alme le cors / Ke jamès ne en istra fors" [1151–52]). Strikingly, his soul did not try to flee from the body at the first hint of death. This is poignantly rendered in the English version:

> For þe soule loueþ þe body so
> Þat neuere heo nule him wende fro,
> For no pyne ne for [no] sore,
> Þauʒ me hit to-hewe euer more,
> Er þe fyf wittes ben loren outriht...
> Ar he wole from þe bodi wende ...
> He ʒaf his soule wiþ loud vois
> Þer he schewede þat he was God so.
> (1171–87)

Christ's calling out in a loud voice is not a sign of his suffering; it is a sign of life and strength. In one of his sermons Grosseteste made this point even more emphatically, asserting that it was not Christ's wounds that caused his death on the cross but the voluntary sundering of his soul from his body.[47] The soul of Christ clung to its body with an infinite love because it desired a lasting and continuous union with the body: "Whence it follows that the love of the bond with the body was infinite, and it follows from that that the suffering in the separation of soul and body was infinite."[48] Christ's suffering is most deeply felt in history, Grosseteste says, "because the greatest suffering is the most deeply felt deprivation of what is most, and most naturally, desired. The most *natural* desire is the union of the soul and the body."[49]

For Grosseteste, the meaning of the incarnation is human dignity, or the reunion of the body and soul in history. By making it the pivotal event of human history, Grosseteste offers his audience an alternative to death as the path to perfection. Human beings can become co-creators with God and nature in the work of creation. But, before the soul can leave the body, that is, before human beings can leave this earth, they first must become like Christ in his act of self-mastery: they must learn to love their bodies again.[50]

2.

Langland and the Four Daughters of God

How well Langland knew Grosseteste's formal theology is difficult to say, but he gives every indication of having been familiar with *Le chateau d'amour*. In passus 18 of the B text of *Piers Plowman* Langland presents his own version of the Four Daughters legend and through it his version of the redemption. Passus 18 contains Langland's answer to the question of why God became a human being, and the Christology of his poem corresponds with Grosseteste's thinking on the subject.[51] Langland's Christ, like Grosseteste's, does not become a human being exclusively or primarily for the purpose of performing the work of the redemption. He has the prior role of embodying human perfection and of teaching human beings that they can fulfill their nature by doing that which is in them. By introducing Langland's version here I do not expect to do justice either to passus 18 or to the poem as a whole.[52] My aim is to show how Langland transforms the Four Daughters story in order to forge a new image of Christ and a new understanding of the redemption that speaks to the needs of his own time.

The redemption of humankind is the main theme of passus 18—perhaps of *Piers Plowman* as a whole—and it is instructive to see how flexible and innovative Langland can be in his adaptation of the Four Daughters legend and in his representation of Christ. In his dream, Will envisions a highly unorthodox or "poetic" Christ who responds to Will's desire to learn more about the nature of charity.[53] Christ appears as a Samaritan, as Piers the plowman, as a knight, and as a giant who can knock down doors. Each configuration brings out another dimension of Christ's multifarious human identity. As the Samaritan he locates Christliness outside of the church and outside of Christendom; as Piers he locates Christ among the poor and disenfranchised. Will's recognition of Christ as "Oon semblable to þe Samaritan, and somdeel to Piers þe Plow[man]" (10) brings the abstract idea of being created in the likeness of Christ to the concrete reality that works of charity, such as those performed by the Samaritan, and daily work, such as Piers performs, make Christ manifest within time. Clothing Christ in these guises, Langland creates another version of the *violent love* tradition, a love that breaks down all barriers and brings to human beings a living example of charity.[54]

Although Langland has the reputation of being a didactic poet, it is obvious in passus 18 that he is not as closed or as authoritative in his views as generally is believed. His commitment to an ethical Christianity, which is manifest everywhere in *Piers Plowman*, does not reduce the poem to the level of a religious polemic, nor does it subordinate his poetry to the demands of theological truth. As John A. Burrow points out, no matter how deeply Langland was concerned with the truth (about faith, his society, and himself), he does not abandon fiction for history or biblical paraphrase, and his fictive imagination remains powerfully at work.[55] Accordingly, the variations Langland adds to the story of the redemption and the various roles he assigns to Christ make for a poet who is willing to play, in Wolfgang Iser's sense, with the theological materials at his disposal, and they make for a poem that is, in Peter Haidu's terms, "unbound and unpredictable."[56] In retelling the Four Daughters legend in the imaginative fashion that he does, Langland opens up his text as a space for play and he leaves ample room for readers to form their own judgment of the events described.[57]

Having the events unfold in Long Will's dream, for example, allows Langland the freedom and distance to arrange things psychologically as well as theologically. Another way that he makes the poem more dialogical is to place theological arguments on controversial topics such as justification, universal salvation, and the devil's rights, in the mouth of Christ or the devils.[58] This displacement lends more force and authority to the arguments, even though the figures speak purely as fictional characters. Another effective technique is the way he cites scripture first in Latin and then repeats the text in English. Here Langland shows that the vernacular is able to convey the central meaning of the Latin and then can develop its own commentary on the passage through the poetic elaboration that follows, showing that the poem does not serve merely as a scaffold for delineation of any of the texts, biblical or Grossetestean, that deals directly or indirectly with the redemption, the Four Daughters, or the devil's rights. When he introduces the Four Daughters sequence in passus 18 with the words *secundum scripturas,* the allusion is not only an authentication of the biblical origins of the legend but also a differentiation. His rendition is not "according to the scriptures" but is a poetic dramatization. Langland underscores the difference between the two discourses, between what is based on scripture and what is based on his poetic imagination. His additions and modifications to the legend, moreover, infuse the story with new values for Mercy and Peace, Truth and Righteousness. Finally, in the passus as a whole, he transforms the notion of charity by extracting from the person of Christ and the life of Christ new lessons on the nature of love and self-sacrifice.

Langland begins his mini-drama of the Four Daughters in darkness. Will has retreated into the pit of hell to escape from the eruption of violence in nature and in society which has occurred after Christ's apparent defeat in his joust with the devil. We learn from the sisters that the darkness is only temporary; Christ has gathered the light of the sun into himself and will use it to blind the devil. In this version the daughters are all attributes of Christ, instead of the Father, and they have been summoned from the four points of the globe to be reunited in him as a sign of his victory over the devil's tenure as lord of the earth. Throughout, Langland keeps Christ as his central focus, relegating the sisters primarily to a choric role. They comment on the actions of Christ, who acts on behalf of human beings out of his shared human nature, and not at the instigation of the sisters, as is the case in Grosseteste's version. As eyewitnesses who are themselves uncertain of the outcome and meaning of the events unfolding before them, the sisters bring tension and immediacy to the moment.

Mercy and Truth appear first, from the west and east respectively. Both look toward hell and toward the strange light and din that emanates from within. Mercy is described as meek, in contrast to her sister, who is described as never fearful. Mercy realizes that the light penetrating the darkness signals the fulfillment of the prophecies and she explains in a series of concrete examples how "man shal man saue þoruȝ a maydenes helpe" (139), sustaining the theme of this passus, which is Christ's "kynde."

Truth scornfully dismisses Mercy's report as a "tale of waltrot" (142), citing Job to the effect that once in hell one never comes out: "Quia in inferno nulla est redempcio" (149a). Truth and Justice speak with great self-confidence because they believe Christ cannot act out of charity for imprisoned humanity without breaking the law. Truth lacks final truth; the law is not fixed and the possibility of universal salvation remains open. Mercy, relying on her "experience," begins the transformation of Truth and Justice. In her most interesting and sustained analogy, that of poison and medicine, she illustrates how Christ is the cure for the most dire of maladies:

> I hope þei shul be saued;
> For venym fordooþ venym, [þer fecche I euydence
> That Adam and Eue haue shul bote].
> For of alle venymes foulest is þe scorpion;
> May no medicyne [amende] þe place þer he styngeþ,
> Til he be deed and do þerto; þe yuel he destruyeþ,
> The firste venymouste, þoruȝ [vertu] of hymselue.
> So shal þis deeþ fordo, I dar my lif legge,
> Al þat deeþ [d]ide first þoruȝ þe deueles entisyng,
> And riȝt as [þe gilour] þoruȝ gile [bigiled man formest]
> So shal grace that bigan [al] make a good [ende
> And bigile the gilour, and þat is good] sleighte.
>
> (151–62)

Mercy lays the foundation for Christ's mercy: it is the devil rather than humankind that has poisoned human nature. Evil will destroy evil; the guiler shall be beguiled; just as the scorpion, though poisonous itself, has the power and virtue to destroy evil.

The poison analogy probably derives from Numbers 21.8–9, where Moses, at the Lord's bidding, makes a bronze serpent whose aspect can cure those who have been bitten by a serpent. What kills, cures; it is a theme Christ picks up himself in the passage where he repudiates Satan's claim to humankind (329–50). Earlier, in passus 16, we learned that Christ was schooled by Piers in the skill of medicine, first to heal himself and then to cure others, "Til he was parfit praktisour" (107). The life he gives for a life, according to the old law (343), remedies the poison Adam ingested when he ate the apple infected by the serpent's venom who appeared in paradise (Christ's "paleis") to rob Christ of the thing he loved best (338).

In his vivid account of the crucifixion earlier in the passus, Langland tells us how the executioners nail Christ to the cross with three nails and then "poison on a poole þei putte vp to hise lippes, / And beden hym drynken his deeþ [to lette and] hise daies [lengþe]" (52–53). When Christ stands before the devil, he offers an antidote in the elixir of his own blood:

> [þe bitternesse þat þow hast browe, now brouke it þiselue];
> That art doctour of deeþ drynk þat þow madest.
> For I þat am lord of lif, loue is my drynke,
> And for þat drynke today, I deide vpon erþe.
> I fauȝt so me þursteþ ȝet for mannes soule sake;
> May no drynke me moiste, ne my þurst slake,
> Til þe vendage falle in þe vale of Iosaphat,
> That I drynke riȝt ripe must, *Resureccio mortuorum.*
>
> (363–70)

Langland's interpretive maneuver with the gospels displays the dexterity with which he welds every event to his theme of Christ's charity and forgiveness. He transforms what has often been read as a defeat or as a negative event into a victory for humankind. Just as Mercy interpreted the eclipse and earthquake at the time of Christ's death as a sign that Christ will triumph over nature and lead humankind out of the darkness, so too we learn Christ's thirst was not a consequence of his extreme suffering; it is a sign of his unquenchable thirst for human souls. The devil must drink the poison he has brewed while Christ yearns to drink to the dregs the wine of life ("vendage"), which becomes the blood of his brethren. The poison vinegar or spoiled wine is transubstantiated into the blood-wine of Christ's sacrifice and healing power.

Peace and Justice confront each other in a similar way. When Peace arrives, richly attired in the clothing of patience, she announces that she and Mercy will sing and dance in honor of the occasion, and she petitions Justice "do þow so, suster. / For Iesus Iustede wel Ioye bigynneþ dawe" (180–81), the latter a reference to the light that is gradually overcoming the darkness. Justice, who has been introduced by Truth as the final authority on God's will because she is the oldest (165), declares that the pain of hell will be perpetual for sinners: "For it is boteles bale, þe byte þat þei eten" (202). If Peace thinks otherwise she must be drunk. The words of Justice are a variation of the poison motif. The death bite of the apple is incurable. As he did with Truth, Langland makes the argument of Justice to be formidable. He shows respect for the old law primarily to celebrate the magnificence of Christ's transformation of the rule of Justice into a metaphysics of Peace, a movement from woe to well-being.

In her response to Righteousness, Peace reveals that Christ became man of a woman and suffered to be sold so that he could know the "sorwe of deying" (214).[59] His death completes his human identity and has bound him closer to his brethren whose future he will now change. Peace announces that she carries with her a warrant, letters she has received from Love (Christ) authorizing Mercy and Peace to protect or be "mannes meynpernour" forever more (184). In his poem Grosseteste reported that nature improved a hundredfold when Christ descended into the flesh in the incarnation. Langland reverses the situation; Peace shows Christ's nature improving its understanding of love through its union with the body. What he learns from the acquisition of human love prompts him to replace Truth and Righteousness with Mercy and Peace, and thus to promise forgiveness to all:

> And þanne shal I come as a kyng, crouned, wiþ Aungeles,
> And haue out of helle alle mennes soules.

Fendes and f[e]ndekynes bifore me shul stande
And be at my biddyng whereso [best] me likeþ.
A[c] to be merciable to man þanne my kynde [it] askeþ
For we beþ breþeren of blood, [ac] noȝt in baptisme alle.
Ac alle þat beþ myne hole breþeren, in blood and in baptisme,
Shul noȝt be dampned to þe deeth that is wiþouten ende.

(371–78)

Thomas D. Hill, who discusses this passage in great detail, notes that the harrowing of hell traditionally is a prefiguration of judgment. He points out that Langland seizes the opportunity in this passage to alter existing thinking about hell.[60] "The appeal of the conception of universal salvation," he says, "is that it affirms God's benevolence and love. The problem with this answer to the great eschatological questions is that it would appear to leave no room for human choice and significant action."[61] Langland sees farther than that.

One of the ways he has enriched the Four Daughters legend is through the role and voice he gives to the devils. We witness and hear what effect the redemption has on them and on their control over human beings. Almost humorously, Langland has the devil account for the timing of the redemption. At first, the devil says, he had wanted to prolong Christ's life in order to postpone the redemption indefinitely. Once Christ began to lure souls away from him through the power and efficacy of his preaching, the devil infiltrated the dream of Pilate's wife in order to set the passion in motion and bring Christ's ministry to an end. The implication is that Christ poses a more serious threat to the rule of the devil in his ministry and his example of charity than he does as redeemer, as formidable as that role obviously is. With the redemption God's revelation of human nature is complete, and in the absence of Christ human beings are expected to carry out his legacy, to emulate the kerygma of his lived existence. His words to the devil "And al þat man haþ mysdo I man wole amende" (341) indicates that human beings have within their nature the power to make the choices Christ made. Langland thus makes it clear that the work of the redemption is ongoing; it no longer involves death on the cross or the harrowing of hell. What secures freedom and restores human beings to their former dignity is the example of Christ's lived existence.

Langland also uses the devils to mitigate the fault of Adam and Eve and along with it the magnitude of original sin. In the foyer of hell Mercy and Peace speak fondly of Adam and Eve and express their desire to be reunited with them. In hell, a parallel debate unfolds that is also four-cornered, among Lucifer, Satan, Goblin, and the devil. Just as the four sisters collectively represent aspects of the one Christ, the several fiends represent the one archfiend. As Christ approaches the gates of hell the consistory of devils dissolves into mutual acrimony and vituperation. They accuse one another of deceiving Adam and Eve and of betraying the creation. The more the devils blame themselves the more Adam and Eve are absolved of guilt. Christ defeats the devils by trickery according to the rule that it is proper for a beguiler to be beguiled. Accordingly, he will judge the devils by the old law "dentem pro dente et oculum pro oculo" (340a), but he will judge human beings by the new law of love. Enrolling Adam and Eve in the new law suggests that the fall no longer should determine the shape or the course of human history.[62]

Christ will not hang a felon twice. He forgives humankind and em-braces his brothers and sisters in one human nature, resolving to bring Mercy and Peace and Love together: "And Pees þoruჳ pacience alle perils stoppeþ" (415). Justice ratifies Christ's promise that Mercy will prevail on the last day when she acknowledges the wisdom of Peace's words that nothing is impossible to him who is almighty. The sequence ends with Peace reciting lines from a poem which bring the light and darkness imagery to a close: "After sharpe shoures, quod pees, moost shene is þe sonne; / Is no weder warmer þan after watry cloudes" (409–10). Grosseteste, too, had the sun, which was dimmed by the fall, return to its former brightness at the reconciliation of the sisters. The song and dance that follow celebrate poetry in its performative aspect, not in its prophetic mode.

The reconciliation of the four sisters at the end of the passus ex-plains why Langland chose to shift the setting of his version from the creation or incarnation to the scene of the redemption. The recovery of what had been lost in the past is as meaningful a part of the redemption as is the opening of the path to salvation. The union of the sisters also makes clear the nature of the paradigm shift from the old law to the new: bondage to sin is not the central truth or defining point of human nature or human history. In his depiction of Christ as an active figure who epitomizes human nature and who defeats the devil through a realization of his human powers and virtues, rather than through an exercise of his divine nature, Langland makes Christ the foundation of an ethical or this-worldly Christianity, and makes passus 18 a significant expression of the poetics of human dignity in the fourteenth century.

THREE

The Pearl-*Poet*

One might maintain, not too paradoxically, that every medieval poetic form (on whatever level one may define it) *tends* toward double meaning: and I don't mean the doubling deciphered by an allegoristic meaning but, superimposing or complexifying its effects, a perpetual *sic et non,* yes and no, obverse / reverse. Every meaning, in the last analysis, would present itself as enigmatic, the enigma being resolved into simultaneous and contradictory propositions, one of which always more or less parodies the other.

Paul Zumthor[1]

1.
"kark and combraunce huge" in Cleanness

With the possible exception of *Sir Gawain and the Green Knight,* all of the *Pearl*-poet's works have been regarded as didactic and imitative of the form and content of a medieval sermon. Charles Muscatine set the course followed by many readers in their approach to the *Pearl*-poet when he declared some time ago that the *Pearl* moralist

> seems from his overt statements to be a surprisingly uncomplicated moralist, and a conservative one as well. Thinking of his having lived in the second half of the fourteenth century, we find him surprisingly untroubled for those troubled times, and surprisingly accepting and unquestioning of the orthodox forms of Christianity and of feudalism.[2]

Muscatine concedes that crisis touches the *Pearl*-poet, perhaps profoundly, "but in these poems it is completely absorbed in his art."[3] While political readings of *Sir Gawain and the Green Knight* have become increasingly heterodox, readings of his "theological politics" have not;

the prevailing opinion on the other three poems is that he uses them to instruct and that he is unfailingly orthodox in his vision.[4] What this has meant for most readers is that the *Pearl*-poet, while an accomplished poet, stands far apart from both Chaucer and Langland when it comes to contesting the vital theological and social issues that erupted in the fourteenth century. Rather than unsettling his readers, as Langland does, he appears to relieve them of the moral and ethical problems that a more questioning theological stance might impose.[5] Yet, as I endeavor to show in my discussion of *Cleanness, Patience,* and *Pearl,* this poet is no apologist for the theological status quo. *Cleanness,* for example, is not a standard defense of cleanness but a critique of purity as a theological ideal. This poet recognizes, I shall argue, that what is most in need of change is the discourse of purity and the association of human sexuality with such offensive notions as "filth of the flesh."

As we saw in chapter 1, this poet is no stranger to controversy, and a number of recent articles and books have shown how his poetry addresses the theological concerns of his day. Nicholas Watson places this poet and these poems in the context of late medieval religiosity and as an integral part of a body of vernacular writing "which was more and more aware of, and anxious to shape, and in turn to be shaped by the needs of lay readers."[6] Nick Davis has called special attention to this poet's concern with ethical issues and shown how his exposition of moral precepts consists mainly "of densely wrought accounts of particular actions and events, whose significance will emerge only on reflection."[7] In his discussion of the *Pearl*-poet's scriptural and devotional sources, Richard Newhauser has shown how the poet's adaptation of biblical narratives, while not denying their allegorical or typological potential, demonstrates his great interest in their literal level, "as stories of understandable human psychology."[8] A. C. Spearing has provided us with a new way of understanding the figure and actions of God in *Patience,* and Elizabeth Keiser has presented a most thorough and insightful treatment of the sexual issues in *Cleanness.*[9]

A re-assessment of the *Pearl*-poet's art, his poetic language, and his relationship to the theological discourse of his day might best begin with a reconsideration of the "fayre formez" that he uses in his poems. In *The Sacred Complex,* William Kerrigan suggests that there are two distinct attitudes toward sacred language and biblical hermeneutics: the legal and the prophetic, and that these divide Augustine from Pseudo-Dionysius, Erasmus from Luther, Anglican bishops from Puritan enthusiasts. The radical issue, he says, is whether the meaning of the Bible can be fixed, or "whether instead the Bible forever anticipates a novel future, open to a widening horizon of interpreters who 'assimilate its significance to that of their own creation.'"[10] Kerrigan's remarks were prepared with an audience for Milton's *Paradise Lost* in mind, but his observations can be applied with equal profit to the *Pearl*-poet, whose poetic invention and skill are brilliantly on display in his mastery of biblical narratives. Although the narratives of *Cleanness, Patience,* and *Pearl* maintain a high degree of fidelity to their biblical originals, the poet's deployment of various narrative comments throughout and his use of realistic, contemporary details call attention to their fictionality. As fictions, his poems resist being reduced to sermons or to "mere" vernacularizations of biblical episodes, leading this reader to conclude that the *Pearl*-poet does not reproduce biblical stories in order to provide a new reading of scripture for his own historical era—thereby preserving the truth of scripture—rather, he infuses the parables with contemporary details in order to test the truth of tradition and to open the text to alternative readings.

Acts of interpretation, Frank Kermode says, are required at every stage in the life of a narrative, and however the work is done, whether by fictive augmentation and change or by commentary, "its object is to penetrate the surface and reveal a secret sense; to show what is concealed in what is proclaimed."[11] These new meanings are but actualizations of the text's hermeneutical potential, which, though never fully available, is inexhaustible. Nevertheless, for Kermode, *parables* might better be translated as "riddles," because only "insiders" are intended to have access to the true sense of these stories.[12] In his retelling of the Bible stories, the *Pearl*-poet turns this notion around by providing a text readily available to the laity as well as the clergy. The availability and contemporaneity of his stories encourage his readers to interpret them, showing that the parables are not reserved for the cognoscenti or the experts. Rather, in all of his poems the *Pearl*-poet is engaged in retelling and resituating events from the past in the here and now of the fourteenth century in order to induce the biblical text to speak anew to an audience that needs to comprehend its kerygma in the context of its own experience and historical moment, both existentially and anthropologically.

Malcolm Andrew recently has shown how medieval poets problematize and subvert well-known (biblical) stories by introducing particulars alongside "the ubiquitous medieval tendency to generalize." This technique, which he terms the *realizing imagination* of late medieval English narrative, enables a poet to bring into view the potential human or existential situations latent in received stories.[13] The *Pearl*-poet particularly excels in the employment of this technique. He approaches biblical material in his poems in a fashion altogether different from that of an exegete, a homilist, or a theologian. Unlike a theologian or homilist, who hollows out biblical texts and turns them into abstractions, this poet takes them existentially, responding to the complexity he finds implicit in the biblical narrative. He attends to the words and the story without attempting to isolate the "divine intention" underlying the biblical text. Where a theologian might be concerned with fixed, allegorical meanings that preserve the original integrity of the text, this poet seeks open readings in which the imagery and detail of the original text are embellished and expanded in order to bring out additional or hidden meanings that may have been ignored or suppressed by the allegorical readings.

Accordingly, in each of the poems that we shall examine—*Cleanness, Patience,* and *Pearl*—I will show that the poet strives to strike a balance between the orthodox or traditional arguments that his narrators or protagonists grapple with and those alternative views that emerge from the experience, doubts, and concerns raised in the course of the narratives, concerns that reflect matters of theological controversy in the fourteenth century. Cumulatively, these poems suggest that although the *Pearl*-poet recognizes scripture as an established source of truth he also questions the proposition that one particular kind of language is the source of rationally accountable truth. Poetry, his poetry, I shall argue, can be and is as serious as scripture in reinterpreting history, in clarifying and in qualifying doctrinal matters, and in pursuing an argument.

What encourages his experimentation with and augmentation of the biblical texts are the poetic and fictional aspects of all Bible stories. Long regarded as incidental to the kerygma or message of the story, these fictional aspects have attracted the interest of modern scholars.

Both Robert Alter and Meir Sternberg, for instance, have argued that focusing on the biblical text as a fiction first does not detract from its religious character but brings attention to it in a nuanced way. Alter has shown how the lifelike details and realistic settings of most biblical stories enhance the moral and ethical character of the lesson and enable the reader to get at the deeper meaning for human existence that is contained therein. If we scrutinize biblical personages the way we read fictional characters, he says, we will see them in the multifaceted, contradictory aspects of their human individuality, underscoring the point that human beings are complex centers of motive and feeling and that God is dependent on human actions for the fulfillment of his plan.[14] It is the fullest grasping of this literary art, Alter says, that "proceeds to the sharpest perception of the theological intention."[15] Sternberg adopts a similar tactic. The fictional dimension of biblical stories, he says, frustrates any effort to limit the stories to any ready-made didactic purpose by allowing us to discern new truths in them. What is didactic not only advances a doctrine but also subordinates the whole discourse—plot, character, and language—to the exigencies of the indoctrination. The stories of the Bible, however, generate ambiguity and introduce complex characters that divert attention away from any predetermined or announced message and theme.[16] In her discussion of narrative in the Book of Judges, Mieke Bal has shown how a number of centrisms (androcentrism, theocentrism, ethnocentrism) conditions readerly perspective. They determine what is marginal or central, for instance. She applauds the fictional retelling of biblical stories because of the way it resists the ideological pull of the established coherence of the biblical text, thereby creating countercoherence. Too often, she says, the biblical text is taken at its word, the characters taken as real, and the events that happen to them as historical without taking the structure of the text as narrative at its word with its specific strategies of representation. The fictive allows figures that are silent or powerless to speak and act for themselves, thus taking on a more complex role or identity.[17]

In the concluding stanza of *Pearl,* for example, the narrator proclaims that it is easy for the good Christian to please the prince or be reconciled with God ("To pay þe Prince oþer sete saȝte / Hit is ful eþe to þe god Krystyin"), even though the *Pearl*-narrator is in the company of Gawain, Jonah, and the frequently perplexed narrator of *Cleanness,* all of whom attest to how difficult it is in fact to please God or to imitate Christ.[18] That is because each of his narrators understands something at the end of his story that he only thought he knew at the outset. Typically, the poet begins with a fixed or well-known truth, which has come to the attention of his narrator through a sermon on the beatitudes, or through a visit to the burial site of a loved one. When the narrator turns to the parable or story that illustrates these truths, the biblical text becomes burdened with the personal doubts and apprehensions of the narrator and we get a narrative that frequently runs counter to the received reading. It would appear, to return to Kerrigan, that for the *Pearl*-poet the Bible does "forever anticipate a novel future, open to a widening horizon of interpreters who 'assimilate its significance to that of their own creation.'" His biblical fictions demystify or demythologize the biblical stories he chooses to retell. His poetic reconstructions do not seek to eliminate the mythological material but to interpret it hermeneutically in order to uncover a new meaning. Biblical hermeneutics thus becomes the vehicle that he uses to inscribe crisis into his poetry.[19]

To illustrate, let me turn to the Daniel episode in *Cleanness,* which serves as a *mise en abîme,* a narrative within the larger narrative that mimics the theme and structure of the poem as a whole. The Daniel episode is about reading and interpretation and works as a primer for situating the reader in relation to the biblical material in the poems. Once we have absorbed the reading lesson of Daniel, we can turn to other episodes in *Cleanness,* specifically the poet's rendering of Matthew's Wedding Feast and his treatment of the destruction of Sodom, and see how he has adapted them to bring out the redemptive design he finds latent in even these harshest of biblical stories.

Daniel enters the poem in the Nabuchodonosor sequence, first as a captive of and then as a counselor to Nabucho, whose reign is enriched and whose reputation is elevated to "god of þe grounde" (1324), as a result of Daniel's counsel. Daniel taught Nabucho "bi samples" (parables) that all good things come from God. He then disappears from the narrative until the narrator restates the theme that all good things come from God, this time in relation to Baltassar who has forgotten this truth and demonstrates it by his desecrating the sacred vessels. Daniel appears as a principal actor in the drama once the disembodied fist writes the strange letters on the walls of Baltassar's hall "As a coltour in clay cerues þo forȝes" (1547). The homey metaphor used here is typical of the *Pearl*-poet; it allows the fourteenth-century reader to visualize the event through an image that is familiar to him. At the same time the language, non-biblical in its flavor, calls attention to itself and may remove some of the mystery from the event. Or it may emphasize mystery by doing a supernatural thing in a natural way. The metaphor of the colter in the clay is at once a subtle allusion to poetry as an act of plowing or "verse making," and a reminder that it is a human hand that makes the marks representing God's word on the scriptural page.

Daniel is nominated by Baltassar's queen to solve the mystery of the engraved letters because, as she tells Baltassar, Daniel receives messages directly from God and he has proven himself adept at uncovering the hidden meaning in things:

> "Kene kyng," quoþ þe quene, "kayser of vrþe,
> Euer laste þy lyf in lenþe of dayes!
> Why hast þou rended þy robe for redles hereinne,
> Paȝ þose ledes ben lewed lettres to rede,
> And hatȝ a haþel in þy holde, as I haf herde ofte,
> Pat hatȝ þe gost of God þat gyes alle soþes?
> His sawle is ful of syence, saȝes to schawe,
> To open vch a hide þyng of aunteres vncowþe."
> (1593–1600)

The ability to open what is closed to the vision of others distinguishes Daniel from the other "readers" in Baltassar's court, those clerks who are "bok-lered" but who have failed to decipher the "Wryt" emblazoned on the wall. These clerks, the narrator wryly remarks, in what may be a crack at the expense of fourteenth-century theologians, looked at the handwriting as if "þay had loked in þe leþer of my lyft bote" (1581).

Baltassar insists he needs someone who can do more than decipher the words; he requires a reader who is able to make "þe mater to malt my mynde wythinne, / Pat I may wyterly wyt what þat wryt menes" (1566–67). He wants the message to penetrate his mind, so that he can comprehend it interiorly, not just superficially. His interpreter must be someone who can do the same before relating the message to Baltassar himself and showing him what it means personally as well as historically. The reward for deciphering the words is, appropriately, a robe of

purple and election to the rank of "prymate and prynce of pure clergye."
Baltassar makes his request of Daniel more explicit: "Fyrst telle me þe
tyxte of þe tede lettres, / And syþen þe mater of þe mode mene me
þerafter" (1634–35). Baltassar shows that he is sensitive to the interplay
between the plain text and its hidden meaning. He wants Daniel to read
the letters to him and then tell him the *materia* of the words, that is, its
subject matter. He wants to know the meaning of the words denotatively,
and afterwards the meaning or the message as Daniel would interpret it,
indicating the necessity to grasp the literal meaning before any allegori-
cal interpretation can be limned.

Prior to making this request Baltassar promised Daniel "If þou with
quayntyse con quere hit, I quyte þe þy mede" (1632). The language here
is both curious and compelling. What does Baltassar mean when he
tells Daniel to "con quere" the text with "quayntyse"? Obviously, he
wants Daniel to use his special skill to uncover meaning. But he seems
to tell him to conquer, overwhelm, or take possession of the text by the
force of his own powers of interpretation and give the enigma some
form of coherence and consistency. The "tede lettres" suggest the idea
of tied or linked letters, like alliterative verse itself, implying some in-
separability, some need to comprehend the message whole, by linking
and holding together its component parts. The sense is that the interpre-
tation may "conquer" the text but it must be grounded in the literal, in
the "tede lettres." Should he do so, Daniel will no longer be "enslaved"
(to the text).

Quayntyse or *coynt* and its cognates function meaningfully in the
Daniel episode and throughout the poem as a whole, helping to give it
internal coherence. Here *quayntyse* means wisdom or cunning, but in
other places it denotes courteousness or fastidiousness. In respect to Lot's
daughters it signifies beauty or elegance, and in the Wedding Feast it
refers to fitting finery or to elaborate clothing or appearance, as in "comly
quoyntis." It also means that which is skillfully or artfully crafted, and
in one instance in the poem refers to Solomon's ability to make beauti-
ful objects for God. Cumulatively, these qualities suggest writing or
poetry making, which entails crafting and clothing a text, tying words
together, laying out a strategy, and, of course, disclosing what is hidden.
Like the prophet, the poet is the visionary who can make meaning. Ac-
cordingly, in the scene described here, Daniel acts as a kind of poet,

reader, and narrator. Instead of (immediately) interpreting the letters, he sets up a theme or context for his interpretation by telling a story. He narrates the story of Nabucho, Baltassar's father.

Daniel fictionalizes Nabucho's rise to power, his fall from grace, his loss of reason, his ordeal in the wilderness, and his final reconciliation with God—a familiar pattern of Old Testament narrative. Throughout the narrative, Daniel adheres to a providential view: God, who guided Nabucho in becoming a powerful ruler, initiated his greatness. It was also God who upheld his authority, as long as Nabucho kept faith with God: "And whyle þat *counsayl* watȝ cleȝt close in his hert / Þere watz no mon vpon molde of myȝt as hymseluen" (1655–56). Editors agree that there is a word missing in line 1655 of the original text and they have substituted the word *counsayl* for what Gollancz was convinced was the word *coyntise.* If Gollancz is correct, and I certainly want him to be, it would mean in this instance that *coyntise* is the faculty by which human beings (without "counsel," as it were) come to know or see God. When Nabucho became proud he lost his *coyntise,* he forgot God's power and boasted that his own might was equal to that of God's:

> I am god of þe grounde, to gye as me lykes.
> As He þat hyȝe is in heuen, His aungeles þat weldes.
> If He hatz formed þe folde and folk þervpone,
> I have bigged Babiloyne, burȝ alþer-rychest,
> Stabled þerinne vche a ston in strenkþe of myn armes;
> Moȝt neuer myȝt bot myn make such anoþer.
>
> (1663–68)

Nabucho regains his throne once he accepts the justice of God's wrath and submits to the wisdom of God's plan.

After he has created the proper context, Daniel then identifies the letters on the wall and explains what they betoken for Baltassar, who, like his father, has defiantly hurled his boasts of mighty power in the face of God. Because Baltassar has abused his power and failed to perform "fayth-dedes," Daniel says, God will deprive him of his kingdom and turn it over to his enemies, the Persians. Nabucho had regained the sight of God, his *coyntise,* but Baltassar, Daniel emphasizes, "Seȝ þese syngnes wyth syȝt and set hem at lyttel," thereby bringing down on himself the anger and fury of God. Baltassar has seen the "text" Daniel has expounded for Baltassar already, as his father's son, but he did not know how to "con quere" or assemble it.

In this scene Daniel presents himself as God's voice or instrument, but his own words reveal a degree of subjective judgment. In reference to the letters on the wall he says, "Þise ar þe wordes here wryten, wythoute werk more, / By vch fygure, as I fynde, as oure Fader lykes: / *Mane, Techal, Phares:* marked in þrynne" (1725–27). Daniel's "as I fynde," as innocuous and rhetorically commonplace as it sounds, nevertheless occasions a shift from the text to the interpreter, making Daniel responsible for the meaning extracted from the text. It functions as a kind of creative insight akin to poetic invention, as in *invenire* or *trovare,* for, in a similar passage early on in the poem, the narrator, when preparing to relate a series of examples of God's hatred of the filth of the flesh and how harshly he dealt with it, remarks, "For, *as I fynde,* þer he forȝet alle his fre þeweȝ / And wex wod to þe wrache for wrath at his hert" (203–4, emphasis mine). In both instances the phrase serves as a cue that places the onus first on the reader or interpreter rather than on God as having lost all of his noble qualities. In the broader space of the latter passage ("Bot neuer ȝet in no boke breued I herde / Þat euer He wrek so wyþerly on werk þat He made. / Ne venged for no vilté of vice ne synne"), the narrator could be saying that he has never found an authority who says that some other sin is punished by God more severely than filth of the flesh. The ambiguous syntax of the passage leads to the possibility that the poet places blame squarely on the learned clerks and their books for propagating the idea of sexual defilement and God's intense hatred of it, and may not be a view either the poet or the narrator shares.[20]

The narrator's ambiguous attitude toward the clerks brings to the forefront the pressure the biblical text and the poet's rendering of it places on the reader. Although it has been said of the *Pearl*-poet that he treats his readers as passive listeners receiving instruction, it is more accurate to say that in *Cleanness* the poet makes every reader his or her own Daniel. The reader occupies the position Daniel or the author of the Daniel story once filled and in imitation of whom he or she gives new form to the preexisting story. Each reader is called upon to assemble his or her own text; that is, to read the signs with his eyes and to "con quere" the text with his "quayntyse." To guide the reader in this activity, this poet interposes between the text and the reader this narrator who is not an authority but a reader himself. Since the world of the biblical parables is bound to have varying degrees of familiarity for its possible readers, the poet's readers must be placed in a position that would enable them to actualize the revisionary perspective he is providing. The text, with its multiple interpolations, excisions, and shifts of emphasis breaks open the biblical story, which allows the reader to grasp things that might never have come into focus as long as his habitual or acquired dispositions were determinative of his orientation.[21]

What marks the narrator in all three poems under examination is this conspicuous lack of authority. He does not present himself as a knower but as an ordinary Christian who is himself in the process of discovery and who is trying to understand the material he is rehearsing. Consequently, events do not unfold in a chronological sequence but come to the reader through a narrator who is struggling to uncover their meaning and who is divided between the traditional understanding of the text and his personal experience with and reaction to the parable, beatitude, or the moral lesson involved. This will become clear below in his recitation of the Wedding Feast parable. The overall effect is to juxtapose the narrator's discourse with that of Daniel. Daniel's story of Nabucho's exile in the wilderness is monological and authoritative; it belongs to an Old Testament discourse that is mythic and archaic, and Daniel himself speaks from a prophetic tradition that envisions human history as the workings of a transcendent, providential God who uses one's enemies as instruments of punishment. Conversely, the narrator's discourse is dialogical; the story of Daniel is interwoven into the fabric of a larger tapestry on the subject of cleanness, some parts of which, particularly the Christ sequence, challenge Daniel's mode of discourse and allow for an alternative idea of both humanity and divinity to emerge, one that may speak more persuasively to the lived experience of a fourteenth-century audience. In this way, the *Pearl*-poet makes his poem less of a homily on sin and repentance and more of a collaborative effort on the part of the poet and the reader to soften the impulse toward a supernatural biblicalism.

The *Pearl*-poet's method of reading is similar to Wyclif's approach to reading scripture, to cite a contemporary practice. Like the author of *Cleanness*, Wyclif was unrelenting in his criticism of priests who were "unclean" or who interfered in any way with the faith of the people. He was especially sharp and impatient with the learned clerks who failed to treat scripture as a living text connected to the ethics and activities of everyday life. In several of his writings, especially in *The Authority of Sacred Scripture,* he argued for widespread access to scripture for the laity and against limiting interpretation to a privileged few. The general prologue of the Wycliffite Bible confidently states that a "symple man," with God's grace and through his own effort, can "expoune myche openliere and shortliere þe Bible in English þan þe elde greete doctouris han expoundid it in Latyn, and myche sharpliere and groundliere þan manic late postillatouris eiþir expositouris han don."[22]

Citing the same text from Matthew that is used in *Cleanness,* "Blessed are the pure of heart, for they shall see God," Wyclif proclaims that any Christian who is morally "clean" can see God through the scriptures— if not as he is, then as he is clothed in his works and deeds. The purity of the reader represents for Wyclif a kind of mature vision, a way of apprehending God's word, without which one may not seek a just interpretation of the text. Intention is the critical issue or aspect of inter-pretation, from the perspective of the text and reader, which is why com-mitment of the heart and rectitude of the will is the first requisite of interpretation.[23]

Even though Wyclif insists that the divine intention is determinative of meaning, he takes into account cultural and linguistic factors when approaching the text. The whole of scripture's meaning is and can be known only by God; for the reader, understanding is perforce histori-cal and thus subject to changes in the way knowledge and reality are constructed.[24]

From the *Pearl*-poet's perspective, to demythologize is to ex-istentialize. To paraphrase Rudolph Bultmann, the meaning of God's mystery is not rooted in ancient time but lies in the sphere of personal experience and in how God chooses to act with human beings at any given moment.[25] Existentializing is a difficult task when it comes to religious fictions, as Kermode has pointed out, because religious fic-tions, unlike literary fictions, are harder to free from their mythical "de-posit."[26] If we forget that fictions are fictive we regress to myth:

We have to distinguish between myths and fictions. Fictions can de-generate into myths whenever they are not consciously held to be fictive.... Myth operates within the diagrams of ritual, which presupposes total and adequate explanations of things as they are and were; it is a sequence of radically unchangeable gestures. Fictions are for finding things out, and they change as the needs of sense-making change. Myths are the agents of stability, fictions the agents of change. Myths call for absolute, fictions for conditional assent. Myths make sense in terms of a lost order of time, *illud tempus* as Eliade calls it; fictions, if successful, make sense of the here and now, *hoc tempus*.[27]

To demythologize is to emphasize the historical. If the effect of retelling or poetically interpreting a biblical story or parable is to bring out its kerygma, then the poems of the *Pearl*-poet serve as a prime example of the humanizing and immediacy of experience available through the fictional or poetic medium. Because a fiction allows for broader development and exploration of meaning, what Alter refers to as the "latitude for the exercise of pleasurable invention for its own sake," the reader of a biblical story retold as a poem is afforded the opportunity to come away from the experience with a clearer idea of the relationship that exists between God and humanity and history.[28] Ever mindful of the eschatological and the future life, the *Pearl*-poet nevertheless localizes and contemporizes biblical events in such a way as to bend the mind of his audience away from any exclusively transcendent disposition or interpretation toward an apprehension and appreciation of a more immanent one.

Earlier I cited Alter and Sternberg to the effect that focusing on a biblical text first as a fiction does not detract from its religious character but brings attention to it in a nuanced way.[29] I want to turn now to a consideration of the parable of the Wedding Feast in Matthew 22.1–14 as a necessary and fitting prologue to this poet's approach to the subject of *Cleanness* and of "cleanness." Matthew's Gospel may be the one most hospitable to fictional analysis because it is structured like a literary text in its plot and themes. Matthew is himself drawn to paradoxes, such as we find in his use of the Vineyard parable. His narrative imprecision leaves ample room for interpretive maneuvering. His parables tend to rely on allegory to smooth over whatever inconsistencies or awkward transitions surface on the literal level of his narratives, such as the time sequence in the Wedding Feast. In it, a king arranges a feast in honor of his son, inviting guests to come immediately for a

meal that he has prepared. He interrupts these preparations to take re-
venge upon those among the first invited who had refused to come and
had killed his servant messengers. He retaliates by destroying these
murderers and burning their city to the ground. When other servants are
then dispatched to ever more remote parts to gather guests for the feast,
the sense of the parable is that all of these events occur within the same
day, an obvious impossibility.

Equally disconcerting is the sequence with the man lacking the proper
wedding garment. Most scholars agree that this episode was taken from
another parable or source and hastily or clumsily tacked on to this one.
The harsh treatment of the guest, casting him into the outer darkness,
raises problems with the king's method of justice, inasmuch as Matthew
makes the guest somewhat of a sympathetic figure, one who has arrived
in accordance with the way the servants found him. If the reader looks
to the moral lesson, "many are called but few are chosen," for satisfac-
tion—a lesson Matthew had employed earlier at the close of the Vine-
yard parable—he is likely to be disappointed or puzzled because its
emphasis on readiness or repentance seems at variance with the main
body of the parable, traditionally read as a celebration of the new
covenant and of the refusal of the Pharisees or the Jews to attend the
feast God had arranged for his son, the Messiah.

For Douglas Hare all of these problems are the product of what he
terms "uninformed readers," who fail to understand the story as an alle-
gory. The Wedding Feast, he says,

> is not the Church but the age to come. The required garment is
> righteousness, that is, behavior in accordance with Jesus' teachings
> (Matthew 28:19). The man is speechless because he has no defense;
> he accepted the invitation of the gospel but he has not lived the
> life of the gospel. The attached saying, "For many are called, but few
> are chosen," should not be taken as a forecast of the proportion of
> the saved to the damned. Its function is not to frighten Christians
> with the thought that the statistical odds are against them but to en-
> courage vigorous effort to live the Christian life.[30]

As Hare indicates, the parable of the Wedding Feast has been heavily
allegorized, usually with an eye toward one of Matthew's favorite
themes—the kingdom of heaven. The punishment of the one guest in

the here and now creates a problem of interpretation, however; it has confused scholars in respect to Matthew's vision: Is the kingdom to be realized in the future, in the present, or only in the other world? Even if Hare's reading reconciles the two parts of the parable it simultaneously points up the fact that there are often irreconcilable differences between allegorical and literal readings, crises that inevitably arise in a text when a formal metaphysical or theological framework is absent that would direct the flow of the allegorical meaning and establish a hierarchy of relationships between the literal and the metaphoric.[31] In such crises it becomes the task of the reader to decide. The tension is acute in respect to the Wedding Feast because we have another version of the parable in Luke 14.16–24. Luke's parables in general appear to be less allegorical than Matthew's and they are a good deal less concerned with angels, hell, or the other world. Luke's parable of the Wedding Feast is more existential; it gives a clear account of why the guests fail to come to the banquet and omits Matthew's stress on punishment.

Augustine, in his account, suggests that there are two feasts: one to which the good and evil come and the other to which the evil come not. The table laid out by the king is open to all, and the man without a wedding garment is representative of a whole class. Unlike Hare, Augustine applies the lesson of the many who are called and few who are chosen to support his idea that many are indeed cast out, that many are evil and only a few are good. All who excuse themselves from the feast are evil, but all those who enter are good. The garment, he says, is in the heart not on the body. The garment is charity, but it must be char-ity out of a "pure heart, of a good conscience, and of faith unfeigned."[32] The wedding garment is taken in honor of the union of Christ and his church.

The wedding feast in *Cleanness* has none of Matthew's controlling theological framework, and the poet's foregrounding of the literal level problematizes whatever allegorical reading might be proffered. For example, attenuating the lesson from the gospel story to "many are called" stresses the universality of the mission. His poem is going to be more about the many who are called than the few who are chosen. Another significant change has to do with the subject of cleanness, or uncleanness, itself. The narrator comes to Matthew's parable through a process that begins with uncleanness; yet the parable has no traditional association with cleanness, nor has it been used theologically to illustrate the beatitude of the clean of heart. The associations are idiosyncratically the narrator's, and the reader is obliged to get in tune with him. The impression he strives for throughout is one of spontaneity, which invites the reader to rethink the parable and the stories that follow in order to arrive at one's own understanding of the Bible message.

At the outset the reader discovers the narrator thinking to himself about cleanness and musing that if anyone should care to write about it "Fayre formes my3t he fynde in forering his speche."[33] These "forms" embrace the various modes of discourse with which the narrator is familiar and which he brings into play, ranging from the Bible to sermons, to clerkly commentaries, and to poems, such as the *Roman de la rose*. Thinking about uncleanness is infinitely more difficult for the narrator, not because there are no "splendid themes" ("kark" and "combraunce" are this poet's specialty), but because it involves the narrator with the wrath of God and the filth of humankind, topics which he seems dispositionally and philosophically reluctant to broach. As W. A. Davenport says, the antithetical presentation of fair formes and "kark" is not just "a treatment of men's actions and destinies but recognition of the opposites in the nature of God who gives with one hand and takes away with the other."[34] The first figures who come to the narrator's mind, however, are priests ("renkez of relygioun. . . . / As be honest vtwyth and inwith alle fylþez" [6–14]) who handle Christ's body, who appear clean on the outside but may be filthy within. They clash with God or with the king who is "so clene in His courte" and clad in "wede3 so bry3t."

Making the analogy between God and the king anticipates the parable the poet will tell about the lord and the anecdote he invents that precedes it. The priests he refers to also anticipate the parable if we count them among the chosen that are cited in the explicit moral lesson of the parable. The reference to the priests concretizes the issue of uncleanness. It makes it specific to a late medieval audience. It also points up the gulf that exists between the magnificent court and city of God and the imperfect world of God's creatures, including his elite or chosen. At this point the narrator is still feeling his way; he has not yet hit upon his main subject. The priestly uncleanness reminds him ("me myne3") that Christ spoke about cleanness of heart in Matthew. After reciting the beatitude, "þe haþel clene of his hert hapene3 ful fayre, / For he schal loke on oure Lorde with a leue chere" (27–28), he fears that the beatitude means that no one will come to that sight who is in any way unclean because God cannot tolerate anyone who is unclean to come near his body in that city. The severity of this judgment provokes him to explore the whole matter in greater detail and we get our narrative. Linking the Matthew parable to the beatitude is evidence of the poet's genius because it helps to contain the allegorical. The beatitudes, as Albert Cook says, return us to history and to time, to human activity as a virtue in itself. Their intent is to make human beings doers of deeds who act out their lives not only before the eyes of God but also before those of their fellow creatures.[35] This is the hidden appeal of the story of the Wedding Feast.

The story begins with the anecdote of the man who appears in court with his hair sticking out in all directions and his clothes in tatters, who presumes to be seated at a dais above dukes in attendance and served dainties—the poet enjoys overstating the man's boldness and is especially effective in directing our attention to the literal level. What earthly man would not take offense, he asks, if such an ill-attired man were to approach the table? Surely he would be dealt with roughly, hurled to the hall door, shoved outside, and forbidden to enter the city ever again, even if he were never to trespass further. This man nicely anticipates the guest who is improperly attired at the wedding feast. The narrator, in his enthusiasm to defend, in advance, God's treatment of the wedding guest in the allegorical reading of the parable, calls added attention to the severity and finality of the punishment that is meted out to the guest.

Malcolm Andrew and Ronald Waldron concede that modern readers may find the lord's reaction extreme or not entirely just, and they assure the reader that the punishment does not appear to have caused anxiety to medieval commentators, perhaps because, they say, the wedding garment could be readily allegorized as good works, which the poet afterwards explicitly informs his readers is the case.[36] Andrew and Waldron seem to have Matthew's version in mind more than the poet's, in which the literal is much more difficult to suppress. Or, they do not distinguish the poem from the gospel, as if Matthew's text controls the spirit and meaning of the poetic version. Ironically, the poem may be one clear instance of the anxiety that they assume did not exist in the Middle Ages. The narrator's gesture at the close of the parable formally explaining to his audience that the clothes in the parable are good works suggests that he is not confident himself that the parable itself makes that clear. Besides, in the anecdote that sets up the parable, the clothing of the man is a matter of his social standing and not an indication of his moral worth, a point not likely to have been suppressed by the reading audience in the Middle Ages, at least a reading audience that encompassed more than clerks.

The anecdote with its attention to clothing does make what is assumed to be an afterthought of Matthew's parable the centerpiece of the poetic version. The poetic version is more cohesive and, thanks in part to the anecdote, builds dramatically to the confrontation between the lord and his guest. The details here encourage the reader to look at the feast as a literal wedding feast. The narrator describes the specific meats that have been prepared, how hot the food is, and the importance the lord attaches to the feast itself. The specific details and familiar descriptions reverse the eschatological thrust of Matthew's text and insert the reader and the characters in the parable into the real and familiar world of the fourteenth century. As in the anecdote, the clothing of the guests refers primarily to their social status. The difference is that whereas the king's court emphasizes the exclusion of the man in tatters, the wedding feast stresses the wide variety of people who have been invited in. At first the lord had sent his servants out into the broad streets of the city and into the surrounding countryside to bring in all kinds of ordinary people and to treat them as if they were royal:

> Þe wayferande freke3 on fote and on hors,
> Boþe burne3 and burde3, þe better and þe wers.
> Laþe3 hem alle luflyly to lenge at my feste,
> And brynge3 hem blyþly to bor3e as baroune3 þay were.
> (79–82)

Disappointed when his house is not full, the lord commands his servants to bring in others, not discriminating between "fre" and "bonde." Once he discovers he has still more room, the lord instructs his servants to search the farthest fields, the most remote regions, for whatever kind of people dwell there and to invite them to his house as well:

> Be þay fers, be þay feble, forlote3 none,
> Be þay hol, be þay halt, be þay on-y3ed,

- And þaȝ þay ben boþe blynde and balterande cruppeleȝ,
Þat my hous may holly by halkeȝ by filled.

(101–3)

When the lord decides to walk among his guests to give them comfort and to increase their joy, he graciously shows his courtesy to the rich and to the poor. In his hall each is given what is proper to him or her and even the plainest is served to the limit. Instead of adverting to a heavenly court for its meaning the poet uses the gathering of all levels of society to break down the otherness of this world to God's world and invites his audience to see that the inclusiveness and social harmony attributed to God's world is realizable in human time. A good example of this is seen when the lord generously makes room for those who were not "alle on wyueȝ suneȝ, wonen wyth on fader," which Vantuono rightly suggests is the poet's provision for the inclusion of the pagans or adherents of other religions in the scheme of salvation—but also to be seated at the earthly table. The spirit of inclusion is made more explicit at the conclusion of the parable when, instead of reciting the entire moral, as it appears in *Pearl* "For mony ben calle, þaȝ fewe be mykeȝ," all the narrator says here is "fele arn to called."

The celebration the narrator has been describing is brought to a sudden and chilling climax at the moment when the lord discovers the man in the soiled garment and punishes him ruthlessly. The man is described as an improperly attired thrall who has arrived with no "festiual frok," but with one "fyled with werkkeȝ" (136). If we follow the allegory or clothing metaphor here then the man's attire signifies unclean deeds. The way the passage depicts him makes it difficult to take him out of his habitual condition as one who is a worker soiled by the dirt of the fields, and an unintended transgressor of the lord's decorum. The reader's sympathy is enlisted by protracting the scene and showing the guest to be dismayed or confounded ("abayst") by the lord's reaction. His silence betokens embarrassment rather than guilt. For the poet to retain the severe punishment meted out in Matthew when he has freely altered so much more makes the severity of it stand out. The poem may mitigate his suffering (making the dungeon more purgatorial than infernal) by implying a limit to his incarceration, and that he is punished in order to teach him a lesson, "to teche hym be quoynt" (160).

In this instance *quoynt* means either courteous or wise, and either way a kind of self-transforming experience is implied. This seems to be the perspective adopted by the narrator in his summation of the parable:

Wich arn þenne þy wedeʒ þou wrappeʒ þe inne,
Þat schal schewe hem so schene schrowde of þe best?
Hit arn þy werkeʒ, wyterly, þat þou wroʒt haueʒ,
And lyued, wyth þe lykyng lyʒe in þyn hert.

(169–72)

Cleanness is in no way a static condition; the narrator plays down the idea of punishment or defilement and links the parable to the beatitude. He proposes a conception of cleanness as a life of moral virtue sustained by works of love and justice. To learn to be "quoynt" is to act in the image of Christ, for, at the close of the poem the narrator will tell us that cleanness is God's comfort and "coyntyse he louyes." Those who have learned it will see God—and be seen by him—and "gon gay in [their] gere," walk gallantly in their attire.

What lingers in the mind at the end of the parable is not only the lesson but also the seemingly arbitrary judgment and violence of the lord toward the astonished guest. The narrative appears to have created as many problems for the narrator as it does for the reader because he finds himself in need of going back to the beginning, to the origins of God's wrath and human sinfulness, in order to effect the transition from God to Christ, from a fear of vengeance to the law of love.

By way of transition the narrator begins with a long list of acts that a human being might perform that would cause him to forfeit his bliss, ranging from sloth to spreading false rumors (lines 177–92). It is also at this point that he cites the high clerks as those who have singled out sexual impurity as most loathsome in God's sight, a theme he develops in several related episodes. After the first two disasters of the fall of Lucifer and the fall of Adam, the third disaster, the Flood, is said to have been precipitated when the first people of the earth discovered the impurity of carnal deeds ("founded þay fylþe in fleschlych dedeʒ"). They defiled their flesh so horribly that the devils, attracted to the daughters of the group, engaged in sexual union with them. Filth of the flesh is not the only kind of impurity cited in the main episodes, but it is the one the narrator, following the discourse of the clerks, associates with uncleanness, and the reader is occasionally admonished not to be found in the filth of the flesh.[37]

As Elizabeth Keiser points out, inasmuch as *Cleanness* represents the Creator as "personally implicated with and vulnerable to the embodied and sexual desires of his human creatures, the poet seems to be in his own way renegotiating differences between the secular and sacred and subverting the distinctions between the two realms that clerical ritual and discourse manipulated."[38] She places the poet in harmony with St. Thomas who, she says, "provides a cheering contrast to the pessimistic dualism that polarized flesh and spirit, nature and grace in medieval ethical discourse."[39] In her argument the *Pearl*-poet singles out filth of the flesh as the worst violation of cleanness and, she says, he represents homosexual deviance as loathsome in order to provide a foil against which the poet "can legitimate the way of life that he sanctifies as the manifestation of God's *clannesse* and his *clene* relations to the world."[40] These are excellent observations, but they may not adequately account for the narrator's self-consciousness and for the poet's desire to make God's wrath an integral part of his critique. For one thing, although the narrator does not offer a defense of homoerotic love that compares in any way with his description of God's gift to human beings of marital love, he does make it clear that he has a serious moral difficulty trying to reconcile God's act of love and generosity then with God's horrible vengeance now. God's compassion in the one instance makes his violence in the other stand out more sharply. According to Regina Schwartz, the Bible's prohibition against homosexuality centers on issues of (God's) power and authority. In biblical texts, she says, there is a palpable fear that when men love one another, they will overthrow their fathers: "As Noah's terrible curse of his son belies and as the general biblical hysteria about homosexuality suggests, the son's desire for the father is also primary in biblical traditions. Only this desire—denied, repressed, suppressed, and punished—explains both the ferocity of biblical injunctions against homosexuality and the ferocity of the deity's determination to punish his children, to stomp out their desire with its threat of parricidal displacement."[41] What her analysis does is shift the focus from human beings or the "sinners" to the wrath and violence of the father, where it belongs.

As he did in the Wedding Feast, the poet uses the emotional responses of his narrator, in the Flood and Sodom sequences, to manipulate our sympathies for the victims of God's violence. As we shall see, the narrator's dismay over God's violence in the Flood and Sodom episodes prompts him to wish for the intervention of Christ in the acts of the Father. In the poem, Christ's love replaces the terrifying and vengeful image of the Father as he is depicted in the Old Testament episodes. The way the poet structures the poem, the incarnation follows the Sodom episode, and with it a new idea of cleanness is born, one that centers on conformity with the life of Christ. The rhetorical emphasis on filth of the flesh and on cleanness or purity is thus presented as a large part of the problem—a symptom of a long-standing hatred and distrust of the flesh in western (religious) consciousness that the poet wants to neutralize by relieving human nature of the stigma of uncleanness and of the idea that we or any specific group of human beings are defined by filth of the flesh.

The narrator's ambivalence about sexual impurity, moreover—condemnation of the sin but sympathy for the sinners—suggests that what stands in need of transformation or demythologization in *Cleanness* is the defilement-purity doublet, and along with it the traditional explanation of human evil and the way it is transmitted, such as through "mannes sperme unclene," in Chaucer's Monk's account. As Paul Ricoeur has observed, the first function of the myths of evil is to embrace humankind as a whole in one ideal history: "The myth makes the experience of a fault the center of a whole, the center of a world: the world of fault."[42] But modern consciousness no longer associates sexuality with defilement (save in those benighted circles where AIDS is deemed a punishment sent by God for sexual sin). Sexuality as defilement is a belief that is pre-ethical in character and not connected to an interpersonal ethics. The way to overcome original dread or God's wrath centers on a demand for a just punishment: the transformation of Truth and Justice to Mercy and Peace, as we saw in Grosseteste and Langland. In a chapter entitled "Christological Poetics," John Milbank speaks of Christ and his ethical works as a poetic text: "As the divine utterance, Jesus is the absolute origination of all meaning, but as human utterance, Jesus is the inheritor of all already constituted human meanings. He is a single utterance in his unified fulfillment of these meanings, such that he becomes the adequate metaphoric representation of the total human intent."[43] Christ, Milbank says, should bring an end to sin or the psychology of human nature as sin-centered because he engenders the new order of charity:

> Original sin can only be defined as hatred of the works and person of Christ. But sin has already been defined as a refusal of the plenitude of creation, the fulness of representation, which can only be received by the succession of humanity as a whole. If sin is exposed uniquely through the works of Christ, this must be because there we see that plenitude, that adequate representation, and, in a sense, the 'whole' of humanity, a person who is *more* everyone of us than we are ourselves. We now have the true poetic bounds of behaviour and sin is located, so potentially nullified. If sin is at an end, then charity is engendered.[44]

In *Cleanness* the poet does not seek to blame God or to exonerate human beings from fault; he aims to dislodge the discourse of cleanness from its association with sexual purity and make it instead a discourse centered on love and on an ethics of human dignity.

In the Old Testament episodes the narrator exaggerates the tension between the human and divine wills by dwelling on the horrific or holocaustic aspects of God's wrath, and by insinuating that the rebellious aspect of human nature is a consequence of a fundamental incompatibility between human understanding and a transcendent God. The contradictory nature of the human will, its desire to please God and carry out his plan over against its impulse to act independently and to satisfy its own appetites, is a favorite theme of this poet's and underlies most of *Patience* and a portion of *Pearl*.

In *Cleanness* we see it in small ways as well as large, in the skeptical laugh of Sarah, in the little defiances of Lot's wife, and in the lapses of the Hebrew people as reported in Daniel's dialogues. The divided will is well illustrated in the Flood episode when Noah sends out the raven to find dry ground. The raven is described as ever rebellious and once out from under the watchful eye of Noah, he feels the surge of his freedom and, like Jonah in the belly of the whale or in the comfort of his woodbine,

> He croukeȝ for comfort when carayne he fyndeȝ
> Kast vp on a clyffe þer costese lay drye;

He hade þe smalle of þe smach and smoltes þeder sone,
Fallez on þe foule flesch and fyllez his wombe,
And sone зederly forзete зisterday steuen,
How þe cheuetayn hym charged, þat þe chyst зemed.
Þe rauen raykez hym forth, þat reches ful lyttel
How alle fodez þer fare, ellez he fynde mete.

(459–66)

Human beings can be obedient, like Noah and the dove; more often they are willful and self-seeking like the raven. In the *Pearl*-poet's imagination it is not only human beings that must change, God also must relent in his judgment.

Prior to the Flood we hear in God's complaint, uttered to himself, his disappointment with his creation and his regret that he ever infused a soul into flesh:

When he knew vche contré coruppte in hitseleun,
And vch freke forloyned fro þe ryзt wayez,
As wyзe wo hym withinne, werþ to Hymseleun:
Me forþynkez ful much þat euer I mon made,
Bot I schal delyuer and do away þat doten on þis molde,
And fleme out of pe folde al pat flesch werez,
Fro þe burne to þe best, fro bryddez to fyschez;
And schal doun and be ded and dryuen out of erþe
Þat euer I sette saul inne; and sore hit Me rwez
Þat euer I made hem Myself.

(281–91)

Shortly afterward, God speaks to Noah and again expresses his bitterness, in "wild, wrathful words": "I schal strenkle My distresse, and strye al togeder, / Boþe ledez and londe and alle þat lyf habbez" (306–7). God repeats his anger and his intent after instructing Noah in the construction of the ark: "Alle þat glydez and gotz and gost of lyf habbez / I schal wast with My wrath þat wons vpon vrþe" (325–26).

After the Flood, God promises Noah that he will never destroy the earth "for mannes synne," and that humankind will be ruled by a new covenant:

He knyt a couenaunde cortaysly wyth monkynde þere,
In þe mesure of His mode and meþe of Hys wylle,

Þat He schulde neuer for no syt smyte al at oneʒ,
As to quelle alle quykeʒ for qued þat myʒt falle,
Whyl of þe lenþe of þe londe lasteʒ þe terme.
Þat ilke skyl, for no scape, ascaped hym neuer.
Wheder wonderly He wrak on wykked men after.

(564–70)

God's wrath will not end with the destructiveness of the Flood but God does show remorse, and the promise of the covenant as a mutual agreement binds God to human beings in a friendly way and confers on human beings an active role in the making of their history.

The Flood sequence is probably the most popular and most frequently discussed episode in the poem; consequently I will discuss it only as a prelude to a more lengthy discussion of the Sodom episode, which has received less attention. Judging from the frequency with which it appears in medieval poetry, drama, and theological commentaries, the Flood story held the medieval imagination in its grip. The humorous or comic treatment it receives in the Chester cycle and in the *Miller's Tale* indicates its typology as God's wrath and introduces the condition of human impatience with it. The poet does not spare his readers any of the horrible or gruesome details; he wants to put a human face on the victims and force the reader to see and acknowledge them as living beings who suffered terribly. In poignant detail he shows us the families and friends drowning and their bodies slowly rotting in the mud.[45] He also shows us touching scenes of human friendship and loyalty, especially when the mass of people who fled in terror to a mountainside simultaneously realize their collective doom and instinctively they embrace one another in a gesture of compassion and unity. In this way the narrator successfully manipulates the reader to see things from the side of the human victims rather than from the perspective of God's "justifiable" anger. As Andrew says, the poet's handling of the Flood sequence "encourages the reader to sympathize with the imagined experience of these representative individuals, and to feel for them, not only compassion but also a certain respect."[46]

Walter Benjamin has observed that the past is suffused with the needs of the present and we redeem the present by revival of images from the past. To be sure, the injustices of the past cannot be undone but the historian or poet can imaginatively redeem the past by constructing a plot out of the inevitable story of that past. *Cleanness* has exactly the kind of plot or construction Benjamin imagines wherein its chronology is modernistically disrupted and its linear segments are stacked spatially together.[47] The poet, moreover, moves backward in order to move forward; he revisits the past, he replots it, in order to transform the present. His reconstruction or reconception of the Sodom episode is his highest achievement. In it he manages to arouse in the reader the same compassion and respect for the Sodomites that he generated for the victims of the Flood, a major achievement.

The Sodom episode is one of the longer ones in the poem, longer than the Flood and the stories of the falls of Lucifer and Adam combined—the three "wrakes" or disasters that befell humankind. It contains all of the themes that we have been discussing, the wrath of God and the love of God, God's vengeance and God's justice. It is sandwiched between the old covenant struck by God after the Flood, and the new covenant of the incarnation that follows the destruction of the cities of the plain. The poet creates the illusion that the incarnation needs to occur in the wake of such horrible violence. The episode is on the dividing line between history and myth. God designates Abraham, as he did Adam, to be the biological as well as spiritual father of the human race. His announcement to Abraham that Sarah shall conceive and bear a son who shall himself beget "Wyth wele and wyth worschyp þe worþely peple / Þat schal halde in heritage þat I haf men ȝarked," (650–51), anticipates both the annunciation to Mary and the incarnation itself. Perhaps there is an echo of Grosseteste and his notion of the absolute predestination of Christ in the poet's use of *heritage* and in the way the incarnation is linked to human dignity. In conferring on Abraham this special honor, God appears to be relinquishing some of his own control of history and bestowing on human beings some of his authority.

In this sequence we catch a glimpse of another side of God, a tender and intimate side, as he sits with Abraham in his garden and dines and converses with him as a guest. The event introduces the theme of hospitality, which plays a prominent role throughout the whole episode. Andrew and Waldron and, more recently, Ad Putter, observe that the *Pearl*-poet is unusually bold in attributing to God emotions, feelings, and actions that belong to human beings, a gesture which they find contrasts sharply with that of most Christian commentators "who normally try to avoid any suggestion of God behaving like a man."[48] Humanizing God could be construed as the poet's attempt to justify God's wrath toward the Sodomites; he also humanizes him to allow the reader the freedom to question God's violence, in the way Abraham does when he negotiates with God to spare the city and the narrator does at the climactic point in the destruction of Sodom.[49] Throughout, we see and experience things first from Abraham's perspective and then from Lot's. Through them the poet makes us eyewitnesses to the events and elicits our sympathy for the victims, as he did in the Flood. He reaches the same emotional tenor that obtained during the flood, first in the expressions of terror and horror in Abraham and Lot at the extreme of God's wrath and violence and in the depiction of the victims who become aware of the inescapability of their doom.

Recently, Allen Frantzen has argued that the reader's identification with the Sodomites is blocked or strained by God's or the poet's preemptive discourse on natural love. I would suggest that Frantzen underestimates the poet and the poem, as well as the reader. It is true that in the interval between the Flood sequence and the destruction of Sodom, the narrator does restate the theme contained in the beatitude that only the clean of heart will see the face of God. He speaks again of the sins of the flesh which annoy God and bring shame upon men, such as masturbation ("heþyng of seluen"). God does complain bitterly to Abraham of the way that the Sodomites have corrupted his "ordenaunce" on earthly or erotic love, and he contrasts the "kynde craft" he has sanctioned with the lust ("of fauteʒ þe werst") practiced by the Sodomites. Nevertheless, sodomy exists here on a continuum of activities approved and disapproved of by God and is not separated out as a thing apart, even if it is from God's perspective the worst of sexual faults. Other sexual sins of a heterosexual kind, cited earlier, are also designated as "agayn kynde":

> Þer watz no law to hem layd bot loke to kynde,
> And kepe to hit, and alle hit cors clanly fulfylle.
> And þynne founded þay fylþe in fleschlych dedez,
> And controeued agayn kynde contraré werkez
> And vsed hem vnþryftyly vchon on oþer,
> And als with oþer, wylsfully, upon a wrange wyse.
> (263–68)

These involve intercourse with creatures of another "kind," in this case angels. These did produce offspring, hence Frantzen's argument about procreation does not apply here.

In the passage in question (695–708), where God describes the gift of sexual intercourse that he has given to human beings, God lavishes praise upon sexual union as a value in itself, as a means to mutual love and satisfaction for the lovers. It is unambiguously erotic love that God speaks of ("Luf-lowe hym bytwene *lasched so hote*"—emphasis mine), finding something of his own pleasure in the play of paramours: "And þe play of paramorcȝ I portrayed myseulen." The syntax of this line is highly provocative, suggesting that it is in this act or union that God's face or image is realized within the lovers as an emulation of his love. William Vantuono cites Kelly and Irwin to the effect that "the sexual drive, when properly channeled in marriage, produces the family unit which, in its relationship of a father to his children, symbolizes the relationship of God to man."[50] This may be true, but at this point the poem seems to be more interested in redeeming erotic love as such.

What I am suggesting is that the discussion on erotic love or sexual union does not close the discussion on sodomy or (necessarily) prejudice the reader against the Sodomites. The poet, as Frantzen readily acknowledges, does something extremely rare in medieval treatments of sodomy: he allows the Sodomites to speak for themselves in defense of their own practices.[51] While this may not legitimate their discourse it does recognize that what they have to say *is a discourse*. The poet inserts what they have to say into a dialogue which is open ended and may be resumed or reevaluated at any time, as the poet is doing through this poem. While the poem does not sanction sodomy it refuses to hide it or deny its existence. And the poet leaves open the possibility that it does not register in the eyes of human beings the way it looks in the eyes of God.

For example, when a group of Sodomites appears before Lot's house, spokesmen for the group demand that Lot send out the young men "Þat we may lere hym of lof, as oure lyst biddeȝ , / As is þe asyse of Sodomas to seggeȝ þat passen" (843–44). The use of *asyse* by the Sodomites and Lot's use of *costoum* to describe the custom these men follow, indicates that it is recognized as a social as well as a personal practice, relativizing it and lessening its association with primal sin, unnaturalness, or some cosmic defiance of God. At one point they challenge Lot with the question "Who joyned þe be jostyse oure japez to blame / Þat com a boy to þis borȝ, þaȝ þou be burne ryche?" Their speaking for themselves, moreover, does give the Sodomites interiority and agency; voice humanizes them and prevents them from being treated simply as abstract examples of the sin of sodomy.

At the same time, it cannot be denied that the entire confrontation outside of Lot's house is a very ugly scene in which everyone behaves badly. The men of Sodom threaten to kill Lot, to cut off his head, and they intend, apparently, to gang rape his guests. No custom grants license to violently seize another person. Lot is no less reprehensible when he offers his daughters as substitutes for the angels. Is the "craft" that Lot wants to teach the men of Sodom, which involves the sacrifice of his daughters, better "by kynde"? Lot is described here as a man of reason, but his conduct seems no more defensible than the actions of the men of Sodom.[52] What helps us to sort through this scene, morally and emotionally, is the perspective of the narrator, who is no neutral observer but himself quite emotionally involved. The narrator certainly does not appear to approve of the behavior of the Sodomites or of their customs but he is equally aware that God is going to destroy the city and all of its inhabitants because of their impurity. As a result, the narrator feels compelled to demonize or vilify the Sodomites to an extreme and the rhetoric of the scene sometimes borders on the cartoonish:

> Whatt! þay sputen and speken of so spitous fyþle,
> What! þay ȝeȝed and ȝolped of ȝestande sorȝe,
> Þat yet þe wynd and þe weder and þe worlde stynkes
> Of þe brych þat vpbraydez þose broþelych wordez.
>
> (845–48)

One is reminded at this point of Jonah's discomfort with God over Ninevah and wonders with him what human beings could have done to warrant extinction or to suffer such mass devastation. Why does God spare Ninevah and destroy Sodom? The destruction of Sodom puts the narrator in the morally awkward position of straining to explain or justify what his own eyes and emotions forbid. Although the high clerks do not count the destruction of Sodom as one of the three disasters that beset humankind as a whole, the narrator ruefully remarks that it is "þe vglokest vnhap euer on erd suffred" (892).

At the end of the Sodom and Gomorrah episode, as the fire rains down upon the cities and the people, roasting and burning them to ashes— "And ferly flayed þat folk þat in þose fees lenged"—the narrator describes how the infernal fiend opened up the earth to swallow the cities:

> Þe grete barreȝ of þe abyme he barst vp at oneȝ,
> Þat alle þe regioun torof in riftes ful grete,
> And clouen alle in lyttel cloutes, þe clyffeȝ aywhere,
> As lauce leueȝ þe boke þat leþeȝ in twynne.
> Þe breth of þe brynston bi þat hit blende were.
> Al þo citees and her sydes sunkken to helle.
> Rydelles weren þo grete rowtes of renkkes withinne.
> When þay wern war of þe wrake þat no wyȝe achaped,
> Such a ȝomerly ȝarm of ȝellyng þer rysed,
> Þerof clatered þe cloudes, *þat Kryst myȝt haf rawþe.*
> (963–72, emphasis added)

The upheaval and destruction described here, which Spearing has compared to a nuclear blast, makes it difficult for the reader to suppress or ignore the sheer terror of the all-too-human victims, and not come away with a sense of the disproportionate punishment descending upon them.[53] The analogy of the burst book adds to the turmoil, suggesting not only the unbinding of the book of nature but also the book of creation, of scripture itself or God's word to Noah that he would not smite humankind all at once in response to human evil.[54] It is the narrator's personal observation, his extraordinary remark that "Kryst myȝt haf rawþe," that most complicates the text and offers some relief to the reader's conscience. His allusion to Christ does not mitigate the horror; it intensifies it. The reference to Christ at this juncture expresses the degree to which Christ is identified with human suffering and brings to the narrator's consciousness the awful presence of Christ's absence.

As we saw in the example of the Flood, the narrator's irrepressible impulse to humanize every episode prompts the reader to put these events into historical perspective and to recognize that what counts as a violation for a conscience at a remote point in time may no longer obtain, at least not in the same way, for those now living under the shadow of the incarnation as well as the shadow of original sin. The victims who suffer so painfully in the Flood, in the destruction of the cities of the plain, and, most brutally, at the hands of Nabuzardan (lines 1233–1308), come to represent not only the few who are chosen by God, such as Noah, Abraham, and Lot, for whom the biblical story exists, but the many who are called, the "sinners" who meet their fate with dignity and therein reveal to us unsuspected depths of human love. It is for them that Christ has "rawþe," and through them we see traces of the incarnation sufficient to redeem the time. Human love, the poem says, redeems the flesh and frees it from any absolute association with procreation on the one hand and, on the other, with defilement or filth of the flesh as somehow endemic to human nature. Human love, specifically erotic love, the narrator says, can help human beings to overcome all the pains and suffering of the world ("Þat alle þe meschefez on mold moȝt hit not sleke") and regain paradise.

Given the reference to Christ at this juncture, it is logical for the narrator to follow the Sodom episode with the story of the incarnation. Like the incarnation itself, the incarnation episode is for the poet the pivotal moment of transformation of the word. Christ is not only the embodiment of cleanness, he is the embodiment of *Cleanness*. In *Cleanness,* the engendering of Christ is itself an act of charity. The birth of Christ fulfills what was promised at the end of the Adam story when it was forecast that Adam's sin would be amended by a maiden who never had a mate, and it offsets God's words to Noah that man's soul is "to malyce enclyned." The birth's dominant theme is one of change, of healing, and of rehabilitation, not of punishment and violent destruction. The narrator self-consciously leads us into the episode by urging his audience to heed the advice of a poet: "For Clopyngnel in þe compas of his clene *Rose* / Þer he expounez a speche to hym þat spede wolde / Of a lady to be loued" (1057–59). The allusion is arresting because it suggests that poets understand that human love, including sexual love, can have an ennobling effect on the lover, and that poetry has played a primary role in making the word flesh. Accordingly, the incarnation is described as a reunion of spirit and flesh, of divine and human. "God kynned þerinne," the poem says, meaning Christ was conceived in Mary. But *kynned* implies more. Christ remains in Mary's womb as he will remain immanent in the womb of the world until charity is engendered in all of humankind. The descent of Christ into flesh, his adoption of a complete human nature, and the assumption of an active life in the world affirms for the poet what Grosseteste calls deification: whatever Christ *is* in relation to human nature he is what human beings are to realize about themselves in time and history.

In the birth sequence Mary purifies all that had been previously marked as unclean: Eve, the body, birth itself. She erases the stain of sexual pollution and restores the old order of intimacy between human and divine:

> And efte, when He borne watȝ in Beþeleu þe rychc,
> In wych puryté þay departed; þaȝ þay pouer were,
> Watȝ neuer so blysful a bour as watȝ a bos þenne,
> Ne no schroude hous so schene as a schepon þare,
> Ne non so glad vnder God as ho þat grone schulde.
> For þer watȝ seknesse al sounde, þat sarrest is halden,
> And þer watȝ rose reflayer where rote hatȝ ben euer,
> And þer watȝ solace and songe wher sorȝ hatȝ ay cryed.
>
> (1073–80)

Pain, foul odor, and groaning may still accompany childbirth, but the incarnation and Mary's role in it transforms the sense of Eve's punishment associated with child labor after the fall. More to the point, the word *rote,* meaning "rot" or "decay" in line 1079, also may have been redeemed. Given the meaning of *root* when seen in context of the whole line, *rote* could refer to Christ as the root of human nature, present at the creation and returned in the incarnation to preserve the dignity of human nature. In the creation story sex and procreation were positive events. God's reiteration of them as his gifts to humankind emphasizes, as we saw, the paradisal aspects. The incarnation and birth of Christ completes the recovery of the human heritage.

If the first half of the incarnation story concentrates on Mary, the second half centers on Christ and his active ministry. We are shown how the ox and the ass acknowledge Christ for his purity and honor him as the king of nature. This indicates their redemption as well, inasmuch as the animals were made to suffer and perish in the Flood. Christ thus heals the wound suffered by the whole of nature when he elects to be born in a stable. When the narrator says that Christ elevates that stable to the level of a sacristy and the manger to the Garden of Eden (the "blysful bour"), we see him in the act of making the unclean clean. Although he will not touch that which is filthy within, he welcomes to himself the sick, the leprous, the blind, the diseased, and the dead, all those with diseases "normally regarded in the Middle Ages as resulting from unclean or incontinent living of one kind or another" :[55]

> He heled hym wyth hynde speche of þat þay ask after,
> For whatso he towched also tyd tourned to hele,
> Wel clanner þen any crafte cowþe devyse.
> So hende watʒ his hondelyng vche ordure hit schonied.
>
> (1098–1101)

Milbank says of Christ that he "seems to recover from his more concrete works a plenitude of significance" and that he "learns from his own works his own nature."[56] This would seem to be the case here too. Christ's welcome of the lame, the repulsive, the paralytic, and the poisoned puts aside the figure of a transcendent God and installs in its place a paradigm of love and forgiveness. After the incarnation there is no limit to Christ's forgiveness and no threat of utter human destruction. Even if we become "al tomarred in myre" we still may "schyne þurʒ schryfte."

The poet does not place the incarnation in the poem chronologically but at the point in the narrative where it is needed most, after the terrifying examples of God's wrath and before the abominations of Baltassar's feast. His point seems to be, to paraphrase Purvey, that Christ is hidden in the scriptures the way wine is contained in grapes, that the lesson or point of the incarnation could have been discovered at any time because the truth or spirit of Christ, God's wisdom or "quayntyse," is always already in scripture waiting for the text to be properly negotiated and assembled. Put another way, Christ's incarnation realizes the potential of life as poetic "quaintise" realizes the potential of language.

Cleanness thus places the reader in the position formerly occupied by Daniel in order to permit the reader to see that the direction history has taken is not inevitable but contingent and open to endless reinterpretation. Awareness of past alternatives works dialectically to produce an additional response, one that exposes the limits of the poet's point of view. The reader in turn is forced to negotiate the interplay of the present text with the texts of the past that might reveal to us the otherness of our

105

own point of view and induce us to search for alternative ways of world making.[57] For *Cleanness* this means that the narrator, by his act of translation / recodification, that is, his ability to "con quere" the biblical text with his "quayntyse" and find Christ in it, leads the reader to see that history is not only God's story but also a human drama and a quest for alternative ways of world making. The transcendent world, in this act of translation, no longer poses a threat to the immanent one.

2.
Vision and History in Patience

> In the darkness and this half-silence which, by contrast with what he had known before, seemed to him the silence of the desert or the tomb, he listened to his own heart. The sounds that reached the loft seemed not to concern him any more, even when addressed to him. He was like those men who die alone at home in their sleep, and in the morning the telephone rings, feverish and insistent, in the deserted house, over a body forever deaf. But he was alive, he listened to this silence within himself, he was waiting for his star, still hidden but ready to rise again, to burst forth at last, unchanged and unchanging, above the disorder of these empty days. "Shine, shine," he said. "Don't deprive me of your light." It would shine again, of that he was sure. But he would have to meditate still longer, since at last the chance was given to him to be alone without separating from his family. He still had to discover what he had not yet clearly understood, although he had always known it and had always painted as if he knew it. He had to grasp at last that secret which was not merely the secret of art, as he could now see. That is why he didn't light the lamp.
>
> *Albert Camus*[58]

The story of Jonah, a minor prophet of the post-exilic era, has fascinated audiences of various kinds from biblical times down to the present. The story of his sojourn in the belly of a whale is the stuff of legend, passing quickly and enduringly into the popular imagination as a metaphor for human suffering, confinement, and abandonment, and inspiring the more theologically minded to forge an analogy with Christ who underwent his own three-day ordeal in the bowels of the earth. Jonah emerges from these analogies as an enigma. He is, on the one hand, a mythological figure, heroic and larger than life, while, on the other hand, he is an odd-acting prophet, diminished and obscure, with no memorable speeches or lessons that issue from his mouth. He is, however, as the opening lines in the Vulgate tell us, the son of Amathai ("Et factum est verbum Domini ad Jonam filium Amathi, dicens") whose name, according to Haimo of Auxerre, means "truth."[59] Hence, Jonah speaks the truth and may be the one who tells us the truth about the human condition. For a modern writer, like Camus, Jonah represents any person marked or endowed with a gift, the meaning of which is different to the person who possesses it in distinction to those who see or admire it from the outside. Camus's Jonas is an artist, the prophet in the modern world, who suffers a fall from which he will recover with a greater knowledge and understanding of his condition than he had beforehand. Like the biblical Jonah, Jonas is disposed toward the solitary life but his talent projects him into public life in ways he cannot fully control. Moreover, like the other main characters in *Exile and the Kingdom,* Jonas illustrates the difficult passage of coming to being when torn between the competing demands of a loyalty to the self and one's personal vision and the obligations imposed by history and the needs of others.

In the Middle Ages, the Jonah story, quite aside from its miraculous elements, may have generated interest because it pitted the obstinate or recalcitrant will of Jonah against the will of God, a theologically hot issue in the fourteenth century, as we have seen. The narrator of *Patience* is no less impressed with the conflict between God's wrath and human freedom than the narrator of *Cleanness.* In unearthing the hidden as well as the conspicuous values embedded in the Jonah story he adds another dimension to it by associating Jonah with the beatitude of patience. His version begins with his narrator, in a pose not unlike Jonah's, meditating on the nature of human happiness and human suffering. He is musing to himself how forbearance may assuage the over-burdened heart and neutralize the impulse human beings have toward evil or malice, for "quo for þro may noȝt þole, þe þikker he sufferes." His initial thoughts are thus somewhat formulaic and commonsensical, arriving at the obvious conclusion that it is better to abide the pain of one's circumstance than to vent one's anger intemperately and have it rebound in one's face. In much the same fashion he turns to a rehearsal of the beatitudes that he had heard recounted "on a halyday, at a hyȝe masse." The narrator is on very safe and sure ground in his rehearsal, although he does embellish Matthew's text with his own flourishes and makes it more familiar to himself and his audience by referring to the beatitudes as ladies whom one might court. Wryly, he acknowledges that a person would be blessed to possess one. All, of course, would be better. Up to this point he is able to be somewhat droll and playful; then he realizes that he is wedded to Dame Poverty and he lacks the patience that should attend upon her. Poverty and patience are of one kind, he thinks, and wherever poverty chooses to reside she will not be evicted, whether one likes it or not. The only antidote is patience: "And þereas pouert enpresses, þaȝ mon pyne þynk, / Much, maugré his mun, he mot nede suffer" (43–44). These lines state essentially the same point the narrator uttered at the outset (lines 4–5), but they have the added poignancy here of applying directly to his own life and experience.

At this juncture the narrator surmises that there is nothing he can do but shoulder his burden as best he can; he has no other choice. Grumbling or protesting one's fate simply worsens one's suffering and may excite the wrath of one's master. "Did not Jonas in Judé suche jape sumwhyle," he asks, rhetorically. For the narrator the story of Jonah is intended to serve solely as an armature or an object lesson in support of the announced narrative focus, that if any one of us is ordained by God to carry out a mission it would do us no good if we acted defiantly. The disingenuousness of the narrator's comments have the effect of raising the prospect of the good that having a choice or asserting one's will can have. This is an unforeseen lesson Jonah may teach. In the course of the narrative, the figure of Jonah grows in stature; his story displaces the intended narrative, transforming both the narrator himself and the narrator's understanding of the beatitude of patience. The way the narrator turns the retelling of the Jonah story into a personal quest for theological illumination becomes the poem's most original and exciting feature.

This self-discovery can be seen at work first in the slight yet important difference between the opening and closing lines of the poem:

"Pacience is a poynt, þaȝ hit displese ofte"; and "Þat pacience is a nobel poynt, þaȝ hit displese ofte." As several readers have observed, one of the more curious and conspicuous stylistic traits of this poet is his habit of linking the ends of his poems with their beginnings.[60] The usual explanation offered for the poet's tendency to restate his theme is that he wishes to reaffirm his commitment to the original moral proposition laid out at the front of the poem. A more compelling reason, I believe, is that it shows that the narrator has arrived at an understanding of his subject that he did not possess when he began. The insertion of *nobel* into the final line alters both the rhythm and the meaning of the line. It shifts the weight from the tentativeness conveyed in the opening line, where the emphasis falls on the second half of the line "þaȝ hit displese ofte," to the narrator's now more confident assertion "þat pacience is a nobel poynt." In the final line the concessive statement acts as an intensifier: patience is a nobel virtue (even) though it may cause discomfort. The appearance of *nobel* in the last line also implies that some change or movement has occurred from beginning to end, some growth or personal realization has been attained by the narrator concerning patience that prompts him to attach an intrinsic value to the beatitude instead of simply submitting to it because the alternative is worse.

What Paul Piehler ascribes to the narrator of *Pearl* may be extended to the narrator of *Patience,* namely, that the central character, at the end of his quest for a principle of authority by which his life may be regulated, achieves "a psychic synthesis in which his emotional and irrational impulses, his intuitive understanding, and his rational principles are brought into harmony."[61] At the same time, the structure of the last line of *Patience* suggests that the relationship between patience and discomfort is ongoing or dialogical and that there is no final close to the poem.

That the various events in the story culminate in a moment of vision or self-realization for the narrator is not an approach shared by most critics who have written on the subject. As a rule they do not distinguish between the authority of the poet and the voice of the narrator, despite the fact that the former is the product of having already undergone what the narrator is now in the process of experiencing. Rather, it is assumed that the narrator remains in control of the Jonah story throughout and that he appropriates examples of Jonah's experience with God as object lessons for the reader, showing how each point of contact with God reveals how far or near Jonah falls from the mark of the beatitude, or from Christ, whose example Jonah prefigures either positively or negatively. Readers have pointed out that Jonah is not known for his association with patience and that the gap between Jonah and God widens rather than narrows at the end.[62] Consequently, readers have felt justified in converting the poem into a sermon *exemplum,* into a meditation on penance or spiritual renewal, or into an instance of the transformation from Synagoga to Ecclesia.[63]

Those who have honored the patience theme have, in general, compromised the issue by regarding Jonah mainly as a negative example or as an embodiment of impatience.[64] Jonah's lack of patience with God, John A. Burrow and Thorlac Turville-Petre tell us, contrasts sharply with God's tolerance of human rebelliousness; Jonah evolves into an antitype to Christ, they say, because, unlike the wind, the sailors, the whale, and the ivy, he steadfastly refuses to obey God's commands.[65] To maintain thematic consistency the poem thus shifts away from Jonah, and the narrator must focus on God as the supreme example of patience and look on his mercy, power, and justice as the primary theme of the poem.[66] Spearing's new and insightful reading of the poem approaches the poem in this way: "a poem that on first reading seems to be about Jonah turns out on reflection to be about God."[67] My aim is to restore the poem to Jonah or to give his voice and experience an equal share in the story. For me, the poem culminates in a redefined poetic conception of the deity and its relation to the human world.

Recently, Sandra Pierson Prior connected the patience theme to the Jonah story by showing how it addresses the very real fourteenth-century theological problem of eschatological delay:

> The poet's definition and use of patience make it an active virtue, a divine quality that characterizes not only God's long sufferance but also his involvement in human history. By extension, patience becomes the virtue best suited to God's servants and prophets in "the middest," those who must work within history, who must cease looking to a distant, timeless future and become instead responsive to the present reality of God and his will.[68]

Through the Jonah story the narrator learns that even if God is outside of historical time and has his own historical plan, he is also in the world and committed to Jonah's and all of humankind's well-being.

For Prior, Jonah ultimately apprehends God's message and internalizes it, coming to an accommodation with God at the end. Her reading gives *Patience* its existential dimension but we lose a great deal if we diminish the import of Jonah's anger with God or impose an accommodation not supported by the conclusion. If God deserves all of the credit for sparing the Ninevites then Jonah is deprived of knowing what effect, if any, his own actions have had. Jonah's sustained resistance to God's will and the narrator's silence in the face of it make the conclusion much more problematical and open ended, subject to future revision or debate.[69]

As I indicated above, the narrator begins on what appears to be solid ground; he is confident that a clear set of lessons can be abstracted from the story of Jonah. He invites his readers to tarry "a lyttel tyne and tent me a whyle," and he will instruct us in the meaning of the story, "as holy wryt telles" (59–60). Once the narrative begins, however, the narrator discovers that the biblical text is too reticent; it does not account adequately for either God's motivations or those of Jonah. The narrator thus feels compelled to embellish the biblical text, personalizing it and making it his own. The play world of the fiction lifts the story, and Jonah, out of the realm of the sacred or, as Davenport says, "out of an ancient world of myth into a world of circumstance, history, and probability."[70] This gesture humanizes Jonah and makes him more vulnerable to misjudgment and available to human identification. What begins as a defense of God evolves into an understanding of and respect for the behavior of Jonah. The correspondence between Jonah and the narrator is enriched further by the way the poem depicts Jonah as undergoing his own act of self-discovery as a prophet.

From the outset the narrator makes us aware that patience strikes him as the most paradoxical of all the beatitudes; it defines for him the complex relationship that exists between human beings and God at the same time that it seems to be the beatitude that runs most counter to human nature. The Jonah story, he thinks, will help him to penetrate that paradox. But Jonah turns the tables on the narrator. Instead of an evaluation of Jonah's career, the narrative implicates the narrator in such a way that he begins to assess his own values in order to determine what kind of personal commitment is demanded of human beings by Christ's Sermon on the Mount. This development gives added impetus to the notion introduced by the narrator that patience is a "point," in this instance a prick or spur to self-renewal.

What exactly does the narrator mean when he says that patience is a "poynt"? The gloss preferred by most editors is "virtue" or, as Gollancz suggested, "essential thing." *The Middle English Dictionary* lists a "small hole," "prick," and "puncture" as alternatives. Laurence Eldredge has shown that *point* had a wide currency in the fourteenth century and that the *Pearl*-poet employs the term multifariously throughout his work. He says that the point "is a superb image for the human virtue of willing acceptance primarily because, like the atomists' point, patience is an indivisible virtue. In effect it is that fundamental virtue that underlies all others, the acceptance of God's will."[71] In this respect we might think of the point as a *cairos,* as the time of the prophet, the intersection of the eternal with the temporal, vision and history. We also might view patience as a punctuation mark—something that stops the flow of the reading (a medieval *punctus* is a time pause more than a syntactic one) but in so doing allows clarity and hence truth to emerge.[72]

Jonah, we might say, becomes the "point" of *Patience* if we think of his role in the same way Roland Barthes has taught us to look at the point or *punctum* of a photograph. The *punctum* is the appearance of an incongruent detail or obtrusive element that either punctures or reframes the central image *(studium)* and has the power of expanding its subject or conferring upon it a new and higher value.[73] The *studium* and the *punctum* are for Barthes the two main features of a photograph. The *studium* is what the picture wants to say, its study or subject, the ground on which we encounter the picture taker's intentions. The *punctum,* on the other hand, is a cut, prick, or detail that illuminates the *studium* while remaining a "point" that nevertheless may fill the whole picture. Like poetic vision, the *punctum* is highly subjective (and highly subversive); it is, Barthes says, what the viewer adds to the photograph and *"what is nonetheless already there."*[74]

In Barthes's analysis, the *punctum* reverses the way we normally approach a subject; instead of relying on a caption or an announced theme to predispose us toward what the picture is about, the "point" diverts our attention with details that at first glance may seem insignificant but which, in retrospect, free the subject from any prescriptive meaning that might be imposed upon it. Barthes's model, however anachronistic, challenges the reader to confront the text of *Patience* in a different way. The narrator's selection of Jonah, instead of the more traditional figure of Job, as a vehicle for his inquiry into patience alerts us to his independence and subjectivity (very much like Jonah himself), upsetting any preconceived notions we might have about the nature of patience. Preachers, such as the one he "herde on a halyday," appear to treat patience as a recipe or formula, a solution or *consolatio* for suffering, implying that once one submits to the beatitude a sense of achievement or transcendence follows (lines 4–6). The narrator's willingness to follow his own intuitions in his evaluation of the beatitude disrupts all assumptions about the text as a seamless whole and allows it to unfold as a series of idiosyncratic or spontaneous intrusions that punctuate the pre-established biblical story. Although he never rejects the authority of the theological argument, his assessment of his personal inventory prevents him from affirming patience as a positive value. Instead, it has made him more acutely conscious that there may be no relief or reconciliation with the condition of suffering itself: "And þereas pouert enpresses, þaȝ mon pyne þynk, / Much, maugré his mun, he mot nede suffer" (43–44).

In his suffering, in his challenges to God, and in his habitual complaints, Jonah comes to life for the narrator as a full-fledged personality who is neither a positive nor a negative *exemplum,* but the human *exemplum,* the one who embodies the problematic itself. From the moment that we meet him, sleeping as usual, Jonah impresses upon us his ability to make the most alien and inhospitable of places a locus of comfort and repose. At first we may be astonished, as are the sailors, to learn that Jonah can sleep soundly in spite of the fury of the storm battering the ship and threatening the extinction of them all. But in episode after episode—ship, whale, and woodbine—Jonah succeeds in making his own quest to avoid pain and to seek comfort seem like the human one. In the whale episode, for example, we see Jonah equally occupied with the claims of the human and the claims of the divine. As he did aboard ship, he secures for himself a clean corner suitable for rest and suitable for prayer. Characteristically, in his petition to God for mercy, Jonah excuses himself for taking so long to incline toward God's will:

Þou schal releue me, Renk, whil þy ryȝt slepeȝ,
Þurȝ myȝt of þy mercy, þat mukel is to tryste.
For when þ'acces of anguych watȝ hid in my sawle,
Þenne I remembred me ryȝt of my rych Lorde,
Prayande Him for peté His prophete to here,
Þat into His holy hous myn orisoun moȝt entre.

(323–28)

Jonah reasons that he, like all human beings, needs a crisis or an ex-treme circumstance ("þ'acces of anguych") to occur before he can put aside his own interests and priorities—a point underscored by the sailors and the Ninevites who themselves advert to God only under the threat of their destruction.

What appeals to this reader is the way that Jonah, while acknowledging that he is the prophet of God (327), pleads the human cause. He announces that he is first and foremost a human being and only after that a prophet. Jonah's immersion for three days in the belly of the whale has been readily allegorized to function as Christ's three days in hell, but the narrator's descriptive skill doesn't allow the allegory to take over and we never lose sight of the literal Jonah who is genuinely concerned about his own life and the humiliation to which God is now subjecting him. The narrator shows less interest in the supernatural or miraculous aspects of Jonah's ordeal—he twice calls attention to its mythological content by reminding the audience that the event would be unbelievable were it not recorded in scripture ("Hit were a wonder to wene, ȝif holy wryt nere" [244], and "What lede moȝt leue bi lawe of any kynde" [259])—and more interest in the internal change taking place in Jonah. One might say that the poet's tendency to emphasize the ordi-nary, human nature of Jonah alongside his divinely ordained or gifted status is consistent with his overall resistance to allegory and with his larger scheme to present Christ in his human identity.[75]

Jonah has arrived at his moment of self-realization by his attempt to evade it. Earlier God had called on Jonah to go into Ninevah "wythouten oþer speche" and bring his word to the Ninevites. Ninevah, like another Sodom, has so angered God by its wickedness that he has determined to avenge himself on the city. Jonah, we are told, is stunned ("stowned") by God's request, partly out of fear for his own safety and, as commentators of the biblical text have argued, partly because he feared it would result in the eventual demise of his own people.[76] The narrator focuses exclusively on the first of these two motives and he shows Jonah reasoning, quite logically and understandably, that his flight is justified on the grounds that God has little understanding of human pain and torment, that he sits too high on his throne to comprehend his, Jonah's, fear of being tortured and blinded or slain:

> "Oure Syre syttes," [Jonah] says, "on sege so hyȝe
> In His glowande glorye, and gloumbes ful lyttel
> Þaȝ I be nummen in Nunniue and naked dispoyled,
> On rode rwly torent with rybaudes mony."
>
> (92–95)

Jonah's impression of God's remoteness is hardly a projection of his febrile imagination but had common currency in theological circles in the fourteenth century, given the notion of a hidden God whose primary qualities were omnipotence and unknowability.

In the enclosed space of the ship Jonah feels protected and undetected ("Watȝ neuer so joyful a Jue as Jonas watȝ þenne"). It is characteristic of his thinking that God can and does accomplish his ends without the aid of human intermediaries such as himself. This thinking allows him to sleep. For the poet, Jonah's regeneration, his awakening, or awakenings, to the responsibility and power that is in him constitutes one of the transferable values for a fourteenth-century audience to be found in the Book of Jonah.

Once Jonah is awakened during the storm he rises to accept his responsibility and to act positively toward it. The terrified sailors press him to tell them what land he has come from, what he seeks on this ship, and, most importantly, what is his mission, "what is þyn arnde?" (200–202). It is inconceivable to them that he has no goal or purpose in life. This question apparently makes Jonah realize that he is not in flight from God but from himself, and he responds by an assertion of his identity as a man and as a prophet of God:

> "I am an Ebru," quoþ he, "of Israyl borne;
> Þat Wyȝe I worchyp, iwysse, þat wroȝt alle þynges,

Alle þe worlde with þe welkyn, þe wynde and þe sternes,
And alle þat woneʒ þer withinne, at a worde one.
Alle þis meschef for me is made at þys tyme,
For I haf greued my God and gulty am founden;
Forþy bereʒ me to þe borde and baþes me þeroute,
Er gete ʒe no happe, I hope forsoþe."

(205–12)

Jonah does the right thing; he sacrifices himself for the welfare of the
sailors. Shortly afterwards, in the belly of the whale, he pledges to make
a gift of his complete self to God and "soberly to do þe sacrafyse." Ironi-
cally, Jonah has arrived at the spot God originally had requested him to
go, but the scene is not as fittingly ironic as the narrator imagines it
when he says, triumphantly, "Þe bonk þat he blosched to and bode him
bisyde / Wern of þe regiounes ryʒt þat he renayed hade" (343–44). Jonah
has emerged from his ordeal with his dignity intact. What is a turning
point for him is also a turning point for the narrator who begins to look
at him in a new light.

The first sign that the narrator has begun to identify more approv-
ingly with Jonah can be seen in his reluctance to interrupt his narrative
with his own moral judgments. Prior to the Ninevah sequence the narra-
tor has taken advantage of several opportunities to intrude upon the nar-
rative with his personal assessment of Jonah's efforts to avoid suffering.
First, when Jonah thinks that he has successfully eluded God's eye by
sailing for Tharsis, the narrator unself-critically observes:

Lo, þe wytles wrechche! For he wolde noʒt suffer,
Now hatʒ he put hym in plyt of peril wel more.
Hit watʒ a wenyng vnwar þat welt in his mynde,
Þaʒ he were soʒt fro Samarye, þat God seʒ no fyrre.

(113–16)

Later, when Jonah is about to be swallowed by the whale, the narrator
confidently intones "Þaʒ he nolde suffer no sore, his seele is on anter"
(242). Again, once Jonah is inside the whale, the narrator triumphantly
avers, "Now he knaweʒ Hym in care þat coupe not in sele" (296). When
Jonah gets to Ninevah this kind of intrusion ceases. From Ninevah to
the conclusion it is God who is pressured to explain himself.

The Ninevah sequence allows Jonah's full personality to flower and it shows that he cannot be reduced to mere willfulness or to a series of selfish evasions. After Ninevah the narrator learns that there are limits to what Jonah, or any human being, can be expected to know and be held accountable for. In the exchange that takes place between God and Jonah on the shore of Ninevah we see that Jonah still feels imposed upon by God, but he concedes that others may benefit from his compliance. In response to God's query "Nylt þou neuer to Nuniue bi no kynneȝ wayeȝ?" Jonah answers with his habitual grumbling, "ȝisse, Lorde,... lene me þy grace / For to go at þi gre: me gayneȝ non oþer." Retention of the original manuscript reading "*mon* oþer," in the passage "me gayneȝ mon oþer" ("other men will profit from me"), as Vantuono recommends, over the usual emendation "*non* oþer" ("nothing else profits me"), adds dignity and purpose to Jonah's conduct in Ninevah.[77] The original wording allows us to see Jonah as a moral character, as someone who does take pride in his role as prophet and who is concerned for the welfare of others, not just for himself. The original phrasing also is consistent with the spirit of self-sacrifice Jonah displayed earlier when he instructed the sailors to cast him overboard. Finally, retention of "mon oþer" supports the impression that Jonah does know in advance that God might forgive the Ninevites, as he recites to God later, and therefore Jonah's (just) anger is not over God's forgiveness of the Ninevites but over the way God chooses to use him to shroud his real intentions in a mystery Jonah cannot penetrate.

Throughout this scene it is apparent that God is fond of Jonah, that he indulges him and is willing to forgive him for his earlier trespass. The affection he shows for Jonah anticipates the shift in attitude toward Jonah expressed by the narrator who has come to recognize that Jonah is indeed a worthy prophet, a voice for human concerns, and not just a wily maker of excuses. When he re-ordains Jonah to deliver his message to the Ninevites, God says to him, "Ris, aproche þen to prech, lo, þe place here. / Lo, me lore is in þe loke, lauce hit þerinne" (349–50). Earlier, when God first had called upon Jonah, he instructed him to go to Ninevah "And in þat ceté My saȝes soghe alle aboute, / Þat in þat place, at þe poynt, I put in þi hert" (66–67). In both of these passages it seems that Jonah is a mere instrument or mouthpiece for God. What is the lore that is locked inside of him? What are the seeds that are planted in his heart? Does God speak through Jonah or is what Jonah has to say of his own invention, his own lore? At this pivotal point in the narrative, the poet makes clear the terms of his theological vision: whatever God's plan, whatever he has in mind for human beings, it can only be implemented and come to fruition through the actions of human beings. That is why God is so patient with Jonah and goes to so much trouble to secure his cooperation. Jonah is the true prophet or poet of God, the one with the seeds to sow and the lore to loose because he does question and transform all pre-existing "truths" about the nature of God, his justice, and the place of human beings in the scheme of things.

As a sign of obedience, Jonah hastens to go: "Þenne þe renk radly ros as he myȝt," words which echo the movement Jonah made when he fled from God: "Þenne he ryses radly and raykes bilyue" (89), indicating his newfound enthusiasm for the task and his regenerated will. As if in defense of Jonah, the narrator builds on the meager details in the biblical story in order to cast Jonah in the act of becoming God's prophet.

I am aware that Jonah's conduct during and after the Ninevah episode has been used to discredit him as a prophet or as a model of patience. Robert Blanch and Julian Wasserman, for instance, criticize Jonah for failing to sympathize or identify with the Ninevites, alleging that "he cuts himself off from the Ninevites and fails to embrace their general human condition as reflective of his own."[78] The poet, however, appears to have taken steps to prevent us from reaching this conclusion. Once Jonah accepts his gift or calling he throws himself into the task with his whole spirit and body. Normally, it takes three days to traverse the city of Ninevah but Jonah accomplishes it in a single day, walking continuously. When he stops he is able to cry so clear (his speech "sprang in þat space and spradde alle aboute") because he does correlate their plight with his flight from God and with his ordeal on the ship and in the belly of the whale. Jonah had internalized his experience after his ordeal in the whale, now he externalizes it, doing that which is in him, being a prophet. The Ninevites are his people (Jonah is the prophet to the Gentiles) insofar as they replicate his relationship to God.

The parallels are revealing. In Ninevah Jonah shows that he is indeed the son of Amathi, the speaker of truth. He holds nothing back, assailing the Ninevites with "þe trwe tenor of his teme." Ninevah, he says, shall be brought down to nothing ("noȝt worþe"). The town will tumble to the ground, be turned upside down, fall into the depths of the abyss and be swallowed quickly by the dark earth: "Vp-so-doun shal ȝe dumpe depe to þe abyme, / To be swolȝed swyftly wyth þe swart erþe" (361–62). This warning corresponds with Jonah's experience when he had been swallowed literally by a whale who had come up from the "abyme" (248) and who had then plunged to the bottom of the sea ("he swengeȝ and swayues to þe se boþem"). As Ninevah will tumble to the ground ("tylte to grounde") so did Jonah "tult in [the whale's] þrote" (252). Jonah, while enduring the whale's rough ride, is said to be "malskred in drede" while the Ninevites who hear his dire words are filled with terror and a "hatel drede." Assuming from his own experience and intuition that God will forgive the Ninevites, Jonah's performance is magnificent. He persists in his theme ("Þe verray vengaunce of God schal voyde þis place!") even as the Ninevites change their demeanor and show reverence in their hearts. Jonah proves he is a very persuasive orator and it is his appeal that motivates, first the people (371–76) and then the king to repent. Like Jonah, the king is confident that his "psalm" of praise and repentance will rise to God, as Jonah's did in the whale, and God will show mercy. Thus in his own "acces of anguych," the king will rise up "radly," like Jonah, and run from his comfortable chair to humble himself in ashes before God.

Jonah's unhappiness following the Ninevah episode introduces the most complex and troublesome section of the poem. His impatience with God tries the patience of most readers and has prompted them to conclude that Jonah places his own reputation ahead of the welfare of the Ninevites or, in extreme cases, that he wants to see the Ninevites destroyed so that his word is upheld.[79] Certainly, Jonah places a high premium on his word, as well he should, but Jonah's quarrel is exclusively with God and he wishes no ill fortune to the Ninevites. His quarrel is personal but at bottom it is theological. Jonah feels that he has been used as a pawn in a game of divine false consciousness.[80] His condition or state of mind at this juncture is akin to Milton's Samson, another Old Testament figure whose experience with God bears a remarkable resemblance to Jonah's, and who, the Chorus informs us, wants for patience. But patience as an absolute value of trusting solely in God's will is questioned in Samson's challenge to the Chorus who, he charges, seems to love bondage more than liberty—"Bondage with ease than strenuous liberty" (271).[81]

Milton's Samson is confused by what Milton terms the "various" and often "contrarious" hand of God, who deals most severely with those he has selected as his champions or prophets. Like the *Patience*-poet, Milton dramatizes the absence or unavailability of moral certainty in human activity, even when one believes one is fulfilling the will of God. Samson's decision to heed his "rousing motions" punctures the Chorus's static conception of waiting for God to act. His self-assertion does not resolve the question of the limits to the human will and God's will but brings into sharper focus the inseparability or covenantal relationship of the two—a point that is inherent in the vision of the *Patience*-poet.

Similarly, Jonah's wish to die or be slain by God is no petulant or idle threat; it is an indication of how seriously he regards his word and his agency:

> Now, Lorde, lach out my lyf, hit lastes to longe.
> Bed me bilyue my bale-stour and bryng me on ende,
> For me were swetter to swelt as swyþe, as me þynk,
> Þen lede lenger þi lore þat þus me les makeȝ.
>
> (425–28)

Jonah has raised the stakes in the human conversation with God; he has called God to account by challenging him to judge himself or, possibly, judge for himself: "I biseche þe, Syre, now þou self jugge" (413). Only a part of Jonah sincerely wants to die; another part of him has learned that this is how one gets God to listen. His clever use of "as me þynk" in line 427 allows him to retreat from an absolute stance. However, his use of "lore" in line 428 serves to remind God of his words when he commissioned Jonah on the beach at Ninevah with the words, "My lore is in þe loke, lauce hit þerinne." Jonah distrusts his word.

What is welcome in this debate is the narrator's shift of allegiance; his silence in the face of Jonah's demand that God now judge himself bespeaks his willingness to see Jonah as a spokesman for a very human complaint. The narrator apparently recognizes that there may be grounds when impatience with God, or the human conception of God, is justified. Jonah deserves our indulgence or our patience; he may, for the narrator and the reader, inevitably prefigure Christ, but Jonah himself is limited in his comprehension of the larger historical purpose God's act of forgiveness serves. Jonah should not be expected to act like Christ nor should he be judged by that standard. What Jonah does at this point is cut off the conversation. When God responds to the challenge by asking if Jonah has a right to be angry, Jonah does not answer but wanders off, kvetching to himself, as is his wont. Nevertheless, a new dialogue has begun.

The narrator's appreciation for Jonah's limited vision and his own difficulty with the proposition that God's mercy lies hidden beneath his wrath reaches his climax in the woodbine scene. In this episode the narrator finds it virtually impossible to maintain his distance. He enters the scene with the same exuberance and eye for detail he exhibited earlier in his description of the ship and its rigging. In his bower Jonah partakes of the same joy and satisfaction that the sailors shared in their routine tasks on board ship:

> Þenne watȝ þe gome so glad of his gay logge;
> Lys loltrande þerinne, lokande to toune,
> So blyþe of his wodbynde he balteres þervnder,
> Þat of no diete þat day þe deuel haf he roȝt!
> (457–60)

Jonah is ready to forget his bitterness toward God; he is thankful for the gift of this beautiful bower which "lylled grene," "þat euer wayued a wynde so wyþe and so cole," that shields him on all sides from the sun yet allows him to look outward toward Ninevah, which means "beautiful" and signifies the world.[82] Perhaps it is no small thing that Jonah, in his joy, is willing to forego eating for an entire day!

Once again, in exile, Jonah finds his kingdom. More than the ship's hold or the belly of the whale, the woodbine epitomizes Jonah's capacity to create a refuge for himself amid turmoil. It brings to the forefront the "sweetness of life" theme that has been running as a powerful undercurrent throughout the poem:

> And euer he laȝed as he loked þe loge alle aboute,
> And wysched hit were in his kyth, þer he wony schulde,
> On heȝe upon Effraym oþer Ermonnes hilleȝ.
> "Iwysse, a worþloker won to welde I neuer keped."
> (461–64)

The narrator makes the woodbine and Jonah's pleasure in it so palpable and attractive that the reader shares Jonah's disappointment when the worm devours it.

So deep is Jonah's attachment to the woodbine that he senses its destruction in his sleep, which is disrupted—unusual for him—by wild or disturbing dreams ("wyl dremes"), a detail entirely of the poet's invention. He is envisioning his own loss of paradise. Is God teaching Jonah a lesson he does not need to learn, one the framers of the Jonah story were committed to but which the poet sees as alienating? As Eldredge has observed, Jonah's attachment to the woodbine expresses a more elemental or primitive urge than a desire for mercy; it is the need to find a comfortable, secure place for oneself in a space one can call home.[83] It is this familiar dimension in Jonah that recommends forgiveness; he continually impresses us with the depth and sincerity of his attachment to earthly things and he proves to us that humankind may never be able to regard the things that they love—for Jonah his booth, for the sailors their feather beds—as insignificant or mere lendings. That is why the narrator finds something to admire as well as lament in Jonah's vehement reply to God's dismissal of the destruction of the woodbine: "Hit is not lyttel ... bot lykker to ry3t" (493).

In the wake of the destruction of his little booth the bitterness returns to Jonah's voice. He weeps tears of sorrow and he is consumed with a "hatel anger and hot" toward God not only for what he perceives is God's injustice or his campaign to break his will, but also because Jonah believes God has abrogated a trust that had been established. This time when he asks to die (488, 494) it is more distressing because his request is rational rather than emotional. He concedes that God has won in their struggle but he cannot find any triumph or victory in it for God who has wearied him so much: "A þou Maker of man, what maystery þe þynke3 / Þus þy freke to forfare forbi alle oþer?" (481–82). He rebukes this God who, he claims, arbitrarily creates "meschef" for those creatures he professes to love. The fact that the narrator again remains silent and then greatly expands the biblical text in the place where God seeks to defend his actions indicates that what goes beyond Jonah's ken has created a problem for the narrator and the reader as well.[84]

Despite its inconclusiveness, or perhaps because of it (this reader is inclined to believe that the ambiguity about voice or speaker at the conclusion of the poem is deliberate), the Jonah story yields a vision for the narrator, even if it is not the one he originally expected. Patience, as the Jonah story has defined it for him, is the experience of, rather than the relief from, pain. The patterns in the story argue that patience is neither an escape from impatience nor a stoic transcendence, but a realization of the irreconcilability of the human will and the divine imperative, that area of distress between the human being and God that Ricoeur calls the tension between an infinite demand and a finite commandment.[85] The point of Jonah's experience, even after the narrator invokes the Christian beatitude or New Testament perspective, is that patience does not narrow the distance between the human being and God but emphasizes that very distance or dissonance as the nature of things. Christianity, moreover, is not a solution in the sense that it changes the human condition or reduces human suffering in this life. On the contrary, there never comes a point where the beatitudes become essential or definitive of one's state. They forever remain existential (*playferes,* the narrator terms them), because one never transcends the human circumstances that necessitate the adoption of the beatitudes in the first place.

But if discomfort persists as a permanent or inseparable part of patience, the narrator also concludes that that is what makes it noble:

> Forþy when pouerté me enprece3 and payne3 inno3e
> Ful softly with suffraunce sa3ttel me bihoue3;
> Forþy penaunce and payne topreue hit in sy3t
> Þat pacience is a nobel poynt, þa3 hit displese ofte.
>
> (528–31)

The passage is worded so that *by* in the next to last line refers to both God and to Jonah. It is as much through Jonah's suffering and pain as it is through God's display of mercy that the narrator has arrived at a heightened level of self-realization. What was offered to Jonah is made concrete for the narrator through the beatitudes. Christ, whose suffering is made more real to the narrator by the parallels with Jonah, is the fulfillment of God's promise to Jonah about forgiveness—what God meant when he assured Jonah that "malyse is no3t to mayntyne boute mercy withinne" (523).[86] The beatitudes in turn are Christ's promise of the incarnate word within human nature, the unrealized "lore" God tells Jonah is locked inside him.

Is there a direct connection to Dante in all of this? Has the *Patience*-poet borrowed from or integrated into his own quest the imagery and theology found in the pilgrim's vision in the *Comedy*? The concluding vision gives us ample reason to think in this way. In canto 28 of the *Paradiso* Dante speaks of God as "un punto" (16) and as "al punto fisso" (95). As a "nobel poynt," patience might be regarded as a part or aspect of the divine point on which, Dante says, "the heavens and all nature are dependent" (42) and "the fixed point that holds them [the celestial sparks], and will forever hold them at the *Ubi* in which they have ever been" (95–96). In addition, in canto 28 Dante, like the *Patience*-poet, asserts the primacy of vision as the source from which all love springs:

> Quinci si può veder come si fonda
> l'esser beato ne l'atto che vede,
> non in quel ch'ama, che poscia seconda;
>   e del vedere è misura mercede,
> che grazia partorisce e buona voglia:
> così di grado in grado si procede.
> (*Paradiso* 28.109–14)

> From which it may be seen that the state of blessedness is founded
> on the act of vision, not on that which loves, which follows after;
> and the merit, to which grace and good will give birth, is the mea-
> sure of their vision; thus, from grade to grade the progression goes.[87]

As with Dante, the *Patience*-poet's truth or vision is an act not just an idea, and it affirms the dialogical structure of the relationship between God's plan and the human will, vision and history, as the distinct but interrelated agents in the scheme of salvation. What the narrator has learned from Jonah's experience is that God is not only "on sege so hyȝe" but also is innermost, and that the beatitudes are designed not only to encourage us to turn toward God and his will but also to get us to turn toward this world and to trust in our own will. Practically speaking, patience is more than submission to God's will; it is the will to continue in the face of human suffering and discomfort, and in the full knowledge that God is and will remain incomprehensible to human understanding.[88]

Jonah is, then, a far better example of the beatitude than anyone could have anticipated at the outset. This prophet, this all-too-human everyman, this visionary and this willful example of short-sightedness, this emissary from eternity and this man mired in human time, is the "point," the dividing line between time and eternity, sacred time and human time, who binds us to God's will at the same time that he liberates us from it. This is the *Patience*-poet's vision. To ensure that the reader's vision coalesces with his own, the last line of *Patience* does not lead us out of this world or out of the poem; it leads us inexorably back to the beginning—back to the world, back to ourselves, and back to Jonah—but, as a new beginning.

3.

The Dreamer Redeemed:
Exile and the Kingdom in Pearl

> To overcome death is to discover in it a meaning which inserts it
> into the significant whole of life.
>
> *Romano Guardini*[89]

Of the three poems written by the *Pearl*-poet that are under consideration, *Pearl* is the one most frequently named as the most controlled and sustained example of his homiletic art. For one reader *Pearl* is about the drama of faith or the "tension of belief" which lies at the core of medieval spirituality; for another it is about the fallen soul and its salvation; for most others it is about the education of the Dreamer, his progress under the guidance of the Maiden toward his learning to shift his focus from earthly to heavenly love, from the Maiden to the love of Christ.[90] What these readings share is a confidence in the authority of the *Pearl*-Maiden's discourse, particularly her interpretation of the Vineyard parable as prologue to her formal instruction of the Dreamer in the traditional theology of salvation and justification. In general, these readings treat the Dreamer as a sympathetic but somewhat naïve figure who does not understand the basic principles of Christian doctrine.

Some new readings have begun to recognize the Dreamer's centrality in the narrative and to award him a more active role in the progress of his spiritual education. After acknowledging the psychological complexity and theological sophistication of the Dreamer, David Aers perceives a degree of Lollard individualism and interpretive freedom in his resistance to the Maiden's reading of the Vineyard parable and in his faith in his own understanding of it.[91] Aers argues that the Dreamer's self-absorption has prevented him from gaining self-transcendence and from renewing his bonds with the human community; the dream and the encounter with the Maiden give the Dreamer the "time, space, and provocation to *change,* to redirect his being from identification with the dead person, to redirect his love."[92]

This approach goes a long way towards redeeming the Dreamer, even if it still leaves him too dependent on the Maiden for his personal renewal, and it allows the Maiden's theological argument or position to stand uncontested. I want to show that the Dreamer's voice counts as much as the Maiden's in the theological discourse of the poem and that he shares the moral center of the poem with her. Accordingly, I am proposing that we read *Pearl* in terms of Bakhtinian dialogic instead of Boethian dialogue, the traditional approach to the poem. In Boethian dialogue, the interlocutor holds unquestioned superiority over the correspondent, whereas in Bakhtinian dialogic no such superiority is apportioned. For Bakhtin, both sides have equal authority, even when the dialogue takes place within only one party, usually as a struggle or interplay between two categories: the authoritative word (religious, political, or moral discourse, the word of the fathers or teachers) and internally persuasive discourse (translating external discourse into one's own words or vocabulary, with one's own accents, gestures, modifications) which, Bakhtin says, is denied all privilege, backed by no authority, and goes unrecognized by scholarly norms or opinions.[93] Applied to *Pearl,* this means that the Dreamer is no mere foil that feeds the Maiden easy questions that permit her to expatiate on doctrine to a passive listener. Once elevated to the level of the Maiden, the Dreamer brings the poem into line with the tenor and terms of the theological discussion that was ongoing outside the poem. His questions, whether they are practical, personal, or economic, enlarge the scope of the debate and stretch the discourse of the Maiden to address the very real concerns that trouble him, not simply those explanations that she has found satisfactory. His voice gives expression to views on justification and salvation that we have seen were current in the fourteenth century and that were in opposition to the Maiden's.

The dialogical structure also allows the reader to assume a more active role in the reception of the narrative. Inasmuch as the theological issues under examination in the poem—salvation and justification, the claims of this world against the claims of the other world—are topics that directly concern the medieval audience, the dialogical structure invites the audience to discriminate among the various positions advanced without having to commit itself to any one of them. This is especially true of the poet's "fictionalization" of the Vineyard parable. In themselves, parables such as the Vineyard or the Wedding Feast appeal to the interpretive skills of any reader, and the *Pearl*-poet does not disappoint in the way that he sustains the tension between the Dreamer and the Maiden through their separate readings and responses to Matthew's text. The Maiden treats the parable primarily as a metaphor for the kingdom of heaven, or as a lesson in the eternal values, in God's love for the innocent, and in the consolation gained by those who resign their will to the supreme will of God. Her vision encompasses the whole scheme of salvation, and her theology centers on the reward of heaven as the free gift of God's grace. The Dreamer responds more existentially and pragmatically: the vineyard is like the human order in its ordinariness and its familiarity. It constitutes an area of human activity that is self-contained and autonomous; it pertains to events or conditions in this world, to matters of justice or merit or proper reward for works rendered. His vision settles first on the sense world of immediate experience and does not separate what is theological from what is social, political, or economic.

Normally in a narrative such as this one, a narrator gains and holds authority as teller by controlling or co-opting the power of the narratee, or the text of the narrator shapes the audience into its ideal narratee.[94] In the Vineyard parable the Maiden-narrator fails to achieve her desired control over the Dreamer-narratee because he continues to trust his reason and sense perceptions throughout, despite her several attempts to wean him from them, and because his practical intellect persistently interrogates the authority of her explanations and conclusions. By interposing himself between the Maiden and the audience through his seemingly naïve questions, the Dreamer mediates the authority of her discourse so that the reader is neither "recruited" nor "seduced" by the Maiden (to borrow the vocabulary of narrative persuasion employed by Ross Chambers) and thus remains free to be an active reader who can search the text for alternative meanings beneath the Maiden's assertion of truth.[95]

I intend to discuss the relationship between the Maiden and the Dreamer in more pointed detail below; first, I want to say something about the place of the Vineyard parable in the theological debates about justification. In this way we can approach the poem with a clearer understanding of how *Pearl* unfolds as a debate within the narrator, wherein the earthbound voice of the Dreamer counters the idealizing voice of the Maiden, and a theology of immanence balances against a theology of transcendence.

The Vineyard parable (Matthew 20.1–16) apparently always has been an enigmatic one, no less so in the fourteenth century, primarily because a literal reading leaves the impression that both sides in the dispute, workers and householder, have a just and reasonable claim. Judging from the commentary it attracted, the parable enjoyed widespread popularity in late medieval discussions of justification, yielding what Paul Zumthor calls a multiplicity of "simultaneous and contradictory propositions."[96] The traditional or orthodox understanding of the parable, articulated by Augustine against the Pelagians, interprets it as a defense of the necessity of God's prevenient grace in the work of salvation. In Augustine's analysis, the workers have no claim to the money in terms of the work done, but they do have a claim on the basis of the promise made to them by the owner of the vineyard. Analogously, human beings have no claim on the grace of God on the basis of their works, only on the basis of the obligation of God to live up to his promise.[97]

Augustine's view remained prominent throughout the fourteenth century but its authority was seriously challenged, first by the nominalist or modern position, and then by Biel. Extrapolating from Ockham's and Pierre D'Auriole's so-called semi-Pelagian treatment of justification, Biel offers an interpretation of the Vineyard parable that epitomizes the modern thinking with its characteristic emphasis on human dignity and reward for meritorious deeds. Biel accepts that both God and human beings are teleologically oriented but avers that God's *telos* and humankind's *telos* may not coincide. Whereas the employee works for his wages, the employer, Biel says, is motivated not by the wages of the employee but rather by the work performed. Biel's analogy, in Heiko Oberman's judgment, emphasizes the intrinsic importance of the life of the *viator* on earth, "the value of which was now less exclusively defined in terms of the *eternal Jerusalem,* the final destination of the *viator,* and more in terms of the journey itself."[98] The concept of the *viator,* as Oberman says, carved out a realm (the dome which excludes all God's nonrealized possibilities) for human beings under which they could come into their own, free to realize their own innate endowment of dignity.[99] The idea of the *viator* enabled theologians in the fourteenth century first to confront then to offset the legacy of "negative progress," whereby the human will is imagined as so weakened by sin it cannot effect its own regeneration, and human nature itself, without grace, can do little more than contribute to the sum of evil in the world.[100]

The cornerstone of humanist thinking on justification was the concept of the covenant, a partnership or legal *pactum* with God that broadened the basis of God's justice and brought it into conformity with a theology of merit. Before covenental theology, Alister McGrath explains, there was no definitive concept of justification in the late Middle Ages. The twelfth century, and scholasticism in general, determined that justification involved an ontological change in human beings, thus requiring an ontological intermediary or intermediate, which was identified with the created habit of grace or charity.[101] Hence, *ex natura rei* such a habit was implicated in the process of human justification. In the fourteenth century, however, both the *moderni* and the *schola Augustiniana moderna* began to conceive of justification in personal and relational terms. In place of the ontological intermediary the *moderni* substituted the *pactum,* wherein God, in his unlimited freedom *(de potentia Dei absoluta),* wills to limit himself within the chosen order *(de potentia Dei ordinata).*[102] The *pactum* idea, McGrath concludes, is the turning point in the doctrine of justification associated with the *moderni* because in it God imposes upon himself the obligation to reward the individual who "does that which is in him" with the gift of justifying grace.[103]

Although formal debate of these issues, and the special language in which they were framed, remained the special purview of the schoolmen, justification, as we saw in chapter 1, concerned everyone and, as

William Courtenay has shown, the themes that occupied the scholars continually crop up in the literature of the fourteenth century. The poetry of the period undoubtedly can take some credit for the shift in discourse in theology after 1350, starting with new "emphases on penance and salvation, biblical faith, preaching, and the preference for a less scholastic style in the numerous defenses of the faith," all matters endemic to the thinking of the *Pearl*-poet.[104]

Pearl is a poem about regeneration and human dignity brought about by human beings doing that which is in them; it is about the Dreamer's self-redemption through his dialogue and through his vision of Christ. Seeing Christ as the Lamb or Christ in his human suffering works as an epiphany for the Dreamer.[105] In Christ he sees something of himself and the source of his own grief. Aers is right when he speaks about the Dreamer's self-absorption and self-mourning.[106] Although his daughter has been dead for some time, the Dreamer is so forlorn that he appears spiritually bereft and has isolated himself from the human community. Yet, at the end of the poem he appears regenerated. He speaks of Christ, who can be seen daily at the Mass, as a friend. The Eucharist is one common way in which the covenant struck by Christ between humankind and God is celebrated, and the Mass is where the human community is formed. The end of the poem suggests his redemption, his restoration to the "mass," as it were, to the human community.[107] Before this can happen, however, the Dreamer must do a very difficult and painful thing. He must bury his daughter.

The prologue of *Pearl* takes place in an erber, a curious mixture of cloister garden and romantic bower, where the Dreamer repairs to commune with his absent pearl. More than a place of contemplation and retreat from this world, the erber stands in for this world as the natural physical environment in which the Dreamer is situated. It is the site where the poet problematizes the figure of the Dreamer before we meet the Maiden and where the Dreamer reveals himself to us as a complex and introspective representative of the human condition. The conversation the Dreamer holds with himself in the erber shows us that he is aware of his loss emotionally and intellectually and that he feels it physically. The appeal of the Dreamer himself, who strikes us as an ordinary layman or bereaved father, draws us into the world of the poem and makes the theological debate that swirls in his mind all the more personal and substantive to our own way of confronting the world.

From the outset it is apparent that the Dreamer refuses to act as a predictable player in a conventional dream vision. In the opening stanza when he tells us that he suffers "fordolked of luf-daungere," we are led to expect one kind of poem only to discover shortly that it is to be entirely of another sort. The open wound or freshness of his hurt is conveyed in the way the first eight lines begin languidly and leisurely only to be cut short by the next "Allas! I leste hyr in on erbere." The suddenness of this reversal suggests the suddenness of his loss. The poet's manipulation of *luf-daungere,* a term familiar to love poetry, has a calculated effect; it acts as a verbal prod that disorients us and sticks in our mind because of its incongruity, both complicating the narrative and individuating the Dreamer. It puts the audience on notice that it has to adjust to his way of articulating and internalizing things. The erotic potentiality in the term is not misplaced if we see it as an expression of the limitations of spiritual consolation and as an admission of the need human love has for the physical or bodily presence of the beloved. The erotic language and images in so much mystical writing supports the experience.[108]

To unpack what the poet has wound so tightly in his phrase "luf-daungere," we may have recourse to the technical vocabulary of modern psychoanalytic theory, especially that of Jacques Lacan. Personal grief, as Lacan describes it, exists in the frame of a discourse. We the living give the dead over to the symbolic order. We bury them, that is, according to the rituals of our society, and we resuscitate them in a discourse. Only the reference to discourse prevents the grief from becoming chronic.[109] Stuart Schneiderman describes this transaction in the Freudian vocabulary of the ego:

> When the experience of love is made out to be primary, the dominion of the ego is extended and death is reduced to a loss of love. The ego denies death by *idealizing* love and life; the dead remain alive in the strong ego, still loving and beloved. Thus the ego may recover from its loss by believing that, through death love has been made eternal.... It is through the symbolic order and through the rituals it prescribes that the object is truly given up, truly buried.[110]

Schneiderman goes on to say that if the deceased is not buried meta-
phorically, which means forgotten, the subject will have no sense of
loss or lack and will be alienated from a desire that can only be seen as
a threat to the perfect harmony of the truest love.

In laymen's terms, what the Dreamer needs to learn is that letting go
of or burying his daughter does not mean obliterating her from his mind
altogether, losing her a second time, which he fears (325–49). Burying
her, in fact, may lead to the release of an even greater capacity to love,
one that could expand the human community to embrace the dead as
well as the living, a lesson Gabriel Conroy—and Gretta Conroy—fails
to learn in Joyce's "The Dead." Consolation then will come not only
from his vision of the New Jerusalem with the Maiden in it, but also
from the regeneration of his "luf-longyng" through his encounter in the
other world. If his vision teaches him that his pearl is lost forever to this
world—living in this world entails the loss of precious things—it also
may teach him that such loss need not result in his surrender of the
whole earthly enterprise. He can learn to see the world as redeemed, as
his kingdom as well as his place of exile.

The Dreamer's reluctance to let go of his daughter is revealed in the
ambivalence he shows toward the erber and his fondness for the image
of the pearl as an everlasting object of beauty. He is drawn to the spot,
even though it fills him with sorrowful reminders, and because it se-
cretly arouses him and energizes him:

> Syþe in þat spote hit fro me sprange,
> Ofte haf I wayted, wyschande þat wele
> Þat wont watz whyle deuoyde my wrange
> And heuen my happe and al my hele—
> Þat dotȝ bot þrych my hert þrange,
> My breste in bale bot bolne and bele.
> Ȝet þoȝt me neuer so swete a sange
> As stylle stounde let to me stele.
>
> (13–20)

The paradoxical state of the Dreamer's mental frame—his sensations
oscillate between near violence and extreme sensitivity—reveals to us
the depth of his attachment to and ambivalence toward his daughter. In
line 10 ("Þurȝ gresse to grounde hit fro me yot") and again in line 13 it

sounds as if he blames himself for her loss, an emotional state rein-
forced by the self-pitying way he describes himself to her shortly after
they meet in the dream:

> Art þou my perle þat I haf playned,
> Regretted by myn one on ny3te?
> Much longeyng haf I for þe layned,
> Syþen into gresse þou me agly3te
> Pensyf, payred, I am forpayned
> (242–46)

He thinks and acts as if he has found his lost pearl, still alive, rather than
being able to confront the fact of her permanent death.

In contrast to the Maiden's comprehensive vision, the Dreamer is
more inductive and particular in his outlook. His mind does not advert
immediately to the symbolic signification hidden beneath the concrete
reality. Whatever meaning readers may assign to the flowers, and to the
pearl itself, the Dreamer sees them first as natural objects of beauty in
their own right and not as shadowy reminders of some higher invisible
reality. His attention to the sights, sounds, and odors of the garden indi-
cate his attunement with the physical world and point to his sensitivity
to human finitude, change, and the enigma of death.

His inability to expel the demons of loss that torment him provoke
the Dreamer to speculate about the resurrection of the body and the pros-
pect of an afterlife. His rational faculties and animal soul seem to under-
stand and accept death and regeneration as an integral part of the cycle
of human nature:

> Flor and fryte may not be fede
> Þer hit doun drof in molde3 dunne,
> For vch gresse mot grow of graynez dede;
> No whete were ellez to wonez wonne.
> (29–32)

However much his "special spyce" may enrich the seed, he wonders
whether some more perdurable quality is due her, and he cannot fully
reconcile himself to the thought that she has dissolved into mere mud or
clay. Yet the comfort he might derive from the resurrection eludes him:
"Þa3 kynde of Kryst me comfort kenned, / My wreched wylle in wo ay

wraȝte" (55–56); it does not master his will and emotions which incline toward the consolations of the erber. The erber in its colors, odors, and natural beauty thus imposes on our consciousness an acute awareness of the Dreamer's presence in his body and in a familiar human setting that remains embedded in our mind even after we take flight with him to traverse the landscape of the other world.

These two currents converge in the Dreamer's mind when he identifies the occasion as both a religious holiday and the height of the harvest season.[111] Aers has shown that the holiday and the suggestion of human activity unfolding outside or beyond the erber poignantly depict the Dreamer's isolation and distance from the community.[112] True enough, but we should see that he is not indifferent to this activity, and the particularity of the Dreamer's language both places him in it and allows us to visualize along with him this particular August, this field of corn, these workers with their sharp sickles. His words, "In Auguste in a hyȝ seysoun, / Quen corne is coruen wyth crokez kene" (39–40), pit the imagery of the coming of winter and impending death against the celebration of life in its plenitude. He is struggling to integrate himself with nature and its rhythms. His consciousness of the organic growth from seed to flower and of the interpenetration of nature and human beings in their coordination of the liturgy with the seasons offsets earlier images of disintegration and decay and serves as a buffer for his loss. The continuity of nature and of the self-renewal of nature in its annual cycles thus vies in his mind with the linear plane of eschatological time or salvation history.[113]

Suffused with the scent of the flowers that engulf him, he drifts into sleep. He dreams of a vineyard, not only because the parable centers on a grape harvest but also because it contains all the conflicting tensions he has been turning over in his mind. When he departs from the erber, for example, he says "my spyryt þer sprang in space," which parallels the departure of his precious pearl from him: "Syþen in þat spot hit fro me sprange." His announcement that his body has been left behind, "My body on balke þer bod" (62), registers his concern that the separation of the soul from the body as prerequisite for entry into the other world is the source of much of his anguish. His eventual return to his body could entail a plea for the "resurrection" of the bodily, an appeal to heal the body-spirit schism and thus restore human nature to its original dignity.

The Dreamer's return to the erber also posits a theology open to this world, and thus a counter to the *contemptus mundi* motif inherent in the Maiden's discourse.

The lines of the dialectic are sharply drawn once the Dreamer meets the Maiden in his dream. What disrupts the joy of their reconciliation is his dismay, first over her counsel that he cease mourning—he busies himself "aboute a raysoun bref"—then over her disclosure that she has been made a queen of heaven, when Christians here on earth accept only Mary as queen. The Maiden patiently explains to the Dreamer that many strive for heaven and many attain it but that there are no "supplanters" within the place and all who arrive are made kings and queens. Then, drawing on Paul's analogy to the body in 1 Corinthians 12.12–31, the Maiden explains to him that the heavenly order differs from the earthly norm. In heaven everyone cares for and belongs to the other:

> Of courtaysye, as saytz Saynt Poule,
> Al arn we membrez of Jesu Kryst:
> As heued and arme and legg and naule
> Temen to his body ful trwe and tryste,
> Ryȝt so is vch a Krysten sawle
> A longande lym to þe Mayster of myste.
> Þenne loke: what hate oþer any gawle
> Is tached oþer tyȝed þy lymmeȝ bytwyste?
> Þy heued hatz nauþer greme ne gryste
> On arme oþer fynger þaȝ þou ber byȝe.
> So fare we alle wyth luf and lyste
> To kyng and quene by cortaysye.
>
> (457–68)

Although the Maiden's aim is to attend to the invisible or heavenly application of the analogy, her language exceeds her announced intention. Christ's body in its physical dimensions obtrudes and takes on a significance of its own. As David Jeffrey has shown in respect to medieval painting, when the natural world is made fully natural, it may no longer signify the spiritual. That is, when the vividness or realism of the visible, physical object that refers is more pronounced than the spiritual or invisible thing to which it refers, the signs cease to function with the same directness.[114] Accordingly, in this passage, we are more likely to register an impression of the physical or material body of Christ than the mystical concept—more so if we have been an audience that had become increasingly exposed to what Ullmann identified as the growing pervasiveness of incarnational images.

Christ's navel, the most unusual and arresting item in the inventory of Christ's physical properties, acts as a *punctum,* arresting one's eye and preventing one from responding passively to an otherwise metaphoric commonplace. Making *naule* a rhyme word with *sawle* and *Poule* draws added attention to it and suggests the inseparable link of the body with the soul. More suggestively, the navel is what connects the audience to and reminds it of their common origins in Adam and redemption in Christ, whose birth from a human mother and acceptance of a complete human nature characterized incarnational devotion at that time.

Incarnational theology was also secular in its outlook, insofar as it sought the political as well as the moral improvement of human society. Paul's exaltation of Christ's body, Peter W. Travis tells us, stimulated the imagination of the poets and artists as well as the theologians, who used it as a metaphor for social unity:

> Recognizing the tendency of social bodies to break up into misaligned fragments, yet appreciating the importance of the most lowly organs [Christ's navel?], Paul's version of Christ's body and the unifying and disunifying function of its discrete parts is a version that ramifies throughout the Middle Ages. Not only was this living metaphor sacralized in peculiarly complicated ways in the idea of the king's two bodies, but it blended with various late medieval ways of conceiving the polis, the city on earth perceived as a sacred human organism of interdependent economic, social, political, and geographic units.[115]

One intention of the incarnational consciousness, then, was to transpose to the human plane, as a this-worldly possibility, the social harmony and spirit of mutuality that the Maiden deems as an otherworldly ideal. Perhaps the best example of this is the way Thomas Aquinas applied to the political, earthly realm the values Augustine reserved for the true *patria* of the Christian, the kingdom of heaven or the celestial city of Jerusalem: "Amor patriae in radice charitatis fundatur."[116]

In his questions and in his attachment to earthly things the Dreamer is unconsciously redeeming them, bringing dignity to ordinary human emotions and activities. Without identifying it as such, his view of the Christian life is incarnational, or based on an imitation of Christ. Those who have endured the trials of this world and have lived their penance in it, he reasons, are the ones most entitled to wear the crown and be at one with Christ:

> What more honour moȝte he acheue
> Þat hade endured in worlde stronge,
> And lyued in penaunce hys lyuez longe
> With bodyly bale hym blysse to byye?
> What more worschyp moȝt he fonge
> Þen corounde be kyng by cortaysé?
> (475–80)

His reluctance to approve the Maiden's heavenly status is not intended to deny her a place in heaven, only that it seems to him that human beings purchase their salvation ("blysse") with "bodyly bale." Indirectly the Dreamer's argument summarizes the view of the *moderni* on justification. His emphasis on work in the world assumes the essential goodness of human nature and the obligation to work in the vineyard as the human side of the *pactum*.[117]

In response to the Dreamer's contention that God's "courtesy" is too generous if it allows someone to be queen who has scarsely lived two years in the world and who, he says, "Þou cowþez neur God nauþer plese ne pray, / Ne neuer nawþer Pater ne Crede" (484–85),[118] the Maiden recites the Vineyard parable as an object lesson (it is she who is didactic, not the poet) that will teach him that there is no "date" or limit to God's mercy:

> For al is trawþe þat He con dresse,
> And He may do noþynk bot ryȝt.
> As Matthew melez in your messe
> In sothfol Gospel of God almyȝt:
> In sample He can ful grayþely gesse
> And lyknez hit to heuen lyȝte.
> (495–500)

Her interpretation of the parable conforms to the Augustinian theme of salvation in the other world, but her homely, familiar recitation of the parable itself pulls against the soteriological meaning she extracts from it. As in her description of Christ's body, the physical object that refers is more pronounced than the invisible thing to which it refers, and we cannot repress the immediate sense impressions that rise before us in the vivid details of a contemporary harvest scene Brueghelian in its realism.[119]

First the householder is given a ring of authenticity by the skill he displays in knowing the most propitious time to secure the vines: "Of tyme of ȝere the terme watz tyȝt, / To labor vyne watz dere þe date. / Þat date of ȝere wel knawe þys hyne" (503–5). Chaucer employs similar language to fix the acumen of his Reeve: "Wel wiste he by the droghte and by the reyn / The yeldynge of his seed and of his greyn" (lines 595–96). The emphasis in both of these passages falls on experience and the knowledge that accrues to human beings that are in harmony with nature and nature's time.

The *Pearl*-poet's attention to human beings engaged in their ordinary tasks, in rhythm with their surroundings and in tune with their work, such as the sailors in *Patience* or the servers, pipers, and the armorers in *Sir Gawain and the Green Knight,* not only heightens the realism of his poems but also gives presence to what is usually simply assumed to be there in many poems and chronicles. Most of these scenes and the workers themselves are peripheral at best to the main focus of the poem, yet they are memorable, and it is precisely through them that the poet is able to incarnate a theme in his poems: how humble, routine labor and those in the margins of society are connected to the vitality of the community. And, since the work activity occurs in poems that revolve around a moral or theological crisis, he appears to be imputing a sacramental purpose to work no matter how remote it may stand from official spiritual activity.

In the parable the poet synchronizes the labor of the vine workers with the rise and fall of the sun and with the canonical hours. Time is measured by the color of the sky and the pleasure or pain the workers feel as they "Wryþen and worchen and don gret pyne, / Keruen and caggen and man hit clos" (511–12). The Maiden's narrative respects, perhaps privileges, the generosity of the householder, but the heat of the day, its length, and its exhausting toll on the day workers, stretched out by the effective use of polysyndeton in the lines just cited, generates sympathy for the disgruntled day laborers, who feel unfairly compensated for their efforts:

> And þen þe fyrst bygonne to pleny
> And sayden þat þay hade trauayled sore:
> "Þese bot on oure hem con streny;
> Vus þynk vus oȝe to make more.
> More haf we serued, vus þynk so,
> Þat suffred han þe dayez hete,
> Þenn þyse þat wroȝt not hourez two,
> And þou dotz hem vus to counterfete."
> (549–56)

The workers evidently believe in a merit system wherein reward is proportionate to performance. To them the householder's generosity appears arbitrary and unjust. That actual day laborers in the fourteenth century often worked exceedingly long hours for deplorably low wages and were systematically exploited by householders or the seigneurial class lends credence to the protests uttered here by the vineyard workers.[120] In the poet's version of Matthew's parable, the workers are granted a greater recognition scene than they get in the biblical text, rooting the poem and the parable more firmly in the social and economic milieu of the fourteenth century and making the question of justice in this world a more immediate one.

The householder defends his actions on the grounds of the covenant, the agreement he struck with the individual groups of workers before they entered the vineyard—although no mention is made of wages in the employment of the one-hour workers:

> Frende, no waning I wyl þe ȝete;
> Take þat is þyn owne, and go.
> And I hyred þe for a peny agrete,
> Quy bygynneȝ þou now to prete?
> Watz not a pené þy couenaunt þore?
> Fyrre þen couenaunde is noȝt to plete;
> Wy schalte þou þenne ask more?
> More, weþer louyly is me my gyfte—

139

To do wyth myn quatso me lykez?
Oþer ellez þyn yze to lyþer is lyfte
For I am goude and non byswykez?

(558–68)

The householder speaks placatingly to the day laborers here, calling their leader "frende," but he stands firm in his conviction that he has the right to reward as he pleases, as long as he does not violate his promise to the first in his generosity to the last. Legally or technically, the householder is correct in his stance, but the strength of any covenant lies in its mutuality, and any sense of injustice or unfairness could result in discontent or loss of respect, as is expressed by the day laborers.

The concept of the covenant itself—no equivalent of which is in Matthew's text—does leave room for some reconciliation of grievances to be negotiated, which the poet underscores by its repetition in lines 562 and 563. In addition to its theological signification as the bond or working arrangement between God and human beings, the concept of the covenant had a rich heritage in English law, dating to the feudal period which united the lord to his vassals in a bond of reciprocal rights and duties.[121] Feudal law had or presupposed the cooperation of both lord and vassal toward a common goal, a cooperation that emanated from a concept of mutual fidelity.[122]

In the poem the vineyard itself is the mutual ground that unites the workers and householder together, and on its growth and development depends the economic salvation of both laborers and landowner. Throughout the parable the householder's repeated injunctions against idleness and his several forays into the marketplace to recruit fresh workers whose "hyre watz nawhere boun," that is, not fixed by covenant, and who are asked to do whatever they can (that which is in them?) (531–36), contributes to the dissatisfaction of the day workers. Alternatively, the householder's actions open the vineyard to the entire community, giving the parable a Dantean turn. It is Dante who contends that only through the effort of all human beings working collectively toward peace and justice will humanity actuate the totality of its *humanitas*.[123] For this enterprise all are called and everyone is chosen.[124]

As is his habit, the *Pearl*-poet does not seek to resolve the dispute between the laborers and the householder openly. He neither privileges the view of the householder nor discredits the complaints of the workers. He prefers to sustain the paradox built into the parable and its several levels of meaning so that the impasse between the parties serves as a provocation that frustrates closure and allows questions about social justice and divine justice to arise naturally from the situation that exists. Additionally, the narration of the parable does not resolve the differences between the Dreamer and the Maiden, each of whom seems hardened in his or her position in the aftermath of the reading. At the close of her recitation the Maiden likens the householder to Christ, who sheds his mercy graciously on the innocent "Þaȝ þay com late and lyttel wore, / And þaȝ her sweng wyth lyttel atslykez" (574–75). She supports her argument by drawing on the moral force contained in the double epigram that concludes the parable: "Þe laste schal be þe fyrst þat strykez" (570) and "For mony ben called, þaȝ fewe be mykez" (572). In her gloss the Maiden alludes to paradigms of universal and timeless significance, preeminently to the ideal of innocence and to the figure of the child as the highest beatitude. Because Christ beckons us to come to him as little children, she says, the innocent receive a greater portion of glory and bliss than all the people of the world might claim by seeking judgment on the grounds of their righteousness. The tag lines that echo throughout sections 11 and 12 respectively carry the burden of her argument: "Þe grace of God is gret innoȝe" and "Þe innosent is ay saf by ryȝt." Her theology is impeccable but her delivery seems designed to provoke the Dreamer and certainly a portion of the audience.

The Dreamer reacts boldly to her interpretation ("Then more I meled and sayde apert"), telling her that her explication is unreasonable. Confidently advancing his own understanding of scripture, he cites David's psalm as a more accurate reflection of the meaning of the parable:

> "Þou quytez as hys desserte,
> Þou hyȝe Kyng ay petermynable."
> Now he þat stod þe long day stable,
> And þou to payment com hym byfore,

> Þenne þy lasse in werke to take more able,
> And euer þe lenger þe lasse þe more.
> (595–600)

It is apparent that the Dreamer identifies with the point of view of the workers; he refuses to treat them abstractly, and his enthusiasm for those who "stand the long day stable," the many who are called, matches her zeal for the few who are chosen. In his persistence the Dreamer should not be dismissed as stubborn or simpleminded, as some have concluded, when his words show that he is as committed to his own theological convictions and moral values as the Maiden is to hers. What the Maiden attributes to the transcendent the Dreamer continues to show is also part of the immanent, the personal, and the human. What counts, of course, is not who is right. They both are. But in the last half of the fourteenth century it is apparent in the poetry that a theology on the side of this world was much needed.

The Maiden continues to expound on the power of God's grace and the redemption of the innocent, urging the Dreamer to abandon "þe world wode" (743). The Dreamer persists in his wonderment—and doubt— that she should be exalted above those who have suffered in Christ "onvunder cambe" (775). The Dreamer's resistance sets the Maiden off on another lengthy disquisition, this time on salvation history. In her lesson the Maiden schools the Dreamer in the sinfulness of earthly life, Christ's suffering in the world at the hands of "boyez bolde" (806), his transformation into the Lamb, and the evolution of the New Jerusalem out of the old one. More and less, she informs him, are not relevant in God's kingdom; what does count is the salvation of one's soul. From her perspective recovery of the pearl in the other world is compensation enough for loss or death in this world. She warns him that no one is righteous enough to warrant heaven (697–700) on his or her own merits: "Forþy to corte quen þou schal com / Þer alle oure causez schal be cryed, / Alegge þe ry3t, þou may be innome" (701–3). She completes her lesson and brings the poem to its climax with an allusion to death and salvation that goes to the heart of the distress experienced by the Dreamer in the erber—his fear of death and bodily decay set against the promise of permanence and the release from all tension in the New Jerusalem. She assures him:

Alþaʒ oure corses in clottez clynge,
And ʒe remen for rauþe wythouten reste,
We þurʒoutly hauen cnawyng;
Of on dethe ful oure hope is drest.
Þe Lombe vus gladez, our care is kest.
(857–61)

The Maiden's appeal situates intimacy—the lost intimacy the Dreamer
had mourned for in the erber—in the New Jerusalem and in the Lamb
who relieves all cares. What is clear to her is obscure still to the Dreamer
and he asks earnestly that she afford him a vision of that city. The
Dreamer's request to see rather than to be told points to one of the prob-
lems with the Maiden's (theological) discourse, and that is her imper-
sonal, legalistic, or doctrinal language. It fails to move the Dreamer or
respond to his needs. His request of her makes this clear. He apologizes
for trying her "wyt so wlonc" and for his own lack of sophistication—"I
am bot mokke and mul among." Then he says he would ask her a thing
directly, "þaʒ I be bustwys, as a blose," and that be that she show him
where she abides.

Some readers have been disappointed with the Dreamer's descrip-
tion of the New Jerusalem; they find it flat and insipid, an example of a
lapse of attention on the poet's part. More likely it is another instance of
his style creating meaning. Throughout the sequence the Dreamer de-
fers his own responses to those he has read in John's Apocalypse. John's
description, like the Maiden's lengthy speech, appeals to him intellectu-
ally but also shows the limitations of theological formulations to per-
sonal crises. The repetition in every stanza of some phrase that acknowl-
edges John's description solidifies the Dreamer's role as reader and in-
terpreter and also his independence as seer. He is no mere conduit for
John's vision, and his own vision does not result in the renunciation of
this world, as the Maiden may have anticipated. Like Dante, the Dreamer
is "rauyste" (1088) by his glimpse of heaven, and also like Dante his
ascent to the pinnacle of the other world does not result in the rejection
of the mutable world. Instead, the vision encourages the viewer (includ-
ing John, another poet figure) to return to this world to work or to write
in order to make this world approximate the heavenly ideal each had the
privilege of seeing.

The Dreamer's personal response enters the moment he sees Christ's body, the wound in his side still spurting blood (1135–37). What is even more transformative for the Dreamer than the wound is the look of serenity on the face of Christ, causing the Dreamer to remark "Þaȝ He were hurt and wounde hade, / In His sembelaunt watz neuer sene, / So wern His glentez gloryous glade" (1142–44). His countenance is of one who has overcome his sorrow and the Dreamer sees how Christ's triumph over death fills his company with new life. The burden of sorrow and despair drop from his shoulders when he spies his daughter in the procession frolicking joyfully with her companions. His sudden impulse to cross the river, "For luf-longyng in gret delyt" (1152), is ambiguous, dividing readers in their response to his act. On the one hand, his impulse is his act of self-transcendence, his desire and determination to be reunited to society, to be part of the human community again. Conversely, it may be seen as a folly that prevents him from seeing more of God's mysteries, and suggests, on one level, that he has learned nothing at all. It is possible that the poet allows for both readings to be true, making the ending of the poem, as was true in *Patience,* an announcement of the incommensurability of earth and heaven. For me, the Dreamer's "luf-longyng" here recalls the "luf-daungere" he felt in the opening passage of the poem, which no longer seems mysterious but identifies itself as that love of the earth which calls him back to his "erber grene" and to the fundamental human desire for the life of the body: back to the harvest, and back to the work that remains in the fields and in the vineyard.[125]

An important feature of dream poems is the awakening; its timing, its motivation, its when and its why.[126] What awakens the Dreamer is his self-assertion, the regeneration of his will (to live). Like Keats's dreamer he awakens to himself. With the vision dissipated. And we are constrained to ask, Is this the fall of man?[127] Does the Dreamer awaken in a "doel-doungoun" or in an "erber wlonk"? Viewed from one perspective, with one eye on his "lyttel quene" (1147) set in a "garlande gay" in the New Jerusalem, and the other eye on the Dreamer prostrate on her grave mound, this world (the "old muck ball," Beckett calls it) may seem indeed a place of exile. Yet the heavenly view need not invalidate the earthly one. At the end the narrator, who is at once the Dreamer and the one who has had the dream, can accept the vision of the eternal world, God's world, and its fulfillment. But he also accepts the fact that there is a real world here and a will to enjoy its pleasures and pains, to understand his purpose in the present life, and to comprehend still further his work here. To love the things of this world, the Dreamer has learned, is not to be overly attached to the material world or to be resistant to God's love. It is to love better by seeing how such love brings about the full realization of one's humanness. He rises from the burial mound and declares, "Now al be to þat Pryncez paye" (1176). The Dreamer has buried his daughter. The immanent world is not a rejection of the transcendent; the presence of the transcendent—the knowledge of her continuity—compensates for the awareness at the root of Western consciousness of a profound sadness, or incurable lack, to human existence.

Reawakened to the world around him, the Dreamer finds that he is not alone in the world. He discovers in the Eucharist, in the unbloody Lamb, "a frende ful fyin" (1204). Calling the Eucharist friend echoes the householder's conciliatory gesture toward the day laborers in the Vineyard parable, making the Eucharist a sign of the covenant reuniting the human and divine in Christ's nature. As Caroline Walker Bynum says of the Eucharist and its devotion in the late Middle Ages, "it stood for Christ's humanness and therefore for ours. Eating it and, in that eating, fusing with Christ's hideous physical suffering, the Christian not so much *escaped* as *became* the human."[128] The Eucharist thus becomes for the Dreamer a daily reminder of his dream, of the vineyard, of the vision of his daughter, and, finally, of a fully human redemption.

Like Dante, then, the Dreamer sees to see better. It is his vision, after all, and not the Maiden's, and the writing or retelling of it affords him the retrospective view that yields meaning. He has lost one vision only to gain another that has always been in front of him. It is the Dreamer himself who draws the link between seed, penny, pearl, and Eucharist, the harvests of grain and grape, bread and wine. He knows he cannot lose himself in the seasons or the cycles of nature, nor can he withdraw to the heavenly Jerusalem. But he now knows who he is and to what kingdom he belongs. That he returns to the erber and reinhabits his body without any sense that he has fallen back into a sinful world assures us that he is not in exile here. Like Jonah in his woodbine, the Dreamer is at home in his "erber wlonk."

4.

The Bishop's Tears: Baptism, Justification, and the Resurrection of the Body (Politic) in Saint Erkenwald

The citizen must love the city more than himself, because the city is his only possible actuation: the whole; the city is more perfect than the individual, and being more perfect, it is more to the image and likeness to God.

Remiglo de Girolami[129]

Let him be just and deal kindly with my people, for the dead are not powerless. Dead, did I say? There is no death, only a change of worlds.

Chief Sealth (Seattle)[130]

Once a poem that relied almost exclusively on its affiliation with the *Pearl*-poet to garner whatever critical attention it received, *Saint Erkenwald* since has emerged as a poem with a level of literary sophistication and theological seriousness that allows it to stand on its own.[131] In concert with the vision of the *Pearl*-poet, this poem also successfully treats some of the more complex and controversial ideas that beset and characterized English theology and religious practices in the fourteenth century concerning doctrine and popular belief, the authority of the episcopacy against the rising power of the laity, and the increasingly important relationship between salvation, justification, and social justice—with special reference to the fate of the virtuous pagans. One of the features that distinguishes it from anything written by the *Pearl*-poet is its London setting: embracing pre-Christian and seventh-century London as well as fourteenth-century London. London in the fourteenth century had begun to emerge as a center that provided many new opportunities for all levels of society, sometimes providing a sense of unity or community absent in the church.[132] Cities like London functioned as ideas as well as physical locales and were celebrated as such in chronicles, legends, poems, and in the popular imagination. Louise Fradenburg has suggested that the late medieval city, "not exclusively but with a particular kind of power, poses the problem of how human beings construct and produce their world." [133] If, as she says, remembering is an attempt to repair the relationship of the human creature to superreality, to transfer an external origin (such as the agency of the Creator) to the interiority of the creature, then how the people of a city choose to honor the dead or to retell the legend of a patron saint may provide us with a supreme example of the ethos of that city and the aspirations of its inhabitants. *Saint Erkenwald* attempts to do just that in developing its own version of civic religion or *citified theology,* Steven Ozment's quaint phrase for a theology of social and ethical concern that stresses responsibility toward this world and not merely salvation from it.[134]

Saint Erkenwald is an anonymous alliterative poem written in the late fourteenth century about Erkenwald, who was a seventh-century bishop of London and the East Saxons and one of London's earliest patron saints. It is also about a pagan lawyer who was buried on the site of St. Paul's Cathedral centuries before Christianity had come to England and who serves as a model of secular English citizenship. What distinguishes the poem is the role the poet assigns to this pagan lawyer, whose discourse gives the poem its polemical edge. Although Erkenwald bears the mantle of ecclesiastical authority—he acts as teacher, pastor, and lawgiver to his congregation and he serves as the instrument through which the Holy Spirit carries out his miracle—the lawyer refuses to act as his mere foil. Instead, he functions to correct Erkenwald and the church on a number of deficiencies in their vision. The lawyer exceeds any conventional defense of his own moral virtue to assume an equal share in the theological burden of the poem's argument. Not content to urge the worthiness and justice of his own salvation, the lawyer's *apologia pro vita sua* makes a direct appeal to Christ and to the Christian community (Erkenwald's congregation) to release all pagans from the limbo of anonymity, to resurrect their bodies, and to reinscribe them in the book of life.

The moral force of the lawyer's argument, which moves the bishop and his congregation to tears, pits the spiritual autobiography of an anonymous public servant against Erkenwald's authoritative discourse on divine justice and salvation in the other world. Through the intervention of the lawyer, the poem advocates the rebirth of the citizen, a figure distinct from but not opposed to the Christian. In citing this distinction I am mindful of the fact that the medieval citizen does not correspond to the modern self-sufficient individual. Nevertheless, the increasing complexity of life in the cities, coupled with greater access to Aristotle's ideas about the nature of the citizen, prompted people at all levels of society in the fourteenth century to think of themselves and their cities in political as well as religious terms.[135] This was equally true in England as it was on the continent.[136] English theology proved no less receptive to Aristotle's influence than Italy had, if only because England had cultivated a long tradition of civic life and civic humanism that complemented existing religious practices.[137] The incorporation of the lawyer and his discourse in the poem makes *Saint Erkenwald* a specifically English example of the continental tradition of *civitas* as a form of *caritas*.[138]

Most readings of the poem, especially those concerned with the fate of the virtuous pagans, have followed one of two fruitful but mutually exclusive avenues of approach, both of which warrant our close attention. The dominant or orthodox view, epitomized by the work of E. Gordon Whatley, privileges Erkenwald's discourse and argues that the poem upholds the long-standing doctrinal proposition that salvation does not exist outside of the church or without baptism.[139] In this reading, Erkenwald, who was celebrated for his devotion to ecclesiastical authority and sacramental Christianity, evinces sympathy for the "impeccable character" of the lawyer, but he never makes the error of presuming God has forgiven the pagan:

> The poet reveals that even such a flawless exponent of rational justice and civic probity cannot be saved outside the sacramental church. Without the church and its consecrated ministers, the best that human nature can achieve is doomed to receive a merely material reward. Moreover, the entire narrative movement of the poem serves to dramatize the limitations and inadequacies of ordinary human powers unaided by the divine grace available through the mediation of the priest and the sacraments.[140]

Alternatively, some readers, notably Ruth Morse, view the poem through the prism of the lawyer whom, she believes, the poet has introduced as an example of justification gained through meritorious works.[141]

Morse's reading points us in the direction of the *moderni* who, as noted in chapter 1, were reformulating justification theology in the fourteenth century and framed the kind of questions raised by the poem, such as, Can God contradict his own ordinances? Is baptism necessary for salvation? Can a soul be liberated from hell if it is presumably there forever?

As we discussed in conjunction with the *Nun's Priest's Tale,* the *moderni* determined that what was freely elicited by a person *ex puris naturalibus* was as worthy of merit as those acts that came about through grace. By his ordained power God's love is reserved for the baptized, but by his absolute power God can accept any moral act performed naturally, including those carried out by a pagan. The distinction is a vital one because it meant that God was not bound by the sacraments, and baptism was not essential for salvation.[142] To be sure, as Gordon Leff cautions, the *moderni* "did not openly deny the *reatus* of original sin, nor the need or efficacy of baptism; they rather, in starting from God's *potentia absoluta,* did not regard man in his actual fallen state but as God could make him."[143] Suggesting that pagans could be saved if they had faith and practiced social justice was one way that the *moderni* made "doing what is in one" grounds for one's final justification.

Much of the thinking toward the pagans on the popular as well as the professional level is distilled in the Trajan legend, the story of the Roman emperor who, long after his death, was redeemed through the auspices of Gregory the Great.[144] The tenacity of the Trajan legend, which resurfaced again and again throughout the early and late medieval epoch, suggests that it struck a responsive chord in the collective spiritual consciousness of medieval Christians, engaging them in the fourteenth century at a moment when concerns relating to forgiveness and charity, the fate of the soul after death, and the meaning of the resurrection of the body had become prominent once more.[145] Marcia Colish has shown how each period in the Middle Ages adapted the Trajan story to suit its needs and ideology. Early versions, she says, stressed the charisma of Pope Gregory, and later ones the power and mercy of God. John of Salisbury places emphasis on the virtue within Trajan himself as the efficient cause of his own salvation, and for St. Thomas, Trajan is but one of an entire cohort of souls who are not finally damned if they adhered to the natural law, led upright lives, and practiced religion out of their rational understanding of natural theology.[146]

Two sources of the Trajan legend with which the author of *Saint Erkenwald* seems to be familiar are Langland's *Piers Plowman* and the *Polycraticus* of John of Salisbury. Langland appropriates Trajan as a figure whose ethical conduct serves as a model for public figures to emulate, and John of Salisbury uses Trajan to show how the good ruler or head of a corporate body is cast in the image and likeness of the deity. Both of these sources mute the theological debate over the necessity of baptism for salvation in order to advance a political concern for the legitimacy of civic activity and the pursuit of social justice as redemptive values.[147] Their intent is not to diminish the importance of baptism or the sacraments but to recognize, in the contemporary environment of the poem, the need for virtuous behavior, particularly among justices.[148]

In his humility and moral virtue, the lawyer in *Saint Erkenwald* resembles these various Trajan incarnations, but he is far more than a composite of earlier versions. The poet, in fact, does not rely on the Trajan legend for the particular circumstances and details of his lawyer's life. There is nothing known about the lawyer prior to his own discourse; allowing him to speak, to tell his own story and to question the very doctrine represented and articulated by Erkenwald is part of what gives the poem its individuality and inventiveness. Neither the eleventh-century *Vita Sancti Erkenwaldi* nor the twelfth-century *Miracula Sancti Erkenwaldi,* the two Latin texts that memorialize Erkenwald's deeds, offers even the faintest hint of any miraculous encounter that could be exploited in the way imagined by the author of the poem. By engrafting the story of the lawyer onto what otherwise is a conventional saint's legend, the poet modifies or modernizes the saint's legend genre so that the genre incorporates the new forms of devotion to the saints that was being generated at the popular level. What the fourteenth century introduced to the cult of the saints, especially in the cities, was a new appreciation of local and patron saints. Erkenwald himself enjoyed a revival of devotion at the time that this poem was written. At the same time a new kind of saint had begun to emerge, one who closely resembled the figure of the pagan lawyer. Unlike the traditional saints nominated by the pope and singled out for their chastity or asceticism, these figures were revered for their active engagement with the world, for their service on behalf of the poor, and for their devotion to social and ecclesiastical reform.[149] Civic religious practices "ensured the survival of devotions which were not imposed from above but instead emanated from the basic constituent elements of urban society."[150] The emphasis on civic virtue in these newly recognized figures of devotion suggests a greater consciousness of civic activity as a social as well as a religious issue, expanding the Christian ideal of charity into an existential ethic in pursuit of the common good.

Given the prominence of the question of the virtuous pagans, then, in both the literary and theological discourses of the fourteenth century, it seems fair to say that the rehabilitation of the pagans was part of a larger effort to expand the freedom and autonomy of human beings in the social and political spheres, and to lay the groundwork for a new anthropology based on the inherent nobility of human nature and its capacity for a virtue that is self-achieved.[151] Revival of interest in pagan systems of law and government, as William Courtenay has argued, brought renewed dignity to the natural or political virtues, and recovery of Aristotle's *Ethics* and *Politics* gave impetus to a new science of the polis which inspired Christian political theologians to think of the earthly city as a corporate organism, the *corpus morale et politicum,* separate from but not incompatible with the spiritual goals of the *corpus mysticum.*[152]

The immediate effect of the revival of Aristotle's political thought, in Walter Ullmann's illuminating analysis, was to dissolve the "total view" of the person in the theocratic system and give the individual standing as a political being.[153] Prior to the recovery of Aristotle, Christianity had seized the whole of the person and directed all of his or her actions toward one goal—salvation. The cornerstone of this unipolar view of human identity was the sacrament of baptism. The baptismal waters washed away the degenerate natural human being and the person emerged from the rite reborn, a member of the church and an adherent of its laws. The *renovatio* of the natural human being, begun in the thirteenth century, conferred on the citizen the same legal standing as had previously been accorded solely to the Christian, the baptismally reborn person. It attributed inborn value, Ullmann says, to the unregenerate human being.[154] In addition to the Pauline understanding of the new man, the individual transformed by grace, the late Middle Ages fashioned an anthropology that conceived of the new man as the old man, human redemption achieved through the powers infused in human nature at the creation.

Accordingly, Baldus, an Italian jurist who died in 1400, defines his citizen as *homo naturalis,* the human being composed of body and soul, in his natural state, living in a city. To him, the person living in the society of a city becomes a special kind of person: a citizen, a figure distinct from but not opposed to the Christian. The individual assumes in congregation a specific characterization that he lacks in isolation. Above all, Baldus's citizen does not derive his rights from above, from a superior, ultimately God. Rather, his rights are inherent in his nature and his status as a citizen.[155] As a result, the Christian gained a temporal or earthly goal to complement his eternal or heavenly one.

Dante, who rewrites the theological project for poetry, makes the redemption of the virtuous pagans an underlying theme of his *Comedy*. The virtuous pagans facilitate his notion that salvation is a collective endeavor that requires the cooperation and involvement of the whole of human time and the whole of humanity, living, dead, and yet to be.[156] To this end Dante borrows from Aristotle and St. Thomas the notion of the city as the supreme form of human association, good in itself, in accord with nature, and necessary for human beings to fulfill their nature. For his efforts Dante the pilgrim is "baptized" by Virgil in canto 27 of *Purgatorio* and, as tokens of his spiritual rebirth, he is given the articles of crown and scepter. Ernst Kantorowicz explains that the crown and miter bestow on Dante royal and sacerdotal dignities "just as on every newly baptized who through the sacrament of baptism was reborn in the original status of Adam and thereby potentially acquired immortality and eternal co-rulership with Christ in the kingdom of heaven."[157] The fact that the lawyer in *Saint Erkenwald* is found in possession of these same articles implies that he had earned the same royal and sacerdotal dignity they conferred on the pilgrim Dante. Perhaps the poet chooses not to name his lawyer in order to further this theme; anonymously he is able to represent all the nameless inhabitants of the city whose lives and deeds will never be "merkid" in the "martilage" or recorded in the "crafty cronecles" preserved by the dean of St. Paul's and his clerks.

Like Dante, the author of *Saint Erkenwald* wants to situate Christianity securely in this world. He begins with the recognition that the traditional Christian emphasis on the afterlife has created a rift between the body and soul, the self and the world, and he needs to find a means to repair it. His citizen-saint of London serves as that bridge. Just as the workmen in the poem will test the "fundement" of St. Paul's and the "fote halde" at the base of its supporting columns, the poet will go back to pre-Christian England and resurrect a figure from its pagan past who, in giving a new account of that past, shows that paganism is not antithetical to Christianity and may be able to make a positive contribution to its renewal.

The narrator is at pains in the prologue, or first thirty-two lines of the poem, to portray Christ's church in England as a historical institution that has undergone constant change. In the first four lines he links the ecclesiastical foundation of Christianity in England with Christ's sacrifice on the cross:

> At London in England noȝt fulle longe sythen—
> Sythen Crist suffride on crosse and Cristendome stablide—
> Ther was a byschop in þat burghe, blessyd and sacryd:
> Saynt Erkenwolde as I hope þat holy mon hatte.
>
> (1–4)

The crucifixion functions first as a historical marker and the repeated use of *sythen* directs our attention to the temporal order. Reference to Christ suffering on the cross prevents the poet from treating Christ or the crucifixion in any purely iconic fashion. We are asked to envision Christianity as emanating from the action of Christ's personal sacrifice. Erkenwald follows in the tradition of someone who is prepared to sacrifice himself to establish Christianity in England. Erkenwald is further identified as the spiritual successor to Augustine, who himself had to reestablish Christianity in England because it had fallen into desuetude under Hengist who is rumored to have "perueted alle þe pepul þat in þat place dwellide" (10). When we meet Erkenwald, he is engaged in the "Newe Werke," a reconstruction of St. Paul's down to its foundation because the temple was reputed to have been the seat of a mighty devil and the site of the most solemn sacrifices in Saxon times. The reader may be forgiven if he smiles at the note of uncertainty about Erkenwald's identity that pops up in the middle of line 4. The narrator's use of "I hope" ("I believe" or "I think") serves as a subtle indication that he is aware that all historical events lack the fixity and stability we desire of them. His uncertainty upsets the equilibrium of the reader about the coherence of the events from Christ to Erkenwald and reveals the inevitable overlap of fact with fiction in any historical enterprise.

Lack of clear origins or boundaries is symptomatic of this poem. Later (lines 205–16), when the lawyer is asked to fix the date of his own lifetime in London, he only manages to create confusion. He misses his calculation by at least one hundred years, and, while identifying Brutus as the builder of the city, he can only imagine the origins of London or the New Troy as a product of some past obscure and remote to him. The poet plays with and frustrates his audience at this point, creating an infinite regress of "founders," from Erkenwald backwards to Augustine, Hengist, St. Paul, and Christ, to the lawyer himself, to Sir Belyn, and to Brutus, depriving his audience of any single source that constitutes the identity of those who are either Christian or of Britain. The effect is to show how difficult it is to fix with any clarity or confidence the shaping power of any single agency in the growth and interiorization of English consciousness and spirituality. What connects each of these figures, however, is the *telos* that drives each of them to build or remake the city in an image that each imagines will restore a former harmony. No new beginning, however, can eradicate the past, no matter how strong or pervasive the ideology, because if one digs deep enough remnants of that past inevitably will surface.

Instead of a discontinuity between the pagan past and the Christian present, the prologue proposes a seamless whole, one that anticipates the blossoming of the Christian godhead out of the pagan deities, as is reflected in the symmetry of their respective temples. The Church of St. Peter naturally corresponds to the temple of Apollo, which it replaces; the Church of the Mother of Christ corresponds to the temple of the sun over which it is built; and the early episcopal sees of York, London, and Caerusk are modeled after the pagan Triapolitan.[158] Clifford Peterson notes that, according to Bede, Pope Gregory wrote to Abbot Mellitus instructing Augustine "to make as much use as possible of pagan temples and festivals, easing the conversion for the English by the retention of much that was familiar."[159] Gregory's instructions reveal sensitivity to the psychological condition of the English people and their need for some sense of continuity with their pre-Christian past.

The poet apparently wants to expand this perspective to include a sense of continuity with the dead because the appearance of the lawyer in his physical form introduces a purgatorial element into the poem. Christopher Dyer has noted that the theology of purgatory spawned new religious attitudes in the late Middle Ages, bringing about a greater emphasis on good works.[160] Jacques LeGoff has outlined the psychological benefits wrought by the "discovery" of purgatory, which took hold in the thirteenth and fourteenth centuries. First, he says, it dissolved the binary pattern of heaven and hell and, second, it promoted a strain of humanism and forgiveness which was directly related both to a weakening of the doctrine of contempt for this world and to a tendency to incarnate in this world values formerly situated in the other world. A third society in the other world, he avers, developed more out of a concern for justice here than for a yearning for salvation there.[161] Doubtless, the release of a soul from hell through the impetus of human prayer would have enormous psychological significance for a late medieval audience.

The resurrectional motif adds meaningfully to the idea of continuity in the poem. As the re-furbishing of the temples suggests, Christianity does not embody a wholly new development so much as it builds on structures already existing. Building over the pagan temples actually perpetuates rather than obliterates the meaning of the pagan tumulus on which St. Paul's sits. Similarly, the lawyer who pre-dates Christ and has been lying at the base of St. Paul's, like a truth waiting to be discovered, shows that the values and ideals nominally identified with Christ are shared by pre-Christian and Christian alike. The lawyer after all built the hall of justice on which St. Paul's now sits and his residing at the foot attests that English Christianity has its roots in the pagan past and that a concept of justice remains at its foundation. His bodily presence, moreover, attests that the *corpus* of pagan history imposes itself on Christian history and consciousness; it refuses to be consigned to a kind of limbo or absent cause, and it refuses to support the illusion of a new beginning, the fiction that the pagan era can be reduced to such theological categories as "the reign of sin." In speaking of how communities are found and defined, David Luscombe points out that the identity of communities was more often explained in historical terms than in territorial terms. Descent myths, he says, traced the origin and progress of different peoples from Noah or from Troy. Such origin stories "assumed that peoples were biologically united, on-going communities; they thereby reinforced a sense of national or tribal solidarity."[162]

At the end of the prologue we are introduced to Erkenwald's London and the excavation ongoing at St. Paul's which leads to the discovery of the tomb. Erkenwald's congregation encompasses all levels of London society, ecclesiastical and civil, and all manner of vocations, right down to the activity of the masons with their "eggit toles" and the ordinary laborers who open the tomb with their "prises," details which encourage the reading audience to enjoy a heightened sense of presence at the event.[163] Those who are not present at the outset hurriedly gather at the spot when the tomb is discovered: "Þer commen þider of alle kynes so kenely mony / Þat as alle þe worlde were þider walon wytin a hondequile" (63–64). At first, the discovery by workmen of a corpse perfectly preserved and arrayed as a king, threatens to undo all that Augustine and Erkenwald have labored to accomplish. The people "crakit euermore" about a corpse, and Erkenwald is summoned to quell their fears.

Confronted by a mystery that he cannot explain, Erkenwald fears that the people will become confused in their faith or lapse into pagan superstition. Providing an example to his people, Erkenwald shows no outward concern for the corpse; instead, he closets himself in his study for the night where he appeals to God to vouchsafe him a vision that will solve the mystery and help him to secure the faith of the people:

> "Þaghe I be vnworthi," al wepande he sayde
> Thurghe his deere debonerté, "digne hit my Lorde
> In confirmynge þi Cristen faithe, fulsen me to kenne
> Þe mysterie of þis meruaile þat men opon wondres."
>
> (122–25)

Following a night of prayer, during which the Holy Ghost answers his petition with an undisclosed vision, Erkenwald confidently enters the church and dismisses the apprehensions of the dean and his fellow clerks who deem the corpse a marvel because they cannot find a record of the man in their rolls of kings and martyrs. The corpse is a wonder, Erkenwald counsels, only to those who underestimate the providence of God.

Erkenwald treats the discovery as an occasion afforded him by God to instruct the people in the wisdom of God's plan. He begins his lesson by cautioning the congregation not to rely on human reason as the instrument to fathom God's secrets:

To seche þe sothe at oure selfe ʒee se þer no bote,
Bot glow we alle opon Godde and His grace aske
Þat careles is of counselle and comforthe to sende,
And þat in fastynge of ʒour faithe and of fyne bileue.
I shal auay ʒow so verrayly of vertues His
Þat ʒe may leue vpon longe þat He is Lord myʒty,
And fayne ʒour talent to fulfille if ʒe Hym frende leues.

(170–76)

For some readers this passage forms the "ideational center" of the poem, inasmuch as it expresses Erkenwald's belief in the agency of God behind all earthly phenomena and it makes Erkenwald's role as intermediary all the more explicit:

> In line 124 the Bishop looked heavenward to the Faith established by God, in confirmation of which the saint would have knowledge of the present mystery. Here, the Bishop turns earthward to the congregation's faith, in confirmation of which they will receive (through the Bishop) not knowledge but counsel and spiritual comfort.[164]

Erkenwald then turns to the corpse and in the name of Christ, who "was bende on a beme quen He His blode schedde" (182), and commands it to speak. In response to the bishop's questions, the corpse provides a moving account of his professional life as a lawyer and judge who sat on the highest cases in the city. He humbly tells the congregation that even though he had led an exemplary life his soul still languishes in limbo. The bishop thinks the lawyer yet may be saved if he is baptized. Before he can perform the formal ceremony, but while he is reciting the words of the rite, one of his tears falls on the face of the lawyer, thereby washing the lawyer clean. His soul flies to heaven and his body disintegrates. The lesson is complete: God answers one miracle (the undecayed body) with another miracle (the baptism with tears) and the truth of the Christian faith is preserved.[165]

The miracle intends to impose closure on the poem, but as is common with any finished meaning or definitive statement, it creates gaps or cuts off dialogue prematurely. In this instance it silences the lawyer at a moment when he has leveled his most devastating remarks (283–308) at the very doctrine that purportedly has saved him, and at a point when he has exerted his most profound effect on the audience, having moved them all to tears:

> Þus dulfully þis dede body deuisyt hit sorowe
> Þat alle wepyd for woo þe wordes þat herden,
> And þe bysshop balefully bere doun his eghen
> Þat hade no space to speke so sparkly he ȝoskyd,
> Til he toke hym a tome and to þat toumbe lokyd,
> To þe liche þer hit lay, wyt lauande teres.
>
> (309–14)

In several respects these tears are the most interesting phenomenon in the poem. At this critical juncture they shift the focus from the divine intervention to the audience, hinting that here is the site where the regeneration will take place. The tears bring the audience back to earth so to speak, to themselves, and to the corpse, and they make closure impossible.

Such tears, Georges Bataille says, are not tears of sorrow but an expression of the "keen awareness of shared life grasped in its intimacy."[166] What Bataille means is that death or the mere appearance of a corpse can provoke in the living a momentary recollection of a state of immanence between the body and the soul, self and the world, that existed before the fall from grace or before the idea took hold of the existence of a separate spiritual realm that separated the mind or soul from the body and turned the body into an object or thing.[167] The essence of religion in Bataille's thinking is the search to recover this lost intimacy. For him, a corpse provides the most complete affirmation of the spirit because it assures the spectator of the indivisibility of the body and the spirit, and the inseparability of human existence from earthly life. "That intimate life which had lost the ability to reach me," Bataille says, "which I regarded primarily as a thing, is fully restored to my sensibility through its absence. Death reveals life in its plenitude and dissolves the real order."[168] The fascination of the fictive audience with the corpse need not betoken the spiritual instability Erkenwald assumes it to be; instead, it may bespeak an intuition that they have uncovered something sacred from their past that renews a lost intimacy.[169]

What I am proposing, with the help of Bataille and the tears, is that *Saint Erkenwald* does not culminate in a miracle as in a moment of awakening during which the distance between the lawyer and the congregation is suspended and the members of the audience confront in the lawyer an image of their mortal selves. For, at the end of his interrogation, when Erkenwald asks the corpse about the disposition of his soul, we are told "Þen hummyd he þat þer lay and his hedde waggyd, / And gefe a gronynge ful grete" (291–92). His groaning brings to the surface in the form of tears something that Erkenwald and the congregation inwardly groan for but which has been lost, buried, or forgotten in the eschatological ideal of the church, namely, the desire to return to intimacy with their bodies. As St. Paul says, the whole of humanity aches for the resurrection of the body: "For we know that the whole creation *groaneth* and travaileth until now. And not only they, but ourselves also, which have the first-fruits of the spirit, even we ourselves groan within ourselves waiting for the adoption, to wit, the redemption of the body" (Romans 8.22–23, emphasis added). The theological problem left unresolved by the miracle is no longer confined to the pagans alone but applies to the audience as well who in suspense yearn to discover the meaning of the redemption and how the resurrection of the body is to be understood.

Traditionally, the Pauline text has been interpreted to refer to the reunion of the body with the soul on judgment day, but in the late Middle Ages theologians sought a clearer distinction between one's glorified mortal body and one's earthly body in order to satisfy their desire for a material and structural continuity of body and soul. "The idea of a person," Bynum says, "bequeathed by the Middle Ages to the modern world, was not a concept of soul escaping body or soul using body; it was a concept of self in which physicality was integrally bound to sensation, emotion, reasoning, identity—and therefore finally to whatever one means by salvation."[170] The idea of the person as a composite, as an organic union of mind and body, instead of a spirit in a corpse, was shaped and developed by St. Thomas, who, in his elaboration on Paul's seed and clothing imagery in 1 Corinthians 15 and 2 Corinthians 5, states, as Bynum reports, that the verb *to clothe* "does not mean that the body is a garment, donned on earth and discarded or replaced in heaven; it means rather that immortality (a quality) is added to what we are—i.e., 'this soul' and 'this body, repaired from the same dust into which it was dissolved.'"[171] Tertullian, whose ideas were revived in the fourteenth century along with the Pauline commentaries, also provides a patristic source most congenial to this idea, partly because he upheld against the gnostics Paul's belief in the unity or inseparability of the body and the soul.[172] Tertullian shows that Paul identifies the body with the self and understood that this life was not merely a period of soul making. Furthermore, Tertullian describes the resurrection as a natural process in distinction to a divinely mediated one in which the new body maintains continuity with the old one: "There will be an additional body, which is built up over the body, and that over which it is built up, is not abolished but increased." He too uses Paul's metaphor of a seed implanted in human nature at the creation which blossoms over time into the glorified mortal body (Romans 8.11):

> for when it is sown it is merely grain, without the clothing of its husk or the foundation of its ear or the defenses of its beard or the pride of its stalk: but when it rises up it has made interest by multiplication, is built up in compactness, is drawn up in rank, fortified with apparel, and clothed in every sense.[173]

Presumably Tertullian is talking about the glorified mortal body after death, but his model of the creation with its seeds ripening over time calls attention to an incarnational view of the world, wherein human beings, under the renewed covenant, are charged with the responsibility of bringing the creation to its completion, building and rebuilding the body of Christ. In the immaculately attired and preserved body of the lawyer the poet virtually reproduces Tertullian's redeemed man, who, when he "rises up," is "fortified with apparel, and clothed in every sense." As the just man, the people of his city paid him the homage he deserved, and when he died after forty years of service the entire city ("þe more and þe lasse") mourned his death. For his righteousness and fidelity to the law, the people dressed him in gold; for his meekness and manliness they mantled him in the finest gown; for his firmness of faith they robed him in furs. For his supreme honesty they crowned him as a king, and because he always judged justly he was awarded the scepter.

For his part, the lawyer identifies himself only as an ordinary citizen, "þe vnhapnest hathel þat euer on erthe ȝode." He stresses that he was neither a king, nor a kaiser, nor a knight, but a simple "lede of þe laghe," who never sought the rank of domesman that was bestowed upon him.

He announces that he lived in dark times, "Þe folke was felonse and fals and frowarde to reule," much like the fabled corruption of fourteenth-century England. He speaks solemnly and humbly of his own adherence to the law and of his refusal to be intimidated into delivering an unfair judgment, regardless of the threats he received from powerful people:

> Bot for wothe ne wele ne wrathe ne drede
> Ne for maystrie ne for mede ne for no monnes aghe,
> I remewit neuer fro þe rizt by reson myn awen
> For to dresse a wrange dome, no day of my lyue.
>
> (233–36)

He took no bribes and he never compromised his conscience for political favor. Nothing deterred him from the path of righteousness and everyone who came before him was treated equally.

Even though he is visibly moved by the lawyer's narrative ("wyt bale at his hert"), Erkenwald makes no comment on the lawyer's virtue and achievements. He marvels instead at the pristine condition of the lawyer's clothing, a conventional Christian sign of the soul's purity. Erkenwald resists the evidence that suggests the lawyer has been preserved in bodily perfection by God and asks instead if he has been embalmed. Patiently, the lawyer assures him that God himself has kept him uncorrupted because God honors justice above all other virtues:

> "Nay bisshop," quoþ þat body, "enbawmyd wos I neuer
> Ne no monnes counselle me clothe has kepyd vnwemmyd
> Bot þe riche kynge of reson þat rizt euer alowes
> And loues al þe lawes lely þat longen to trouthe.
> And moste he menskes men for mynnynge of riztes
> Þen for al þe meritorie medes þat men on molde vsen;
> And if renkes for rizt þus me arayed has
> He has lant me to last þat loues ryzt best."
>
> (265–72)

The lawyer's assertion that God has preserved him poses a serious challenge to Erkenwald's belief that the body has been preserved and exhumed solely to accommodate the lesson the bishop wants to teach to the people. The lawyer's discourse has reversed the message Erkenwald delivered to the people on the limits of human reason and initiative, and his confidence that God preserved his body because he honors most those who practice justice affirms that human beings are carrying out the will of God when they do that which is in them. This point is reinforced nicely, and appropriately, by Erkenwald himself in a gesture that turns out to be *extra ecclesiam,* that is, in his personal response to the lawyer's story, as opposed to his official response as bishop, Erkenwald's tears reunite the body and soul of the lawyer before the formal sacramental ritual can be performed.[174]

The poet inscribes a few more lessons that would have had a special resonance for a fourteenth-century English audience bent on secular and ecclesiastical reform. At one point in the discussion of his administration of justice, the lawyer remarks that he would show no partiality toward his father were he to come before his bench, nor would he treat his father's murderer more severely than he would the murderer of any other citizen:

> Ne for no monnes manas ne meschefe ne routhe
> Non gete me fro þe heghe gate to glent out of ryȝt,
> Als ferforthe as my faithe conformed my hert.
> Þaghe had been my fader bone, I bede hym no wranges
> Ne fals favour to my fader, þaghe felle hym be hongyt.
>
> (240–44)

His administration of social justice centers exclusively on the merits of the case, on the matter of justice itself, without concern for institutions, hierarchies, or the social or religious status of the individual. His unremitting perseverance in the face of political opportunism, furthermore, serves as a reproach to the lawyers of medieval London who were notorious for their greed and lack of civic responsibility.[175] What is significant about the widespread corruption in clerical and legal quarters is that it did proliferate despite Christian revelation and the sacramental system, suggesting that Christian *renovatio* in and of itself has not made a material difference in ethical conduct and stands in need of the lawyer's embodiment of *civitas* as a form of *caritas.*

More to the point, human beings have not been allotted, in eschatological and salvation theology, enough responsibility or incentive to participate actively in the realization of a better world here and now, whereas the ideal of the good citizen places that goal within the reach of every person. As Hans Blumenberg has observed, too much of

Christian theology was formed in the shadow of the Parousia and by the fourteenth century was badly in need of transformation.[176] What needed to be implemented, he argues, was a new arrangement on the side of this world, one that would shift the burden that devolves on human beings from an original offense in the past, to responsibility for the world relating to the future, what Hans Jonas describes as the "levelling of divine grace into an instructive power working toward progress in the whole of human history and increasingly bringing men to the consciousness of their freedom and responsibility for themselves."[177] This last point is made more forcefully in the closing sequence of the poem.

To this point the lawyer has been patient and measured in his tone. But when Erkenwald, in words mindful of the psalm of the just man (Psalm 287), poses the long-deferred question about the disposition of his soul, the lawyer turns away from Erkenwald and demands that Christ answer why pagans have been judged by a law they could not possibly have known:

> Maȝty maker of men, thi myghtes are grete—
> How mayȝt þi mercy to me amounte any tyme?
> Nas I a paynim vnpreste that neuer thi plite knewe,
> Ne þe mesure of þi mercy ne þi mecul vertue,
> Bot ay a freke faitheles þat faylid þi laghes
> Þat euer þou Lord wos louyed in? Allas þe harde stoundes!
>
> (283–88)

Why, he charges, have so many "plyȝtles pepul" been poisoned forever by Adam's bite of the apple, yet deprived of the "medecyn" that should be available to all of Adam's offspring?[178] The word *plyȝtles* (296), if "blameless," continues the lawyer's petition against unjust punishment, but coupled with "plite" (285) it points to the covenant or *pactum* which joins the whole of humanity to God and serves as a reminder that history is a collective endeavor that requires the cooperation and involvement of the whole of human time and humanity to realize its perfection. With that in mind, the lawyer makes a plea to have his "well deeds" and the works of his fellow pagans serve as a substitute for baptism and to be recognized as an expression of their obedience to the law, to their "doing what is in them." His appeal to Christ makes it clear that pagan judges hungered after justice, that he faithfully practiced his particular *ergon,* and that he, like the patriarchs of the Old Testament, upheld the ancient covenant of law and religion as the backbone of his community.

Why lead a just life, he asks, if nothing can be garnered from one's good deeds?

> Quat wan we wyt oure wele-dede þat wroghytn ay riȝt,
> Quen we are dampned dulfully into þe depe lake
> And exiled fro þat soper so, þat solempne fest
> Þer richely hit arne refeted þat after right hungride?
> My soule may sitte þer in sorow and sike ful colde,
> Dymly in þat derke dethe þer dawes neuer morowen,
> Hungrie in-wyt helle-hole, and herken after meeles
> Longe er ho þat soper se oþir segge hyr to lathe.
>
> (301–8)

By citing the sixth beatitude (line 304) in this moving passage, the lawyer picks up on Erkenwald's use of the psalm of the just man and places before the audience the record of his life and the present state of his suffering. The passage involves a kind of inversion of the Wedding Feast in Matthew 22.1–14; here the lawyer has on the appropriate garment, but he has not been invited ("lathe") to join in the feast.

The lawyer's outburst reaches its emotional and theological climax in his witness to the harrowing of hell, in the work of what he calls the "blo rode," the sad or dark cross:

> I was non of þe nommbre þat þou wyt noy boghtes,
> Wyt þe blode of thi body vpon þe blo rode;
> Quen þou herghedes helle-hole and hentes hem þeroute,
> Þi loffynge oute of limbo, þou leftes me þer.
>
> (288–92)

Christ, or the body of Christ, is the other corpse in the poem, also in need of being reunited with its spirit. The poet refers to the crucifixion three times in the poem, at the beginning, in the middle, and here at the end (lines 2, 182, and 290). On each occasion he appropriates Christ's body as a sign of his complete humanity. The graphic descriptions of his "blode vpon þe blo rode" and how Christ "was bende on a beme quen He His blode schedde" direct the audience to his body and, coupled

164

with the eucharistic image of the banquet table, make his body a signifier of the redemption in the poem. The lawyer's identification with this body suggests that he too bears in his being the image and likeness of Christ. The cross is a "blo rode" or "dark cross" because the full meaning of Christ's sacrifice has not yet been interpreted or penetrated, any more than the clerks at the beginning of this poem were able to decipher the letters or comprehend the meaning of the lawyer's insignia. The harrowing of hell should have made the crucifixion a general amnesty that would include the whole of history and the whole of humanity in its quest for justice.[179] The last four words of the passage, "þou leftes me þer," as poignant and heart wrenching a passage as there is in the poem, remind the audience of the gulf that still separates them. In the idea of the "blo rode," the poet realizes that the opportunity was available for Christianity to redeem human nature completely and to restore to humankind a dignified image that, Blumenberg avers, would have been medieval Christianity's noblest endeavor.[180] In making the incarnation and the crucifixion the dividing line between Christianity and paganism, however, and consigning the pagans to limbo, Christianity cut itself off from its historical roots and failed to see in the incarnation the promise of human deification or the pledge that God's relation to the world is properly conceived in terms of love.

In granting the lawyer his own agency and historical identity, the poet suggests that the whole of English history, not just Christian history, has a voice in the dialogical partnership with God. The rehabilitation of the pagans as a part of this consciousness makes the incarnation a sign of human progress not only as a miraculous descent from above but also as a product of human generations laboring to bring forth a paradigm of virtue that epitomizes the collective goal of human history.

By the end of the lawyer's narrative, the audience no longer sees him as a marvel but as a fellow human being—an Englishman!— with whom they can and do identify. If he began as the epistemological other, the "not-Christian," he has become the moral other, the one who in his sameness and difference reflects back to them an image of themselves, "the keen awareness of a shared life grasped in its intimacy." Literally, the tears they shed are a sign of self-judgment, a recognition that it is they who are in limbo, and they who are in need of regeneration.

Symbolically, their tears are the loosing of the waters, for the lake in which the lawyer says he is immersed can only be Cocytus, Dante's lake of frozen tears.

Finally, in the *Ethics* Aristotle distinguishes between what is fair or proper and what is lawful. The bishop chooses to baptize the lawyer according to the law (line 320), but the involuntary flow of his tears betrays a deeper impulse toward charity, and it is his tears that perform the work of redemption. Instantly the lawyer's soul is delivered to heaven, although the poet explicitly says that the lawyer is seated at a table in the "cenacle," the room where the apostles gathered for the Last Supper and where they reassembled at Pentecost—the feast in honor of which this poem was written, and a suitable resting place for this "famished ghost."[181] Placed among other bearers of the law, the lawyer is located where he belongs, and his inclusion in the *corpus mysticum* readies the church to take its proper place in the *corpus morale et politicum.*

The vision is only momentary. Amid mourning and mirth, the congregation forms a procession of all the constituent parts of the community, with the bishop and the mayor at the head (351), and then "alle þe pepulle folowid," as if the souls ("þe more and þe lasse") who had attended his original funeral had been resurrected with him, the work of the harrowing of hell symbolically completed. In a communal outpouring of emotion, like the leap of his soul that "sprent" with "unsparid murthe," all the "belles in þe burghe beryd at ones."[182] The very last words of the poem, "at ones," signal the union of past and present, pagan and Christian, and they connect with the very first, "At London," to bring to fruition the initial impulse to unify, to make one, what had been fragmented or cut off. The poem thus opens and closes with direct references to the city of London, implying that the events begin and end within the framework of the earthly city. If so, the lawyer's case has served to test the limits of Erkenwald's salvation theology, and the fictive audience has served as a court of equity in the disposition of the appellant. The principle that has been at work is Aristotle's *epikeia,* the correction of a defect in the law. Even though the lawyer had been excluded from forgiveness because of a situation that is legally correct, the act resulted nevertheless in an injustice. Here, at the end of the poem, the lawyer is acquitted and welcomed into the community, which underscores the need for Christianity to incorporate pre-Christian concepts and practices of justice into its doctrine if it is to be renewed or made whole.

Once he is incorporated into the community, the lawyer is free to die.[183] The real order asserts itself and the flesh of the lawyer disintegrates, but not before its disappearance in death reveals the brilliance of a life that is not a thing. The poet leaves the question of what constitutes human salvation an open dialogue, one to be resolved by human beings in their history, for history is always a matter of tears, of human forgiveness, not divine.

FOUR

Chaucer

1.

Pilgrimage and Storytelling in the Canterbury Tales

My sone, be war, and be noon auctor newe
Of tidynges, wheither they been false or trewe.
Whereso thou com, amonges hye or lowe,
Kepe wel thy tonge and thenk upon the crowe.

Canterbury Tales 9.359–62

Chaucer's theological outlook is the most varied and comprehensive of all the major poets of the fourteenth century, and the most difficult to pin down. Unlike Langland or the *Pearl*-poet, who readily identify and directly address the theological problems that concern them, Chaucer approaches these matters indirectly. His response to the theological issues of his day is deeply embedded in the language of his poetry. What is conspicuously absent from his poetry, particularly the *Canterbury Tales,* is any unifying or overarching theological vision that ultimately binds all of the tales together in a singular point of view. The lack of a unifying theological vision is a strength rather than a weakness of the poem because its absence prevents the poem from becoming tendentious or wedded to a specific ideology that might turn it into a polemic or have it serve some end other than its own discourse. Modern critical practice has taken to sorting the tales into homogeneous categories such as the "religious tales" or the "marriage group."[1] However convenient or attractive this practice may seem, our experience with the tales has taught us that no one of these categories is comprehensive enough to contain the tales within it under a single rubric. Besides, this practice runs the risk of subordinating the poetry to a predetermined theological or moral function, of suppressing some features of the tale to make it conform to the moral argument, and of making those tales not included under the heading *theological,* tangential to the moral and theological concerns Chaucer does engage.[2] Tales such as those told by the Miller and the Reeve, while not listed among the religious tales or the marriage group, nevertheless have a great deal to tell us about marital love and sexuality, and both are as committed to theological topics as any of the tales commonly listed as religious.

It is possible, of course, to treat any given tale independently of the pilgrimage frame in which it is cast, or to isolate its theological content for separate analysis, but the tales belong primarily to the pilgrimage frame and represent one decisive measure Chaucer has initiated to defeat any attempt to privilege any tale or teller as voicing his own personal view. He goes to great lengths to create the illusion of an actual pilgrimage, a spontaneous drama in which the pilgrim-tellers appear to spring to life, select their own tales, and relate them directly to the audience. Chaucer, to borrow from the language of M. M. Bakhtin, does not think in thoughts but in points of view, in consciousnesses, and in voices.[3] He chooses not to separate ideas from the person conceiving or expressing them; instead, he "allows" each figure to develop and to substantiate the validity of his or her own position, without authorial interference.[4] Allowing each individual pilgrim to speak for him- or herself, instead of using a master narrator, dialogizes the poem, leaving us with a multiplicity of discourses, no one of which functions as a master text that serves as a vision of the whole.[5] By dispersing the discussion of theological issues throughout the poem, he implies that all of the pilgrims, from all levels and vocations in society, have a stake in the religious or doctrinal matters that impinge upon their lives.

The irony generated by having different narrators whose characters are at least partially known and who belong to a heterogeneous company that is also the audience is pervasive in the *Canterbury Tales* and makes it difficult to take any of the stories straight. As Lisa Kiser has observed, the *Canterbury Tales* is Chaucer's most complex commentary on the nature of human fictions, "for not only does the work offer a variety of representational strategies in the pilgrims' individualized narratives, but it also foregrounds the political and social management of 'reality' that motivates human discourse."[6] Pilgrimage proves to be an excellent vehicle for pursuing these interests. His collection of pilgrims, gathered from a wide number of occupations, social ranks, and geographical locales, presents Chaucer with the opportunity to explore and display the "extraordinary plasticity" of human beings who, precisely because they do not have a determinate nature, can expand into an almost "unlimited range of culture-bound patternings."[7] What this means for the *Canterbury Tales* is that Chaucer opens up the field of moral theology and religious doctrine for broad discussion. He reserves some of his more provocative theological speculations for his least likely tellers, such as the Pardoner.

As a practical matter, the Pardoner's personal viciousness ought to modify the moral truth or value of what he has to say. His claim that a vicious man can tell a moral tale—a poetic version of the Donatist controversy that was revived in the fourteenth century—threatens the stability of the moral structure we assume exists, in which there is some relationship between what one is and what one says. The Pardoner insists that all we have or are is language; it is his tale and not the teller who speaks: language speaks, not the author. The legitimacy of the Pardoner's claim does not mean that the pilgrims are unnecessary or merely incidental to their tales. The individual person to whom Chaucer assigns the tale matters significantly and forms part of the theological critique he may be presenting through the tale. The moral authority of the teller, which may be a consequence of education, social position, or religious training, no longer takes precedence over the content of the tale itself. We might prefer to be given moral instruction from the Parson, who practices what he preaches, but the moral tenor of his life does not determine the quality of his moral instruction.

Writing himself in as a storyteller on his own pilgrimage, Chaucer addresses the matter of authority and morality openly in the link between the two tales he tells. Once Chaucer's narrative of the doughty (or doughy) knight, Sir Thopas, is cut short by Harry Bailly, who rudely interrupts him and dismisses his storytelling with the disdainful comment "Thy drasty rymyng is nat worth a toord!" Chaucer agrees to tell another tale, the heavily didactic *Melibee*. Chaucer identifies the *Melibee* as a "moral tale vertuous," and as a tale the Host, who feigns enthusiasm for tales of an overt moral or religious kind, ought to like well. Chaucer scholars have been at turns amused and perplexed at

Chaucer's assignment of these particular tales to his literary persona because they lack the literary sophistication evident in most of the other stories. Yet these two tales do have their serious dimension (*Melibee* may be an example of a failed didactic poetics) and in the context of the tale-telling game, Chaucer's stories may represent one pilgrim's rebellion against Harry Bailly's aesthetic and his attempt to sort stories into one of two categories, "sentence" or "solaas." *Melibee* becomes a means for Chaucer to defend fiction as a way to argue hermeneutical issues, without relying exclusively on traditional modes such as the Man of Law's saint's legend or the Prioress's story of a martyred innocent.

Prudence's copious use of scripture in the tale as a form of moral discourse or instruction raises several interesting questions for Chaucer's fiction. Does her incorporation of scripture into a tale alter the way scripture ordinarily functions? Does the authority of scripture change once it appears in a poem? Does the fiction alter its epistemology, its truth claims, and its hermeneutical status? Do the pagan authors, who are cited with equal force alongside the biblical and patristic figures, further modify the privileged status of scripture? The added fact that Prudence applies scripture to the secular world throughout her narrative shows that for her its signification is not exclusively the question of salvation. Based on the *Thopas* and the *Melibee,* it would seem that the whole thrust of the *Canterbury Tales* is to free poetry from such delimiting categories as romance escapism and moral didacticism.

Chaucer's commitment to the autonomy of his fiction is manifest in the tale-telling game that takes over the pilgrimage. The mix of the serious and the playful, of earnest and game, is characteristic of the *Canterbury Tales* as a whole and of its pilgrimage. Chaucer sets this dialectic in motion in the familiar and enchanting opening lines of the poem. The condition he describes is general throughout Christendom: the urge to travel, to get outside of one's habitual self, takes over and impels folk to seek distant lands and, especially, distant shrines. This centrifugal motion is countered by a centripetal one, a desire for *compaignye* and *felaweshipe,* or a need for *communitas,* which Victor Turner aptly describes as a temporary merging of the self with the rest of creation. If *communitas* is one of the spiritual benefits of pilgrimage, storytelling helps to build it. When the Host announces his storytelling game to the pilgrims at the end of the prologue, he appeals to the same basic impulses expressed in the first eighteen lines:

> Ye goon to Caunterbury—God yow speede,
> The blisful martir quite yow youre meede!
> And wel I woot, as ye goon by the weye,
> Ye shapen yow to talen and to pleye;
> For trewely, confort ne myrthe is noon
> To riden by the weye doumb as a stoon;
> And therefore wol I maken yow disport,
> As I seyde erst, and doon yow som confort.
>
>   (1.769–76)

In effect, the Host proposes that the pilgrims suspend the usual social rules and enter into a game or play world in which they relate to one another as players. Their social roles can never be completely forgotten—indeed, one's customary identity with its actual and latent prejudices may be brought out with greater intensity, as we witness in the links as well as in the individual tales. What distinguishes the play world is its gratuitousness or inconsequentiality, which is not to say it is frivolous or non-serious. Reality, not seriousness, is the opposite of play, and the play world set up by Chaucer resembles Michael Oakeshott's idea of a conversation, a circumstance in which there is no truth to be discovered, no proposition to be proved, or conclusion to be sought, and the voices involved do not compose a hierarchy:

> Each voice represents a serious engagement and without this seriousness the conversation would lack impetus. But in its participation in the conversation each voice learns to be playful, learns to understand itself conversationally and to recognize itself as a voice among voices.[8]

Even though the Host's plan dissolves after the first tale, the new model that emerges, one of spontaneous play, more closely captures the spirit of conversation desired by the pilgrims.

In giving their assent, Chaucer's pilgrims recognize, as Boccaccio's storytellers did, the attractiveness of tale telling as a group activity; it involves everyone and elicits from them their point of view on an unlimited number of moral and social issues. In the game, the tales and the tellers speak to one another, expanding, refining, and contradicting various points. Each tale also acts as a miniature pilgrimage in itself, as a quest or adventure for the teller in his or her construction of meaning, and is either enabling or disabling for the teller in the effort to attain the kind of self-discovery and self-renewal promised by the pilgrimage. In the poem the pilgrims are presented to us as incomplete selves, wounded by desire. The act of tale telling does not complete the self (there is always the prospect that another tale will follow) or give us a "true self," as a theological project would demand. The experience may, nonetheless, confer on the teller a new sense of his or her being in the world.

The Clerk is an interesting example of what I mean. When the Host calls on the Clerk to tell his tale he reminds him that when a man is entered in a play "He nedes moot unto the pley assente." He then urges him not to preach "as freres doon in Lente," and, above all, to "Speketh so pleyn at this tyme, we yow preye, / That we may understonde what ye seye" (4.19–20). The Host has every reason to fear that the sober Clerk will tell a tale that is not appropriate to the occasion. The reader is thus surprised to see that the Clerk, by the end of his tale, has fully entered the play world and that his concession to the Host, "As fer as resoun axeth, hardily," has altered our perception of him and his tale. Although the Clerk emerges from his tale firmly established as one of Chaucer's more orthodox narrators, affirming in his narrative the value of humble submission to divine authority and the value of patience in the face of events often incompatible with or "inportable" to human reason, his narrative also manages to put these same values and virtues in question. Instead of concluding in harmony with his mentor, Petrarch,[9] the Clerk cancels the example he has been delineating ("Griselde is deed, and eek hir pacience") and installs in its place the example of the Wife of Bath, who is both impatient and unsubmissive:

> This storie is seyd nat for that wyves sholde
> Folwen Grisilde as in humylitee,
> For it were inportable, though they wolde,
> But for that every wight, in his degree,
> Sholde be constant in adversitee
> As was Grisilde; therfore Petrak writeth
> This storie, which with heigh stile he enditeth.
>
> (4.1142–48)

For the Clerk, telling his story in the vernacular and within the context of the tale-telling game brings out unsuspected depths in Griselde that problematize the tale. In his dual capacity as narratee of the Wife's discourse and as narrator of the story of Griselde, the Clerk, as an experienced dialectician, comes to appreciate the limits of Petrarch's ideal model and he elevates the Wife of Bath to Griselde's status as a worthy alternative. For the reader, the Clerk's performance illustrates two important points about the *Canterbury Tales* and the way we read the individual tales. The first is the intertextuality that exists between the tales and the second is the way the tale-telling game releases unsuspected depths in the pilgrim-tellers, as it does in the Clerk, transforming the individual described to us by the pilgrim Chaucer in the *General Prologue* and by the Host in the prologue to the Clerk's tale.

We've learned a great deal recently about the Chaucerian subject, about the construction of the self and the disenchantment of the self in Chaucer's poetry. One of the more dramatic changes in regard to the self that occurred in the late fourteenth century involved an inversion of the Platonic ideal:

> The center of the self is no longer reached, as in the ancient inheritance, by moving away from that which is temporal and particular to that which is universally intelligible and 'other'; the center now somehow embraces all these temporal particulars and complicates them within itself.[10]

The way this works in the *Canterbury Tales* is that each pilgrim reaches the center of the self by a radical act of de-centering the self. Each pilgrim enters his tale in the same way Chaucer enters his poem, inhabiting all of the various figures that people it and experiencing the multiple perspectives afforded by the narrative. As we saw in chapter 1, the Nun's Priest became visible to us and to Chaucer's narrator through his fiction; we gained a sense of who the Nun's Priest was as an individual apart from his social role. The recognition of the Nun's Priest by the Host and the company validated his existence and made him an integral part of the (evolving) community. His own self-awareness, as it were, arose from his act of positioning himself in relation to his fellow pilgrims and their tales, and through that engagement he came to shape or recognize his own subjectivity.

This pattern repeats itself throughout the tales. Storytelling acts as a catalyst that accelerates the presumed spiritual benefit of the pilgrimage. The tale telling both facilitates and frustrates the aim of the pilgrimage by intensifying the tension between its centrifugal and centripetal impulses, its transcendent and immanent elements.

For some readers, even those enthusiastic about the play element in the poem, the tale-telling game is detrimental to the spiritual goals of the pilgrimage. Previous studies of the relationship between pilgrimage and storytelling, earnest and game, have treated the terms and the activities as antithetical. Charles A. Owen, for instance, believes that "the storytelling contest supplants the pilgrimage,"[11] and Edmund Reiss contends that the realism Chaucer employs to make the pilgrimage resemble a real one defeats the purpose of the carefully structured pilgrimage frame:

> As a consequence of this concretization, fragmentation, and emphasis on the human, the characters in the *Canterbury Tales* do not strike us as essentially pilgrims. Most of them do not belong on a spiritual journey or even appear conscious that they are on such a journey. Perhaps the best way of viewing them is as varieties of true and false seekers (or even as stages on the road to the heavenly Jerusalem).[12]

Both authors fail to respect the difference between pilgrimage as an ideal or abstract concept—or there is too much reliance on an outmoded model—and its actual practice as a religious activity in the late fourteenth century.[13] In the *Canterbury Tales,* Chaucer uses Harry Bailly to balance the tension between earnest and game. As Richard Lanham has observed, the Host's "natural sphere of life is the play sphere, and he is practiced in keeping high spirits in order without too much dampening them."[14] The Host intuitively understands play to be an essential ingredient in a human being's ontological composition, and under his guidance the journey to Canterbury becomes a vast social game which demonstrates the extent to which life—Christian life at least—is a dialectic between what is transcendent *(Pilgerfahrt)* and what is earthbound *(Wallfahrt).*[15] Participation in the sacred ceremony at the shrine reveals man's desire for transcendence but the play of the outward journey and the return to the homestead reveal a love and appreciation for the things of this world and a desire to affirm the things of this life.

Normally when we think of a pilgrimage we think of the sacred goal. Most pilgrimage literature reinforces this impression by concentrating rather exclusively on the sacred shrine with only passing reference to the special and separate character of the journey. In any enterprise, however, the outcome is not the only significant event; the actual play counts for something too. After all, the ceremonies conducted at the pilgrim shrines could just as easily have been dispensed at one's local parish church. What gives a pilgrimage its unique character and makes the ceremony at the shrine all the more efficacious is the journey itself—the transition from place to place. The journey provides both a sense of detachment from one's normal routine and the psychological refreshment *(refrigerium)* to embrace anew the spiritual values offered at the shrine.

To be sure, the mass pilgrimage movements of the late Middle Ages were not conducted as austerely as the earlier solitary and ascetic practices, but pilgrimages never ceased to be an earnest activity even when they were conducted in the spirit of play. As Edmond-René Labande has observed, pilgrims in the fourteenth century still pursued the same ideals as religious travelers of an earlier era and were motivated by the same impulses. Curiosity was not a motivational excrescence peculiar to late medieval pilgrimages in the first place; traces of its presence exist from the beginning, even in the most holy of anchorites.[16] Despite having extrareligious motives, late medieval pilgrims still set out with the sacred goal very much in mind and they continued to define themselves as religious travelers. They may not have consciously envisioned themselves as en route to the New Jerusalem, as the *peregrini* did, but they could derive a keen sense of their own participation in the Christian community at large as a result of their journey.

For Leon Zander the primary purpose of pilgrimage is to promote "forgetting" of one's present state of mind; by participating in the journey the pilgrim achieves a temporary triumph over time and a liberation from the vicissitudes of the world.[17] Since it is entirely possible to journey without undergoing any significant regeneration or relief from the pressures of everyday life, especially if the journey is a brief one, as the Canterbury pilgrimage was for most English pilgrims, the ability to shed one's usual habit of mind is diminished considerably by the knowledge that one will shortly reassume it. On such occasions, play or storytelling may act as an impetus to detach oneself from one's habitual cast of mind by activating another aspect of the self not readily accessible or required in one's everyday role.

According to Freud, tale telling is an adult form of child's play or a sophisticated form of make-believe. A story creates the real world we wish to inhabit and rearranges reality so that it conforms to what we would like it to be. In one's tale one can be whoever one aspires to be. As a player the tale teller is able to assume any number of identities without the onus of responsibility connected with his actual identity. In addition to playing out his traditional role in society, one is free to test new or provocative attitudes toward life. One may even choose to confess or expose his private, inner self but in so doing he is not committed to the kind of firmness of amendment or new way of life that is implied in a religious confession.

Chaucer's willingness to mix play with the sacred thus is not an attempt to demean the sacred or, simply, to satirize late medieval pilgrimage mores. He was not content to use pilgrimage merely in the traditional literary context as a metaphor for the journey of life when it encompassed so much more of human experience. Besides the symbolic representation of the journey and the goal, he chose to include something of the personal character and motivations of individual pilgrims, including their impulse to play. Chaucer acknowledges that an eschatological strain inheres in all pilgrimages but he also recognizes that coextensive with the urge to direct all of one's activities toward some specific end or goal is the urge to allow things to happen unpredictably or at random.

As I see it, then, the pilgrimage frame is more than a convenient device to gather together a diverse group of men and women; it radically informs the way the pilgrims encounter and interrogate their world. By formally introducing the tale-telling game in the *General Prologue* and having all of the pilgrims assent to participate in it, Chaucer makes it an integral part of the pilgrimage. His preference for a pilgrimage as an ordering device, as opposed to any other structuring principle available to him, acknowledges both the intrinsic value of a theological purchase on life and an appreciation of storytelling as a liberating force through which his pilgrims can freely express themselves on whatever social, political, or theological issues concern them.

In the four tales that follow, beginning with the Prioress's tale and the Second Nun's tale and continuing with the tales of the Reeve and the Pardoner, I want to show how each tale acts as a miniature pilgrimage, as a quest or adventure for the individual pilgrim-teller that turns out to be either an enabling or disabling experience for the teller in her or his effort to attain the kind of self-discovery and self-renewal promised by the pilgrimage. All of the tales, as I outlined earlier, deal to one degree or another with a concept of the church in the fourteenth century and with versions and perversions of human love.

2.
The "greyn" and the "fruit of thilke seed of chastitee" : Charity and Chastity in the Prioress's Tale *and the* Second Nun's Tale

> For Iames þe gentele iugeth in his bokes
> That fayth withouten þe feet is feblore then nauiht
> And as ded as dore-nayl but yf þe dedes folowe:
> *Fides sine operibus mortua est.*
> Chastite withouten charite worth cheyned in helle;
> Hit is as lewed thyng as a laumpe þat no liht is inne.
> *Piers Plowman,* C text, passus 1.181–85[18]

THE PRIORESS

If the Pardoner is a vicious man who can tell a moral tale, the Prioress seems a moral woman who surprises us with the viciousness of her tale. Both tales raise serious questions about the teller's responsibility for the content of his or her tale, including Chaucer's responsibility for the content of the *Canterbury Tales.* As countless readers have demonstrated in their response to the *Prioress's Tale,* it is extremely difficult to affix blame or to separate the fruit from the chaff in this tale. The Prioress (and her defenders) would have us believe that the intent is all; her tale should be taken for what she says it is: a hymn of praise to the Virgin. It is true that Chaucer presents her as innocent (though hers is a studied or willed innocence) and unaware of the race hatred that surfaces as if it were incidental in her tale. The language of her tale tells a very different story, however. What is disturbing about the Prioress ("And al was conscience and tendre herte"), perhaps about sentimentalists in general, is her distance from any genuine emotional or intellectual engagement with the events of her tale. Her responses to the brutal as well as the precious

179

moments are affected and impersonal.[19] We see this first in the ease with which she moves from the sweet sentiment of her appeal to Mary in her prologue, highlighted by her self-effacement as a child of twelve months old or less, to the sharp and critical tone of the opening stanza:

> Ther was in Asye, in a greet citee,
> Amonges Cristen folk a Jewerye,
> Sustened by a lord of that contree
> For foule usure and lucre of vileynye,
> Hateful to Crist and to his compaignye;
> And thurgh the strete men myghte ride or wende,
> For it was free and open at eyther ende.
>
> (7.488–94)

In some places her language is coldly logical, such as occurs when the Provost determines that evil shall receive what evil deserves; the stanza concludes syllogistically and dispassionately, "*Therefore* with wilde hors he dide hem drawe, / And after that he heng hem by the lawe" (emphasis added). In other places the violent images and events as well as her emotional appeals to the shared witness of her audience (see the passages beginning at 7.579, 7.607, and 7.684, respectively) conflict with or deconstruct the tone of simplicity and mode of piety she affects in her narration, making it difficult to exonerate her completely from the moral judgment of the tale.

Blaming the Prioress (or Chaucer) for the anti-Semitism in the tale does not do justice to the case, however; it is more important, as Alfred David has pointed out, to locate the conditions and practices that made this kind of religious intolerance conventional.[20] By assigning this tale to the Prioress, Chaucer appears to want to go beyond blaming the Prioress in order to look at the way the church transmits doctrine (by rote memory), at the way it idealizes certain modes of piety (the cult of the Virgin), at the way it exaggerates the danger or threat to the faith from external enemies, real or imagined, such as the Jews, and at its failure to attend to the internal threats to the faith that stem from the gap in the Prioress's example, the gap between belief in Christ and an imitation of his love and forgiveness.[21]

Rote learning implies knowledge that is unsifted or unanalyzed. In his prologue the Pardoner boasts that his theme is always one and the

same, *radix malorum est cupiditas,* "For I kan al by rote that I telle."
The Pardoner's admission comes across as a parody of the church prac-
tice, whereas the Prioress, in the second stanza of her tale, speaks ap-
provingly of the rote-based indoctrination of the children:

> That lerned in that scole yeer by yere
> Swich manere doctrine as men used there,
> That is to seyn, to syngen and to rede,
> As smale children doon in hire childhede.
> (7.498–501)

The Prioress, like the boy in her tale, seems to have learned by rote her
hymn of praise to the Virgin, just as she summons from memory frag-
ments of songs and bits and pieces from the Bible and church services
that honor Mary. Her reverence for Mary is epitomized by her recitation
of a segment of Bernard of Clairvaux's hymn to the Virgin as a part of
her invocation. Whether these words are merely drawn from memory or
expressed with heart-felt sincerity, the Prioress does implore the Virgin
Mary to help her with her tale and through its telling to "getest us the
lyght" and to "gyden us unto thy Sone so deere."

Louise Fradenburg has suggested that "criticism on the *Prioress's
Tale* has failed to appreciate the intimacy of the connection between
anti-Semitism and medieval legends of the Virgin."[22] One aspect of the
problem can be found in the late medieval cult of Mary, the language
and devotion of which centers on Mary's virginity and the miracles
that flow from devotion to it. As Hyam Maccoby points out, the rela-
tionship of the worshiper to the Virgin Mary in the cult tended to be
of "an ecstatic and sentimental kind," which fits the Prioress well.[23]
From this approach, the Prioress's limited *amor* or lack of forgive-
ness is more a consequence of the triumph of an ascetic concept of
Mary and less a deficiency in her character. Her submission to Mary as
a supernatural or mythological figure, despite her inclination to em-
brace a figure of Mary who could accommodate her own womanly and
earthly desires, a Mary reconciled to Eve, may go further to explain the
contradictions that appear in her and in her tale than the notion that
she is in some way disaffected from her religious vows. A reconsidera-
tion of the cult of the Virgin, first in late medieval culture and then in the
Prioress's tale, may explain how one and the same tale can move some

readers to commend it for its spiritual insight and others to condemn it for its moral blindness.

Critical discussion of the Virgin Mary theme in the tale has been vitiated by a tendency to underestimate the diversity of the role Mary played in the art, literature, and doctrine of the late Middle Ages.[24] To simplify matters, I have identified two main traditions or concepts of Mary that obtained in both the iconography and devotional practices of the period. The first portrays Mary as the semi-divine mother of Christ whose virginity is stressed as her most salient feature and who, accordingly, becomes a symbol for religious asceticism, monasticism, and mysticism, disciplines that center on the other or heavenly world. The second image depicts Mary as the mother of Christ whose humanity is stressed and who serves Christianity with a more this-worldly orientation. It is this Mary who is so prominent in the devotional lyrics of the late medieval epoch, in much of the drama, and who serves as a basis for the "sacred parody" in the secular lyric of the same era. This Mary also enjoys a sisterly relationship with Eve.

Prior to the eleventh century, Mary's image in art and doctrine was primarily an abstract or symbolic one. Most often she was portrayed as Reason or as a symbol of the contemplative life.[25] In this concept, Mary and her perpetual virginity are treated as counterimages to Eve and the ills that are supposed to have emanated from Eve's capitulation to the flesh. The image of Mary standing on the head of the serpent became one of the more popular manifestations of this theme. Mary's submission to the voice of the angel who entreats her to embrace God's will to be the Mother of God was juxtaposed to Eve's surrender to the blandishments of the serpent. "Mors per Evam; vita per Mariam" was a commonplace by the beginning of the twelfth century.[26] This Mary, as the antithesis of Eve and foe of the devil, became known as the *Virgo immaculata,* and her eternal purity was cultivated in order to sponsor various moral doctrines and reform movements in the church.[27] The Immaculatists promoted many of the miracles that celebrate Mary's virginity because they wanted to establish her extrahuman dimension and her control over natural forces. Her perpetual virginity elevated her to the station of Queen of Heaven.[28] The sublimation of her femininity into the dual aspects of maidenly purity and motherly self-denial made Mary the paradigm for all women to emulate in the work of salvation.

But, as Robert Hanning has shown, the impulse to deify Mary usually resulted in a corresponding tendency to stigmatize Eve.[29] Whenever Mary came to be associated with the superiority of the contemplative life or functioned solely as the symbol of obedience or some such ideal, then Eve stood apart as human nature in all its carnality and weakness.

In contrast to this transcendent idea of Mary is the image of her in her earthly naturalness. During the eleventh and twelfth centuries a new concept of Mary began to emerge as pressure increased for a figure who was more accessible to human identification and who could fill the role of mediatrix.[30]The older, hieratic image of Mary as Queen of Heaven gave way to the development of Mary as nurturing mother. In this role she became the figure most closely identified with the theme of forgiveness, replacing her Son, who had gradually assumed the role of Judge. The Mother tenderly fondling or nursing her child quickly established itself as the dominant expression of Mary's love for humanity and gave impetus to the impulse to naturalize the incarnation by depicting an ever more real and human Mary. Simultaneously, we get an ever more real and human Christ. In *La Vierge et l'Enfant,* Ambrogio Lorenzetti depicts the child in the arms of his mother, but the infant looks away from his mother toward the view of the spectator, all the while eating an apple, suggesting that the incarnation itself has reversed original sin. Previously humankind had been said to have been made in the image and likeness of God, but until the appearance of the incarnation paintings it had not been shown to be so.[31]

In concert with Mary's descent from heaven and her recovery of the features of a flesh-and-blood woman, Eve began her ascent from oblivion and to display more individuating feminine characteristics. Her image carved on the lintel of the north portal at Autun during the eleventh century attests to the growth of a new attitude toward the representation of natural things, including the human body.[32] At this point, Eve still suggests sexuality and the body in much of the art and iconography, but great care is taken to portray her as a positive image of human and feminine nature. As a consequence of this humanizing trend, Eve and Mary are no longer depicted solely as antithetical to one another: a new configuration emerges which places them in a sisterly relationship.[33] This development attributes a transformative power to Eve—and thus to all human beings—as well as to Mary: the will to rise.

Traces of this new configuration first appeared allusively in the Madonna paintings: Eve is shown nursing her infant while Mary nurses Christ; or Mary's loss of her son and her accompanying grief is foreshadowed and paralleled in Eve's loss of Abel.[34] The appearance of Abel as a forerunner of Christ in his suffering and death reflects a shift in doctrinal emphasis from themes of the fall and judgment to those of reconciliation and forgiveness. In two striking examples, Ernst Guldan shows that by the fourteenth century the traditional contrast of Eve and Mary found in the Annunciation paintings and in the fruits of the one tree has been transformed into a typological parallel. The Eve / Mary triptych at San Marino attributed to Petruccioli shows Mary holding Christ and beneath her Eve reclines with Cain and Abel. Instead of the usual contrast of Eve's painful birth (Cain) with Mary's painless birth of Christ, the artist shifts the focus to one of reconciliation by placing Abel in the foreground caressing his mother, a scene reminiscent of countless Madonna paintings. In the Hanover triptych, based on Bonaventure's *lignum vitae*, Eve appears as one of the penitents present at the crucifixion. The words from Luke 7.47, traditionally associated with Mary Magdalene, are here put into the mouth of Eve: "I am forgiven much for having loved much."

What is most remarkable about the late medieval Eve / Mary paintings is the way that they fuse the erotic with the sacred image patterns. The presence of Eve afforded the artist a greater freedom to portray the full humanity of women in sacred subjects and to depict Mary in a whole new range of commonplace activities that underscored her humanness. Eve's presence permitted them to keep intact the physical contours and sexuality of Mary that certain reformers preferred to efface when they placed her outside the realm of sinful flesh. In these scenes Eve often appears as highly erotic but not as a temptress; her physical charm both complements and illuminates the eroticism and inherent femininity of Mary, introducing delicate shadings that Mary eventually absorbed as her own. Ambrogio Lorenzetti's experiments with Mary's eyes, for example, bring out an unmistakable sensuality in her at the same time that they accent a new dimension of maternal tenderness that heightens her human likeness and draws her closer to Eve.

In the lactation paintings that proliferated in the thirteenth and fourteenth centuries, the figures of Mary and Eve converge. Mary becomes the nursing Mother of God and the spiritual mother of all the living (numerous churches and shrines in the late Middle Ages claimed to have phials of Mary's milk). Lorenzetti's *Madonna del latte* epitomizes the type. Mary appears as an alluringly beautiful young woman and the child is shown deriving obvious physical pleasure while sucking at the breast. The pressure of the child's hand on the breast and the mother's sensual response betokens what Leo Steinberg describes as a powerful erotic communion.[35] Mary's identification with Eve's fertility also corrects a popular misconception about Mary's virginity. Depicting Mary in her human wholeness, as mother as well as virgin, implies that her virginity is meant to signify a triumph over lust and concupiscence, not over sex and womanhood.[36] The distinction is an important one because it suggests that the idea of Mary as virgin and mother is not only a mystery or paradox but also a Christian affirmation of a complete womanhood.

The assimilation of Eve and Mary is celebrated in a series of paintings based on the theme of Lorenzetti's *Maesta*. In it, the *Mater virtutum* cedes to the *Mater viventium* her central place at the feet of the *Mater pulchrae delectionis*. Eve is readmitted into the garden and Mary is depicted as enthroned but now seated on the ground, her descent from heaven complete.[37] By the fifteenth century Eve will have acquired a halo, bringing to a climax the tradition that Eve was the first figure Christ led from hell after the harrowing.[38]

The idea for the *Maesta* originates in Dante's *Paradiso,* a source for a number of Lorenzetti's creations.[39] As did Dante, Lorenzetti treats his female figures as complete human beings. The *Maesta* reveals what Joan Ferrante has cited as Dante's intention to make human love the essential first step in gaining knowledge of the divine and to praise the female side of God as the means through which humanity is saved.[40] Dante speaks of Eve's great physical beauty and Lorenzetti brings it stunningly to life. He does not present Eve in an attitude of shame; instead she appears as a resplendent embodiment of erotic human nature with her own dimension of humility. Her bountiful hair and casual attitude of repose, her sensual gaze and pronounced femininity, together with her air of comfort at the feet of Mary enhance the point that her sexuality is meant to serve exalted womanhood, not to detract from it.

The Prioress's devotion to Mary is not to be doubted. We see it from the outset in the *General Prologue* when she identifies Mary with the love that conquers all; it continues in her prologue with the dedication of her tale to Mary, and culminates in the tale with the miracle Mary performs for her devotee. But the Prioress's understanding of and identification with Mary is as vexed and divided as the image of Mary that I have just been describing. The figure of the Prioress that we meet in the *General Prologue* seems thoroughly devoted to her profession yet willing, in innocuous ways, to violate the rules of her convent. Her extravagant manners, her meticulous concern for her appearance, her treatment of her pets, and her physical charm—all have led critics to view the Prioress as alienated from her vocation. But is she a nun who strains against her vows to be a woman, or is it more accurate to say that she is a woman who struggles desperately, and fails, to be a nun? What does her devotion to Mary and her desire to imitate Mary's virginity tell us about her? If her brooch with its famous inscription is an indication that she is torn between opposing concepts of love—eros and agape, Eve and Mary—is her impulse to affix the brooch to her rosary beads evidence of an inward disposition to join the opposing forces within her and thereby imitate the unity or wholeness enjoyed by Mary in her motherhood and in her virginity?

In the prologue to her tale the Prioress speaks of how Mary, in her human nature and identity, had the power to "ravish" the godhead down from heaven:

> O mooder Mayde, O mayde Mooder free!
> O bussh unbrent, brennynge in Moyses sighte,
> That ravyshedest doun fro the Deitee,
> Thurgh thyn humblesse, the Goost that in th'alighte,
> Of whos vertu, whan he thyn herte lighte,
> Conceyved was the Fadres sapience,
> Help me to tell it in thy reverence!
>
> (7.467–73)

In some of the art of the period Mary is depicted as terrified of the angel and shrinks from the awesome responsibility his presence betokens. In the Prioress's version Mary is depicted as the aggressor. Her Mary is a dynamic figure, rooted in this world (God comes down to her), one who acts on the behalf of human beings even before they have prayed to her

(7.474–80). Her use of the verb "ravyshedest" has more than a hint of the erotic attached to it. This is a promising image of Mary as one who has the power to turn the "Fadres sapience" into flesh, into human nature. We see the Prioress searching for or tending toward this Mary, first in the images of the nursing mother in her prologue, then in the *Alma redemptoris,* the song that courses through the tale from beginning to end. The *Alma redemptoris* is a song of liberation. It celebrates Mary as mother of the redeemer, as gate of heaven, and as star of the sea, attributes Mary earned in her role as mediatrix. The *Alma redemptoris* presents a more human and humanistic Mary than the Mary of the *Gaude, Maria,* the song associated with some sources for the tale. In the *Alma redemptoris,* Mary is said to lift up her fallen people ("þou sterre of se rer of þe uolk / þat rysing haueht in munde"), including Eve, who is reconciled with Mary in the redemption as Adam is with Christ.[41] This side of Mary remains "untranslated" or inert in the tale, however, partly because the Prioress is no more capable of translating or understanding the words of the song than the boy is and partly because the Prioress identifies emotionally with the boy instead of with his mother.

In her tale, the Prioress shrinks from the responsibility of bearing the word. Her worship of Mary's virginity, as the specific source of the love that conquers all, places emphasis on the miraculous side of Mary rather than on forgiveness or on what the miracle and song are intended to mediate. The Prioress fails to apprehend the genuine mystery that the birth of Christ in the virgin soul is a miracle akin to his bodily birth from Mary. She worships the female principle that enslaves her, not the serene womanhood of the Virgin. Such a figure as the Wife of Bath, a kind of Eve and natural foil of the Prioress in her refusal to remain a virgin or to extol it as a virtue, expresses confidence in the regenerative power of human love by introducing the Hag as her surrogate, who then shows the power of her love to transform. Her tale also culminates in a miracle, although hers emanates from the depths of the Hag's humanity and from a difficult but rewarding submission to the way of *kynde.* Chaucer deftly sharpens the contrast by reversing the traditional concepts of the nun and the *vieille.* He attributes to the Wife of Bath the generosity of spirit ordinarily found in the nun and he places in the Prioress the convoluted sexuality that has distorted her understanding and exercise of charity.

In her tale the Prioress introduces a widow and her only son. They represent the Prioress's conception of the Holy Family: the child is a Christlike innocent devoted to his mother and the mother has no earthly husband. Instead of identifying with the mother who would be her natural self-projection, the Prioress projects her feelings onto the chorister, who embodies an uncomplicated example of virginity and a single-minded devotion to Mary. Her enthusiasm for the boy's virginity ("O martir sowded to virginitee") might pose no serious problem were she to view it as one of the several forms innocence can take. Throughout her tale, however, she treats virginity, specifically virginity of the sexual organs, as if that constituted an appropriate imitation of Mary's virtue. The simplicity and sentimentality of her narrative, especially her fondness for the word *litel* reflects the depth of her desire to sublimate her femininity into childlike innocence.

As a child might, the Prioress exaggerates both the power of evil in the world and the weakness of human beings to oppose it. She imagines Christendom as beset by powerful enemies, like the little Christian schoolhouse trapped in a hostile environment of wicked Jews. Everyday the boy must travel through this "Jewerye" to reach the school located on a street she describes as "free and open at eyther ende." The openness of the Jewish district disturbs her. It offends her sensibilities, awakening in her fears of the world in all its ugliness and materiality. The open space is the opposite of her cloister; it is an unfamiliar realm, a place of strangers that are foreign to her experience and embody the unknown. We might see the Prioress's anxiety about the street to be emblematic of her tale and her person. She distrusts an open narrative or an ambiguous lesson, preferring instead a story whose meaning or theology is already established and secured. Her vision of Mary is also static and fixed. Her tale, like the Second Nun's tale, with which it will be compared below, is not a new version or interpretation of a legend adapted for the pilgrim audience in order to acquaint them with a new manifestation of Mary and her love. Rather, the Prioress's tale is marked by its absence of kerygma; that is, it lacks an appreciation of the Christian message contained in the song and it shows the Prioress as closed off to its meaning. Like the boy who, when dead, is encapsulated "in a tombe of marbul stones cleere," the Prioress remains insulated from the community (of pilgrims or seekers of the new) around her. As a result, her appeal to God for mercy in the closing stanza of her tale sounds all the more hollow and formulaic, without practical value or spiritual conviction.

In her tale the Jews and the district exist solely for the material principle, for "foule usure and lucre of vileneye."[42] Her most visceral impression is the "stewe" into which the child is thrust. She is perversely fascinated with it, judging from the attention she accords it. She repeats the horror of his being thrown into the privy, as if this indignity were more heinous than the murder itself:

> This cursed Jew hym hente, and heeld hym faste,
> And kitte his throte, and in a pit hym caste.
>
> *I seye* that in a wardrobe they hym threwe
> Where as thise Jewes purgen hire entraille.
> (7.570–73, emphasis added)

For the Prioress, the world at any time can become a pit that engulfs us. Yet for one so dainty of speech and fastidious of manners, she cannot resist the temptation to sink herself verbally in the awful physicality of earthly existence. The Prioress has made the assault on the boy an assault on her, an invasion of her security that will be restored only by the intervention of Mary.

The gap that exists between the impersonal stance of her narration and the emotional fervor of her language lays bare the several layers of conflict within her. Her excessive fear of the world and her view of the mother and child as powerless innocents, along with her concept of the Jews as irredeemable agents of Satan, impel her to embrace a concept of Mary as an avenging angel. Mary never comes to life in the tale as the *Alma redemptoris,* the loving mother of the redeemer who embraces all of humankind as her children. Without her example of forgiveness, the Christians dispense their justice with the same crudity and dispatch that they have condemned in Herod's slaughter of the innocents and the Prioress condemns in the Jews, her "cursed folk of Herodes al newe."

There is nothing exceptional about the Prioress's tale in its violence toward the Jews; a minority of the tales in the genre end with violence or some form of vicious treatment of the Jews.[43] They are not representative of the Marian theology that inspired these stories, however. In most miracles of the Virgin, especially those involving Jews, conversion is a central motif. Conversion ratified the power of Mary to restore the community to wholeness and affirmed the universality of her motherhood. This Mary, as I indicated earlier, is the focus of the song. Her mercy or conquering love remains untranslated, as foreign and obscure to the Prioress's sensibility as the Latin on her brooch, because Mary remains ever the disembodied Queen of Heaven or the miraculous bush that burns "unbrent." The pressure to declare the theology of the song does emerge in the tale from the chorister himself, who wants to understand the meaning of the song, not just to memorize the words and then repeat them.

Early on in the tale, after the clergeon has learned "by rote" the first verse of the *Alma redemptoris,* he implores a schoolmate "T'expounden hym this song in his langage, / Or telle hym why this song was in usage" (7.526–27). Upon "his knowes bare" he petitions his fellow "to construe and declare" the meaning of the song. These are unusual or technical words for a boy his age; they have a Latinate or clerkly ring to them. *Expound* can mean to set forth or to state in detail some aspect of doctrine or to explain that which is difficult and obscure. More commonly, especially in regard to scripture or religious formularies, it means to interpret or comment upon. (See, for comparison, the use made of the term by the Monk, especially in relation to the daughter's interpretation of the dream of Croesus.) *Construe* also means to interpret or to translate, and *declare* means to explain, with a strong suggestion of to proclaim. The boy demands a full explication of the song. His desire to know why this song was in usage goes beyond rote learning and to the heart of the moral problem of the tale. To answer his question would require an explication of the song and Mary's role in giving birth to Christ or the Word of God.

His fellow has himself only memorized the song, content in the knowledge that the song was made to greet "oure blisful Lady free." He concludes by telling the boy "I kan namoore expounde in this mateere. / I lerne song; I kan but smal grammeere" (7.535–36). His "smal grammeere" refers to his lack of training in Latin, a language noted for its clear grammatical structures and stable system. The key to understanding Latin is through its grammar, its rules; without it one is deprived of access to its inner workings and to the parsing that constitutes so much of the subtlety in exegetical and biblical writing. When it comes to Latin, apparently, the Prioress also has but "smal grammeere." She has mastered the language and the theology of the church about as well as she has mastered the French of her social class, leaving the reader with the impression that she has a lazy as well as a limited intellect. Just as the boy determines that it is more important for him to memorize the song in a language he cannot understand, "Though that I for my prymer shal be shent," the Prioress has not become a nun so much as she has mastered the gestures. She has not internalized her vocation anymore than she has internalized the habit of charity, salving her tender conscience with lavish displays of love and sentiment for animals.

Toward the end of the tale, once the boy has had his throat cut and has been thrown into the pit, his song is the means by which his mother discovers him. He sings the song again when he is lying on the bier and he is sprinkled with holy water. The repetition of the song, untranslated, reminds the audience of the absence of its message. Sung at the end of the tale, the song has gained a new urgency because the boy has had a vision of the Virgin Mary who has placed a grain on his tongue and instructed him to sing until the grain is removed. The song has now been contextualized as a message from Mary. The boy makes that much clear:

> as by wey of kynde
> I sholde have dyed, ye, longe tyme agon.
> But Jesu Crist, as ye in bookes fynde,
> Wil that his glorie laste and be in mynde,
> And for the worship of his Mooder deere
> Yet may I synge *O Alma* loude and cleere.
> (7.650–55)

The boy himself does not expound the text of the song; whatever is proclaimed in the song is left to the reader to construe and declare. First it is left to the Prioress to declare, since the boy's message is directed at her. As a message from Mary, the song tells the Prioress to grow up, to cease sublimating her love and femininity into childlike innocence. If she wishes to bear fruit, if she wishes to effect an imitation of Mary, she must remove the ambiguity embossed on her rosary. The clue to the mystery lies in the "greyn" that Mary has placed in the boy's mouth, but which neither the Prioress nor the monk who is present appears to understand.

Placed in the mouth of the boy, the grain is like the seed implanted in Mary, impregnating her with the Word while allowing her to remain a virgin. The grain permits the boy to proclaim the word of God, "as ye in bookes fynde." The incarnation, giving birth to the Word, is the central theme of the *Alma redemptoris*. In her discussion of this grain, Sister Nicholas Maltman, O. P., cites a passage from the second vespers in the Mass of the Holy Innocents which contains the words *Jacet granum oppressum palea,* "the grain lies crushed from the chaff."[44] In this context the grain functions as a "symbol of the soul winnowed or purged from the body, of the spirit as distinct from the body."[45] In the Prioress's tale, Mary places the soul or grain back into the body, the fruit enclosed in the chaff, and keeps the boy alive, even though his throat is cut to the "nekke boon." Identifying the grain as seed suggests the parable of the Sower and the Seed (Mark 4.1–29). According to Frank Kermode, the parable of the Sower is a great crux because in it Jesus explains the nature of his parables as stories told to them without—to outsiders—"with the express purpose of concealing a mystery that was to be understood only by insiders."[46]

The parable tells how some of the seed of the sower falls by the wayside and is eaten by birds, some falls upon rocky ground and does not flourish, some falls among thorns and yields no fruit, and some falls on good ground, "and yielded fruit that grew up, made increase and produced, one thirty, another sixty, and another a hundredfold" (Mark 4.8–9). Jesus explains to the Twelve that the sower "sows the word." The Twelve are chosen to know the kingdom of God but to those outside all things are treated in parables, that "seeing they may see, but not perceive; and hearing they may hear, but not understand; lest perhaps at any time they should be converted, and their sins be forgiven them" (Mark 4.12). The last part of the lesson is Jesus' instruction to insiders, whom he expects will see, hear, and understand his message. As bearers of the word, they must comprehend its meaning and not merely recite it. As Kermode says, the Sower parable can make outsiders of insiders: "Only those who already know the mysteries—what the stories really mean—can discover what the stories really mean."[47]

Applied to the tale, the boy is cast like a grain into the pit of the world. Throughout the tale, but especially in the scene of his death, there is a strong sense of the earthly that the Prioress tries to make repugnant.

During his ordeal or suffering the boy sees Mary and comes to understand that she is the mother of the redeemer, the gate of heaven, help to those who have fallen—all characteristics of Mary that are celebrated in the song. With the grain on his tongue the boy has given birth to the word; he now is a sower of the word, an insider, and when he sings at the end of the tale the meaning of the words no longer are a mystery to him. When the grain is plucked from his mouth he dies, but his dying words are seeds that will bear fruit.

The Prioress is also like a grain of wheat that has fallen into the convent. She does not "die" to the world nor does she bear fruit. She has ears to hear the song but she understands not. She has eyes to see, but she perceives not. For the Prioress, who identifies with the boy, her "song" is her tale (she calls her tale a song in the prologue); it is the fruit or grain on her tongue. She needs to retell it and this time get the ending and the meaning right. Her narrative makes this insider into an outsider. To see and to hear rightly she needs to see how the mother of the boy, particularly in her role as Rachel, brings the human Mary, the suffering Mary, the Mary of the love that conquers all, to the forefront. Rachel is the figure in whom the suffering women, Jew and Christian alike, converge. She looks backward to Eve and forward to Mary in the loss of her children and she stands as the one authentic or unsentimentalized figure of grief in the tale. She is a judgment on the Prioress herself, a sign of Madame Eglentine's failure to see in Rachel a reflection of herself and of the shared humanity of the Jews. All of the Jews, including the assassin, remain faceless; Satan is the only one who speaks for them. The Rachel reference forces the tale to see the Jews, and the Jewish children sacrificed by Herod, in a literal way. They cannot be transposed into the innocent martyrs of the church. Neither the Christian community, nor the Jews, nor the Prioress is transformed into the New Testament image of Rachel as the church weeping for its innocent martyrs because the miracle works only for the boy. The spirit of forgiveness that reverberates throughout in the *Alma redemptoris* is forsaken for mere admiration of the fact of the miracle itself. The Prioress's exclusive embrace of celestial love and her concomitant fear of the earthly confirm her own divided and unregenerated condition because they show that she has not yet realized that the world itself has been regenerated, that is to say, conquered by love.

THE SECOND NUN

> As soon as we enter the symbolic order, the past is always present
> in the form of historical tradition and the meaning of these traces
> is not given; it changes continually with the transformations of the
> signifier's network. Every historical rupture, every advent of a new
> master-signifier, changes retroactively the meaning of all tradition,
> restructures the narration of the past, makes it readable in another,
> new way.
>
> *Slavoj Žižek*[48]

The Prioress's tale ends, as we have seen, in a failure of love and in the absence of forgiveness. As it stands it poses one of the more serious threats in all of the *Canterbury Tales* to the moral integrity of the church and to any idea it has of itself as a community open to all. It is thus fitting that the Second Nun, a nun from the same convent as the Prioress, is the instrument Chaucer uses to answer the Prioress's tale, although the Second Nun is more intent upon establishing her own idea of the church in the fourteenth century than she is in responding directly to the Prioress. More immediately apparent to the reader is the link, in word and theme, that her tale forges with the Canon's Yeoman's tale, a union which brings greater clarity to the notions of *communitas* and *caritas* that are central to her tale, and which gives us new insight into the nature of conversion in her tale. Together, the Second Nun's tale and the Canon's Yeoman's tale support the foundation for a Chaucerian anthropology or soteriology based on human dignity that is initiated in the *General Prologue*. The link between the two tales will be discussed in detail below. I want to look first at some parallels with the Prioress's tale.

In her tale, the Second Nun reverses the situation of the Christians and the church from the way they are depicted in the Prioress's tale: the Christians stand in relation to the Romans where the Jews stood in the Prioress's tale in relation to the Christians. Unlike the Prioress, who locates her tale in some remote and unnamed city in Asia, the Second Nun sets her story in Rome, seat of the church and emblem of Augustine's earthly city. Placing her story in pagan Rome, when the church was still in its infancy and not yet institutionalized, is not her attempt to distance the tale from the present or from England but to give it a voice in an ongoing theological or ecclesiological debate in the fourteenth century. According to Gordon Leff, nothing fueled fourteenth-century ecclesiological controversy more than the meaning of the historical apostolic church for the medieval one, whether the primary significance of the former for the latter lay in its juridical organization or in its simple charismatic way of life.[49] For the reformers in the fourteenth century, including Wyclif, the threat to the church no longer came from the outside but from the inside, and they held up the primitive church as a model of poverty, community, and charity. They also saw in the primitive church an opportunity to diminish the power of the papacy, advocating a shift from the structural body or hierarchy of the church in favor of its teaching role. In her tale, the Second Nun holds up the primitive church as a model of *communitas* and *caritas,* and she attributes to Cecilia all of the qualities associated with the primitive church: poverty, community, and charity. In the course of the tale, Cecilia gives away all of her earthly possessions; she converts her house into a church open to everyone; and she burns in charity. Cecilia and the apostolic church become the vehicles through which the Second Nun would transform the medieval church from the suprapersonal institution it has become to its original role as the community of the faithful.

If, in the Prioress's tale, chastity is associated with innocence, in the Second Nun's tale it is converted into works and deeds. We see this in one of the more poignant and lyrical passages in the tale, when Urban praises Cecilia for her emulation of Christ and Mary:

> "Almighty Lord, O Jhesu Crist," quod he,
> "Sower of chaast conseil, hierde of us alle,
> The fruyt of thilke seed of chastitee
> That thou hast sowe in Cecile, taak to thee!
> Lo, lyk a bisy bee, withouten gile,
> Thee serveth ay thyn owene thral Cecile."
>   (8.191–96)

The idea of Christ as a bee that pollinates or goes about planting seeds evokes once more the parable of the Sower and the Seed, but to very different effect here. The language is both procreational and incarnational.

What failed to take root in the Prioress's tale, the love of Christ, fully blossoms and bears fruit in the Second Nun's story. Cecilia, like Mary, is shown here as impregnated with the seed of Christ. She does not shrink from bearing and sowing the Word; the fruit of the seed of chastity fills her and she brings it to fruition in her works of charity. The willingness of Christ to humble himself, to serve his "owene thral," Cecilia, introduces one of the more important themes in the tale, also connected to the parable of the Sower, that of service to others.

The Second Nun sees (sight is a major motif in her tale and a link with blindness in the Canon's Yeoman's tale) and understands the meaning of Christ's message, and the telling of her tale becomes a form of service to others. Through her tale she will restore the word *martyr* to its original meaning (Greek *mártus, martur*) of "witness"; she will bear witness to Cecilia's life of "bisynesse" as a personal and a theological ideal. In the process, the Second Nun makes the narrative of Saint Cecilia her own story, in contrast with the Prioress, whose rote narrative never allows her to become an authentic or conscious witness. Apparently, the Second Nun locates in the Cecilia legend a re-enactment of the Christ drama. Cecilia's imitation of Christ, especially in her three-day death and in the scene of confrontation with Almachius, shows her that the incarnation and redemption are ongoing events capable of repetition. She sees that they are not exterior to her as static, mythical events but form part of her personal history and that she too can participate in the redemption through her "revision" of the Cecilia story. One of the truly innovative features of her tale is the way her narrative transforms the work of redemption and salvation from an emphasis on the (bloody) sacrifice of Christ, and of those martyrs like Saint Cecilia—or of the little clergeon and young Hugh of Lincoln—to works of charity, to service to this world.

For some readers, however, the Second Nun's tale is not remarkably different from the Prioress's tale, inasmuch as both tales seem to rely on miracles and divine intervention as the means to affirm religious faith. It has been argued that at every turn Cecilia forsakes the opportunity to discuss doctrine in any detailed form in favor of the mere fact or event of conversion, which leads to the conclusion that the many conversions in the Second Nun's tale are a supernatural phenomenon imposed by God rather the consequence of Cecilia's instruction or the force of her example.[50] Yet, the Second Nun does state in each instance that those who are converted are schooled or instructed in the articles of faith, at some point, either by Cecilia, Urban, or St. Paul, indicating that she is aware of not providing such details.[51] While it is true that she foregrounds the miracles, and the appearance of the angel or St. Paul, the miracles are more of a narrative device to illustrate that the conversion experience is a form of self-discovery, a way of seeing that what was believed to be "yhid in hevene pryvely" is really concealed in oneself, a point which the Canon's Yeoman's tale confirms. For the Second Nun, the conversion experience is a privileged kind of seeing, like that of the blind Briton in the Man of Law's tale who sees, apparently without fully realizing the gift that he possesses, "with thilke eyen of his mynde / With whiche men seen, after that they ben blynde."[52] More to the point, St. Paul, who haunts the Second Nun's tale, personifies the kind of sight one gains through one's conversion, a seeing which is shared by Valerian and Tiburce.[53] In any case, Cecilia's gesture of good works and her instruction in the faith precedes divine impetus and does not depend on it; Christ responds, like a bee, to the energy of her love.

To resolve the seeming contradictions in the Second Nun and her tale, I would suggest that we approach the Second Nun as someone involved in an intense personal struggle, torn between centripetal and centrifugal impulses which are apparent from the outset in her "portrait." There is of course no portrait of the Second Nun in the *General Prologue* that contains the kind of rich and provocative detail that Chaucer lavished upon the Prioress, a sign perhaps of this nun's greater identification with her vocation. As was the case in the example of the Nun's Priest, the reader is forced to rely on the prologue and tale to piece together an image of the woman and the concerns that consume her, a hint that in her anonymity she stands closer to the Nun's Priest in her spirituality than she does to the Prioress. Like the Nun's Priest, the Second Nun is a person whose identity is defined by an external authority figure. The Second Nun's immediate superior is the Prioress, but Cecilia is really the "first" nun, the internal model who generates an ideal of virginity and a way of being in the world that contrasts with the example of the Prioress. As a saint, Cecilia embodies not only the monastic or conventual ideal of chastity and holiness, the *via negativa,* she also embodies the virtue of an active lay piety through charitable work

197

in this world. She does not advocate or practice ascetic withdrawal so much as she aspires to pursue the conventual ideal in this world.

It is apparent that the Second Nun wants to strike a similar balance in her own life. On the one hand she appears to view the world as a hostile place still in need of Mary's protective and regenerative love. She also appears to be committed to the notion of conventual *peregrinatio,* when she speaks of herself as a "flemmed wrecche" imprisoned in a "desert of galle" where she is afflicted with the foul contagion of her body. On the other hand, she worries about conventual idleness, respects the active life, and states flatly that faith without good works is dead (8.64). The vehemence of the Second Nun's expressions of alienation reveals how profoundly she experiences her immersion in her flesh. Her conscious-ness of the weight of earthly lust and false affection indicates that these are not mere abstractions for her; rather, they underscore the degree of personal struggle involved and show that she feels the presence of her own body in a way that prevents her from withdrawing from the flesh or the physical world no matter how severe the spiritual discipline she prac-tices.[54] We might treat her more extreme statements about alienation and exile from this world as formulaic, the zeal of a young woman com-mitted to her vocation. As she moves into her tale she will move away from these expressions of alienation, just as Cecilia will gradually let go of the angel who protects her from harm at the outset of the tale. The Second Nun's admission of her struggle with her body both humanizes and personalizes her, bringing her closer to us and sharpening the image of her that is beginning to form.

The Second Nun may also envy the freedom and ecclesiastical sup-port Cecilia receives from Urban in her pursuit of the active life. That she calls herself a son of Eve may be more politically astute than has been appreciated, in that she shows her readiness to bend gender cate-gories as a first step toward gaining for nuns, if not medieval women in general, a more active and meaningful role in the church, such as Cecilia enjoyed.

What the Second Nun may immediately respond to in Cecilia, then, is the capacity Cecilia has to unite within herself seemingly irrec-oncilable opposites: chastity and procreation (of charity), spirit and matter, citizen and saint, a gold robe and a hair shirt. Her double identity as citizen and saint is especially evident in her confrontation with

Almachius near the end of her tale. When she meets Almachius, Cecilia responds to his query by identifying herself as a Roman citizen: "'I am a gentil womman born,' quod she." Several readers have commented on the disproportionate space the Second Nun gives to this confrontation. H. Marshall Leicester acutely observes that the Second Nun derives great enjoyment from Cecilia's aggressiveness and challenge to male authority.[55] Paul Beichner comments on the importance the Second Nun accords to the Almachius scene, remarking that the Second Nun promotes the drama of the confrontation at the expense of spiritual or doctrinal edification.[56] Not quite. The scene is part of the edification or moral argument of the tale. Placing Cecilia, or emphasizing Cecila's place, in a specific social matrix insures that her religious activities are not isolated from the community in which she lives. Her moral conscience is not merely private; it has to be translated into social conduct.[57] Despite her defiance here, Cecilia does not seek her death or martyrdom and does not suggest that a true Christianity means renunciation of this world. In answer to Almachius's demand that she deny her Christianity (8.442–48), she says:

> "Yowre princes erren, as youre nobleye dooth,"
> Quod tho Cecile, "and with a wood sentence
> Ye make us gilty, and it is nat sooth.
> For ye, that knowen wel oure innocence,
> For as muche as we doon a reverence
> To Crist, and for we bere a Cristen name,
> Ye putte on us a cryme and eek a blame."
>   (8.449–55)

In her view, being a good Christian is no obstacle to being a good citizen.

The Second Nun's invocation of Mary at the close of her prologue also has strong centripetal and centrifugal elements. In it, she stresses Mary's humanity as well as Christ's. When the Second Nun invokes Mary's aid it is no mere formality. Borrowing liberally from Bernard's hymn in Dante's *Paradiso,* but putting her own stamp on it, the Second Nun imagines the incarnation as a work of collaboration between the human and the divine.[58] She appears to write herself into the event by describing Mary's womb as a blissful "cloistre" ("infinite riches in a little room") where love and peace take "mannes shap." In this version,

Christ is neither seduced nor "ravished" down from heaven but, as we saw in Grosseteste's rendition of the Four Daughters, Christ descends of his own will, in loving union with Mary. Christ gladly takes up his abode in Mary's womb and adorns himself with human flesh ("God for bountee chees to wone"). Mary, she says, "baar of her body" the Creator of every creature, a view that affirms that Christ derives his human nature wholly from his earthly mother. Above all, Christ suffers no indignity by assuming human nature because God has no disdain "His Sone in blood and flessh to wynde." Mary's womb, like an alchemical alembic, distills the eternal love and peace into temporal forms of charity and forgiveness, in this her *magnum opus*.

As much as the Second Nun identifies with Cecilia, she also realizes how antiquated the legend is. She knows that the era of the martyrs is over, that Christianity is no longer a minority religion in its cities, and that in the fourteenth century conversion no longer defines the primary mission of the church in the world. Consequently, throughout her tale she maintains a critical distance from her sources, editing and reshaping them as she narrates. In the closing stanza of her prologue she makes explicit her compositional technique and she invites the reader to collaborate with her in the reconstruction of her story:

> Yet preye I yow that reden that I write,
> Foryeve me that I do no diligence
> This ilke storie subtilly to endite,
> For bothe have I wordes and sentence
> Of hym that at the seintes reverence
> The storie wroot, and folowe hir legende,
> And pray yow that ye wole my work amende.
>
> (8.78–84)

This passage has been cited as evidence that Chaucer had not fully adapted the material of the Second Nun's tale to the *Canterbury Tales,* but her self-consciousness as a reader, writer, and narrator (see the propensity she has to qualify her observations with comments such as "As I writen fynde" or "as I understonde") indicates that she is aware of the subjectivity of her version and that she intends to choose her own emphases for the tale, omitting some details and foregrounding others. Besides, mimesis produces more than a weakened image or copy of pre-existing things. Rather, as Paul Ricoeur says, mimesis brings about an augmentation of meaning in its field of activity.[59] In this passage the Second Nun reveals herself to be an interactive reader who rehearses the past in order to provoke fresh insights. For good measure, she follows this stanza with the *Interpretacio nominis Cecilie,* which expresses her sense of Cecilia's multifariousness and shows us how Cecilia's name can be played with poetically to yield numerous meanings. The passage informs the reader that there may be no authoritative version of Cecilia's life and that every version, including her own, is open to interpretation.

The Second Nun's call for the reader to amend or correct her work implicates the reader in her act of recuperation. She dislodges the Cecilia story from the genre of strict hagiography and turns it into a more critical text that applies to her present needs. She is not reciting the "legend of Saint Cecilia," but constructing the narrative now known as the *Second Nun's Tale,* a poem that is part of a larger poem, the *Canterbury Tales.* Once liberated from its legend status and its theological function as the Cecilia story, it enters into dialogue with the other stories in Chaucer's poem, where both the narrator and her readers are free to question its vision. The obvious example is the relationship that exists between the Second Nun's tale and the Canon's Yeoman's tale, whereby the latter helps us to see some of the finer points of the Second Nun's tale in sharper detail.

Fragment 8 provides us with a thematic principle that shows that the Second Nun's tale not only belongs with the Canon's Yeoman's tale but also shares in its philosophical outlook. The fragment also serves as a principle of unity for the relationship that exists between tales and between fragments throughout the *Canterbury Tales.* In the Canon's Yeoman's tale the alchemical quest is described as the effort to unite matter and spirit through "multiplicacioun," the process by which the spirit concealed in matter is brought to maturity or fruition.[60] It is not unlike the pollinating work of the bee in Urban's metaphor, or the work of the incarnation itself. The essential and stabilizing element in the process is the elusive philosopher's stone or *prima materia.* In theory, the aim of alchemy is the old dream of *homo faber,* of human cooperation in the perfection of matter. The alchemist puts himself in the place of time to effect through his operations what by itself would take nature aeons to accomplish.[61] In practice, as we shall learn from the Yeoman, the alchemists never realize their goal: "We concluden everemoore amys," he laments.

Heretofore, nearly every attempt to establish a principle of unity between the two tales has rested on the assumption that the Second Nun's tale was intended to function as a critique of the Canon's Yeoman's tale and that alchemy serves only to represent the futility of a soulless striving with matter. The difficulty with this reading is that it deprives the Yeoman's language of much of the freshness and vitality it brings to the *Canterbury Tales* and prevents his scientific discourse from occupying its rightful place alongside all other discourse, including where it may act as a critique of other discourses. For, regardless of what alchemy may have meant in the popular imagination in the fourteenth century, Chaucer, by adopting the subject for a story in the *Canterbury Tales,* has made it a serious topic. Treating the Canon's Yeoman's tale as having its own autonomy also relieves the Second Nun's tale of having to be expressive of Chaucerian truth when it is only one more tale told by another pilgrim-teller.

Taken alone, the vocabulary and the perspective of the Second Nun are self-limiting. Once placed beside another tale, however, particularly one that uses a set of terms identical to those in the Second Nun's tale but meant to signify different things, the tale is dialogized. The fusion of the two sign systems relativizes the text and brings out the doubleness or ambiguities in the words, images, and alchemical signs that serve as well-established parallels that bind the two tales. The fact that all the alchemical parallels that appear in the Second Nun's tale are not original to her tale but first occur in her sources suggests that she is not consciously criticizing alchemy, and the fact that the Yeoman's response is made without benefit of hearing her tale relieves him of any intent to "quite" her narrative. All of which adds to the point that Chaucer's design for the *Canterbury Tales* is therapeutic, that is, instead of supplying answers or solutions to problems, he sets up the various tales and fragments as different sets of problems in need of reconsideration. His design encourages tales like the two involved here to talk to one another and to create a circumstance in which neither one can fully mean without the other. At the same time, each opens the other tale to new levels of signification.

For example, when the Yeoman quotes Arnold of the New Town, "Ther may no man mercurie mortifie / But it be with his brother knowlechyng" (8.1431–32), we are expected to recall Valerian's first request after his conversion, "I pray yow that my brother may han grace / To knowe the trouthe as I do in this place" (8.237–38), pitting alchemical discourse against religious discourse or, more accurately, uncovering their mutual interest and intention. The juxtaposition of the passages hints at a *caritas* in alchemical language, and Arnold's description of what it means to "multiplie" brings out a dimension in Tiburce's conversion not immediately apparent in the Second Nun's tale. As a form of "multiplicacioun," Tiburce's cry that he has changed "al in another kynde" suggests more than a religious conversion. He has undergone a change in his very being. And, still relying on the alchemical analogy, the change comes about as a consequence of drawing from one's brother what exists in a companion form in oneself. Conversion in the Second Nun's tale emerges less as a change in belief and more as a refinement or perfecting of a pre-existing condition—the result of the release of a *caritas* already rooted in human nature.

This theme of brotherhood has additional resonance in the Second Nun's tale that touches on Augustine's vision of the two cities and on the two loves associated with each. Cecilia, as we have seen, identifies herself as a Roman citizen and sees her dual identity as commensurate with her Christian faith. Earlier, in our discussion of *Saint Erkenwald*, we spoke of the lawyer as an example of *civitas* as a mode of *caritas*. The Second Nun shows Cecilia inverting this model by making *caritas* a mode of *civitas*. I want to pursue the theme of *civitas* and *caritas* a bit further because it links the *Second Nun's Tale* with an important theme in the *Canterbury Tales* as a whole. In *Chaucer's London*, D. W. Robertson observes that all of the cities that appear in Chaucer's poetry are, in one form or another, versions of London. Troy serves as the most obvious example, inasmuch as Londoners regarded their city as the New Troy, enjoying the glory of Old Troy but subject to the vices that left Old Troy in flames. London is Chaucer's earthly city in the same way Rome is Dante's, and in the *Canterbury Tales* Chaucer seeks to define and preserve London's ethos and ideology while striving to prevent it from suffering the internal and moral erosion which befell Troy—and Rome. Thus, for Robertson, the journey to Canterbury in quest of the "hooly blisful martir," who had helped men restore their moral integrity "whan that they were seeke," was "at once a reminder to Londoners of their highest ideals and an invitation to renewed dedication."[62] Thomas Becket, Robertson adds, was London's most celebrated citizen-saint. The mayor, aldermen, and men of the mysteries participated in regular processionals from the hospital of a military order dedicated to him to the grave of his parents at St. Paul's, and a little chapel was erected in his honor on London Bridge that greeted citizens and wayfarers of all kinds on their way to and from the city. When Chaucer decided "to create a fictional pilgrimage to the shrine of St. Thomas at Canterbury beginning on the outskirts of London, he was making a deliberate appeal to the *pietas* of the City of London and, indirectly, to that of the realm as a whole."[63]

Pietas is one of those terms Robertson concedes is not easily translatable into English, particularly in its political signification. Its religious understanding is obvious enough: it implies religious piety, an inclination toward mercy, and a willingness to help the miserable and the needy. Its political meaning, which dates back at least to the time of Virgil, is associated with an awareness or feeling of responsibility for the traditions of one's own people or city. *Pietas,* moreover, is just one of a number of terms or concepts, such as *patria, amicitia,* and *koinonia* (Aristotle's word for community) that had been adopted from classical antiquity by the church fathers, who then de-politicized them and Christianized them. Augustine uprooted the idea of *patria,* originally meaning the aggregate of all the political, moral, religious, and ethical values for which one might choose to live or die, from its association with *civitas* in order to establish the celestial city of Jerusalem as the true *patria* of the Christian. Under Augustine's rubric, once the Christian pledges to be a citizen of the city in the other world, then his final return to that spiritual and eternal fatherland is the *natural* desire of the Christian soul peregrinating on earth.

Again, as was discussed in relation to *Saint Erkenwald,* in the late Middle Ages, following the recovery of Aristotle, an effort was made to redeem these concepts and restore them to their original valence. The aim was to wed the political with the theological in order to repair the rupture between the city and justice.[64] Ptolemey of Lucca boldly compares the love of one's city to the ties of charity and love that bind Christian society together. Love for the fatherland, he says, is founded in the root of a charity that puts not the private things before those common but the common before the private. As Ernst Kantorowicz says, the idea of the state as *patria* became in the late Middle Ages an object of political and semi-religious devotion. The martyr who offered himself up to the invisible polity and dies for his lord (or in the case of Cecilia, for her city) *pro fide* became a model of civic self-sacrifice, *pro patria*. He cites Geoffrey of Monmouth who had the temerity to compare to martyrs warriors who died *pro patria* in battle against the Saxons; their deaths were interpreted as self-sacrifice *pro fratribus*. Therein a death *pro patria* appeared as a work of *caritas*.[65]

In my reading of the *Second Nun's Tale,* the Augustinian ideal does not disappear, as one reader puts it, so much as it is transmuted. In book 15, chapter 5 of the *City of God,* Augustine rejects the city of man because Cain, who committed an act of fratricide, founded it. It comes as no surprise then, Augustine says, that long afterward in the founding of that city which dominates so many peoples and becomes the capital of the earthly city, Rome, that it corresponds to the original in a fratricidal crime at its foundation. Augustine is referring to the death of Remus at the hands of his brother Romulus. What Augustine sees in the quarrel between Romulus and Remus is the way in which the city of man is divided against itself; in the example of Cain and Abel we see the enmity between the two cities, the city of man and the city of God.[66]

The Second Nun reimagines the fratricide in Almachius's sacrifice of the Christians—his fellow Romans in Cecilia's view—and she uses the theme of *amicitia,* the brotherly love of Valerian and Tiburce, to compensate for the fratricide of Romulus and Remus and thus restore the city to its moral foundation. The love Valerian has for Tiburce awakens the spark of agape or *caritas* latent in him and brings him to the realization that human love is redemptive: "The sweete smel that in myn herte I fynde," he says, "Hath chaunged me al in another kynde" (8.251–52). We learn that the flowers that had been produced by the angel have been brought from paradise, and "Ne nevere more ne shal they roten bee," which suggests that the flower is uncorrupted human nature—created in paradise in the image and likeness of Christ, the "Creatour of every creature," redeemed by Christ here on earth—and can be recovered by the charity or *amicitia* the brothers share.

The marriage between Cecilia and Valerian is still another form of *amicitia,* as is her union with Tiburce.[67] During the ceremony in which Cecilia marries Valerian, she also pledges herself to Christ. The line, "whil the organs maden melodie," evokes the opening lines of the *General Prologue* suggesting the naturalness of the two alliances. The double wedding betokens both a civic virtue and a sacred commitment. A second "marriage" or union occurs at the end of the tale when Cecilia requests that her house be converted into a church. The union of her church with Rome embodies a kind of Thomistic vision in which *amicitia* and *communitas* emerge as temporal beatitudes. The downward or centripetal thrust of converting her house to a church, which is to remain in the city perpetually, epitomizes her commitment to her work in this world, and is a sign of the Second Nun's idea of a church that is abuzz in "bisynesse."

Saints' lives were, after all, stories designed to teach the faithful to imitate actions which the community had decided were paradigmatic.[68] The martyr, as Jeffrey Schnapp has shown, is the one who translates the language of faith into the language of exemplarity, the eternal mysteries into historically immediate terms, the universal cross of Christ into an individualized one in the community's own image. The martyr also served as a natural earthward projection of the cross, and the specific qualities of the martyr, in her witness or struggle against malign forces, makes her an exemplary citizen of the human city.[69]

Once again, the Canon's Yeoman's tale helps us to see the centripetal movement of the Second Nun's tale, as well as the ideal community she envisions. It also helps us to see how dramatically her tale differs from that of the Prioress in its concept of Christian love. The themes of marriage and brotherhood, for example, and the self-sacrifice of Cecilia, gain in meaning once we witness how fraternal strife and personal betrayal disrupt the alchemical wedding in the Canon's Yeoman's narrative. Literally, the hoped-for wedding of *sol* and *luna* terminates in an explosion, "The pot tobreketh, and farewel, al is go" (8.907).[70] Symbolically, a similar disintegration occurs. The explosion signals the end of the collaborative effort by the various figures involved to forge an authentic brotherhood. In the aftermath of the explosion each begins to blame the other, causing the Yeoman to lament, "But wel I woot greet strif is us among" (8.931). The strife resulting from the failed experiment leads to the real concern of *secunda pars:* alchemy as a threat to community. The story of the Yeoman's fall into alchemy becomes a paradigm for the betrayal of humankind. The Canon of the tale is likened to Judas whose lust for gold "wolde infecte al a toun." He is a "theef" and, like Satan, the

> roote of al trecherie,
> That everemoore delit hath and gladnesse—
> Swiche feendly thoghtes in his herte impresse—
> How Cristes peple he may meschief brynge.
> God kepe us from his false dissymulynge!
> (8.1069–73)

These theological parallels combine with the exclusively clerical status of the alchemists to suggest that in the Yeoman's mind alchemy is, in the final analysis, an allegory of the role of the church in society. The Canon's vow to "doon a maistrie er I go" (8.1060), presumably to produce the philosopher's stone, amounts to a claim that he controls the mysteries of creation, incarnation, and redemption. At the same time his vow comes to be seen as a betrayal of "Cristes peple," because implicitly the Canon imputes to himself the power that through the incarnation was bestowed on all.

The particular character of the Canon's "false dissymulynge" is made clear in a parallel passage in *Inferno* 29, where Dante shows us that the moral issue of alchemy is the vanity of the alchemists who induce humankind to believe that they have the power to alter nature and thereby arrogate to themselves a dominion that belongs to God. Dante's alchemists, like Master Adam in canto 30, suffer in hell because they are at root simoniacs. Unlike Cecilia, they distort the image or work of Christ by materializing the spiritual quest and by seeking to deify the self at the expense of the community. Earlier, in canto 19, Dante described Simon as a kind of alchemist:

> O Simon Magus! O his sad disciples!
> Rapacious ones, who take the things of God,
> that ought to be the brides of Righteousness,
> and make them fornicate for gold and silver!
> (*Inferno* 19.1–4)

In the prologue to his tale, the Yeoman ceases to be the Canon's "sad disciple." By remaining on the pilgrimage, moreover, and joining in on the tale-telling game, he breaks free of the Canon's influence and comes to understand that his kind of alchemy is a form of simony. At the same time, the act of tale telling has drawn him into the pilgrim group, with the subtle implication that here he will find the brotherhood he was seeking among the alchemists. Tale telling thus has acted as a form of vision for the Yeoman—as it does for the Second Nun—and enables him to bear witness, for, the Yeoman is led, at the end of his tale, to the discovery both of the philosopher alchemists, who are quite distinct from the Canon, and of an alchemy that, like pilgrimage, constitutes an authentic spiritual quest.

As Arnold of the New Town says, the philosopher alchemists thrive because they understand the first principle of "multiplicacioun," that no man can perform the work without the help of his brothers. By identifying with these alchemists, the Yeoman realizes that he need not repudiate alchemy altogether because he sees that an ideal purpose remains in it, namely, that the pursuit of the philosopher's stone is valuable even if one never reaches a conclusion, because the quest culminates in Christ. What appears to be a purely materialist endeavor turns out to be joined to spirit after all. Or, in the metaphor employed by the Yeoman, Christ is the truth embedded in a Platonic dialogue, a mode of discourse which is like the alchemical project itself insofar as it transmutes language into meaning and it too has no conclusion. In the dialogue Plato tells his disciple why the philosophers will not reveal the secret of the stone:

> For unto Crist it is so lief and deere
> That he wol nat that it discovered bee,
> But where it liketh to his deitee
> Men for t'enspire, and eek for to deffende
> Whom that hym liketh;...
>
> (8.1467–71)

The historical discovery of Christ, so to speak, does not bring the philosophical project to an end, but, as is true in the Second Nun's tale, it shifts the locus of human activity from a preoccupation with the other world to an increased concern for this one.[71] These alchemists accept human imperfection as a starting point for reform of the human image, and because Christ holds out the possibility of new encounters, they remain committed to the perfection of the material principle as the human side of the compact with the divine.

In her tale, the Second Nun performs her own work of transmutation. The lesson she teaches through her tale is that all human beings have within them the philosopher's stone, the power to incarnate or join spirit and matter in their original union. This is revealed in the conversation that transpires between Cecilia and Tiburce at the scene of his conversion. Tiburce confesses that Cecilia confuses him when she speaks of there being one God and then of there being three. To explain the concept of the trinity to him she adverts to this analogy: "Right as a man hath sapiences three— / Memorie, engyn, and intellect also— / So in o beynge of divinitee, / Thre persones may ther right wel bee" (8.338–41). She then goes on to instruct him in the incarnation, passion, and redemption of Christ. The analogy she uses corresponds closely with Grosseteste's idea of the *minor mundus*. Grosseteste, the reader will recall, insisted that God created the world *ex nihilo* in order that the entire created order from the smallest speck of dust ascending upwards expresses the unity and diversity of the Trinity. Human beings, among all creatures, including the angels, most closely approximate that image because they combine in their nature "free intelligence and the dust of the earth." The *minor mundus,* or natural image of God, has the special prerogative to reproduce within himself the cosmic order as it was revealed in the incarnation.

In the prologue to her tale, the Second Nun observes that Christ, the "tryne compas lord and gyde," whom "erthe and see and hevene, out of relees, / Ay heryen," is the *minor mundus*. Cecilia, cast in his image, is called the "hevene of the peple." Just as people may see in the heavens the sun, the moon, and the stars in every direction, so they may see in Cecilia, this "mayden free," of faith "magnanymetee," radiant wholeness and "sondry werkes, bright of excellence." As the *minor mundus,* Cecilia, "brennyng evere in charite ful brighte," and like Heaven, swift, round, and "eek brennynge," reproduces in her being the first light or *prima materia* out of which human beings were formed in the divine image. Her integrity and wholeness are revealed in the closing sequence of the tale.

In a stunning reversal of the conclusion of the *Prioress's Tale,* the Second Nun has Cecilia, "with her nekke ycorven there," exactly like the Prioress's "litel clergeon," deliver a message of love and forgiveness designed to bring the pagans into her church, the very people the Prioress had excluded from hers. In the bath of flames Cecilia internalizes and thus completes the alchemical quest. She brings together spirit and matter in a process of sublimation that does not break down or flee under the heat of the fire. All her energy is directed centripetally: she does not lose a drop of sweat and her head cannot be severed from her body. Even after her death her spirit remains incarnate in the world, in Rome (that has become her true *patria*) and in her house, that has become her church: "In whiche, into this day in noble wyse, / Men doon to Crist and to his seinte servyse."

It is most fitting that the last word of the Second Nun's tale is *servyse* (in effect, her tale moves from idleness to service), conveying a sense of devotion and charity, spiritual obligation and social consciousness. The Second Nun has done her service to Saint Cecilia and to her own time; she has borne witness. In her noble effort to articulate the kerygma contained in the story of Cecilia, she has managed to show that Cecilia's death and the sacrifice of Valerian and Tiburce and the nameless others continue to mean by being regenerated in the here and now as *amicitia* and as *caritas,* as service to this world.

3.

From Caritas *to Love:*
The Reeve's Tale *and Fragment 1*

"Allas, allas! That evere love was synne!"
Canterbury Tales 3.614

Although the Wife of Bath bemoans the fact that love has been confused with sin, particularly in the discourse of the clerks, she insists that it did not prevent her from using her "instrument" in marriage, "As frely as my Makere hath it sent," she says (3.150). Her robust defense of her own sexual practices makes it clear that as far as she is concerned the prohibitions or restraints imposed on sexual love in marriage are strictly man made, as in not woman made, and are not in harmony with human nature as it was given at the creation (hence her use of "Makere" rather than God in the line cited). In the war of words she carries on with the clerks throughout her prologue and tale, the Wife of Bath makes sure that a woman's voice and experience will not be excluded from the discussion of love and marriage that takes place on the road to Canterbury.

Before the Wife of Bath can tell her tale of the woe that is in marriage, we hear first from the Reeve, another old-timer who uses his prologue to talk about his personal sexual history. Like the Wife of Bath, the Reeve acknowledges that he has always had a "coltes tooth."[72] But, where the Wife of Bath has boldly resisted the clerkly model of marriage, with its emphasis on procreation as the primary purpose of sexual union, the Reeve appears to have committed himself to it wholeheartedly. He emerges from his prologue and tale as a "burning" example of what can happen if one takes too literally the model of marital love as it is outlined in the penitentials.[73] Judging from the level of sexual frustration he shows in his prologue and his tale, his "tribulacioun" is written on his flesh.[74] The Reeve may well be the most unjustly maligned character among all the pilgrims in the *Canterbury Tales*. Certainly he is not the first pilgrim who comes to mind when one thinks of Chaucer's love debate; yet, by its end, his tale proves itself to be as moving an appeal as the Wife of Bath's to transform the theological ideal of married love. If we approach the Reeve as if he were one of the Wife's first three husbands, a role in which the Miller in fact does cast him, he may gain from us the sympathy he deserves. A fresh approach to the Reeve in the light of that ideal and in the light of the Wife of Bath's narrative gives us a new understanding of the Reeve and a new appreciation of the scope of Chaucer's love debate.

Let me begin my revisionist perspective of the Reeve by identifying the context in fragment 1 in which his tale arises and the particular circumstances that provoke him to make what turns out to be a very personal confession. Starting with his appearance in the prologue to the Miller's tale, I shall argue, the Reeve shows himself to be deeply committed to marital and sexual concerns, and he too suffers from the same cultural prejudice that frustrates the Wife of Bath when it comes to speaking with authority on these matters. Chaucer had addressed the issue before of who is authorized to speak on the nature of love, most notably in the love debate in the *Parliament of Fowls*. In that poem, the "gentil tercelet" rebuked the duck for his crude and pragmatic approach to the subject of courtship and love, saying "Now fy, cherl ... / Thy kynde is of so low a wrechednesse / That what love is, thow canst nouther seen ne gesse" (596–602). The *Canterbury Tales* is also a kind of parliament, but one in which the "churls"—such as the Miller, who will "abyde no man for his curteisie"—are not so easily silenced. In the *Canterbury Tales* Chaucer democratizes the discussion of love and marriage to an unprecedented degree. His poem recognizes that love and marriage are topics that cut across class and gender lines to engage the passions of all the pilgrims and, in the spirit of the Wife of Bath's opening foray on "auctoritee" and "experience," Chaucer empowers the socially disenfranchised or "lewed," to challenge, through their experience, the established views of the church and its clerks.

At the close of the Miller's prologue, for instance, Chaucer's narrator cautions every "gentil wight" not to expect anything that "toucheth gentillesse / And eek moralitee and hoolynesse" in the two tales that follow the Knight's tale:

> The Millere is a cherl; ye knowe wel this.
> So was the Reve eek and othere mo,
> And harlotrie they tolden bothe two.
> (1.3182–84)

Readers no longer take the narrator's remarks at face value, nor do they treat Chaucer's fabliaux as if they were just elaborate bawdy jokes. Nonetheless, the Miller and especially the Reeve have not been adequately appreciated for the contribution each makes to Chaucer's love debate. We still are inclined to look at the sequence of tales in fragment 1 in a descending order of value, in part because the dominant view of love in the fourteenth century does not include the experience of love in the marriage bed of the lower classes.

The Miller's tale has been discussed often enough as a response to the Knight's tale. It has been justly praised for its broad good humor and for the aplomb with which the Miller demystifies the courtly notion of love presented by the Knight. The Reeve's tale, on the other hand, all too often has been regarded as a mean-spirited and humorless response to the Miller's tale, and it certainly has not been examined as a serious statement about fundamental human relationships.[75] The Reeve is forever linked with the Miller and the two tales complement one another in important ways. But the Reeve's tale can stand on its own merits, even as it looks forward to the Wife of Bath's prologue and tale as well as back to the Miller's.

We might begin our "redemption" of the Reeve and his tale by refusing to view the tale as an act of retaliation against the Miller. The Miller and the Reeve may be poles apart in their personalities and in their social conduct, but the familiarity they display toward one another—they are on a first-name basis—suggests a playful as opposed to a bitter rivalry between them. The rough play that obtains between them may even imply a bond of friendship. If we overlook for the moment the Reeve's "choleric" nature, we will see that his tale responds to the larger theological and marital issues raised by the Knight's tale as well as the Miller's, and that it projects the Reeve's distinctive vision on these matters.

One indication that the Reeve understands the issues is that he too has a pair of young lovers, a young attractive woman and an older figure whose moral authority is the central thematic concern of his tale. In all three tales an accident occurs at a crucial juncture of the plot—a fall from a horse, a misdirected blow to the head, or the tail—that helps bring into focus the concept of justice envisioned by the tale. Instead of being third in the series of Chaucer's conversational game, the Reeve, upon closer inspection, may provide us with an important synthesis of the previous two tales.

It appears at first that the Reeve intends to avoid a personal reponse to the Miller's tale by delivering a sermon on the four "gleedes" that "longen unto eelde." It is only after the Host rebukes him that he announces his intention to "quite" the Miller with his tale. Just what it is in the Miller's tale he intends to answer has not been asked, although it is clear from the moment that they begin bickering that the Reeve is concerned with an ideal of marriage that he fears the Miller will abuse. When he hears Robyn announce that he will tell "a legend and a lyf," an adulterous and potentially blasphemous tale about a carpenter duped by a clerk, the Reeve protests in the name of a marital *pryvetee:*

> Stynt thy clappe!
> Lat be thy lewed dronken harlotrye.
> It is a synne and eek a greet folye
> To apeyren any man, or hym defame,
> And eek to bryngen wyves in swich fame.
> Thou mayst ynogh of othere thynges seyn.
>   (1.3144–49)

Here it looks as if it is the Reeve more than the Miller who links John and himself with Joseph, a union that is hard to deny or resist. Both the Reeve and Joseph are carpenters; both are old; both practice chastity; both are grumpy; and both see marriage as a sacred trust.[76]

The Reeve's fears are not realized by the Miller's performance, but in his own prologue the Reeve shows that the Miller's tale has touched a profoundly personal nerve. One indication of this is in his introspective sermonizing and his exaggerated bluster over the Miller's story (he is the only one not laughing). The sermonizing and anger are intended, I believe, to divert attention from the unexpected wound inflicted on him by the Miller's tale, the precise nature of which I will elucidate in the course of my discussion of his tale. First, let me return to the marriage theme.

The most compelling reason to treat the Reeve's tale as a serious statement on love and marriage is the way in which he embodies, as no other pilgrim does, the very real conflict that existed in the fourteenth century between the theological ideal of marriage and the fact of human nature, between procreation and sexual desire, *caritas* and *cupiditas*. The terms of this debate are well established in the *Canterbury Tales*. The *Knight's Tale*, which begins and ends with a marriage, represents the institution as a prerequisite to personal and social order, a sentiment echoed by the Merchant when he has the old knight January, a double for the Reeve, remark that "Mariage is a ful greet sacrement. / He which that hath no wyf, I holde hym shent" (4.1319–20). The *Parson's Tale* neatly summarizes the theological ideal bequeathed by Paul and Augustine to the Middle Ages: "For certes, in so muche as the sacrement of mariage is so noble and so digne, so muche is it gretter synne for to breken it, for God made mariage in paradys, in the estaat of innocence, to multiplye mankynde to the service of God" (10.882). The Parson goes on to say that the true purpose of wedded love is to cleanse one from fornication, to replenish holy church of "good lynage," and to "chaungeth deedly synne into venial synne bitwixe hem that been ywedded" (10.918).

For the Parson, as for Paul and Augustine, God sanctioned marriage in order to bring lust *(cupiditas)* under a lawful bond. It was instituted so those partners could help one another overcome their random physical urges by "canalizing them into the safety of the marriage-bed."[77] Accordingly, even if the first natural bond of society is between man and wife, the purpose of marriage, even before the fall, is the procreation of children. In Augustine's view, marriage is concerned more with the birth of children than with their conception through intercourse, and woman was created as man's helpmate for the express purpose of bearing children.[78] For Augustine it follows that celibacy is the highest good and procreation is the only justification for sexual intercourse in marriage.

As I suggested earlier, Chaucer's most impassioned voice on the subject of marriage, the Wife of Bath, takes issue with the theological ideal on the grounds that it fails to recognize that sexual pleasure is an essential component of marital love. Chaucer uses her prologue and tale as a veritable "mirror of marriage," not to dismiss the theological ideal (the Wife tells us both in her prologue and in her tale that she married all of her husbands at the "church door"), but to transform it by bringing it into conformity with human nature and human experience. What makes her testimony so important to the *Canterbury Tales* is that she insists that the erotic is consistent with the Christian ideal. Hugh of St. Victor, in his discussion of marriage, presents the traditional patristic argument of an inverse relationship existing between sexual activity and *caritas*. He cites those marriages where sex does not occur as especially productive of grace and charity, "As in old people, when fleshly ardor disappears the order of charity nevertheless flourishes."[79] If Hugh's idea is to convert love into *caritas*, the Wife of Bath, employing an incarnational metaphor, finds a way to include *caritas* in marital love:

> I nyl envye no virginitee.
> Let hem be breed of pured whete-seed,
> And lat us wyves hoten barly-breed;
> And yet with barly-breed, Marke telle kan,
> Oure Lord Jhesu refresshed many a man.
>
> (3.142–46)

In her prologue the Wife confesses that she could not withhold her "chambre of Venus" from a good fellow, "Al were he short, or long, or blak, or whit; / I took no kep, so that he liked me, / How poore he was, ne eek of what degree" (3.624–26). From her perspective, sexual activity increased her level of generosity and made each encounter an act of *caritas* as well as *cupiditas*. When she alludes shamelessly to her sexual organ as her "bele chose" (3.447, 3.510) and boasts that all of her husbands assured her that she had the "beste *quoniam*"[80] that might be, she aims to offset Jerome's remark that a woman casts her shame away "Whan she cast of hir smok" (3.782–83).

Yet, for all of the use the Wife of Bath has made of her instrument she appears to have no offspring. For her, marriage has been more for delight than for the world to multiply. Early on in her prologue she indicates that she is familiar with the biblical text where God bids human beings to increase and multiply, and she turns it inside out by interpreting it to mean women can use marriage to increase their wealth and multiply the number of marriage partners they can have. Perhaps the boldest defense she makes of her sexual practices occurs after she has debated with herself all the pros and cons of chastity and concludes with the assertion that she will "bistowe the flour of al myn age / In the actes and in fruyt of mariage" (3.113–14). Her appreciation of fruit and seed centers wholly on erotic pleasure. For her, as for the narrator of *Cleanness,* the erotic passions of marriage recall the good bestowed upon human beings by God in paradise. She reiterates this point later in her prologue when, in her reverie, she resolves to sell the "bran" as she best can now that the "flower" is gone. In her old age the Wife of Bath intends to continue her "praktike" of taking her pleasure in the marriage bed—"Welcome the sixte, whan that evere he shal." All of this is repeated and highlighted in her tale of transformation where the Hag insists on consummating her marriage to the knight, an act he finds more repugnant and onerous than the marriage itself. The Hag summons all of her rhetorical powers to persuade him to transform his *cupiditas* (rape) into *caritas* (acknowledgment of her desire).

The Reeve, conversely, confides that he has not used his instrument in marriage as fully as he might. The rusty blade that hangs idly by his side bears mute testimony to his physical restraint and sexual abstemiousness and may account for his choler more than any bodily humor does. He is one of those husbands who might benefit from both the Wife of Bath's "scoleiyng" and from her "praktike." If the Reeve and the Wife of Bath appear to make for a very odd couple, there are significant parallels between them. Both are now old, both are readily given to moralizing, both have risen within their class to a level of economic prosperity that sets them apart from most members of their respective vocations, both speak of marriage as a means to social advancement, and both talk openly and confessionally about their sexual appetites. What the Wife of Bath has to say in defense of sexual pleasure gives us a keener sense of the Reeve's personal affliction, the "nayl" in his will. What we learn about him from his *General Prologue* portrait—his work habits, his secretiveness and his furtiveness, and his manner of dress—solidifies the impression of a deep conflict between the Reeve's desires and his religious discipline.

First we learn that the Reeve affects the style and demeanor of a preacher: his hair is "round yshorn" about his ears, his top is "dokked lyk a preest biforn," and his surcoat is tucked in his girdle "as is a frere aboute." The parallels to members of the clergy are less conjectures by the pilgrim Chaucer and more projections by the Reeve himself. The Reeve's propensity to moralize has prompted A. C. Spearing to remark that the Reeve is a person who appears to have listened to many sermons and "perhaps preached a few himself to his neighbors."[81] His asperity, reformer's zeal, and fetish for proverbial wisdom may suggest a cold New England Puritan or, as Spearing proposes, the Reeve may serve as a mild caricature of a lower-class Lollard.

Given what we know of reeves and this reeve in particular, Spearing makes a very plausible suggestion. Chaucer's Reeve is extremely competent at his job and he approaches his duties as if they were a religious calling. He manages the workers under his supervision with aplomb, although his workers as well as the auditors and bailiffs who deal with him are "adrad of hym as of the deeth." Striking fear in workers may have been required of reeves because they occupied an awkward position in the farm hierarchy. If they were regarded by the workers as affiliated with the seigneurial class, they were regarded by the lords of these farms as affiliated with the peasants. Reeves had to be very skillful at their jobs because their work was carefully audited and they were held financially responsible for any shortfall in crops or deficiencies that came about as a result of pilfering by workers or as a consequence of error in their prediction of yield.[82] They were expected to keep watch over all kinds of things, especially the activity of carters who were inclined to cheat. Not only did they have to oversee the work of others, they also had to keep records, an activity that would frequently involve them with clerks (there is strong evidence that most reeves could read and write).[83] Traffic with clerks may account for some of the Reeve's biblical knowledge and vocational aspirations.

Most reeves were elected to their position by a vote of those peasants who held significant land parcels and who were relatively well off themselves. Apparently, Chaucer's Reeve has held his post for many years and has protected himself in his dealings with his lord by having a contract, referred to as a covenant. He, like other reeves, was responsible for supervising the communal activities on the farm and was charged not only with enforcing regulations in regard to farm labor but also with enforcing the moral standards established by the group of peasants who had elected him.[84] Given the Reeve's enthusiasm for morality, perhaps the caricature Chaucer has in mind for the Reeve owes something to Langland and to Piers Plowman. In passus 19 of the B text, Grace makes Piers a reeve (260). She gives him a team of four oxen identified as the four evangelists. She also gives Piers four stots to harrow after the oxen have plowed. These stots are Augustine, Jerome, Ambrose, and Gregory. Chaucer describes the Reeve as riding on a stot, a possible allusion to the Reeve's spiritual pride, or to Augustine, who enjoyed his own triumph over animal appetites. The image of the slender Reeve riding on his stallion called Scot is impressive and perfectly illustrates the enormity and drive of his "coltes tooth," as well as the control he exercises over it.[85]

Although he has succeeded through his self-discipline to increase the amount and worth of his lord's livestock and crops, his economic regimen has resulted in a corresponding conservation of his bodily fluids:

> For sikerly, whan I was bore, anon
> Deeth drough the tappe of lyf and leet it gon,
> And ever sithe hath so the tappe yronne
> Til that almoost al empty is the tonne.
> The streem of lyf now droppeth on the chymbe.
>   (1.3891–95)

The Reeve's penchant for storing grain also has its counterpoint in the storing of his own seed. Thief that he is, he has "stolen" the sexual pleasure due to his wife because of his economic and conservationist habit of mind—and body. The most negative outcome of this discipline occurs in the tale with the commodification of marriage or commodification of the body, where Symkin and the parson (doubles for the Reeve) control both Malyne's body and her marriage prospects.

Throughout his prologue we hear in the Reeve's voice a note of resignation, which humanizes him and makes him sympathetic even if not likable. In both his prologue and his tale, the Reeve's contempt, as Winthrop Wetherbee has observed, is directed more toward himself than it is toward the world.[86] Beneath the biblical / sermonic voice that he affects we can hear that for the Reeve as well as the Wife of Bath old age has not proved to be the refuge from sexual ardor it was promised to be by Hugh and Augustine. He knows in the flesh what Freud has since taught us about sex: with age desire increases:

> We olde men, I drede, so fare we:
> Til we be roten, kan we nat be rype;
> We hoppen alwey whil the world wil pype.
> For in oure wyl ther stiketh evere a nayl,
> To have a hoor heed and a grene tayl,
> As hath a leek; for thogh oure myght be goon,
> Oure wyl desireth folie evere in oon.
>
> (1.3874–80)

What prompts this sudden outburst? These admissions seem out of character for the secretive Reeve. Apparently, the sexual energy released in the Miller's tale, especially the willing participation of the carpenter's wife in the encounter and the liberating effect sexual pleasure appears to have had on her—she initiates making Absolon the butt of her joke—provokes the Reeve to look at himself and at his own sexual attitudes. The Miller's depiction of John as a religious fanatic who is sexually inactive, has stung the Reeve in a personal way; moreover, from the Miller's point of view, it is John who violates the marriage code ("He knew nat Catoun") and it is he who restrains Alison's animal appetite by holding her "narwe in cage." He and not Alison is responsible for her adulterous encounter with Nicholas. The Reeve may "grucche" loudly that he is not amused because he was once a carpenter, but the "truth" of the Miller's tale cuts deeper. The Reeve is more like John than he wants to admit, and however disagreeable on moral grounds he may find the Miller's tale, it brings home to him the fact of women's sexuality and desire as independent from his own.

In his complaint the Reeve names the source of his affliction: a divided consciousness. He is, as he says, like a leek with "an hoor heed and a grene tayl." In keeping with the Augustinian ideal, he places the blame for his discomfort entirely on his green tail when, in actuality, the problem resides more in his head. The lesson he can learn from his own tale is how to restore some balance between his head and his tail. Ironically, what allows him to engage the sexual issue in its naked form in his tale is the fabliau discourse, those very "cherles termes" he associated earlier with the Miller, as if that idiom were not his own. More than its supposed parody or imitation of the Miller's tale and its discourse, the Reeve's use of churlish language works to release his own suppressed drives and desires. In the fabliau discourse of the tale the Augustinian stot becomes the horse which is set free to frolic in the meadow with the mares. The unfettered stallion is a telling shift in gender from the mare found in most sources to the tale and suggests that in this version of the story it is the male libido of the Reeve that has been tethered too tightly. The Reeve's identification with horses in his portrait and in his prologue connects the stallion to his own inner desires and allows us to see the stallion among the mares as a fulfillment of the Reeve's desire to experience sex once in his life as a romp. The "wehee" of the stallion (1.4066) recalls Alison's playful "tehee" (1.3740) in the Miller's tale, suggesting the Reeve shares John's (and Nicholas's) desire for Alison as well.[87] Like the horse, the Reeve's narrative gets away from him and works in an independent way. The tale unfolds as if it were a dream where contradictions and doubleness abound and what is unresolved in one's head rights or corrects itself through one's tail—or tale. The deeper concerns of the Reeve, what is truly personal to him, are worked out as he packs his tale with his own moral ambivalence. Not only will the stallion be released, but also Malyne and Symkin's wife will experience the sex they have desired and the demons of the marriage bed will be exorcised.

The Reeve, who aspires to anonymity ("And evere he rood the hyndreste of oure route"), is nevertheless found everywhere in his tale.

The first place we find him is in the parson, the Reeve's "first mover," who functions in the tale as a paterfamilias or the head of a noble family arranging the marriages of, first, his daughter and, now, his grand-daughter. The parson betokens the intergenerational social climbing of the contemporary clergy's abuse of religious authority and the economic basis of the marriage institution, despite its sacramental status. The Lollard in the Reeve severely criticizes, in the most cutting sarcasm, the parson's abuse of what is sacred: his appropriation of the goods of the church and his identification of his own blood with the blood of Christ.[88] This fornicating parson never appears in person in the tale to receive at firsthand the punishment he deserves for his pride and the abuses he has perpetrated, but his social ambitions collapse with the defeat of Symkin.

If the Reeve, like the parson, is old, hidden from view, socially ambitious, and convinced of his holiness, he is, oddly enough, even more like Symkin. Although Symkin has the Miller's physical characteristics, he has the Reeve's habits of mind, his yeoman's status, his pride, cunning, and affiliation with the church. Symkin's marriage with its "many a panne of bras" and his "greet sokene" with the college is parallel to the Reeve's business enterprise and resourcefulness. Like the Reeve, Symkin can be a clever thief, outwitting the manciple of the college, and when he pits his practical man's ingenuity against the subtle calculations of the clerks, we see the Reeve's scorn for youthful masters. In the tale Symkin is also likened to a horse. Through Symkin, the Reeve will experience the punishment and epiphany he deserves.

It is clear from the start of the Reeve's tale that marriage plays a vital role in it that it does not in the Miller's tale, most graphically illustrated in the respective households depicted in the two tales, particularly the bedrooms. Contrary to the prevailing view of these two tales—the Miller's bright, the Reeve's dark—it is Symkin's house that gives us a carpenter's eye view of the well-ordered interior. In retrospect, it is John's house that is full of dark corners and Symkin's that projects an appealing sense of comfort, coziness, and belonging. The scene with Symkin sitting by the fire and offering hospitality to the clerks (he makes their bed for them himself), and the communal meal, a roast goose ("They soupen and they speke hem to solace, / And drynken evere strong ale atte beste"), all point to a congenial marital and family life. The differences between the two households are epitomized in the sleeping arrangements, which are crucial to the resolution of the two plots.

In the Miller's tale the sleeping arrangement in the tubs mirrors the actual marital relationship in John's house. Throughout, the Miller conceives of the sexual configuration as triangular, or quadrangular, if we include Absolon ever present at the shot window when John and Alison are in bed—and when Nicholas and Alison are. The three tubs aligned in the gables reveal the separateness of the principals involved, the absence of any intimate connection that binds any combination of two people in the tale. The triangularity in the male consciousness—ranging from John's expectation that he will become a cuckold, to Nicholas's insistence that he possess Alison while John is in the room, and that he too trick Absolon—indicates that the Miller regards it as a norm, an interesting variation of Freud's observation that there are never only two people in bed.

In the Reeve's tale Symkin invites the clerks to sleep in the one communal bedroom, "Noght from his owene bed ten foot or twelve." The presence of Malyne in the room adds to the snugness of the interior and she shows her unity with her parents in a most befitting way. I refer to what is one of the more amusing yet serious examples of "compaignye" in all of the *Canterbury Tales,* the night music emanating from the three adults as a sign of their mutuality or habitual bodily proximity:

> This millere hath so wisely bibbed ale
> That as an hors he fnoreth in his sleep,
> Ne of his tayl bihynde he took no keep.
> His wyf bar hym a burdon, a ful strong;
> Men myghte hir rowtyng heere two furlong;
> The wenche rowteth eek, *par compaignye.*
>
> (1.4162–67)

The scene deliberately invites the derision of the clerks, or that aspect of the Reeve that aspires to be one, and then defends itself against their disdain by contrasting the natural bodily responses of the family to the unnatural schemes for revenge in the minds of the clerks.

The placement of the cradle in the bedroom completes the picture of domestic harmony. Before retiring, the wife sets the cradle at the foot of the bed "to rokken, and yeve the child to sowke," details that establish her maternal care and affection. The infant also attests to the primacy of the procreational, with the offspring spaced some nineteen years apart. The cradle becomes the focal point of the bedroom scene, a signpost by which the wife, and later Aleyn, guides her steps in the dark and upon whose positioning the plot hinges. The displacement or movement of the cradle is at once the premeditated trick equivalent to Nicholas's flood scheme and the symbol of the clerks' disruption of Symkin's domestic order. The sexual "auntres" initiated by the individual clerks come to be seen in the nature of a violation of an invisible order of a domestic unity that is integral with the values of love and marriage. The night maneuvers of the clerks bring to the forefront the sexual anarchy that is, from the Reeve's perspective, resident in the Miller's "punishment" of John. The Reeve's comment at the end of his prologue to the "balke" in the Miller's eye refers to the Miller's blindness to the social and marital implications—what the Reeve perceives to be the Miller's lack of disapprobation—in Nicholas's behavior. Once we see Symkin as the Reeve we see how painful the Miller's joke has been to him.

It is the women, however, who force the Reeve to confront his own "sins" (of omission), by an explosion of their own erotic energy. The women may start out as objects of exchange but they quickly become active figures who turn their individual sexual encounters into their own adventure.[89] The Reeve makes a special point of reporting the wife's feelings and the sense of pleasure she derives from her frolic with John:

> Withinne a while this John the clerk up leep,
> And on this goode wyf he leith on soore.
> So myrie a fit ne hadde she nat ful yoore;
> He priketh harde and depe as he were mad.
>   (1.4228–31)

This scene may be both exciting and distressing to the Reeve. We might have expected such explicit detail in the encounter between Aleyn and Malyne, but it is the wife that interests him more. "So myrie a fit ne hadde she nat ful yoore," which implies that sex has been merry in the past but perhaps not practiced enough for her satisfaction. John's frenzied reaction, "He priketh harde and depe as he were mad," gives further impetus to the exquisite joy the wife takes in an act of sheer sexual abandon. It is difficult to imagine the Reeve as distanced from the scene. He protects the innocence of the wife by suggesting that she is too drunk ("hir joly whistle" is "wel ywet"), to realize her lover is not her husband, and the sleep of contentment she lapses into after her fit invokes the whole atmosphere of domestic tranquillity witnessed earlier, only now the sexual is included as part of that harmony.[90]

In encompassing the women's point of view the Reeve is led to an unforeseen conclusion. Malyne's enjoyment of her (k)night's "auntre" does not fit into the Reeve's marital perspective but it does compel him to recognize that it may be an integral part of a love relationship. Without fully embracing what he terms the Miller's "dronken harlotrie," the Reeve makes a concession to the more uninhibited life of the body.

The carnivalesque conclusion that follows, in which Symkin is dealt a blow on the head, is reminiscent of the uproarious ending of the Miller's tale. The misdirected blow becomes a well-directed blow, just as Absolon's coulter hits the appropriate if not the intended target, because the wife strikes at the source of Symkin's problem. She is the agent of justice in the tale, not of revenge. As she readies herself to deliver the stroke, she espies a "whit thyng in hir ye," which she imagines is a voluper worn by one of the clerks. If we recall the Reeve's self-description in the prologue as a "white top" and as a leek with a "hoor heed and a grene tayl," then the wife's blow has greater resonance. All of his life the Reeve has imagined that it is his green tail that is the source of his affliction. The wife's blow shows that it is his head not his tail that needs remediation. The wife's blow replaces the Reeve's earlier determination to establish a moral truth—the "verray sooth" with which he began his tale—with a personal truth about the consequences that ensue when we separate the head from the tail.

Thus far I have been talking about the wife's blow in essentially personal and psychological terms. Now we can see it in relation to the Knight's tale as a comic inversion of the metaphysical rationale of chivalry. The Knight conceives of chivalry as the imposition of order: social, political, and marital. In his tale this order is represented by the will of the gods, the Boethian design, the hierarchy of the gods and its human counterpart in the political structure articulated by Theseus in his speech on the "faire cheyne of love." These structures make their appearance in the Reeve's tale in the social, economic, and ecclesiastical institutions that dominate and control the lives of the characters, especially the women. At the beginning of the tale Symkin is part simple-minded victim of and believer in some or all of these structures and their imperatives. In the Reeve's vision, however, these authority structures are not beyond human control, as they appear to be in the Knight's tale. The wife's blow is a momentary suspension or loosening of the bonds of that order. What is glimpsed is the subversion of the order of money, social advancement, and power and necessity that allows for a manifestation of *caritas* not readily discoverable in the Knight's tale.

If we return to the bedroom we can see the entire scene that is played out there as christological, from Symkin's falling backward onto his wife to her waking with the words of the crucifixion, "in manus tuas," on her lips. Her invocation of Christ and the cross of Bromeholm places the scene in the context of a psychomachia in which she functions as the divine instrument of redemption. First, she liberates herself; that is, she keeps her own head and tail intact. It is fitting that she should mistake Symkin and Aleyn, her husband and a clerk, for fiends who are oppressing her on both her head and her womb—both places where women are oppressed by their husbands and by clerks—for they are the demons that haunt the marriage bed. The theater or vast arena created by Theseus to display the noble emotions ("for love and for encrees of chivalrye") of the aristocratic world are here compressed into the narrow bedroom of Symkin's house, and it is the marriage bed (the site of reciprocal love or marital *pryvetee*) that serves as the microcosm of human experience.

In this, Chaucer follows the example of Eustache Deschamps who, in his *Miroir de mariage,* compares the marriage bed to a forge, at once a workshop or a mill and a place where things are given shape and form. As a forge, the marriage bed, "La recept pour chascun forgier," is both the means to procreation and the sanctuary of utmost intimacy. Deschamps speaks of the forge as "secret place," with the Middle English sense of *pryvetee.* As the site of procreation, the forge is one way that humankind escapes from death or extinction. The marriage bed also allows individual human beings to experience through sexual love a psychological triumph over death. This is why Deschamps sees pleasure as a necessary part of the forge. If human beings had no pleasure in forging ("Car, s'en forgant ne delitassent"), he says, then human beings would leave the forge and forging would not be important to them and to their nature.[91]

The aubade effects for Malyne a moment of grace and discovery akin to her mother's. Her offering of the cake to Aleyn is her act of liberation. It may even be eucharistic or christological, once we realize that medieval women associated the gift of food with the gift of love and both with Christ's gift of self.[92] In the farewell Malyne asserts her own will. Free for once from the parson and from Symkin and the whole order of theological and social restraint that they represent, she shows a generosity and depth of feeling not manifest in any of the male figures, particularly the clerks. The clerks, those notorious demystifiers of *pryvetee*, double in the Reeve's tale as embodiments of the aristocratic perspective. They set out from the college like a pair of young Quixote's eager to tilt at Symkin's mill. After suffering a setback in their first skirmish with Symkin, they renew their assault by preying upon the women and justifying their revenge by concocting a quaint turn on the law of reciprocity. The clerks succeed in their humiliation of Symkin, possessing the women and administering a thorough, if gratuitous, beating to him after he has tripped and fallen to the ground. The violence and triumphant escape of the clerks exemplifies the Reeve's parody of the chivalric ethos. In so doing, the Reeve proves to be more realistic than either the Knight or the Miller. In his tale, as in life, not everything balances out, nor does everybody get what he or she deserves.

In his peroration the Reeve, in keeping with his personality and profession, cannot resist moralizing and rendering an account of everything that Symkin, this "proude millere," has lost. The proverb he chooses to summarize his view, "A gylour shal hymself bigyled be," indicates that whatever anger the Reeve had toward the Miller has subsided, since this proverb is much milder, and applies in equal measure to himself, than the one he started out with, "For leveful is with force force of-showve," which sounds ominously like the logic and legalese of the clerks in his tale. It would be too optimistic to assume that the Reeve undergoes a transvaluation of values through the telling of his tale, but it is not too much to say that his little journey to the mill or forge at Trumpyngtoun has put him back in touch with his peasant origins and the life of the body. There is a nostalgia, return of the repressed, or search for a lost intimacy in the Reeve's tale and the fabliau discourse as a whole

that Chaucer suggests transcends the tale and speaks to a deeper long-
ing in the Canterbury pilgrims and their audience. This nostalgia is
what Bakhtin calls the *folkloric*. Folkloric time is connected to the
communal and to a work-oriented, agricultural base. It involves a feel-
ing for time that has as its heart "a taking-apart and putting-together of
social everyday time, the time of holidays and ceremonies connected
with the agricultural labor cycle, with the seasons of the year, the
periods of the day, the stages in the growth of plants and cattle."[93] In
folkloric time human life and nature are perceived in the same catego-
ries, as are their subcategories involving copulation, pregnancy, ripen-
ing, old age, and death.[94] Bakhtin recognizes that the late Middle Ages
are beyond the folkloric or pre-class society but that the immanent unity
of time is preserved in the "treasure house of language," and in a con-
cept of collective labor.[95]

It has been said of the Reeve, in contrast to the Miller, that he betrays
his class interests, that he has clerical ambitions, and that he acts as an
agent of seigneurial control.[96] This is only partly true. We have seen that
in his work the Reeve is still closely attuned to nature and its rhythms:
"Wel wiste he by the droghte and by the reyn / The yeldynge of his seed
and of his greyn" (1.595–96). His habit of comparing himself to a horse,
a leek, and a medlar fruit speaks to his affinity to the natural world, and
it is appropriate for someone who has been a carpenter to describe his
moral struggle as a nail in the will rather than as a thorn in the flesh. The
Reeve's tale is also filled with folkloric elements related to the commu-
nal, especially in the bedroom and sleeping arrangements of Symkin's
house where individual life sequences have not yet been made distinct
and where the private sphere has not yet fully evolved. The traces of
communal life also appear in the rituals of eating, drinking, farting, and
copulation that take place as an integral part of the little world of Symkin's
house. Symkin's "fall" with his cry of "harrow" suggests a symbolic
death, rebirth, and redemption. The lesson or the "schooling" offered by
Symkin's wife could lead Symkin (and the Reeve) to a reintegration
with the feminine (nature) and with his origins. The christological refer-
ences that abound combine with the folkloric elements to place the Reeve
and his tale into the larger narrative of the Christian epic of salvation.

In retrospect, the Miller and the Reeve may be somewhat at an ad-
vantage in Chaucer's love debate. As peasants, they exist apart from the

dominant discourse of love, and the medium of the fabliau affords them an unorthodox vocabulary with which to address the issue. With this discourse, the Miller and the Reeve alter the terms of the love debate in fragment 1; they show that Chaucer does locate in the "churls"—in the rhythm of work and play and in the familiar structures of marriage and family life—a source of *caritas* more commonly associated with the Knight's aristocratic or the Parson's theological view.

4.
"Com hider, love, to me!" :
The Pardoner's Untransformed Discourse

> Those who do not have power over the story that dominates their lives, power to retell it, rethink it, deconstruct it, joke about it, and change it as times change, truly are powerless because they cannot think new thoughts.
>
> *Salman Rushdie*[97]

The Pardoner endures as one of Chaucer's more fascinating creations, appealing to scholars and students alike and enjoying a popularity today that surpasses the enthusiasm of any previous era. We respond to him because he is one of us. Cynical, alienated, and forlorn, we meet him as the antihero in the pages of the modern existentialist novel, reminiscent as he is of one of Fyodor Dostoevsky's tortured souls or of Albert Camus's garrulous Jean-Baptiste Clamance. The Pardoner shares an unconsecrated affinity with scores of outcast, disillusioned, and homeless fugitives (the medieval *vagabundus*), all of whom are animated by ego, paralyzed by guilt, obsessed with the enigma of Christ, and eager to confess their faults. While no one sees the Pardoner any longer as the one lost soul among the pilgrims or as an embodiment of evil, a corresponding effort has not been mounted to view the Pardoner as undergoing any awakening or experiencing an epiphany that might result in a repudiation of his theological outlook or way of life. Chaucer gives the Pardoner a legitimate place on the pilgrimage; he does not suddenly burst upon the scene to sell his wares and just as suddenly disappear, like that utter materialist, the Canon. The Pardoner remains on pilgrim-age, even after his disastrous encounter with Harry Bailly at the end of his tale, suggesting that he still is a quester, still is in search of some-thing, and that he does not reside on the far side of despair. What the Pardoner seeks, emanating from a region of the self beyond conscious desire, is epitomized by the song he sings, "Com hider, love, to me" (1.672). On the surface the lyric comes across as typical of the Pardoner's cynicism and parody. Its association with the Song of Songs and with a passage from Paul (Ephesians 5.27), both of which imply a union with the church, may suggest that for all his apostasy the Pardoner is ambiva-lent about his alienation from the church or, more likely, he desires the sense of community it promises. The song is also a (Prufrockian) love lyric, in which the Pardoner situates himself in a passive role, wanting love but unable or unwilling to achieve or pursue it himself ("And how should I begin?"). Seeing the Pardoner as at least receptive to love is important because it means that the Pardoner's prologue and tale are more than a register of his misdeeds; they are also an attempt at self-understanding and tell us that the issues he raises in them, however per-sonalized, are not peculiar to him alone but are, as we know from all the other tales, symptomatic of his society and the pilgrim audience as a whole.

The Pardoner may be an outcast, then, perhaps a self-appointed one, but Chaucer not only gives him a voice, he makes it an eloquent one, indicating that what the Pardoner has to say contributes to the conversa-tion in a meaningful way. In keeping with the tenor of his sermons, the Pardoner's discourse will raise important questions about sin and redemp-tion, about original sin, and about the conception of Christ as the medi-eval church fostered it. It is important to remember, as David Aers points out, that those activities in which the Pardoner is engaged—the traffic in indulgences and the selling of relics—were activities sponsored and sanc-tioned by the church. Pardoners were official agents of the church in the late Middle Ages, and Chaucer's Pardoner "dramatises fundamental prob-lems about contemporary religious life, the status of official authority, the nature of the church and its claims to keep the only path to indi-vidual salvation."[98] His discourse, as Lee Patterson has shown, contains many of the issues central to the theological and ecclesiastical debates in the fourteenth century on indulgences, relics, and pilgrimages.[99] In his prologue and tale the Pardoner parodies, by practiced imitation, the discourse of theological belief prominent in the sermons of late medieval England. It is this aspect of the Pardoner's person and performance on which I will concentrate. Taken together, the Pardoner's person, prologue, and tale constitute Chaucer's most complete statement of the crisis confronting the church: its image, its discourse, and its moral deficiency.

Although some of the best writing and thinking on the Pardoner has been advanced in recent years, illuminating some of the dark corners of his existence, he remains as elusive as ever, refusing to yield all of his secrets to us.[100] For some readers, of course, the real mystery surrounding the Pardoner involves his sexual condition and his largely unsuccessful attempts to conceal the true nature of his sexual identity. Certainly the Pardoner's sexual nature is an inseparable part of who he is and accounts for some of his paradoxical behavior, but his problems are at least as much intellectual and theological as they are sexual and psychological. Throughout the *Canterbury Tales,* from his portrait in the *General Prologue* through his interruption of the Wife of Bath, his confessional prologue, his tale proper, and the epilogue to his tale, the Pardoner appears more intent upon projecting a positive image of himself than concealing what is perceived as a negative one. This is no small distinction. We are made aware of this by Chaucer's narrator who, at the end of the Pardoner's *General Prologue* portrait, concludes his description with the observation "But trewely to tellen atte laste, / He was in chirche a noble ecclesiaste" (1.707–8). However ironic this comment was intended or turns out to be, it does link the Pardoner with the church in its ecclesiological or institutional role, an identification he is eager to cultivate in the minds of his Sunday audiences and one that he pursues with equal vigor in his performance before the pilgrim audience. Although the two performances are fundamentally the same in content, there are differences in setting, circumstance, and intent that obtain in one and not in the other. The reader is thus obliged to keep one eye on his sermon in its presumed "real" context—the church on Sunday—and the other on its immediate setting in the tale-telling game. The doubleness of this vision permits the reader to discern aspects of the Pardoner's motivation not apparent in the Pardoner's own account or in that of the narrator.

One of the Pardoner's secrets, apparently, is his ability to believe, at least temporarily, in the image of himself that he projects during his Sunday performances, which may explain why he never varies the nature of his presentation, "For I kan al by rote that I telle" (6.332). Something visibly happens to the Pardoner during his performances; he literally becomes The Pardoner, affecting a special voice and employing a set of carefully rehearsed gestures calculated to overwhelm his audiences. Not surprisingly, he becomes caught up in the whirlwind himself:

> I stonde lyk a clerk in my pulpet,
> And whan the lewed peple is doun yset,
> I preche so as ye han herd bifoore
> And telle an hundred false japes moore.
> Thanne peyne I me to strecche forth the nekke,
> And est and west upon the peple I bekke,
> As dooth a dowve sittynge on a berne.
> Myne handes and my tonge goon so yerne
> That it is joye to se my bisynesse.
>
> (6.391–99)

The Pardoner emerges as his own best audience, in love with the image of himself that he has created. It is this figure who speaks so powerfully and persuasively, and it is this image to which his audiences respond, reinforcing his own belief in this vision of himself.

By his account, his Sunday audiences have been only too eager to affirm him in the role of "noble ecclesiaste." At the end of each of his exhortations they turn him into a kind of sacred shrine, surrounding him as they do in order to be shriven by his "heigh power." He exults in the role, dispensing pardons, and showing his miraculous relics as if he were Christ himself. Presenting himself in the role of someone who can heal, pardon, and absolve, and then to be affirmed in that role by one's audience, allows the Pardoner his moment of transport and sense of self-actualization.

The Pardoner's hold on his public identity is tenuous at best because it does not arise from inside himself; it exists only in the eyes of his audience. The Pardoner needs to perform in order to be. He needs his audience to affirm and authenticate his existence. Accordingly, he returns to church each Sunday to preach. Although he preaches exceptionally well, and moves some members of his audience to repent, the Pardoner would have us believe, as he would like to believe himself, that avarice is the sole motive for his preaching:

> For myn entente is nat but for to wynne,
> And nothyng for correccioun of synne.
> I rekke nevere, whan that they been beryd,
> Though that hir soules goon a-blakeberyed!
> (6.403–6)

To avoid seeing himself for who he is, to avoid confronting the emptiness and insubstantiality of his life, the Pardoner has created a fancifully rapacious figure who is willing to impute the most vicious of impulses to himself, such as starving a widow and her family by unflinchingly snatching her last penny from her. As a sign of his superiority, he places himself outside the bounds of conventional morality, "beyond good and evil":

> Thus kan I preche agayn that same vice
> Which that I use, and that is avarice.
> But though myself be gilty in that synne,
> Yet kan I maken oother folk to twynne
> From avarice and soore to repente.
> But that is nat my principal entente;
> I preche nothyng but for coveitise.
> Of this mateere it oghte ynogh suffise.
> (6.427–34)

But it does not suffice. The Pardoner goes on to batter us with his transgressions and to boast of how he inverts the Christian ideal. He will not live in poverty; he will do no labor with his hands; he will have money, cheese, and wheat; he will not imitate the life of the apostles; he will drink liquor from the vine and have his wench in every town. By the end of his prologue the Pardoner sounds like someone in rebellion against whatever life has meant to him. His world is everything and it is nothing. He contends that he does not adhere to the Christian schema of salvation that he preaches about, but he cannot tolerate the reality of what it means simply to be human and to die. Each performance thus becomes a desperate attempt to forestall the onset of what Jean-Paul Sartre aptly calls *nausea,* the taste of one's own existence, the realization of one's superfluousness, of being *de trop*.

If the adulation of his audiences represents the triumph of the outer person over the inner, of the professional pardoner over the human, individual self, each triumph is also a kind of personal defeat. Despite the brilliance of his performance the reader—and the Pardoner himself—realizes how empty he has become, "hollow at the core." The Pardoner's real secret is that he no longer wishes to be the self that he is but that he refuses to become the self that he wants to be, a condition well illustrated in his (self-)representation of the Old Man.

The encounter between the rioters and the Old Man, the central episode in the Pardoner's tale, has been thoroughly and perceptively analyzed.[101] My interest in the scene centers on the theological implications of the Pardoner's *exemplum* and what it reveals about his own existential dilemma and that of the church. The Old Man has many identities: the old Adam, Paul's *vetus homo,* death itself, but always the Pardoner. As James Joyce says, "Every life is many days, day after day. We walk through ourselves, meeting robbers, ghosts, giants, old men, young men, wives, widows, brothers-in-love, but always meeting ourselves."[102] Is the Old Man a reflection of who the Pardoner is or is he the nightmare from which the Pardoner wants to awake? Certainly he gives us access to the Pardoner's inner self, his "agenbite of inwit." As do the rioters. Though guilty of every form of avarice, the rioters set out on their mission with the right intention. Their desire to conquer death may be interpreted as a desire to overcome the burden of the past, the legacy of original sin. They are poorly equipped for this task because they are not armed with the true image of Christ. Their meeting with the Old Man, who appears holy on the surface with his hair "clowt" and meek demeanor, should be transformative for them but results in a betrayal. The Old Man presents a false dilemma to the rioters. For one thing, he has control over his destiny. While he cannot return to his mother, the earth—that is, he cannot return to his original clay anymore than Christ, once born of his mother, can return to the Father without enduring a human death—there is someone who is willing to exchange his youth for his old age, and that is Christ. The Old Man does not deliver that message. No sincere seeker of Christ is denied his youth, as St. Paul explains it, because his redemption is available for all. But, like the Pardoner in his "youthful" garb, the Old Man is paralyzed, poised between alternative modes of being: unwilling to make the sacrifice of self in Christ and unable to accept physical death as an utter finality, the truth of which might allow him to accept the world in its fallen, finite, and imperfect state. The Old Man knows the landscape he traverses; he is in familiar territory. He knows the way to death and, more importantly, he knows the way to new life. He is not yet ready or willing to abandon his present condition.

For the "lewed peple," perhaps, the chief flaw in the Old Man's proposition is the literal interpretation of its terms. The church has insisted on a literal resurrection of the body of Christ. Part of the need for a transformation of its discourse is a clearer understanding of Christ's work and what his triumph over death entails. Even for Christ, whose words on the tree are "consummatum est,"—it is finished—death is the end of life. Christ, however, experiences his death as a fulfillment and not as a punishment. His life and work have come to an end; he has done that which is in him. In his *exemplum* the Pardoner does not direct his audience to that tree to contemplate that image. Instead, in sending the rioters to the tree of temptation, the site of the original sin, the Old Man sends them to their deaths, echoing the words of the Pardoner: "God save yow, that boghte agayn mankynde, / And yow amende" (6.766–67).

Under the tree the rioters do not simply kill one another in mutually self-defeating plots. They also subvert the fundamental bonds of community and fellowship that sustain human existence. The youngest, who is sent to procure bread and wine, purchases first a powerful rat poison to contaminate the wine. As a result the articles of the Offertory or of Christ's body and blood are never transformed into the real presence; Christ's being is never made immanent and instead of regeneration we get the death of the body and the spirit in this perversion of the Communion of the Mass. The instrument of death in the tale is rat poison because human life in the tale is reduced to the value of a rat. The Pardoner's personal viciousness and envy of human communities seeps through in his assault on human dignity. Neither the Old Man nor the Pardoner is interested in saving anyone from cupidity here, and both find it easier to prey upon human appetites and expose weakness than to embark on the true way themselves. The Old Man is no more inclined to embrace the rioters as fellows, however inhospitable they are toward him, than the Pardoner is the "lewed peple," the bitterness of their loneliness or the aimlessness of their wandering notwithstanding. Accordingly, the rioters kill one another once they let go of their pledge of brotherhood. We see the Pardoner take satisfaction in the disintegration of the vows the rioters proudly made at the outset: "Togidres han thise thre hir trouthes plight / *To lyve and dyen* ech of hem for oother, / As though he were his owene ybore brother" (6.702–4, emphasis added). In the same tenor, once the rioters discover the gold at the foot of the tree, the Pardoner remarks "No longer thanne after Deeth they soughte." They carry out their schemes under the guise of acts designed to secure the other's trust. The youngest bears the articles of hospitality and the other two allay the younger's fears by approaching him in play ("Arys as though thou woldest with hym pleye," the one rioter counsels the other). In this way the Pardoner's tale perverts the natural as well as the supernatural bonds which bind human beings together.

The darker side of the Pardoner's performance, which involves more than his making money by taking advantage of human weakness, is his betrayal of the people by perverting the purpose of the Mass and the figure of Christ at the center of it. As Eamon Duffy has shown, the liturgy "lay at the heart of medieval religion, and the Mass lay at the heart of the liturgy."[103] The central idea of the Mass is that the redemption of the world is re-enacted and Christ himself becomes present on the altar. At the elevation of the Eucharist the expectation is that the congregation is taken to Calvary and through their witness gathered into the passion and the full scope of salvation history.[104] Of all the sacraments, Duffy says, "the Mass was supremely the sacrament of Christ's blood." Prayers attendant on the Eucharist called for Christ's blood to wash away sin, for the old Adam to die, and for a new life to begin.[105] Centering on the Eucharist, on food and drink, and on Christ's blood, the Mass was, ideally, a social ritual that promoted communal wholeness and accommodated community spiritual needs.[106] As Duffy says, "the language of Eucharistic belief and devotion was saturated with communitarian and corporate imagery."[107] In practice, however, much of the congregation may have had difficulty feeling an integral part of the Mass without the invaluable guidance of something like *The Lay Folks Mass Book*. The Mass was conducted in Latin, the priest was often inaudible, and in large churches he was often not visible to a great portion of the congregation.[108] Little wonder that the elevation of the Eucharist became such a climactic focal point for the congregation, allowing it to participate directly with the priest in this act of communion. The emphasis that the church placed on salvation and penance and the role of the sacraments did little to promote the image of the church as a community or as the "totality of its believers," and did much to identify its true nature as the hierarchy of the priesthood and as the sole guardian of the sacramental system.[109]

For every congregation, but especially for the illiterate or "lewed peple," the sermon might well be the most dominant and memorable part of the service. Here the speaker was visible, spoke directly to the congregation, and in their own tongue. According to R. N. Swanson, these sermons were closely related to the confessional and penitential functions of the church, focusing primarily on sin, salvation, and reform of the self rather than on theological issues. Many of them were little more than what he describes as "horror stories" designed to frighten and warn the laity through bad examples.[110] If we use the Pardoner and his sermon (or the Parson with his manual on the seven deadly sins) as an index, we get a clear idea of the penitential and salvational emphasis of both the Mass and homiletic discourse. The Pardoner makes a point of separating himself from the people, placing himself high above them in the pulpit, and he makes a very visible display of the patents, seals, and bulls that grant him the authority to play a leading role in the Mass. The Pardoner may exaggerate but he does not deviate from the themes that are already written into the Mass and the discourse of the church, which begins in Adam's sin and ends in Christ's blood.

The Pardoner's sermon and *exemplum* help us to see how the church has emphasized theology at the expense of Christology. His theme is always and only *cupiditas,* never *caritas.* For the Pardoner, avarice is the first sin, "Adam oure fader, and his wyf also, / Fro Paradys to labour and to wo / Were dryven for that vice, it is no drede" (6.505–7), and human nature has been corrupted ever since:

> O glotyne, ful of cursednesse!
> O cause first of oure confusioun!

> O original of oure dampnacioun,
> Til Crist hadde boght us with his blood agayn!
> Lo, how deere, shortly for to sayn,
> Aboght was thilke cursed vileynye!
> Corrupt was al this world for glotonye.
>
> (6.498–504)

The corruption of the world is conveyed in the life of flagrant excess embodied in the rioters who habitually rend the body of Christ anew with their curses. Even the oath they swear to solidify their pact of brotherhood ends with the words: "And Cristes blessed body they torente" (6.709). The body of Christ, whose blood he says is spilt in human ingratitude, is used by the Pardoner to play upon the guilt of his audience and to exploit shamelessly their psychological needs. The Pardoner is at his cynical best when he speaks of the pathos of Christ's sacrifice, which he invokes at the end of his sermon and, most movingly, here:

> Allas, mankynde, how may it bitide
> That to thy creatour, which that thee wroghte,
> And with his precious herte-blood thee boghte,
> Thou art so fals and so unkynde, allas?
>
> (6.900–903)

In the Pardoner's presentation, the dominant image of Christ's body is the body in bits and pieces, torn and bloody. Christ's body should be the foundation stone for the community or union with God and the creation as celebrated in the Mass. In the Pardoner's tale the human body in general, as well as the flesh and body of Christ and of the Old Man, is presented as repulsive. It has been said of the Pardoner, based on the images that he adverts to, such as his famous eructation, "O wombe! O bely! O stynkyng cod, / Fulfilled of dong and of corrupcion! / At either ende of thee foul is the soun" (6.534–36), that he has a hatred of the flesh. That may well be, but the Pardoner's language here and in other examples is consistent with the dominant ethos of the church in its contempt for this world and for the flesh.[111] If we make the degradation of the human body a product of the Pardoner's perfervid imagination or psychological obsession we lose sight of the fact that he is the end product of this discourse as well as its purveyor.

The critical issue facing both the Pardoner and the church is the refusal of both to transform their discourse from the sin-centered theology of the Father (or fathers of the church) to the regenerative love of the Son, a refusal to stake all on Christ's humanity and his embodiment of *caritas*. In his sermons the Pardoner abstracts the idea of the fall into sin from any concept of reconciliation. As Hans Blumenberg has argued, "The sharper the accent finally placed by medieval theology on the topics of original sin and divine grace, the more precisely it had to differentiate between the lost paradisaic, unmediated enjoyment of the world and the hostile opposition of nature to man's claim to dominate it in his condition of exile from that paradise."[112] Had medieval theology placed more emphasis on Christ's humanity, Blumenberg goes on to say, and on the likeness of all human beings to that Christ, it would have been its noblest endeavor. Without a theology of reconciliation with Christ, the implication is that death still needs to be conquered. Only the boy who informs the rioters of the omnipresence of death seems to have grasped what death is. The Pardoner himself encourages men to strive against one another in the same way that each rioter plotted to gain a larger share for himself. The inevitable death of the rioters implies that death is not the cessation of one's physical being so much as it is the dissolution of any animating principle of human life and dignity. Their deaths raise the question, Is the church in its discourse leading its people to a "new life" here and now through a theology of forgiveness and human dignity or is the mission of the church primarily to conquer death? Is its commitment to this world or to the other world?

As we saw in *Pearl*, the Dreamer comes to terms with his own finitude and manages to see death as a part of life that helps him to do that which is in him. During the Mass, specifically in the showing of the Eucharist, Christ, he says, becomes a "friend," whose own human death teaches him to accept both his daughter's death and the value of his own life. The idea, of course, is not only to die like Christ but also to live like him. Emphasis on Christ's humanity would enhance human dignity and it would change how we experience this life, transforming it into the highest possibility human beings could expect to experience. As Aers points out in his discussion of *Piers Plowman,* Holy Church, in Langland's idea of it (which was not a reflection of the dominant theology in fourteenth-century England), promises that one can become "ylik to oure lord" by being true of tongue, doing the proper works, and maintaining justice in the community.[113]

Even though the Pardoner prominently displays the *vernycle* on his cap, it appears to have become just another of his many authenticating props and no longer signifies the *vera icon* or the true image of Christ as a human being. Strictly speaking, a *vernycle* is the badge pilgrims received when they journeyed to St. Peter's in Rome to view the imprint of Christ's face that hung in the Chapel of St. Veronica.[114] Reputedly, the *veronica* was the most popular pilgrim attraction in Rome in the late Middle Ages. Aside from its denoting a pilgrim badge, the *veronica* also referred to the countless paintings that depicted the sacred face. In the *veronica* the face of Christ is depicted in a tranquil and mild composure, without pain or suffering, a fact reflected in the Ellesmere portrait of the Pardoner's *vernycle*. Though the tranquil image of Christ is contrary to modern conceptions of the Veronica image and story, the evidence derived from medieval iconography shows that the Veronica story in all of its forms was not actively connected to the crucifixion until some time in the late thirteenth or early fourteenth century and only at that time did Christ's face assume the expression of suffering.[115] Prior to that time, the story was that Veronica received the image from Christ during the time of his public ministry, when Christ, according to the *Mors Pilati,* the chief source for the version that appears in the *Legenda aurea,* was an itinerant preacher.

In the story Veronica speaks to a young man named Volusian who has come to Jerusalem at the request of Tiberius, who is sick, in search of Christ whose reputation for curing the ill has reached Rome. Volusian has arrived in Jerusalem shortly after Christ's death, and a now terrified Pilate had concealed both the fact of Christ's death and his own role in it lest he fall out of favor with Tiberius. Veronica informs him that she has a cloth with the image of Christ on it and merely to look at it has the power to restore people to health. Volusian asks if this image can be purchased with gold and silver and Veronica replies that its power can be bought only with pious affection.[116] Veronica's emphasis on the miraculous power of the cloth and on the inner disposition of the recipient—that is, that only true piety and not gold and silver can restore one to wholeness—suggests that the activity involved is the recovery of the image and likeness of Christ implanted in human nature at the creation. Her emphasis on the desire and disposition of the spectator and not on the power of the cloth alone, identifies the central message of Christ's ministry to be the internalization of his image of love.

The Pardoner, as we have seen, brings no such message to his audiences. The image of Christ can be bought, and one need not endure any great hardship to acquire it. The *General Prologue* tells us that the Pardoner made "the person and the peple his apes." In the Pardoner's view it is his audience and not he who is degraded by the success of his performances. Their greed and cupidity, stoked by the kind of temptations he throws their way, allow him to do a brisk business in relics and indulgences and to earn more in a day than the parson garners in two months. As he has argued all along, the people do not want to hear about Christ's own struggle when they can be "saved" by his miracles. The poverty and sacrifices of those parsons who attempt a sincere imitation of Christ is, in the Pardoner's view, wasted on the "lewed peple" who prefer the Christ the Pardoner impersonates.[117] He uses their lack of steadfastness to justify his own apostasy and to give or take from the people the Christ they deserve.

Naturally, the Pardoner is projecting his own shallow materialism onto their less convoluted motives. Either he cannot see or will not see the sincere love of Christ that is involved in the desire to possess a relic or sacred object. Like the various pilgrim badges that signify more than the mere fact that one has been to Rome, Jerusalem, or Canterbury, relics may express the will of the supplicant to participate in the event symbolized by the token. It is a hunger for something spiritually authentic that is apprehended if not comprehended as absent from their lives. The Pardoner misses all this genuine, albeit unconscious, imitation of Christ because he can only see the selfish or material element at work. While that always may be a part of one's motivation, it is secondary to the simple reverence the individual may have for the sacred object and the story that goes with it. As the Pardoner says, the "lewed folk" love "olde stories," not only, as he thinks, because they are gullible but also because these stories help them to understand in practical terms the abstract vocabulary of formal theology. As a rhetorician and storyteller of uncommon accomplishment, the Pardoner is in a position to offer the people some clearer understanding of their earthly condition. He could replace old stories with new stories, but he sticks to the tried and true. That is more profitable. *Corruptio optimi pessima.* The Pardoner persists in this discourse, no matter how tired and atrophied it has become, because it gives him control over the emotions of his audience and their hope of salvation. What he conveys to his Sunday audiences is the divine power of his pardons and the role he plays as surrogate for Christ, whose place he occupies at the end of his sermons, as if he himself possessed the power of divine absolution:

> Youre names I enter heer in my rolle anon;
> Into the blisse of hevene shul ye gon.
> I yow assoile, by myn heigh power,
> Yow that wol offre, as cleen and eek as cleer
> As ye were born.
>
> (6.911–15)

The forgiveness of Christ is always extended in his sermons because the companion theme to sin and fallenness is redemption. He offers nothing short of a pledge of rebirth or regeneration without undergoing the pain and suffering of purgatory. He'll "save" his audience now if they will save him in exchange. And they do. He emerges triumphant every time, victorious over the simple-minded "lewed folk" but no closer to self-mastery or victory over himself and those compulsions for authenticity that force him to go out and establish his mastery all over again. As a result, he effects no transformation of himself or of his discourse. Just the same old story, over and over again.

The Pardoner is willing to reveal his secrets and admit his viciousness to the pilgrims because he has no intention of duping them. He is aware that the theological content of his tale is too simplistic and inadequate for the moral and ethical problems that face society and Christianity in the late fourteenth century and he reserves it exclusively for the unlearned. Among the pilgrims he is all jokes and of very low seriousness. His confession, it might be said, begins as early as the *General Prologue* where Chaucer's narrator learns of his pig's bones, his flattery and japes, and his outrageous claim that he has a fragment of Peter's sail and a relic of Mary's veil. Rather than a state of despair, the Pardoner appears to be in a playful frame of mind, singing his song, interrupting the Wife of Bath, and, in the aftermath of the Physician's tale, bantering with Harry Bailly. He is amused at the irony of his situation when the *gentils* demand that he forego his japes in favor of a moral thing from which they might learn something. In effect, they have demanded that a vicious man tell a moral tale. His confession is a kind of revenge on the *gentils* for their demand of a moral tale, but the real inspiration for his confession comes from the Wife of Bath.

It is obvious that the Pardoner envies the Wife of Bath, whether it be her financial success or her skill as a preacher and her success as a storyteller. The ripple effect of her story has made the Wife of Bath a focal point and won for her something of the fellowship that she covets, another facet of the Wife's performance that the Pardoner may envy. If we look, briefly, at the Wife of Bath's tale from the perspective of the Pardoner's tale we see its value to the Pardoner and to his tale, first as a model, then as a critique. The Wife of Bath's "theology" exposes the poverty of the Pardoner's vision and we discover that the Pardoner's tale is in the end a misreading of the Wife of Bath's performance.[118]

The first sign of his enthusiasm for the Wife occurs in his interruption of her prologue, where he addresses her as a "noble prechour." He misreads her "praktike" as a defense of her own *cupiditas;* he fails to see her critique of St. Paul and clerkly discourse as a call for a transformation or expansion of *caritas* that would exonerate women of the first and original of sins. What registers on the Pardoner is her demand for *maistrie.* When he asks her to teach him of her practice or technique, he seems not to have heard her answer in the form of an apology to her audience. Her intent, she avers, "nys but for to pleye," a lesson lost on the Pardoner, whose "entente is nat but for to wynne."

Like the Pardoner, the Wife of Bath favors "olde stories." The structure and content of her tale is a template for his. Following her tale, the Pardoner's is set in a fairy land of magical enchantment. It too involves a symbolic quest of life and death, a wisdom figure of great age and experience who corresponds to its teller, and a conclusion that emphasizes the primary affliction obsessing each narrator—regeneration.

Through her fiction the Wife of Bath strips away the layers of her outer self, like so many articles of her own clothing, and lays bare the inner self. Her tale deepens her humanity and leads the audience to perceive a larger truth about her and themselves, that what is beautiful may lie enchanted beneath a veil of ugliness. The revelation of hidden beauty corresponds with the transformation of discourse from prologue to tale. In the *General Prologue* the Wife is said to be "out of alle charitee" if any other wife should go to the offering before her. There and in her prologue she shows herself to be highly conscious of social differences. In her tale a very different idea emerges, indicating that the Wife has internalized a christological notion of social rank and of poverty. As in her fifth marriage, she chooses love over money; that is, she chooses *caritas* over *cupiditas*. Christ, who "ne wolde nat chese a vicious lyvyng," is her model and the example for all women: "Crist wole we clayme of hym oure gentillesse" (3.1117). In this way she insists that women be also made in the image and likeness of Christ and not just a copy of Adam. Her identification with Christ allows her to overturn or to rewrite the theology of the fall by reconstructing the figure of Eve as a true and faithful wife who initiates reconciliation with Adam. The Hag, a kind of Eve, transforms herself into a young woman; she renounces her earlier proposition (the question the Hag poses to the knight corresponds to the problem the Old Man poses to the rioters), and declares, "I prey to God that I moote sterven wood, / But I to yow be also good and trewe / As evere was wyf, syn that the world was newe" (3.1242–45).

In having the Hag transform herself into a young woman and then pledging to be both beautiful and true, the Wife of Bath has been accused of capitulating to the norms of the culture and what it values in women. Perhaps so, but there is a Camusian courage in her willingness to choose this life to live over again in this world, despite all the suffering and travail that she has undergone in her life. If there is a sin against life, Camus says, "it consists perhaps not so much in despairing of life as in hoping for another life and in eluding the implacable grandeur of this life."[119] The Wife's tale, her fiction, does not end with herself, it provokes new thoughts, not only for her but also for a number of other pilgrims who feel inspired to address the issues of her tale. The Hag's surrender of *maistrie* generates a new discourse or, optimistically, a new theology on marriage. It effects a reconciliation of opposites, and through the Hag the Wife of Bath is able to experience a kind of regeneration, a reconciliation with this world (she has had the world in her time), with old age ("But yet to be right myrie wol I fonde"), and with death. In the language of Theodor Adorno, the Wife of Bath breaks "the power of oblivion engulfing every individual life" by salvaging life, as an image, from the throes of death.[120]

The Pardoner also had the opportunity to entertain an alternative vision of himself. In Salman Rushdie's terms, he had the opportunity through his fiction to think new thoughts by playing with or deconstructing the dominant story of his life. Instead he chose one of his canned performances, with disastrous consequences. He will not be able to escape his nausea this time. If he had followed his impulse to imitate the Wife of Bath, as he started out to do, his story might have had a different ending. Instead, the Pardoner finds himself in an awkward position. He is unable to retire into his own thoughts because his entire performance was designed to provoke a response from without. For him, there are no inner pleasures or consolations of the text. In the absence of the adulation of those congregants who gather around him on a Sunday, the Pardoner solicits the approval of the pilgrim audience to his performance. He makes no serious attempt to sell his relics; rather, he offers himself and his routine as a parody of the penitential pilgrimage, exhorting the pilgrims to show their gratitude for their having among them a "suffisaunt pardoneer" who can absolve them of their sins, should one or two fall from his horse and break his neck in two. He risks offending the *gentils,* treating them as he does as only slightly more sophisticated than the "lewed peple." The Pardoner will have his japes after all.

He does not pick on Harry Bailly to embarrass or insult him. The Host is the obvious choice to enlist at tale's end for some reaction. With his invitation to the Host to "kisse the relikes everychon," the parody of the Mass in the Pardoner's narrative continues. With his wallet open in his lap, the Pardoner offers the Host his body to eat, a gross inversion of the Eucharistic offering. The Host, correctly operating on the premise that the Pardoner has dropped all pretenses and invited japes of his own, responds in kind:

> "Nay, nay!" quod he, "thanne have I Cristes curs!
> Lat be," quod he, "it shal nat be, so theech!
> Thou woldest make me kisse thyn olde breech,
> And swere it were a relyk of a seint,
> Though it were with thy fundement depeint!

But, by the croys which that Seint Eleyne fond,
I wolde I hadde thy coillons in myn hond
In stide of relikes or of seintuarie.
Lat kutte hem of, I wol thee helpe hem carie;
They shul be shryned in an hogges toord!"

(6.946–55)

As Harry himself is wont to say, "A man may seye ful sooth in game and pley." Unerringly, the Host has uttered the most devastating truth possible at a moment when the Pardoner had seen himself as invulnerable. But I do not believe that the Host acted out of revenge or with foreknowledge.

The most satisfying reading of the exchange assumes that Harry Bailly only stumbles on the Pardoner's sexual secret. The Host comes off as the least likely candidate to take serious offense at the characterization of being "envoluped in synne." As always, the Host is ready for play and on the face of it his riposte is quite humorous and not simply because it deflates the Pardoner. Besides, it is the Host who is chagrined to learn that the Pardoner grows sullen over what the Host had deemed a clever retort. His remark "Lat kutte hem of, I wol thee helpe hem carie," strongly suggests that he thinks the Pardoner to be physically intact and only realizes his gaffe amid the laughter of the pilgrims. We are unfair to Harry Bailly when we impute to the Host the same kind of motives that are characteristic of the Pardoner. Whenever he hears things he does not like he freely expresses his displeasure, as he did in regard to the tales of Chaucer and of the Monk. On each of those occasions, however, he criticized the tales and not the tellers.

The Pardoner, for his part, is shocked into silence by the sudden reversal of his fortune. What the Host has inadvertently done is shatter the image that the Pardoner has flamboyantly been constructing; he has shifted the focus from the image to the person himself. The reaction of the pilgrims is gratifying. They do not laugh at the Pardoner's sexual condition so much as they are amused at the Host's befuddlement and the Pardoner's vain belief in the subtlety of his disguises. The pilgrims rightfully take pleasure at seeing someone fall on his face after he has boasted of his superior stature and his imperviousness to public censure. The wisest course for the Pardoner to follow under the circumstances would be for him to join in the laughter. But he has turned all of his substance into accident; he stands exposed, to his own eye, for what he is, a "shiten shepherde," to borrow a term from the Parson, the very opposite image of the one he has put forth. In its comic irony, Harry Bailly's "excremental vision" makes the Pardoner acknowledge the shame he feels about his own existence.

Without making any extravagant claims of conversion, I submit that the Pardoner's silence may betoken some sort of awakening. He has journeyed in his narrative from a point of boasting about his contempt for humankind to a moment of horrific alienation (the Old Man's desire to enter his mother's womb may be construed as a desire never to have been born) to arrive at a point where he no longer can hide behind empty words and gestures. The contradictions of the man, of this Pardoner, this "noble ecclesiaste," are now apparent for everyone to see. Most conspicuous is his obsession with or ambivalence toward Christ. The Pardoner pretends to imitate Christ by wearing the *veronica* prominently on his cap and by dispensing his pardons freely in the Mass. But he refuses to look inside of himself lest he see the *vera icon* within. Were he to look inside, he would see a Christ as sexless as he is but one who, with his *caritas,* does triumph over death, does redeem sinners, and does bring new life to them. The Pardoner takes no such risks with his life or his discourse. He denies that *caritas,* an authentic life of service to one's fellow human beings, is a greater power than *cupiditas.* For, every time that he tells his tale, the three rioters will forsake their bond of brotherhood in favor of the gold beneath the treasure tree. The Pardoner has learned nothing from the Wife of Bath's *praktike;* he takes the chaff and lets the fruit be still. That is why his theme is always one and the same, *radix malorum est cupiditas,* why he continues to spit out his venom under the hue of holiness, and why he still waits, sadly and fruitlessly, for love to come to him.

Despite the humiliation he suffers, the Pardoner remains on the pilgrimage. He accepts the kiss of peace urged by the Knight—one of the truly singular grace notes in the whole of the *Canterbury Tales*—an act that brings the allusions to the Mass in his tale to a fitting close. The kiss of peace comes just before the Communion rite, indicating that the Pardoner has not been excluded from the "compaignye" (literally, "to break bread with"). Assenting to kiss the Host occasions a meaningful shift of values. It implies a movement, of some significance, away from the violence and viciousness that defined human relations in the Pardoner's tale. When the Knight invites the Pardoner to draw near and join the group in laughter and in play (6.966–67), he mitigates the derisive laughter that followed the Host's blunder and opens the road to Canterbury anew to the Pardoner. We should be able to do as much. We too can prevent the Pardoner from becoming a frozen medieval—or modern—stereotype. We can locate the man breathing beneath the cloak of his professional identity, let him tell his tale again and exorcize some of the demons that plague him, if only by the instrument of laughter. We too can invite him to draw near and enter into our company if we have the courage to look to ourselves and call him our fellow—for the Pardoner is that, far more than the Knight or the Parson.

Qui tacet consentit.

Notes

Preface

1. For the entire passage, see *Canterbury Tales* 2.1174–90.

2. Theodor W. Adorno, *Notes to Literature*, 2 vols., ed. Rolf Tiedemann, trans. Shierry Weber Nicholsen (New York: Columbia University Press, 1992), 249.

1.
Poetry and Theology

1. Roland Barthes, "Authors and Writers," in *A Barthes Reader,* ed. Susan Sontag (New York: Hill and Wang, 1982), 187–88.

2. An impressive number of texts come to mind. The ones that I have relied on most heavily in this study, all listed in the bibliography, are works by David Aers, Hans Blumenberg, Caroline Walker Bynum, Janet Coleman, Eamon Duffy, Alister McGrath, Heiko Oberman, Miri Rubin, Walter Ullmann, and Nicholas Watson.

3. *Literary interest,* as Steven Knapp defines it, is the interest literature takes in representations "that construct new compositions of thought and value out of pre-existing relations between words and objects and the responses associated with them (where the 'objects' in question are actually types of persons, actions, and situations as well as of 'things')" (*Literary Interest: The Limits of Anti-Formalism* [Cambridge: Harvard University Press, 1993], 89).

4. Janet Coleman, *Medieval Readers and Writers: 1350–1400* (New York: Columbia University Press, 1981), 274.

5. For the prominence and importance of incarnational theology in the fourteenth century, see Nicholas Watson, "Conceptions of the Word: The Mother Tongue and the Incarnation of God," in *New Medieval Literatures,* vol. 1, ed. Wendy Scase, Rita Copeland, and David Lawton (Oxford: Clarendon Press, 1997), 85–124. Watson remarks that "the late Middle Ages was a period in which incarnational theology played as important a cultural role as, for example, the doctrine of grace was to do in the sixteenth and seventeenth centuries" (89).

6. For the connection between modernity and late medieval art and literature, see Louis Dupré, *Passage to Modernity: An Essay in the Hermeneutics of Nature and Culture* (New Haven: Yale University Press, 1993), 1–15.

7. I am using *humanism* in much the same way that it is employed by James Simpson, who uses it to cover a broad range of cultural positions found in many works of western European writing composed between the twelfth and the fourteenth centuries. Two of the characteristics Simpson mentions stand out in particular: the profound confidence in the powers of human reason and in the capacity of reason to promote human perfection insofar as that is possible; a corresponding confidence in the constructive powers of human nature and nature more broadly speaking (*Sciences and the Self in Medieval Poetry: Alan of Lille's* Anticlaudianus *and John Gower's* Confessio Amantis [Cambridge: Cambridge University Press, 1995], 18).

8. For the *metamorphosis of scholastic discourse,* see Gordon Leff, *William of Ockham: The Metamorphosis of Scholastic Discourse* (Manchester: University of Manchester Press, 1975). Leff credits Ockham with changing the terms of scholastic discourse by confining himself to what could be ultimately derived from evident knowledge of individual existence or implied from revealed truth (xxii). Compare with Lisa Kiser's comment that Chaucer's poetry raises very real doubts about any poetic project that claims to have "discovered, recorded, or in any way represented truth, especially truth that transcends the limited and contradictory data visible in everyday life" (*Truth and Textuality in Chaucer's Poetry* [Hanover, N.H.: University Press of New England, 1991], 113).

9. Monica McAlpine, "The Triumph of Fiction in the *Nun's Priest's Tale,*" in *Art and Context in Late Medieval English Narrative,* ed. Robert R. Edwards (Woodbridge, Suffolk: D. S. Brewer, 1994), 87.

10. Richard Rorty, *Contingency, Irony, Solidarity* (Cambridge: Cambridge University Press, 1989), 73. Rorty defines *final vocabulary* as the words "in which we tell, sometimes prospectively and sometimes retrospectively, the story of our lives." The vocabulary is final in the sense that if doubt is cast on the worth of these words, "their user has no noncircular argumentative recourse" (73).

11. On *redescription,* see Rorty, *Contingency, Irony, Solidarity,* 75–77.

12. See the remark of C. W. Marx, that Grosseteste's poem is "a valuable example of the way theological ideas could be transmitted into vernacular writing" (*The Devil's Rights and the Redemption in the Literature of Medieval England* [Cambridge: D. S. Brewer, 1995], 65).

13. John A. Burrow, *Langland's Fictions* (Oxford: Clarendon Press, 1993), 4.

14. Richard Newhauser, "Sources II: Scriptural and Devotional Sources," in *A Companion to the* Gawain-*Poet,* ed. Derek Brewer and Jonathan Gibson (Cambridge: D. S. Brewer, 1997), 259.

15. See Giorgio Agamben, *The Man without Content,* trans. Georgia Albert (Stanford: Stanford University Press, 1999), 7. The entire first chapter, entitled "The Most Uncanny Thing," has an incisive discussion of the relationship of poetry to society.

16. See Lucretius, *On the Nature of the Universe,* trans. Ronald E. Latham (Harmondsworth: Penguin Books, 1960), 130–31. Also, for an excellent discussion of Lucretius's use of poetry and its therapeutic effect, see Martha Nussbaum, "Beyond Obsession and Disgust: Lucretius' Genealogy of Love," *Apeiron* 22 (1989): 1–59.

17. See especially "Part One: Authorizing Text and Writer," in *The Idea of the Vernacular: An Anthology of Middle English Literary Theory, 1280–1520,* ed. Jocelyn Wogan-Browne, Nicholas Watson, Andrew Taylor, and Ruth Evans (University Park: Pennsylvania State University Press, 1999), 1–19.

18. Marcia Colish, *The Mirror of Language: A Study in the Medieval Theory of Knowledge* (Lincoln: University of Nebraska Press, 1983), 161.

19. Miri Rubin, *Corpus Christi: The Eucharist in Late Medieval Culture* (Cambridge: Cambridge University Press, 1991), 83–89; 98–105.

20. See Nicholas Watson, "The *Gawain*-poet as a Vernacular Theologian," in *Companion to the* Gawain-*Poet,* ed Brewer and Gibson, 295. See also Watson's companion articles, "The Politics of Middle English Writing," in *Idea of the Vernacular,* ed. Wogan-Browne, Watson, Taylor, and Evans, 331–52; "Visions of Inclusion: Salvation and Vernacular Theology in Pre-Reformation England," *Journal of Medieval and Early Modern Studies* 27 (1997): 145–87.

21. Watson, "*Gawain*-Poet," 295. See his characterization of the *Pearl*-poet as a "communicator of religious teaching in the vernacular" (294).

22. Monica Brzezenski Potkay, "*Cleanness*'s Fecund and Barren Speech Acts," *Studies in the Age of Chaucer* 17 (1995): 109.

23. Ibid., 109.

24. For Langland and others, see Coleman, *Medieval Readers and Writers,* 32–43. For a general discussion of audience, see "Part Two: Addressing and Positioning the Audience," in *Idea of the Vernacular,* ed. Wogan-Browne, Watson, Taylor, and Evans, 109–16.

25. See Peter Haidu, "Repetition: Modern Reflections on Medieval Aesthetics," *Modern Language Notes* 92 (1977): 883–84.

26. Ibid., 886.

27. In relation to this point, see Larry Scanlon's comment that the narrative voice may not be attempting to subvert clerical authority but to "laicize it"

(*Narrative, Authority, and Power: The Medieval Exemplum and the Chaucerian Tradition* [Cambridge: Cambridge University Press, 1994], 21). Scanlon discusses in pointed detail how Chaucer widens the distinction between the two discourses (see especially 14–15).

28. Bakhtin finds polyphony most characteristic of Dostoevsky's novels, wherein the voices are not only objects of the author's word but subjects of their own directly significant word. See M. M. Bakhtin, *Problems of Dostoevsky's Poetics,* trans. Caryl Emerson (Minneapolis: University of Minnesota Press, 1984), 4. See also Michael Holquist, *Dialogism: Bakhtin and His World* (London: Routledge, 1990), 34.

29. See Nicholas Watson, *Richard Rolle and the Invention of Authority* (Cambridge: Cambridge University Press, 1991), 26; 7–9.

30. See Holquist, *Dialogism,* 69.

31. See Wolfgang Iser, "Feigning in Fiction," in *Identity of the Literary Text,* ed. Mario J. Valdés and Owen Miller (Toronto: University of Toronto Press, 1985), 209.

32. All citations from Chaucer's works are from *The Riverside Chaucer,* ed. Larry D. Benson, 3d ed. (Boston: Houghton-Mifflin, 1987).

33. Giovanni Boccaccio, *The Decameron,* selected, trans., and ed. Mark Musa and Peter Bondanella (New York: W. W. Norton, 1977), 69–73.

34. In representing Iser's argument I draw heavily on three of his texts: "Feigning in Fiction," 204–28; *The Fictive and the Imaginary: Charting Literary Anthropology* (Baltimore: Johns Hopkins University Press, 1993); "The Play of the Text," in *Languages of the Unsayable: The Play of Negativity in Literature and Literary Theory,* ed. Sanford Budick and Wolfgang Iser (Stanford: Stanford University Press, 1996), 325–39. This last essay contains Iser's most complete statement on the play element, which he says satisfies both epistemological and anthropological needs: "Epistemologically speaking, it [play] imbues presence with adumbrated absence by denying any authenticity to the possible results of play. Anthropologically speaking, it allows us to conceive that which is withheld from us" (338).

35. Iser, "Play of the Text," 327.

36. Iser, "Feigning in Fiction," 204.

37. Iser, *Fictive and Imaginary,* xvii.

38. In "Play of the Text," Iser explains this process further: Textual play is carried out by "negativity," although negativity is far from negative in its effects. That is, textual play not only undercuts the position presented in the text, it also undercuts the status of that which transformation has moved from absence into presence. Negativity epitomizes the interrelation between absence and presence. Play produces and at the same time allows the process of production to be observed. "It is through this incessant hovering between the closed

and the punctured illusion that the transformation effected by the play of the text makes itself felt to the reader" (336).

39. Iser, *Fictive and Imaginary,* 4.

40. Iser, "Feigning in Fiction," 211–12.

41. Iser, *Fictive and Imaginary,* 297.

42. Ibid., 296–97.

43. See Rita Copeland, *Rhetoric, Hermeneutics, and Translation in the Middle Ages: Academic Traditions and Vernacular Texts* (Cambridge: Cambridge University Press, 1991), 156.

44. Ibid., 158

45. Iser, "Play of the Text," 326–27.

46. *Boccaccio on Poetry: Being the Preface and the Fourteenth and Fifteenth Books of Boccaccio's* Genealogia Deorum Gentilium, ed. Charles B. Osgood (New York: Bobbs-Merrill, 1956), 53.

47. The complete quotation in Latin is "Quis tam sui inscius, qui, advertens nostrum Dantem sacre theologie implicitos persepe nexus mira demonstratione solventem" (232). See Giovanni Boccaccio, *Vita di Dante e difesa della poesia,* ed. Carlo Muscetta (Roma: Edizioni dell'Ateneo, 1963).

48. Boccaccio has a great deal to offer on the relationship between poetry and theology. Watson reports that Boccaccio's *Trattatello in laude di Dante* sets out a daring claim for poetry: "that far from being mere fable-making, it has the same purpose and dignity as theology" (*Richard Rolle and the Invention of Authority,* 266). Elsewhere, Boccaccio says that fable has an honorable origin, derived from the verb *for, faris,* hence "conversation" *(confabulatio),* which means "talking together," (*Boccaccio on Poetry,* 47), a useful point for approaching Chaucer's pilgrim storytelling game.

49. For a discussion of Dante's reliance on Aristotle's *Ethics* and his views on moral virtue, see Kenelm Foster, O.P., *The Two Dantes and Other Studies* (Berkeley: University of California Press, 1977), 197–217.

50. Erich Auerbach, *Dante: Poet of the Secular World,* trans. Ralph Manheim (Chicago: University of Chicago Press, 1961), 178.

51. In this context, see Dante's encounter with the poet Bonagiunta da Lucca in canto 24 of *Purgatorio.* Bonagiunta says to Dante, "O frate, issa vegg' io, diss' elli, *il nodo* / che 'l Notaro e Guittone e me ritenne / di qua dal dolce stil novo ch'i' odo" (55–57, emphasis mine) ("O brother, now I see, he said, *the knot* / that kept the Notary, Guittone, and me / short of the sweet new manner that I hear"). The passage lends force to Boccaccio's observation that Dante surpassed all others in his ability to untie knots. For the translation, see *The Divine Comedy of Dante Alighieri: Purgatorio: A Verse Translation,* trans. and ed. Allen Mandelbaum (New York: Bantam Books, 1982). Unless otherwise indicated, all translations are from this edition.

52. Dante's link to both Virgil and Statius reflects his desire to restore poetry to its authentic, classical status as the fabric of history. Chaucer echoes this sentiment at the close of the *Troilus* when he remarks that his own work in the future will "subgit be to alle poesye" (5.1790).

53. See Ernst Kantorowicz, *The King's Two Bodies : A Study in Medieval Political Theology* (Princeton: Princeton University Press, 1957), 485.

54. For discussion of this point, see R. A. Shoaf, "*Purgatorio* and *Pearl*: Transgression and Transcendence," *Texas Studies in Literature and Language* 32 (1990): 152–68, in which he discusses the importance of literature as evidence. See also his fine essay, "'Noon Englissh Digne': Dante in Late Medieval England," in *Dante Now: Current Trends in Dante Studies,* ed. Theodore J. Cachey, Jr., William and Katherine Devers Series in Dante Studies 1 (Notre Dame: University of Notre Dame Press, 1995), 189–203. See also the argument posed by Richard Neuse in the introductory chapter of his book, *Chaucer's Dante: Allegory and Epic Theatre in the* Canterbury Tales (Berkeley: University of California Press, 1991), 1–17; and, most recently, the study by David Wallace, *Chaucerian Polity: Absolutist Lineages and Associational Forms in England and Italy* (Stanford: Stanford University Press, 1997).

55. See Anne Middleton, "The Idea of Public Poetry in the Reign of Richard II," in *Medieval English Poetry,* ed. Stephanie Trigg (London: Longman, 1993), 25–28. Middleton also says that what distinguishes Ricardian poetry from earlier forms is that it speaks "as if" to the entire community rather than "as if" to the court or to a patron (27).

56. On this point, see Watson's observation that the poetry of the period "is full of images of communality which can be seen as symbols for fourteenth-century English society, bound together not only by common (if bitterly contested) faith and social structure but now also (despite dialect differences) a common language" ("*Gawain*-Poet," 295).

57. See R. W. Southern, *Medieval Humanism and Other Studies* (Oxford: Blackwell, 1970), 29–60; see also his *Scholastic Humanism and the Unification of Europe* (Oxford: Blackwell, 1995), vol. 1, 21–24.

58. For an informed and informative discussion of the diversity of theology and thought in the fourteenth century, see David Luscombe, *Medieval Thought* (Oxford: Oxford University Press, 1997), 133–70.

59. See Gordon Leff, *The Dissolution of the Medieval Outlook* (New York: New York University Press, 1976), 118.

60. See Walter Ullmann, *The Individual and Society in the Middle Ages* (Baltimore: Johns Hopkins University Press, 1966), 100–153. For the relationship between scholasticism and innovations in education, see B. B. Price, *Medieval Thought: An Introduction* (Cambridge: Blackwell, 1992), 141–44.

61. Heiko Oberman, "The Shape of Late Medieval Thought: The Birthpangs of the Modern Era," in *The Pursuit of Holiness in Later Medieval and Renaissance Religion,* ed. Charles Trinkaus and Heiko Oberman (Leiden: E. J. Brill, 1974), 15. For extended discussion on this point, see Coleman, *Medieval Readers and Writers,* 235–47. My use of the terms *moderni* and *via moderna* follows the example established by Coleman, McGrath, Oberman, and Courtenay, among others, who have made common use of these terms to identify a specific set of theologians and theological positions pertaining to justification, human dignity, the covenant, and the two powers of God. William Courtenay recently has explained the common valence of the terms in the fourteenth century ("*Antiqui* and *Moderni* in Late Medieval Thought," *Journal of the History of Ideas* 48 [1987]: 3–10). See also Alister McGrath, *"Iustitia Dei": A History of the Christian Doctrine of Justification* (Cambridge: Cambridge University Press, 1989), 170–71; Janet Coleman, *Ancient and Medieval Memories: Studies in the Reconstruction of the Past* (Cambridge: Cambridge University Press, 1992), 541–58; and Heiko Oberman, "Some Notes on the Theology of Nominalism with Attention to Its Relation to the Renaissance," *Harvard Theological Review* 53 (1960): 47–76.

62. Leff, *Dissolution of Medieval Outlook,* 15.

63. Leff, *Metamorphosis of Scholastic Discourse,* xx.

64. For a comprehensive discussion of the "crisis in language" that occurred in the late Middle Ages, see Nancy Struever, *The Language of History in the Renaissance: Rhetoric and Historical Consciousness in Florentine Humanism* (Princeton: Princeton University Press, 1970), 44–52. Struever shows that both the nominalists and the humanists saw language mediating reality, and this led them to recognize the active, independent power of language, producing a revolution in sensibility.

65. See C. H. Lohr, "The Medieval Interpretation of Aristotle," in *The Cambridge History of Later Medieval Philosophy: From the Rediscovery of Aristotle to the Disintegration of Scholasticism 1100–1600,* ed. Norman Kretzmann, Anthony Kenny, and Jan Pinborg (Cambridge: Cambridge University Press, 1988), 90. The task of the medieval exegete, who believed himself to be in possession of truth by dint of God's revelation, was not the discovery of new truths but the unveiling of truth already contained in the words of the sacred text. For this same exegete, Lohr says, Aristotle's works, "even where ideas conflicted with faith, were an invitation to go beyond himself in a search for new truths" (89).

66. Gordon Leff, *Bradwardine and the Pelagians: A Study of His* De Causa Dei *and Its Opponents* (Cambridge: Cambridge University Press, 1957), 257.

67. See William Courtenay, *Schools and Scholars in Fourteenth Century England* (Princeton: Princeton University Press, 1987), 253.

68. See Alan Gewirth, "Philosophy and Political Thought in the Fourteenth Century," in *The Forward Movement of the Fourteenth Century,* ed. Francis Lee Utley (Columbus: Ohio University Press, 1961), 137.

69. Walter Ullmann, *The Medieval Foundations of Renaissance Humanism* (Ithaca: Cornell University Press, 1977), 29–54.

70. See Dupré, *Passage to Modernity,* 3.

71. See Erwin Panofsky, *Gothic Architecture and Scholasticism* (New York: New American Library, 1957), 13.

72. Ockham's thought, Leff says, does not show a distrust in the reliability of God or nature; his concern was with the inherent contingency of all creation and hence the limitations upon natural certainty, in light of the certainty of God's omnipotence (*Metamorphosis of Scholastic Discourse,* xxi).

73. For a sensible and accessible discussion of these points, see Steven Ozment, *The Age of Reform 1250–1550: An Intellectual and Religious History of Late Medieval and Reformation Europe* (New Haven: Yale University Press, 1980), 32–42.

74. Hans Blumenberg, *The Genesis of the Copernican World,* trans. Robert M. Wallace (Cambridge: MIT Press, 1987), 143–68.

75. For a discussion of this point, see Hans Blumenberg, "An Anthropological Approach to the Contemporary Significance of Rhetoric," in *After Philosophy: End or Transformation?* ed. Kenneth Baynes, James Bohman, and Thomas McCarthy (Cambridge: MIT Press, 1988), 441.

76. See Alister McGrath, *The Intellectual Origins of the European Reformation* (Oxford: Blackwell, 1993), 11: "all the indications are that piety and religion, if not theology itself, were becoming increasingly laicized towards the end of the medieval period."

77. For further discussion of this point, see Jean Leclerq, "The Renewal of Theology," in *Renaissance and Renewal in the Twelfth Century,* ed. Robert L. Benson and Giles Constable, with Carol D. Lanham (Toronto: University of Toronto Press, 1991), 68–87.

78. On this point, see André Vauchez, *The Laity in the Middle Ages: Religious Beliefs and Devotional Practices,* trans. Margery Schneider, ed. Daniel Bornstein (Notre Dame: University of Notre Dame Press, 1993), 97–115.

79. See Sarah Beckwith, *Christ's Body: Identity, Culture, and Society in Late Medieval Writings* (London: Routledge, 1993), 38.

80. See Southern, *Scholastic Humanism,* vol. 1, 8.

81. See Herbert Workman, *John Wyclif: A Study of the English Medieval Church,* 2 vols. (Hamden, Conn.: Archon Books, 1966), vol. 2, 149–200.

82. Miri Rubin, *Charity and Community in Medieval Cambridge* (Cambridge: Cambridge University Press, 1987), 56.

83. See Watson's point that vernacular texts not only derive material from an array of Latin systems of thought, "they generate their own systems" ("Visions of Inclusion," 146).

84. Ullmann, *Medieval Foundations,* 84.

85. Ibid., 3–12.

86. See "The Notion of Vernacular Theory," in *Idea of the Vernacular,* ed. Wogan-Browne, Watson, Taylor, and Evans, where it is asserted that English is a language "with immediate access to people's feelings and easily comprehensible—as Latin is not, even to those who can understand it. Writing in English can thus do rather more than provide a practical vernacular means of access to knowledge; it can *signify* clarity and open access and do so in texts whose projected audience is relatively narrow" (325).

87. Aers suggests that we recognize this period as a time "when the terms, images, rituals, and ideas of holiness became the object of unprecedented *public* and *vernacular* contestation in England" (David Aers and Lynn Staley, *The Powers of the Holy: Religion, Politics, and Gender in Late Medieval English Culture* [University Park: Pennsylvania State University Press, 1996], 4). See also Aers's earlier comment, that the late fourteenth century was a time when orthodoxy and tradition were opened for study and when "religious language was both powerful and extraordinarily flexible, because of its enmeshment in the social and political networks of conflicting communities and interests, which were encountering a very specific, unprecedented, and thoroughly contingent set of problems" (3).

88. On this point, see Margaret Aston, "Wyclif and the Vernacular," in *From Ockham to Wyclif,* ed. Anne Hudson and Michael Wilkes, Studies in Church History, Subsidia 5 (Oxford: Blackwell, 1987), 281–330.

89. See Coleman, *Medieval Readers and Writers,* 157.

90. See Erich Auerbach, *Literary Language and Its Public,* trans. Ralph Manheim (Princeton: Princeton University Press, 1995), 271–313. For a more recent argument, see Brian Stock, *Listening for the Text: On the Uses of the Past* (Philadelphia: University of Pennsylvania Press, 1996). Stock suggests that heresy and dissent offered considerable stimulation to theological thought and change in the late Middle Ages (118).

91. See Iser, *Fictive and Imaginary,* 296–97.

92. See McGrath, *"Iustitia Dei,"* xi.

93. See Margaret Aston, *Lollards and Reformers: Images and Literacy in Late Medieval Religion* (London: Hambledon, 1984), 130.

94. For the term *ex puris naturalibus,* see Heiko Oberman, *The Harvest of*

Medieval Theology: Gabriel Biel and Late Medieval Nominalism (Grand Rapids, Mich.: Eerdmans, 1967), 47–49.

95. Coleman, *Ancient and Medieval Memories,* 549.

96. Ibid., 531.

97. On this point, see Francis Oakley, *The Western Church in the Later Middle Ages* (Ithaca: Cornell University Press, 1979), 132–57. Oakley offers a cogent and perceptive analysis of the various views on the topic.

98. For added discussion on Chaucer's relationship to truth, see Kiser, *Truth and Textuality,* 1–4.

99. For further discussion of this topic, see Bernard L. Jefferson, *Chaucer and the* Consolation of Philosophy *of Boethius* (New York: Gordian Press, 1916), 72–80. Jefferson states that unlike Boethius, Bradwardine, Augustine, Jean de Meun, and Dante, Chaucer leaves the question of necessity an open one.

100. See McGrath, *"Iustitia Dei,"* 141.

101. See McAlpine, "Triumph of Fiction," 79.

102. Donald Howard, *The Idea of the* Canterbury Tales (Berkeley: University of California Press, 1976), 281.

103. See Gerhart B. Ladner, *"Homo Viator:* Medieval Ideas on Alienation and Order," *Speculum* 42 (1967): 236–39.

104. Wallace, *Chaucerian Polity,* 312.

105. Auerbach, *Literary Language,* 313.

106. Neuse, *Chaucer's Dante,* 157–59.

107. See John Milbank, *The Word Made Strange: Theology, Language, Culture* (Oxford: Blackwell, 1997), 85–86

108. For a discussion of this point, see Walter Benjamin, "On Language as Such and on the Language of Man," in *Reflections: Essays, Aphorisms, Autobiographical Writings,* trans. Edmund Jephcott, ed. Peter Demetz (New York: Schocken Books, 1978), 322–27; see also Richard Wolin, *Walter Benjamin: An Aesthetic of Redemption* (New York: Columbia University Press, 1982), 39–42; Michael Jennings, *Dialectical Images: Walter Benjamin's Theory of Literary Criticism* (Ithaca: Cornell University Press, 1987), 94–97.

109. See Benjamin, "On Language as Such," 323.

110. See Wolin, *Walter Benjamin,* 43; see also Benjamin, "On Language as Such," 328–29. See Wolin's additional comment: In Benjamin's analysis, literary works of art as well as scripture "are legitimate objects of the exegetical quest for the key to redemption" (43).

111. Tom Hahn, "Chaucer and Academic Theology," paper presented at the Seventh International Congress of the New Chaucer Society, 6–11 August 1990, University of Kent, Canterbury.

112. Robert O. Payne, "Chaucer and the Art of Rhetoric," in *Companion to Chaucer Studies,* rev. ed., ed. Beryl Rowland (New York: Oxford University Press, 1979), 42.

113. For a pointed discussion of the Lancelot reference, see McAlpine, "Triumph of Fiction," 81–83.

114. See Howard Caygill, "Benjamin, Heidegger, and the Destruction of Tradition," in *Walter Benjamin's Philosophy: Destruction and Experience,* ed. Andrew Benjamin and Peter Osborne (London: Routledge, 1994), 1–31, especially 17.

115. Giorgio Agamben, *Infancy and History: Essays on the Destruction of Experience,* trans. Liz Heron (New York: Verso, 1993), 104–5.

116. For further discussion of this point, see David Williams, *The* Canterbury Tales: *A Literary Pilgrimage* (Boston: Twayne, 1987), 88–100.

117. In the English edition of Barthes's *The Pleasure of the Text, pleasure* and *jouissance* are frequently translated as "bliss." See the selection in *A Barthes Reader,* ed. Sontag, 404–14.

118. See A. S. McGrade, "Ockham on Enjoyment: Towards an Understanding of Fourteenth-Century Philosophy and Psychology," *Review of Metaphysics* 33 (1981): 706–28. See also his "Enjoyment at Oxford after Ockham: Philosophy, Psychology and the Love of God," in *From Ockham to Wyclif,* ed. Hudson and Wilkes (Oxford: Blackwell, 1987), 63–88.

119. McGrade, "Ockham on Enjoyment," 713. See McGrade's comment, in "Enjoyment at Oxford," that Ockham believed that human beings were capable of loving God by nature, *ex puris naturalibus,* whereas Bradwardine insisted that without grace we can love only ourselves. McGrade goes on to say that the kind of debates being held at Oxford could have provided a framework for human understanding which poets and others could have utilized in concrete ways, both in understanding how poetry itself affects us and in understanding or depicting the behavior of actual fictional characters (86).

120. For *bliss,* see Norman Davis, Douglas Gray, Patricia Ingham, and Anne Wallace-Hadrill, eds., *A Chaucer Glossary* (Oxford: Clarendon Press, 1979), 16.

121. For a discussion of this point, see Bernard Levy and George R. Adams, "Chauntecleer's Paradise Lost and Regained," *Medieval Studies* 29 (1967): 178–92.

122. Lee Patterson, "The *Parson's Tale* and the Quitting of the *Canterbury Tales,*" *Traditio* 34 (1978): 379.

123. For a penetrating analysis of the Nun's Priest's use of the citation from St. Paul and for the Retraction, see Peter W. Travis, "Deconstructing Chaucer's Retraction," *Exemplaria* 3 (1991): 135–58.

2.

Grosseteste and Langland

1. William Langland, Piers Plowman: *The B-Text,* ed. George Kane and E. Talbot Donaldson (London: Athlone Press, 1975), passus 18, line 341. Unless otherwise designated, all citations will be to this edition.

2. For a discussion of this point, see Richard Swinburne, "Could God Become Man?" in *The Philosophy in Christianity,* ed. Godfrey Vesey (Cambridge: Cambridge University Press, 1989), 53–70.

3. For this point, see C. W. Marx, *The Devil's Rights and the Redemption in the Literature of Medieval England* (Cambridge: D. S. Brewer, 1995), 2. Marx provides the most complete and detailed discussion of the whole history and concept of the devil's rights.

4. Alister McGrath, *"Iustitia Dei" : A History of the Christian Doctrine of Justification* (Cambridge: Cambridge University Press, 1989), 38–39.

5. For discussion of the full title of Anselm's *Why God Became Man,* see *Anselm of Canterbury: The Major Works,* ed. Brian Davies and G. R. Evans (Oxford: Oxford University Press, 1998), 261n2.

6. See Anselm, *Why God Became Man,* 1.282–88.

7. Anselm, *Why God Became Man,* 1.282–3.

8. For further discussion of Anselm's views on justification, see McGrath, *"Iustitia Dei,"* 55–60.

9. For further discussion of this point, see Marx, *Devil's Rights,* 15. When Anselm criticized the notion of the devil's rights, Marx points out, he was questioning the idea that "God should choose to respect the Devil with justice in depriving him of his possession of human kind."

10. See Marx, *Devil's Rights,* 4 and 65–77.

11. Peter Abelard, *Commentary on Romans,* cited in M. T. Clanchy, *Abelard: A Medieval Life* (Oxford: Blackwell, 1999), 273.

12. For more on this point, see Marx, *Devil's Rights,* 21.

13. See Allan Wolter, "John Duns Scotus on the Primacy and Personality of Christ," in *Franciscan Christology: Selected Texts, Translations, and Introductory Essays,* ed. Daniel McElrath (St. Bonaventure, N.Y.: Franciscan Institute, 1980), 153.

14. See Heiko Oberman, *The Harvest of Medieval Theology: Gabriel Biel and Late Medieval Nominalism* (Grand Rapids, Mich.: Eerdmans, 1967), 234–35.

15. Thomas Aquinas, *Articles of Faith,* article 3, in *An Aquinas Reader: Selections from the Writings of Thomas Aquinas,* ed. Mary T. Clark (New York: Fordham University Press, 1988), 464–66.

16. See Thomas Aquinas, *Commentary on the Gospel of St. John,* trans. James A. Weisheipel, O.P., S.T.M. (Albany: Magi Books, 1980), John 1.14a (lecture 7, p. 85). See also Josef Pieper, *Guide to Thomas Aquinas,* trans. Richard and Clara Winston (New York: New American Library, 1964), 106–9.

17. See Thomas Aquinas, *On the Power of God (Quaestiones disputatae de potentia dei),* trans. by the English Dominican Fathers (Westminster, Md: Newman Press, 1952), question 5, article 10, reply to the fifth objection (p. 149).

18. For a brief discussion of Grosseteste's concept of *deification,* see R. W. Southern, *Robert Grosseteste: The Growth of an English Mind in Medieval Europe* (Oxford: Clarendon Press, 1988), 179. See also James McEvoy, *The Philosophy of Robert Grosseteste* (Oxford: Clarendon Press, 1982), 420. For the idea of deification in the Middle Ages, see II. L. Weatherby, "Dame Nature and the Nymph," *English Literary Renaissance* 26 (1996): 243–58, for example, Weatherby's comment: "If one answers the question *cur deus homo?* with 'deification' rather than 'justification' as the Eastern Fathers did and the Eastern Church generally does, the distinction between nature and grace comes into question; a deified creation is clearly less radically different from God than a merely redeemed or justified one" (248).

19. McEvoy, *Philosophy,* 399–400. See especially Grosseteste's *Hexaemeron* 8.5.7 and 8.12.2 and 3.

20. The concept of the absolute predestination of Christ has not been neglected in Grosseteste studies. See especially Southern, *Grosseteste,* 219–25; James McEvoy, "The Absolute Predestination of Christ in the Theology of Robert Grosseteste," in *Sapientiae Doctrina: Mélanges de théologie et de littérature médiévales offerts a Dom Hildebrand Bascour, O.S.B.,* Recherches de théologie ancienne et médiévale 1 (Leuven: Abbaye du Mont Cesar, 1980), 212–30; D. J. Unger, O.F.M.Cap., "Robert Grosseteste, Bishop of Lincoln (1235–1253), on the Reasons for the Incarnation," *Franciscan Studies* 16 (1956): 1–36.

21. See McEvoy, "Absolute Predestination," 219; for seed imagery, see Caroline Walker Bynum, *The Resurrection of the Body in Western Christianity, 200–1336* (New York: Columbia University Press, 1995), 1–18, and especially 3–7.

22. Robert Grosseteste, *On the Six Days of Creation,* trans. C. F. J. Martin (Oxford: Oxford University Press, 1996), 8.1.1. See also Robert Grosseteste, *Hexaemeron,* ed. Richard C. Dales and Servus Gieben, O.F.M.Cap. (Oxford: Oxford University Press, 1982). See also McEvoy, *Philosophy,* 380–86.

23. See McEvoy, *Philosophy,* 382

24. See Richard C. Dales, *The Intellectual Life of Western Europe in the Middle Ages* (Leiden: Brill, 1992), 245–46. Dales provides the most concise definition of Grosseteste's idea of the *minor mundus,* which is summarized here: The rational soul shares with angels the possession of rationality, and its vegetative and sensitive aspects share with the animal and vegetable kingdoms their functions. The human body is composed of the four elements and thus shares their qualities with the rest of the material universe. And since the rational soul is naturally suited to the perfection of the organic body, it is joined to it in a personal unity; the entire created universe, corporeal and spiritual, is thus summed up in the human being. And the totality of creatures could be united to the Creator, not by any natural bond, but only by God's assuming humanity in the unity of person. This, even, more than the redemption of man from sin, is the reason for the incarnation.

25. In the *Hexaemeron* 8.1.2 Grosseteste says, "human beings are in all things God's closest likeness in resemblance" (et homo, omnibus eius propinquissima similitudo imitatoria).

26. Grosseteste refers to these matters in two works, *De artibus liberalibus* and *De impressionibus aeris.* For a discussion of these works, see McEvoy, *Philosophy,* 165.

27. For the marriage of metals, see Joseph Grennen, "St. Cecilia's 'Chemical Wedding': The Unity of the *Canterbury Tales,* Fragment VIII," *Journal of English and Germanic Philology* 65 (1966): 466–81.

28. McEvoy provides a lengthy discussion of Grosseteste's appropriation of Aristotle's notion of the quintessence and his radical transformation of it to suit his own interests (*Philosophy,* 180–88).

29. Grosseteste, *De cessatione legalium,* 3.2.1. Cited in Southern, *Grosseteste,* 223.

30. The relevant Latin passage is as follows: "Nec sine expressa auctoritate aliquid in tam ardua quaestione disserere volo vel audeo, quia parvitatem ingenii mei et scientiae meae cito potest fallere verisimilis ratiocinatio" (see Unger, "Grosseteste," 16). Unger has edited a significant section of Grosseteste's *De cessatione legalium.*

31. See *The Middle English Translations of Robert Grosseteste's* Chateau d'amour, ed. Kari Sajavaara, Memoires de la Société Néophilologique de Helsinki 32 (Helsinki: Société Néophilologique, 1967), 36–48, 102–9.

32. Marx, *Devil's Rights,* 74.

33. Thorlac Turville-Petre says that the three languages existed in harmony, not just side by side, that is, in a "symbiotic relationship, interpenetrating and drawing strength from one another"; his point is that there were not three cultures but one culture with three voices (*England the Nation: Language, Literature, and National Identity, 1290–1340* [Oxford: Clarendon Press, 1996], 181).

34. All citations to the Anglo-Norman text are from Robert Grosseteste, *Le* Chateau d'amour *de Robert Grosseteste évêque de Lincoln,* ed. J. Murray (Paris: Champion, 1918).

35. On prologues, see Ruth Evans, "Historicizing Postcolonial Criticism: Cultural Difference and the Vernacular, " 366–70, and "An Afterword on the Prologue," 371–78, in *The Idea of the Vernacular: An Anthology of Middle English Literary Theory,* ed. Jocelyn Wogan-Browne, Nicholas Watson, Andrew Taylor, and Ruth Evans (University Park: Pennsylvania State University Press, 1999). See also, Turville-Petre, *England,* 22.

36. Lines for the English text are taken from *Middle English Translations,* ed. Sajavaara.

37. McGrath describes the theory of the devil's rights in this way: "While the death of Christ is a free act of divine love, the choice of the means employed to effect man's deliverance from the devil is necessarily dictated by the fact that the devil is *justly* entitled to punish sinners" (*"Iustitia Dei,"* 58). See also Richard Firth Green, *A Crisis of Truth: Literature and Law in Ricardian England* (Philadelphia: University of Pennsylvania Press, 1999), 347–50. Green distinguishes among three types of the devil's rights concept that obtained in late medieval England. The concept remained popular, he says, because "when Christ dissolves his bargain with the devil, he strikes another with the human race, and his human dependents have every reason to expect that the same punctilious legalism will be exercised in defense of their own rights" (351). The concept would promote confidence in the efficacy of the new covenant.

38. The relevant section in Grosseteste's *Hexaemeron* is 8.12.1 and 2.

39. Richard C. Dales, "Robert Grosseteste on the Soul's Care for the Body," in *Robert Grosseteste: New Perspectives on His Thought and Scholarship,* ed. James McEvoy, Instrumenta Patristica 27 (Steenbruges: Brepols, 1995), 314.

40. See Green, who says Grosseteste shows "intimate knowledge of common-law procedure" (*Crisis of Truth,* 348). The situation between God and the devil is set up as a property dispute, imagined as a writ of right case, in which Christ will represent human beings.

41. Susan Reynolds, *Fiefs and Vassals: The Medieval Evidence Reinterpreted* (Oxford: Oxford University Press, 1994), 20.

42. For a discussion of the origin and history of the legend in the Middle Ages, see Hope Traver, "The Four Daughters of God: A Study of the Versions of the Allegory with Special Reference to Those in Latin, French, and English" (Ph.D. diss., Bryn Mawr, 1907).

43. See McGrath, *"Iustitia Dei,"* 57–59.

44. I have relied here on Southern's translation and his emendations (*Grosseteste,* 227).

45. Southern, *Grosseteste,* 227–28.

46. James Weisheipl, O.P., "Aristotle's Concept of Nature: Avicenna and Aquinas," in *Approaches to Nature in the Middle Ages,* ed. Lawrence Roberts (Binghamton: MRTS, 1982), 140.

47. See James McEvoy, "Grosseteste on the Soul's Care for the Body: A New Text and a New Source for the Idea," in *Aspectus and Affectus: Essays and Editions in Grosseteste and Medieval Intellectual Life in Honor of Richard C. Dales,* ed. Gunar Freibergs (New York: AMS Press, 1993). The critical issue in Christ's death is the voluntary sundering of his soul from his body, which, McEvoy says, "entailed infinite suffering because so long as the body is not vanquished by its own inherent tendency to material dissolution, no finite power is sufficient to cancel the natural care of the soul for the body it vivifies" (37).

48. See McEvoy, "Soul's Care for the Body," 39.

49. Ibid., 43.

50. Is there a Lacanian element in Grosseteste's version of the incarnation? Jane Gallop says that Lacan, in his description of the mirror stage, writes another version of the tragedy of Adam and Eve. In the foregoing, Grosseteste refers to the creation as a mirror and assigns Christ, who reflects the creation, the role of improving nature. Human beings have a sense of their own incompleteness and see in the idea or image of Christ something of their former, original unity and wholeness. If Christ restores the totality of the body in the incarnation he functions like Lacan's mirror stage in which one anticipates in a mirage the maturation of one's own powers. It is also the stage which, Gallop says, projects one into history. As the completed *imago,* Christ reclaims the former unity and wholeness of human nature. See Jane Gallop, *Reading Lacan* (Ithaca: Cornell University Press, 1985), 85.

51. For a discussion of Langland's debt to Grosseteste, see Ronald Waldron, "Langland's Originality: The Christ-Knight and the Harrowing of Hell," in *Medieval English Religious and Ethical Literature,* ed. Gregory Kratzmann and James Simpson (Cambridge: Boydell and Brewer, 1986), 66–81.

52. Those studies of Langland's poetry in general and passus 18 in particular which have shaped much of my thinking on this passus are: John A. Burrow, *Langland's Fictions* (Oxford: Clarendon Press, 1993); James Simpson, Piers Plowman: *An Introduction to the B-Text* (New York and London: Longman, 1990); Thomas D. Hill, "Universal Salvation and Its Literary Context in *Piers Plowman* B. 18," *Yearbook of Langland Studies* 5 (1991), 65–76; and, especially, David Aers, "The Humanity of Christ: Representations in Wycliffite Texts and *Piers Plowman,*" in David Aers and Lynn Staley, *The Powers of the Holy: Religion, Politics, and Gender in Late Medieval English Culture* (University Park: Pennsylvania State University Press, 1996), 65–70.

53. See Aers, "Humanity of Christ," 65–70.

54. For the violent love tradition, see Nicholas Watson, "Conceptions of the Word: The Mother Tongue and the Incarnation of God," in *New Medieval Literatures,* vol. 1, ed. Wendy Scase, Rita Copeland, and David Lawton (Oxford: Clarendon Press, 1997), 114. See also Watson's discussion in *Richard Rolle and the Invention of Authority* (Cambridge: Cambridge University Press, 1991), 19–20.

55. See Burrow, *Langland's Fictions,* 2–4.

56. See Peter Haidu, "Repetition: Modern Reflections on Medieval Aesthetics," *Modern Language Notes* 92 (1977): 883–85.

57. For an alternative point of view, see Simpson, who suggests that Langland's initial commitment in the poem is not to poetry as a self-justifying art (*Introduction to the B-Text,* 14). Simpson then talks about the choices Langland makes in his art in contrast to Chaucer and concludes "whereas Chaucer's reader is brought into play by the narrator's irony, Langland's reader is not invited to participate in the process of judgment"; the reader is simply presented with a judgment completed (22).

58. See also Hill, "Universal Salvation," 65–76. Hill notes that one of the most common, and erroneous, critical assumptions about *Piers Plowman* is that the poem is "a religious poem written in an age of faith and that faith is to be identified generally with the modern Roman Catholic tradition" (65).

59. For an excellent discussion of this point, see David Aers, Piers Plowman *and Christian Allegory* (London: Edward Arnold, 1975), 107–9.

60. See Hill, "Universal Salvation," 66–68. See also Nicholas Watson, "Visions of Inclusion: Salvation and Vernacular Theology in Pre-Reformation England," *Journal of Medieval and Early Modern Studies* 27 (1997): 154–60, especially 157.

61. Hill, "Universal Salvation," 75.

62. For a further discussion of this point, see Barbara Raw, "Piers and the Image of God in Man," in Piers Plowman: *Critical Approaches,* ed. S. S. Hussey (London: Methuen, 1969), 143–79.

3.

The Pearl-*Poet*

1. Paul Zumthor, *Speaking of the Middle Ages,* trans. Sarah White (Lincoln: University of Nebraska Press, 1986), 63.

2. Charles Muscatine, *Poetry and Crisis in the Age of Chaucer* (Notre Dame: Notre Dame University Press, 1972), 37.

3. Ibid., 69.

4. See, for example, Malcolm Andrew and Ronald Waldron, eds., *The Poems of the* Pearl *Manuscript:* Pearl, Cleanness, Patience, Sir Gawain and the Green Knight (Exeter: University of Exeter Press, 1987). Although they contend that his poetry is not something superadded to the theology or morality, that it is analytical and exploratory as well as illustrative and persuasive, they argue that two of the poems—*Patience* and *Cleanness*—are in an overt and unambiguous way didactic, and that the body of intellectual and moral beliefs assumed and analysed in his poetry is in essence that of orthodox Christianity: "At lowest estimate we have in these poems a number of very skillful exercises in the translation of moral didacticism into distinct forms of art" (16–17). Unless indicated otherwise, all citations to the poems will be from this edition.

5. On this point, see David Aers, "Christianity for Courtly Subjects: Reflections on the *Gawain*-Poet," in *A Companion to the* Gawain-*Poet,* ed. Derek Brewer and Jonathan Gibson (Cambridge: D. S. Brewer, 1997), 91–101.

6. Nicholas Watson, "The *Gawain*-Poet as a Vernacular Theologian," in *Companion to the* Gawain-*Poet,* ed. Brewer and Gibson, 294.

7. Nick Davis, "Narrative Form and Insight," in *Companion to the* Gawain-*Poet,* ed. Brewer and Gibson, 329.

8. Richard Newhauser, "Sources II: Scriptural and Devotional Sources," in *Companion to the* Gawain-*Poet,* ed. Brewer and Gibson, 259.

9. See A. C. Spearing, "The Subtext of *Patience:* God as Mother and the Whale's Belly," *Journal of Medieval and Early Modern Studies* 29 (1999): 293–323; Elizabeth Keiser, *Courtly Desire and Medieval Homophobia: The Legitimation of Sexual Pleasure in* Cleanness *and Its Contexts* (New Haven: Yale University Press, 1997).

10. William Kerrigan, *The Sacred Complex: On the Psychogenesis of* Paradise Lost (Cambridge: Harvard University Press, 1983), 93.

11. Frank Kermode, *The Genesis of Secrecy: On the Interpretation of Narrative* (Cambridge: Harvard University Press, 1979), ix–x.

12. Ibid., 2–3.

13. See Malcolm Andrew, "The Realizing Imagination in Late Medieval English Narrative," *English Studies* 76 (1995): 117. Andrew defines the *realizing imagination* as "the process by which the imagination of a creative writer gets to work on a received story—developing, elaborating, and bringing to imagined life; particularizing general issues, realizing the abstract, and drawing out potential implications" (115).

14. Robert Alter, *The Art of Biblical Narrative* (New York: Basic Books, 1981), 12.

15. Robert Alter, cited by Paul Ricoeur, "Interpretative Narrative," in *The Book and the Text,* trans. David Pellauer, ed. Regina Schwartz (London: Blackwell, 1990), 238.

16. Meir Sternberg, *The Poetics of Biblical Narrative: Ideological Literature and the Drama of Reading* (Bloomington: Indiana University Press, 1987), 38.

17. Mieke Bal, *Death and Dissymmetry: The Politics of Coherence in the Book of Judges* (Chicago: University of Chicago Press, 1988), 34.

18. *Pearl,* lines 1201–2.

19. For a recent discussion of the significance and value of retelling biblical stories, see Regina Schwartz, *The Curse of Cain: The Violent Legacy of Monotheism* (Chicago: University of Chicago Press, 1997), 148–59.

20. The passage is a good example of the *Pearl*-poet's occasionally ambiguous syntax, which can be playfully impressionistic rather than precise when it suits him to be so. I want to thank Malcolm Andrew for his private clarification of this passage and for his helpful comments on the complexities of the *Pearl*-poet's syntax.

21. See Wolfgang Iser, *The Act of Reading* (Baltimore: Johns Hopkins University Press, 1978), 127–28.

22. Prologue to the Wycliffite Bible, chapter 15, in Anne Hudson, ed., *Selections from English Wycliffite Writings* (Cambridge: Cambridge University Press, 1978), 69.

23. See David Lyle Jeffrey, "John Wyclif and the Hermeneutics of Reader Response," *Interpretation* 39 (1985): 278.

24. David Lyle Jeffrey, "Chaucer and Wyclif: Biblical Hermeneutics and Literary Theory in the XIVth Century," in *Chaucer and Scriptural Tradition,* ed. David Lyle Jeffrey (Ottawa: University of Ottawa Press, 1984), 136–37.

25. See Rudolf Bultmann, *Jesus Christ and Mythology* (New York: Charles Scribner's and Sons, 1958), 35–36.

26. Frank Kermode, *The Sense of an Ending: Studies in the Theory of Fiction* (Oxford: Oxford University Press, 1967), 40. Literary fictions belong, in Kermode's analysis, to the "consciously false" and thus are not subject, like hypotheses, to proof or disconfirmation, only, if they come to lose their operational effectiveness, to neglect.

27. Ibid., 39.

28. See Alter, *Art of Biblical Narrative,* 46.

29. See, in this context, Alter's remark: "Genesis is not *Pale Fire,* but all fiction, including the Bible, is in some sense a form of play. Play in the sense I have in mind enlarges rather than limits the range of meanings of the text" (*Art of Biblical Narrative,* 46).

30. Douglas Hare, *Interpretation: A Bible Commentary for Teaching and Preaching* (Louisville: John Knox Press, 1993), 252.

31. See Richard Neuse, *Chaucer's Dante: Allegory and Epic Theatre in the* Canterbury Tales (Berkeley: University of California Press, 1991), 61.

32. See Saint Augustine, *Sermon 40,* in "Sermons on Selected Lessons of the Gospels," *The Nicene and Post-Nicene Fathers of the Christian Church,* ed. Philip Schaff, vol. 6 (Grand Rapids, Mich.: Eerdmans, 1974), 394.

33. On the "fayre formes," see Sarah Stanbury, *Seeing the* Gawain*-Poet: Description and the Art of Perception* (Philadelphia: University of Pennsylvania Press, 1991), 44–45.

34. W. A. Davenport, *The Art of the* Gawain*-Poet* (London: Athlone Press, 1978), 84.

35. Albert Cook, *History / Writing: The Theory and Practice of History in Antiquity and in Modern Times* (Cambridge: Cambridge University Press, 1988), 169.

36. See Andrew and Waldron, eds., *Poems of the* Pearl *Manuscript,* textual note to line 139ff.

37. Andrew points out that the primary sense of the Middle English noun *clannes* is freedom from sin, especially sexual sin, although the poet uses it to suggest other meanings such as propriety, balance, and moderation ("Realizing Imagination," 115).

38. Keiser, *Courtly Desire and Medieval Homophobia,* 181.

39. Ibid., 29.

40. Ibid., 8.

41. Schwartz, *Curse of Cain,* 111.

42. Paul Ricoeur, *The Symbolism of Evil,* trans. Emerson Buchanan (Boston: Beacon Press, 1969), 162–63.

43. John Milbank, *The Word Made Strange: Theology, Language, Culture* (Oxford: Blackwell, 1997), 136.

44. Ibid., 137.

45. For an insightful discussion of this scene, see Stanbury, *Seeing the* Gawain*-Poet,* 54–56.

46. Andrew, "Realizing Imagination," 117.

47. I am relying here on Eagleton's comment on Benjamin. See Terry Eagleton, "History, Narrative, and Marxism," in *Reading Narrative,* ed. James Phelan (Columbus: Ohio State University Press, 1989), 279.

48. Andrew and Waldron, eds., *Poems of the* Pearl *Manuscript,* note to lines 197ff. See also Ad Putter, *An Introduction to the* Gawain*-Poet* (London: Longman, 1996), 208–9.

49. In her treatment of the role of women in the Book of Judges, Mieke Bal notes that even if all narrative agents treat women horribly, the "voice of the deity is often invoked to save the ideological tenor of the overall text." Narrative theory, she says, does not share such a view: "It places the divine character on the same level, *as a character* that is, as other characters. It is precisely this methodological rigor that allows a narratological analysis to become truly critical. It also allows the analysis to become historical, in contrast with analyses based on the realistic fallacy that cannot allow for historical analysis unless factual truth can be proven" (*Death and Dissymmetry,* 34). A poem, unlike its original, does not seek to embody a universal truth; it is an act of *poesis* that breaks with its mimetic counterpart.

50. See William Vantuono, ed., *The Pearl Poems: An Omnibus Edition,* 2 vols. (New York: Garland Publishing, 1984), vol. 1, n697.

51. See Allen J. Frantzen, "The Disclosure of Sodomy in *Cleanness,*" *Proceedings of the Modern Language Association* 111 (1996): 452.

52. Putter points out that Lot's boast of the beauty of his daughters, especially his comment in line 868, "þaȝ I hit say," is not moral compunction but parental pride (*Introduction to the* Gawain-*Poet,* 207).

53. See A. C. Spearing, *Readings in Medieval Poetry* (Cambridge: Cambridge University Press, 1987), 189.

54. For an alternative discussion of this passage, see R. A. Shoaf, "'Noon Englissh Digne': Dante in Late Medieval England," in *Dante Now: Current Trends in Dante Studies,* ed. Theodore J. Cachey, Jr., William and Katherine Devers Series in Dante Studies 1 (Notre Dame: University of Notre Dame Press, 1995), 189–203.

55. See Andrew and Waldron, eds., *Poems of the* Pearl *Manuscript,* note to lines 1093–1108.

56. Milbank, *Word Made Strange,* 135.

57. See Brook Thomas, *The New Historicism and Other Old-Fashioned Topics* (Princeton: Princeton University Press, 1991), 211.

58. Albert Camus, "The Artist at Work," in *Exile and the Kingdom,* trans. Justin O'Brien (New York: Random House, 1957), 152–53.

59. See Haimo of Auxerre, *Commentary on the Book of Jonah,* trans., introduction, and notes by Deborah Everhart (Kalamazoo, Mich.: Medieval Institute Publications, 1993), 6: "The Hebrews say that Jonah was the son of a widow in Zarephath; Elijah raised him from the dead, and when he had been returned to his mother, she gave thanks, and said, 'Now by this I know that you are a man of the Lord, and the word of the Lord in your mouth is true' (3 Kings 17:24). For this reason, Jonah was called 'son of Amittai.' 'Amittai' means 'truth,' and because Elijah spoke the truth, Jonah was called 'the son of truth.'"

60. See, for example, John A. Burrow, *Ricardian Poetry: Chaucer, Gower, Langland and the* Gawain-*Poet* (New Haven: Yale University Press, 1971), 64–65.

61. Paul Piehler, *The Visionary Landscape: A Study in Medieval Allegory* (London: Edward Arnold, 1971), 20.

62. For representative examples, see F. N. M. Diekstra, "Jonah and *Patience:* The Psychology of a Prophet," *English Studies* 55 (1974): 205–17; J. J. Anderson, ed., *Patience* (New York: Barnes and Noble, 1969), 11ff.; and Myra Stokes, "'Suffering' in *Patience,*" *Chaucer Review* 18 (1984): 354–63.

63. For the penitential theme, see Lynn Staley Johnson, *The Voice of the* Gawain-*Poet* (Madison: University of Wisconsin Press, 1984), 5; for the typological view, see John B. Friedman, "Figural Typology in *Patience,*" in *The Alliterative Tradition in the Fourteenth Century*, ed. Bernard Levy and Paul Szarmach (Kent, Ohio: Kent State University Press, 1981), 99–129.

64. Nearly all major criticism tends toward this judgment of Jonah. Davenport, *Art of the* Gawain-*Poet,* is a notable exception. See, for example, David Benson, "The Impatient Reader of *Patience,*" in *Form and Matter: New Critical Perspectives on the* Pearl-*Poet,* ed. Robert J. Blanch, Miriam Youngerman Miller, and Julian Wasserman (Troy, N.Y.: Whitson Publishing, 1991), 147–61; and, in the same volume, Lorraine Kochanske Stock, "The 'Poynt' of *Patience,*" 163–75.

65. *Patience,* ed. John A. Burrow and Thorlac Turville-Petre, in *A Book of Middle English,* 2d ed. (Oxford: Blackwell, 1996), 162.

66. See Jonathan Nicholls, *The Matter of Courtesy: Medieval Courtesy Books and the* Gawain-*Poet* (Woodbridge, Suffolk: D. S. Brewer, 1985), 83; Jay Schleusner, "History and Action in *Patience,*" *Proceedings of the Modern Language Association* 86 (1971): 959–65; and David Williams, "The Point of *Patience,*" *Modern Philology* 68 (1970): 127–36.

67. Spearing, "Subtext of *Patience,*" 293.

68. Sandra Pierson Prior, *The* Pearl-*Poet Revisited* (New York: Twayne Publishers, 1994), 77.

69. For the view that *Patience* depicts humankind's powerlessness at its most extreme, see Putter, *Introduction to the* Gawain-*Poet,* 136–37.

70. Davenport, *Art of the* Gawain-*Poet,* 130.

71. Laurence Eldredge, "Late Medieval Discussions of the Continuum and the *Point* of the Middle English *Patience,*" *Vivarium* 17 (1979): 114–15.

72. I'd like to thank Nicholas Watson for suggesting this last "point" to me.

73. See Roland Barthes, *Camera Lucida: Reflections on Photography,* trans. Richard Howard (New York: Hill and Wang, 1981), 42–50.

74. Ibid., 55.

75. A contemporary audience of the poet's would be familiar enough with the allegorical dimension of the Jonah story and may bear out Brian Stock's observation that allegory "which initially gave rise to new understanding, also spawned alienation—that is, the feeling that the more one interpreted, the further one got from actualities" (*Listening for the Text: On the Uses of the Past* [Philadelphia: University of Pennsylvania Press, 1996], 36).

76. See Haimo of Auxerre: "He did not flee because he envied the salvation of the Ninevites, but because he refused to destroy his own people, the Jews. For he knew that the penitence of the Gentiles would be the ruin of the Jews.... For he had learned by the spirit of prophecy that when the Gentiles would receive an understanding of God, Israel would be reproved" (*Commentary*, 8).

77. See Vantuono's discussion in his commentary on this line in his edition, Pearl *Poems,* vol. 2, Patience *and* Sir Gawain and the Green Knight, 225. Vantuono argues, persuasively to my mind, that the manuscript reading can be retained in place of the more common emendation "non oþer" if one considers inverted word order: "*oþer* modifies *mon,* used collectively; *gayneʒ* 'will profit' if fut. t.; and *me* 'from me' is dative.... Rendering *me gayneʒ mon oþer* 'Other men will profit from me' adds to the significance of Jonas as a prefiguration of Christ who preached the salvation of mankind."

78. See Robert Blanch and Julian Wasserman, *From* Pearl *to* Gawain: *Forme and Fynisment* (Gainesville: University of Florida Press, 1995), 33.

79. See Blanch and Wasserman, who suggest that Jonah wishes the death of the Ninevites and that he is angry because God does not live by the letter of the law (*From* Pearl *to* Gawain, 32–33).

80. For a discussion of this point in relation to the biblical Jonah, see Terry Eagleton, "J. L. Austin and the Book of Jonah," in *The Book and the Text: The Bible and Literary History,* ed. Regina Schwartz (Oxford: Blackwell, 1990), 232.

81. John Milton, *Samson Agonistes: A Dramatic Poem,* in *John Milton: Complete Poems and Major Prose,* ed. Merritt Y. Hughes (New York: Odyssey Press, 1957).

82. See Haimo of Auxerre, *Commentary,* 7.

83. Laurence Eldredge, "Sheltering Space and Cosmic Space in the Middle English *Patience,*" *Annuale Mediaevale* 21 (1981): 124.

84. See, for example, Williams, who says, "Jonah calls into question the entire plan of God's justice" ("Point of *Patience,*"135). Davenport also asks, "Is God's lesson adequate to the destruction and the kind of deception employed?" (*Art of the* Gawain-*Poet,*127).

85. Ricoeur, *Symbolism of Evil,* 54–63.

86. For an extensive discussion on the scope and significance of line 523, see R. A. Shoaf, "God's 'malyse' Metaphor and Conversion in *Patience,*" *Journal of Medieval and Renaissance Studies* 11 (1982): 261–79. Shoaf says, "In the new metaphor which God has dictated, 'malyse' and 'mercy' are one and the same, just as indeed they were in the case of His treatment of the Ninevites. To show mercy to the Ninevites, God had to show 'malyse' toward them. He had to begin with 'malyse' in order to move them to repentance, but their desire to repent then called forth His mercy, which, as commentary on the book of Jonah has it, was His will (His intention) toward them all along" (262).

87. Dante Alighieri, *The Divine Comedy,* trans. Charles Singleton, 3 vols. in 6, Bollingen Series 80 (Princeton: Princeton University Press, 1980, 1982), *Paradiso* 28.109–14.

88. For a recent discussion of transcendence, God's otherness, and the dialogical relationship between the human and divine wills that fits nicely with *Patience,* see Karl Rahner, *Foundations of Christian Faith: An Introduction to the Idea of Christianity,* trans. William V. Dych (New York: Seabury Press, 1978), 44–90 and 138–78. On God's mystery Rahner has this to say: "Mystery, therefore, is not something provisional which is done away with or which in itself could be non-mysterious. It is rather the characteristic that always and necessarily characterizes God, and through him characterizes us. This is so very true that the immediate vision of God, which is promised to us as fulfillment, is the immediacy of the incomprehensible…. For in this vision we shall see God in himself, and no longer in the infinite poverty of our transcendence, that God is incomprehensible. But the vision of the mystery in itself, accepted in love, is the beatitude of the creature" (217).

89. Romano Guardini, *The Death of Socrates: An Interpretation of the Platonic Dialogues:* Euthyphro, Apology, Crito, *and* Phaedo, trans. Basil Wrighton (New York: World Publishing, 1969), 89.

90. See Theodore Bogdanos, Pearl: *Image of the Ineffable: A Study in Medieval Poetic Symbolism* (University Park: Pennsylvania State University Press, 1983); A. C. Spearing, *The* Gawain-*Poet : A Critical Study* (Cambridge: Cambridge University Press, 1970); Ian Bishop, Pearl *in Its Setting: A Critical Study of the Structure and Meaning of the Middle English Poem* (Oxford: Blackwell, 1968); Patricia Keen, *The* Pearl: *An Interpretation* (London: Routledge and Kegan Paul, 1967); Johnson, *Voice of the* Gawain-*Poet.*

91. David Aers, "The Self Mourning: Reflections on *Pearl,*" *Speculum* 68 (1993): 54–73, esp. 65–66.

92. Ibid., 59.

93. See M. M. Bakhtin, *The Dialogical Imagination: Four Essays,* ed. Michael Holquist, trans. Caryl Emerson and Michael Holquist (Austin: University of Texas Press, 1981), 342–46.

94. See Marie MacLean, *Narrative as Performance: The Baudelairean Experiment* (London: Routledge, 1988), 20.

95. Cited in MacLean, *Narrative as Performance,* 20.

96. Zumthor, *Speaking of the Middle Ages,* 63. See the epigraph at the beginning of this chapter for Zumthor's complete statement.

97. For a detailed discussion of Augustine's argument and its influence in the later Middle Ages, see Alister McGrath, *"Iustitia Dei": A History of the Christian Doctrine of Justification* (Cambridge: Cambridge University Press, 1989), 53–70.

98. See Heiko Oberman, *The Harvest of Medieval Theology: Gabriel Biel and Late Medieval Nominalism* (Grand Rapids, Mich.: Eerdmans, 1967), 214 (emphasis added).

99. Ibid., 215.

100. For a discussion of this point, see Gordon Leff, *Bradwardine and the Pelagians: A Study of His* De causa dei *and Its Opponents* (Cambridge: Cambridge University Press, 1957), 140–59.

101. McGrath provides a detailed and informative analysis of this entire subject in *"Iustitia Dei,"* 109–55 and 166–80. In *The Intellectual Origins of the European Reformation* (Oxford: Blackwell, 1993), 69–93, McGrath provides a more incisive discussion, which I rely on here, that superbly conveys the gist of the matter as it applies to the social and political issues involved.

102. McGrath, *Intellectual Origins,* 80–82. For related discussion, see William Courtenay, *Covenant and Causality in Medieval Thought* (London: Variorum Reprints, 1984), especially 94–115; and Courtenay's other work, *Schools and Scholars in Fourteenth Century England* (Princeton: Princeton University Press, 1987), 250–307.

103. McGrath, *Intellectual Origins,* 81. See also Janet Coleman, Piers Plowman *and the "Moderni,"* (Rome; Edizioni di Storia e Letteratura, 1981), 201–2, n30, where she cites Ockham: "God of his own free will can accept as meritorious an act arising *ex puris naturalibus* without the *habitus* of *caritas.*"

104. See Courtenay, *Schools and Scholars,* 324.

105. For the wounds of Christ and their function as a sign of his humanity, see Miri Rubin, *Corpus Christi: The Eucharist in Late Medieval Culture* (Cambridge: Cambridge University Press, 1991), 302–6; David Aers and Lynn Staley, *The Powers of the Holy: Religion, Politics, and Gender in Late Medieval Culture* (University Park: Pennsylvania State University Press, 1996), 26–27;

Sarah Beckwith, *Christ's Body: Identity, Culture, and Society in Late Medieval Writings* (London: Routledge, 1993), 42.

106. See Aers, "The Self Mourning," 55–59.

107. The particular properties of the Eucharist, as Miri Rubin describes it, make it especially "friendly" to the needs and psychological condition of the Dreamer: "It was this-worldly in emphasizing that channels of regeneration and salvation were available and attainable, renewable and never exhaustible. It possessed little of the eschatological pull which informed the cultural worlds of late antiquity, or of the early modern era, but was geared toward the present, was fulfilled here and now, offering powerful and tangible rewards to the living in the present, as well as to their relatives the dead" (*Corpus Christi,* 348).

108. On this point, see Lynn Staley Johnson, "The *Pearl* Dreamer and the Eleventh Hour," in *Text and Matter,* ed. Blanch, Miller, and Wasserman. The author of *Pearl,* Johnson says, "seems to be conscious of the ties between the *Romance of the Rose* and the biblical imagery of desire, since he adapts certain key elements of Amant's experience in ways that highlight the *Pearl* Dreamer's state of mind" (5).

109. For a general and insightful introduction to Lacan's ideas as they relate to this discussion, see Stuart Schneiderman, *Jacques Lacan: The Death of an Intellectual Hero* (Cambridge: Harvard University Press, 1983), 150–55; see also Malcolm Bowie, *Freud, Proust, and Lacan: Theory as Fiction* (Cambridge: Cambridge University Press, 1988), 99–135.

110. Schneiderman, *Lacan,* 151–52 (emphasis added).

111. For a discussion of the possible liturgical dates, see Elizabeth Petroff, "Landscape in *Pearl:* The Transformation of Nature," *Chaucer Review* 16 (1981): 181–93.

112. Aers, "The Self Mourning," 57–58.

113. For a discussion of this point, see Aron Gurevich, *Medieval Popular Culture: Problems of Belief and Perception,* trans. Janos M. Bak and Paul A. Hollingsworth (Cambridge: Cambridge University Press, 1988), 99–103.

114. David Jeffrey, "Postscript," in *By Things Seen: Reference and Recognition in Medieval Thought,* ed. David Jeffrey (Ottawa: University of Ottawa Press, 1979), 251. See also Jeffrey's earlier suggestion (240) that with the appearance of Aristotelian thought the current from being to becoming reverses and it is the rich experience of the created order which leads people to an apprehension of its eternal model. Immanence itself, he says, does not prevail until vertical organization—the principle of reference—gives way to horizontal order.

115. Peter W. Travis, "The Semiotics of Christ's Body in the English Cycles," in *Approaches to Teaching Medieval English Drama,* ed. Richard

Emmerson (New York: MLA Publications, 1990), 72–73. See also Peter W. Travis, "The Social Body of the Dramatic Christ in Medieval England," *Acta* 13 (1985): 17–36.

116. "Love for the fatherland is founded in the root of a charity which puts, not the private things before those common, but the common things before the private." Cited in Ernst Kantorowicz, *The King's Two Bodies: A Study in Medieval Political Theology* (Princeton: Princeton University Press, 1957), 242. The words are those of Tolemeo of Lucca but, Kantorowicz says, were attributed to Aquinas.

117. See "Our Daily Work: A Mirror of Discipline," in *The Law of Love: English Spirituality in the Age of Wyclif,* ed David Lyle Jeffrey (Grand Rapids, Mich.: Eerdmans, 1988), 236–64. The anonymous author emphasizes the value of work to salvation and likens Christians to servants in God's vineyard who are called upon to work; he says, "that person prays without ceasing who is always doing good" (246).

118. The Dreamer's allusion to "Pater" and "Creed" indicate that he took seriously the responsibility to learn the minimum that was required of the laity in one's understanding of the faith, and early on instructing his daughter in the rudiments. In addition to the Creed and Paternoster, the laity were expected to know the Ave Maria, the sacraments, the seven deadly sins, works of charity, acts of mercy, and the seven virtues, all of which attested to a concerted desire to have a more active as well as a better informed laity. See R. N. Swanson, *Church and Society in Late Medieval England* (London: Blackwell, 1993), 275–99.

119. Those critics who have linked the Vineyard parable to the harvest or who have recognized the special appeal of its language to the agricultural society of fourteenth-century England are Piehler, *Visionary Landscape,* 150–52; Spearing, Gawain-*Poet,* 101; Bogdanos, *Pearl,* 91.

120. In fourteenth-century France the vineyard day laborers had a widespread reputation for standing up for wage and work reform against strong opposition from their noble and ecclesiastical employers. See Jacques LeGoff, *Time, Work, and Culture in the Middle Ages,* trans. Arthur Goldhammer (Chicago: University of Chicago Press, 1980), 47, n25. For a discussion of labor conditions, clocks, and the social impact of both the Ordinance of Labourers and the Statute of Labourers, see Christopher Dyer, *Standards of Living in the Later Middle Ages: Social Change in England, c. 1200–1520* (Cambridge: Cambridge University Press, 1989), 27–86 and 219–32.

121. In this regard, see the arrangement between the Reeve and his master in Chaucer's *General Prologue* portrait: "His swyn, his hors, his stoor, and his pultrye / Was hooly in this Reves governynge, / And by his covenant

yaf the rekenynge" (598–600). For a more comprehensive discussion of covenants, see Richard Firth Green, *A Crisis of Truth: Literature and Law in Ricardian England* (Philadelphia: University of Pennsylvania Press, 1999), 338–426.

122. See Walter Ullmann, *Principles of Government and Politics in the Middle Ages* (London: Methuen, 1974), 297.

123. See Gerald Groveland Walsh, "Dante's Philosophy of History," *Catholic Historical Review* 20 (1934): 117–34.

124. As was the case in the Wedding Feast in *Cleanness,* the poet may be making an accommodation for the virtuous pagans, those who have done what is in them, to be included as laborers in God's vineyard.

125. Lee Patterson's comment about Chaucer's poetry seems equally apt to apply to the Dreamer and the *Pearl*-poet himself: "the characteristic location of Chaucerian poetry is precisely the middle ground, the space between the atemporal beginning and a transcendent end.… Man is a creature of the middle, a historical being who dreams of a moment before and after history that he can never finally attain" ("'What man artow?': Authorial Self-Definition in *The Tale of Sir Thopas* and *The Tale of Melibee,*" *Studies in the Age of Chaucer* 11 [1989]: 174).

126. See John A. Burrow, *Langland's Fictions* (Oxford: Clarendon Press, 1993), 12.

127. Bogdanos, *Pearl,* 114, among others, answers this question affirmatively.

128. Caroline Walker Bynum, *Fragmentation and Redemption: Essays on Gender and the Human Body in Medieval Religion* (New York: Zone Books, 1991), 44.

129. Cited in Kantorowicz, *King's Two Bodies,* 479. Remigio de Girolami was Aquinas's pupil and Dante's teacher.

130. Sealth (Seattle), chief of the Suquamish and Duwamish tribes, in an address to the governor of Washington territory. Sealth was a convert to Catholicism. See "The White Man Will Never Be Alone," in *Literature of the American Indian,* ed. Thomas Sanders and Walter W. Peck (Beverly Hills: Glencoe Press, 1973), 285.

131. Critical commentary on the poem is still slight when compared to the works of the *Pearl*-poet, but a number of new editions of the poem have appeared that may stimulate interest. The text used for citations to the poem is that of Clifford Peterson, ed., *Saint Erkenwald* (Philadelphia: University of Pennsylvania Press, 1977).

132. On this last point, see Maurice Keen, *English Society in the Later Middle Ages 1348–1500* (London: Penguin Books, 1990), 70–79.

133. Louise Fradenburg, *City, Marriage, Tournament: Arts of Rule in Late Medieval Scotland* (Madison: University of Wisconsin Press, 1991), 8–9. See also her remarks on the primal scene (10) as a means of encountering one's own createdness, mortality, and finitude.

134. See Steven Ozment, *The Reformation in the Cities: The Appeal of Protestantism to Sixteenth-Century Germany and Switzerland* (New Haven: Yale University Press, 1975), 7. According to Berndt Moeller, *Imperial Cities and the Reformation: Three Essays,* ed. and trans. H. C. Erik Midelfort and Mark U. Edwards, Jr. (Durham, N.C.: Labyrinth Press, 1982), 66–71, although civic religion or citified theology is more visible in the sixteenth century, its origins are clearly discernible in the fourteenth century through what Moeller refers to as the strong medieval belief in the city as a unified *corpus Christianum* (49).

135. See Jean Dunbabin, "The Reception and Interpretation of Aristotle's *Politics*," in *The Cambridge History of Later Medieval Philosophy: From the Rediscovery of Aristotle to the Disintegration of Scholasticism,* ed. Norman Kretzmann, Anthony Kenny, and Jan Pinborg (Cambridge: Cambridge University Press, 1988), 732–34. For a related discussion of the growth of the cities and the emergence of citizen consciousness, see David Nicholas, *The Later Medieval City: 1300–1500* (New York: Longman, 1997), 288–302.

136. Although English cities and towns were smaller than their continental counterparts, they did participate in urbanization and were an integral part of the wider political and social changes of the late medieval–early modern era. What distinguishes England from the continent is the rich interplay and integration of the sacred and the secular realms. See *The English Medieval Town: A Reader in English Urban History,* ed. Gervase Rosser and Richard Holt (New York: Longman, 1990), 1–4.

137. See David Luscombe and G. R. Evans, "The Twelfth-Century Renaissance," in *The Cambridge History of Medieval Political Thought c. 350–c. 1450,* ed. J. H. Burns (Cambridge: Cambridge University Press, 1988), 314, 338; see also Luscombe, "City and Politics before the Coming of the *Politics: Some Illustrations,*" in *Church and City, 1000–1500: Essays in Honour of Christopher Brooke,* ed. David Abulafia, Michael Franklin, and Miri Rubin (Cambridge: Cambridge University Press, 1992), 41–55. By the end of the thirteenth century, in the estimation of Peter Riesenberg, the push for citizenship in London compares favorably to that in Florence (*Citizenship in the Western Tradition* [Chapel Hill: University of North Carolina Press, 1992], 117).

138. For *civitas* as *caritas,* see Volker Breidecker, *Florenz oder "Die Rede, die zum Auge spricht" : Kunst, Fest und Macht im Ambiente der Stadt* (München: Wilhelm Fink Verlag, 1990), 41–2. Also, Jeanne Quillet, "Community, Counsel,

and Representation," in *Cambridge History of Medieval Political Thought,* ed. Burns, 526–27; Antony Black, "The Individual and Society," also in *Cambridge History of Medieval Political Thought,* ed. Burns, 596–99.

139. See E. Gordon Whatley, "Heathens and Saints: *St. Erkenwald* in Its Legendary Context," *Speculum* 61 (1986): 330–63; *The Saint of London: The Life and Miracles of St. Erkenwald,* ed. and trans. E. Gordon Whatley (Binghamton: MRTS, 1989).

140. Whatley, "Heathens and Saints," 360–61.

141. See Ruth Morse, "Introduction," in *St. Erkenwald,* ed. Ruth Morse (Cambridge: D. S. Brewer, 1975), 18–21.

142. For a discussion of this point, see McGrath, *"Iustitia Dei,"* 49.

143. Gordon Leff, *Bradwardine and the Pelagians,* 153. See also Marcia Colish, "The Virtuous Pagan: Dante and the Christian Tradition," in *The Un-bounded Community: Conversations across Times and Disciplines,* ed. Duncan Fisher and William Caferro (New York: Garland Publishing, 1995), 1–66. Colish cites Peter Lombard on the point that God's power is not constrained by the sacraments (5).

144. See E. Gordon Whatley, "The Uses of Hagiography: The Legend of Pope Gregory and the Emperor Trajan in the Middle Ages," *Viator* 15 (1984): 25–30. See also Cindy L. Vitto, *The Virtuous Pagan in Middle English Literature,* Transactions of the American Philosophical Society 79:5 (Philadelphia: American Philosophical Society, 1989), 41–42.

145. On this point, see Caroline Walker Bynum, *The Resurrection of the Body in Western Christianity, 200–1336* (New York: Columbia University Press, 1995), xvii–xviii, 326–29.

146. Colish, "Virtuous Pagan," 12–15, 34–35.

147. For Langland, see *Piers Plowman,* the B Text, 11.141–69, 12.281–92. For John of Salisbury, see *Policraticus* 5.8. See also, Colish, "Virtuous Pagan," 12.

148. For an insightful discussion of the political dimensions of the poem, see Frank Grady, *"Piers Plowman, St. Erkenwald,* and the Rule of Exceptional Salvations," *Yearbook of Langland Studies* 6 (1992): 61–86.

149. See André Vauchez, *The Laity in the Middle Ages: Religious Beliefs and Devotional Practices,* trans. Margery Schneider, ed. Daniel Bornstein (Notre Dame: University of Notre Dame Press, 1993), 51–60. For an English example, see J. W. McKenna, "Popular Canonization as Political Propaganda: The Cult of Archbishop Scrope," *Speculum* 45 (1970): 609.

150. Vauchez, *Laity,* 167.

151. For a discussion of the way the pagan question was intertwined with questions concerning the natural law and inherent human virtue, see Janet Coleman, Piers Plowman *and the "Moderni,"* 36–38 and 108–33; see also

Kenelm Foster, O.P., *The Two Dantes and Other Studies* (Berkeley: University of California Press, 1977), 198–99 and 220–22.

152. See especially William Courtenay, "Nature and the Natural in Twelfth-Century Thought," in *Covenant and Causality in Medieval Thought* (London: Variorum Reprints, 1984), 1–26. See also, in the same edition, his "Covenant and Causality in Pierre D'Ailly," 94–119. In addition, see Kantorowicz, *King's Two Bodies,* 210–11. For a discussion of the way justice was linked with the common good, see Nicolai Rubenstein, "Political Ideas in Sienese Art: The Frescoes of Ambrogio Lorenzetti and Taddeo di Bartolo in the Palazzo Pubblico," *Journal of the Warburg and Courtauld Institutes* 21 (1958): 179–207. The theme existed before the revival of Aristotle, Rubinstein says, but it achieved unprecedented importance after the translation of the *Politics;* in the legal formation of *utilitas publica* the theme played an important role in canonist and legist theories (184).

153. See Walter Ullmann, *The Medieval Foundations of Renaissance Humanism* (Ithaca: Cornell University Press, 1977), 7–8; see also Ullmann, *Principles of Government and Politics,* 232–34.

154. Ullmann, *Medieval Foundations,* 7–8.

155. See Joseph Canning, "A Fourteenth-Century Contribution to the Theory of Citizenship: Political Man and the Problem of Created Citizenship in the Thought of Baldus De Ubaldis," in *Authority and Power: Studies on Medieval Law and Government Presented to Walter Ullmann on His Seventieth Birthday,* ed. Brian Tierney and Peter Linehan (Cambridge: Cambridge University Press, 1980), 197–212.

156. See Walsh, "Dante's Philosophy of History," 117–35.

157. Kantorowicz, *King's Two Bodies,* 489.

158. Peterson provides a more extensive list of parallels in his edition of *Saint Erkenwald,* 86–87, nn19–22.

159. *Saint Erkenwald,* ed. Peterson, 86, n15.

160. Dyer, *Standards of Living,* 239.

161. See Jacques LeGoff, *The Birth of Purgatory,* trans. Arthur Goldhammer (Chicago: University of Chicago Press, 1986), 226.

162. See David Luscombe, "Introduction: The Formation of Political Thought in the West," in *Cambridge History of Medieval Political Thought,* ed. Burns, 163.

163. See Rosser's point that activities like the rebuilding of a church were forms of collective behavior through which the urban community is given tangible form or is able to recreate itself (*English Medieval Town,* 2–3).

164. *Saint Erkenwald,* ed. Peterson, 102, n176. See also T. McAlindon, "Hagiography into Art: A Study on *St. Erkenwald*," *Studies in Philology* 67 (1970): 491.

165. See *St. Erkenwald,* ed. Morse, 21; see also Arnold Davidson, "Mystery, Miracle, and Meaning in *St. Erkenwald," Papers on Language and Literature* 16 (1980): 37–44.

166. Georges Bataille, *Theory of Religion,* trans. Robert Hurley (New York: Zone Books, 1989), 48.

167. In *Theory of Religion,* Bataille comments on the body in its material and spiritual balance: "Insofar as it is spirit, the human reality is holy, but it is profane insofar as it is real. Animals, plants, tools, and other controllable things form a real world with the bodies that control them, a world subject to and traversed by divine forces, but fallen." Today, the animal has lost its status as man's fellow creature, he says, and man, perceiving the animality in himself, regards it as a "defect" (38–39).

168. Bataille, *Theory of Religion,* 47.

169. The bishop's tears and the "resurrection" of the lawyer may have echoes of the Lazarus episode in *Piers Plowman* B. 16. There Christ brings Lazarus back from the dead and has the added detail of showing Christ weeping before he performs the miracle, "Ac [er] he made þe maistrie *mestus cepit esse* / And wepte water with hise eiʒen; þer seiʒen it manye" (115–16). If so, Erkenwald's tears and those of his congregation amount to a kind of Christlike compassion and forgiveness of a "brother."

170. See Bynum, *Resurrection of the Body,* 11.

171. Ibid., 235.

172. See Tertullian, *Treatise on the Resurrection,* ed. and trans. Ernest Evans (London: SPCK, 1960), xi–xii.

173. Ibid., 153–55.

174. The version of the Trajan story adapted here is the Thomistic, or "orthodox," version, where the lawyer has to be alive to be baptized before he can be redeemed, so that his salvation won't be precedent setting. This is very different from Langland's version. I want to thank Nicholas Watson for making this distinction clear for me and wish to add that it is Erkenwald who insists on bringing the lawyer back to life. The narrator, I would suggest, may not see things as Erkenwald does and may be closer to Langland's outlook.

175. Langland's depiction of the lawyers in *Piers Plowman* adds ample testimony. See also Sylvia L. Thrupp, "The City as the Idea of Social Order," in *Society and History: Essays by Sylvia L. Thrupp,* ed. Raymond Grew and Nicholas Stenech (Ann Arbor: University of Michigan Press, 1977), 89–100.

176. See Hans Blumenberg, *The Legitimacy of the Modern Age,* trans. Robert M. Wallace (Cambridge: MIT Press, 1985), 131.

177. Cited in Blumenberg, *Legitimacy,* 54.

178. Dante also uses *medicina* in *Paradiso* 20.141 as his term for baptism.

179. Thomas D. Hill points out that "an implicitly universalist eschatology underlies *any* account of the Harrowing in which all of the souls of the lost are freed after Christ's descent into the lower realms of death and punishment" because it would limit the power and efficacy of the passion if only a select number of souls are liberated from hell ("Universal Salvation and Its Literary Context in *Piers Plowman* B. 18," *Yearbook of Langland Studies* 5 [1991]: 70, emphasis mine). Hill goes on to say that "certain medieval eschatological legends (such as the Theophilus legend) in which some particularly notorious sinner is rescued by the essentially gratuitous mercy of the Virgin Mary are fundamentally universalist in their implications, although the framework of the legend is still the traditional Christian cosmology of heaven, purgatory, and hell" (70).

180. Blumenberg, *Legitimacy,* 177.

181. Bynum points out that Christ ate food after he had risen from the dead to show that his body also had been resurrected (*Fragmentation and Redemption,* 353, n96).

182. The ringing of the bells and the regeneration of the spirit of the community is reminiscent of the conclusion of the harrowing in passus 18 of *Piers Plowman.* For further comment on the simultaneous ringing of the bells as a mark of solemn or joyful moments, see *St. Erkenwald,* in *A Book of Middle English,* ed. John A. Burrow and Thorlac Turville-Petre, 2d ed. (Oxford: Blackwell, 1996), note to line 352.

183. See Bynum's discussion of Aquinas's authoritative definition of the person wherein "the full person does not exist until body (matter) is restored to its form at the end of time" (*Fragmentation and Redemption,* 228). Similarly, the poet has practiced his own redemption, piecing together the body of this poem from the fragments he gathered from the "crafty cronecles," thereby reconciling the pagan lawyer, or all pagans, to the community by the memorial of the poem.

4.
Chaucer

1. For a review of this topic, see the collection of articles entitled *Chaucer's Religious Tales,* ed. C. David Benson and Elizabeth Robertson, Chaucer Studies 15 (Cambridge: D. S. Brewer, 1990).

2. For a discussion of this point and for a critique of the approach sponsored by Benson and Robertson in *Chaucer's Religious Tales,* see David Aers, "Faith, Ethics, and Community: Reflections on Reading Late Medieval English Writing," *Journal of Medieval and Early Modern Studies* 28 (1998): 341–69.

3. M. M. Bakhtin, *The Dialogical Imagination: Four Essays,* ed. Michael Holquist, trans. Caryl Emerson and Michael Holquist (Austin: University of Texas Press, 1981), 55.

4. M. M. Bakhtin, *Problems of Dostoevsky's Poetics,* trans. Caryl Emerson (Minneapolis: University of Minnesota Press, 1984), 76.

5. See Michael Holquist, *Dialogism: Bakhtin and His World* (London: Routledge, 1990), 69–70: "Heteroglossia is a way of conceiving the world as made up of a roiling mass of languages, each of which has its own distinct formal markers....The idea of heteroglossia comes as close as possible to conceptualizing a locus where the great centripetal and centrifugal forces that shape discourse can meaningfully come together."

6. Lisa Kiser, *Truth and Textuality in Chaucer's Poetry* (Hanover, N.H.: University Press of New England, 1991), 5.

7. Wolfgang Iser, *The Fictive and the Imaginary: Charting Literary Anthropology* (Baltimore: Johns Hopkins University Press, 1993), 296–97.

8. Michael Oakeshott, "The Voice of Poetry in the Conversation of Mankind," in *Rationalism in Politics and Other Essays* (New York: Basic Books, 1962), 201.

9. For a discussion of the relationship between the Clerk's tale and Petrarch's original, see Richard Neuse, *Chaucer's Dante: Allegory and Epic Theatre in the* Canterbury Tales (Berkeley: University of California Press, 1991), 221–41.

10. See F. Edward Cranz, "Cusanus, Luther, and the Mystical Tradition," in *The Pursuit of Holiness in Late Medieval and Renaissance Religion,* ed. Charles Trinkhaus and Heiko Oberman (Leiden: E. J. Brill, 1974), 99.

11. Charles A. Owen, *Pilgrimage and Storytelling in the* Canterbury Tales: *The Dialectic of "Ernest" and "Game"* (Norman: University of Oklahoma Press, 1977), 8: "Strangely enough, the strongest element in the interacting parts that absorbed the creative energies of Chaucer's last years is not the powerful medieval motif of pilgrimage. Once the Host has made a community of the group at his inn, the pilgrims become storytellers.... In a sense, the storytelling contest supplants the pilgrimage."

12. Edmund Reiss, "The Pilgrimage Narrative and the *Canterbury Tales,*" *Studies in Philology* 67 (1970): 300.

13. Those who think of pilgrimage mainly as *peregrinatio,* the term favored by the church fathers and which epitomizes a radical spirituality, a posture of alienation and exile from this world, will come away from literary and theological accounts of late medieval pilgrimages with the impression that late medieval pilgrimages had suffered a remarkable moral decline. On *peregrinatio* and related matters, see Gerhart B. Ladner, "Greatness in Medieval History,"

Catholic Historical Review 50 (1964): 1–26, and *"Homo Viator:* Medieval Ideas on Alienation and Order," *Speculum* 42 (1967): 233–59.

14. Richard Lanham, "Game, Play, and High Seriousness in Chaucer's Poetry," *English Studies* 48 (1967): 11.

15. German eliminates much of the confusion associated with the single English word *pilgrimage* by supplying two words to designate separate notions and experiences: *"Wallfahrt* obtains when someone, from a religious motive residing within his own being, leaves his community to visit a certain sacred place, with the intention of returning home. A *Pilgerfahrt* need not possess this intention of returning; it may even, from ascetic motives, explicitly renounce such an intention and last until the end of life. The motive is one of a religious nature, that is obvious, but it must also be subjective, otherwise one could call the visit to a council *Wallfahrt;* and the leaving of the community is necessary, otherwise one could call each churchgoer a *Wallfahrer"* (Bernhard Kötting, *Peregrinatio Religiosa: Wallfahrten in der Antike und das Pilgerwesen in der alten Kirche* [Münster: Antiquariat Th. Stenderhoff, 1980], 11).

16. Edmond-René Labande, "Recherches sur les pèlerins dans l'europe des XIᵉ et XIIᵉ siecles," *Cahiers de civilisation médiévale* 1 (1958): 164.

17. See Leon Zander, "Le pèlerinage," *Irenikon* (issue: *L'église et les églises*) (1955): 469–86.

18. *Piers Plowman by William Langland: An Edition of the C-Text,* ed. Derek Pearsall (Berkeley: University of California Press, 1978), passus 1.181–85.

19. For a discussion of the Prioress's harmful sentimentalism, see Ruth Ames, *God's Plenty: Chaucer's Christian Humanism* (Chicago: Loyola University Press, 1984), 200–201. I am especially impressed with Ames's comparison of the Prioress with many kind and well-mannered ladies in twentieth-century middle America who are moved to sorrow for murdered children that they read about, whose hearts, she says, "bleed especially for those murdered sensationally by Reds or Blacks, but not for Yellow children slain in a pit in My-Lai" (201). Ames also has some useful comments on the relations that existed between Jews and Christians in the late Middle Ages that bear meaningfully on the Prioress's tale (see 192–99).

20. See Alfred David, "An ABC to the Style of the Prioress," in *Acts of Interpretation: The Text in Its Contexts 700–1600: Essays on Medieval and Renaissance Literature in Honor of E. Talbot Donaldson,* ed. Mary J. Carruthers and Elizabeth Kirk (Norman, Okla.: Pilgrim Books, 1982), 156. See also Louise Fradenburg, "Criticism, Anti-Semitism, and the Prioress's Tale," *Exemplaria* 1 (1989): 69–115; and Richard Rex, *"The Sins of Madame Eglentyne" and Other Essays on Chaucer* (Newark: University of Delaware Press, 1995).

21. For an overall discussion of several of these points, see Fradenburg, "Criticism," 88–108.

22. Ibid., 88.

23. See Hyam Maccoby, *The Sacred Executioner: Human Sacrifice and the Legacy of Guilt* (New York: Thames and Hudson, 1982), 158.

24. For a discussion of the role of Mary, see Marina Warner, *Alone of All Her Sex: The Myth and the Cult of the Virgin Mary* (New York: Alfred Knopf, 1976); Caroline Walker Bynum, *Jesus as Mother: Studies in the Spirituality of the High Middle Ages* (Berkeley: University of California Press, 1982), 125–26 and 224–30; R. Howard Bloch, *Medieval Misogyny and the Invention of Western Romantic Love* (Chicago: University of Chicago Press, 1991), 93–112; Elaine Pagels, *Adam, Eve, and the Serpent* (New York: Random House, 1988), 78–97; Michael P. Carroll, *The Cult of the Virgin Mary: Psychological Origins* (Princeton: Princeton University Press, 1986).

25. See Hilda Graef, *Mary: A History of Doctrine and Devotion,* vol. 1 (New York: Sheed and Ward, 1963), 180 ff.

26. See Ernst Guldan, *Eva und Maria: Eine Antithese als Bildmotiv* (Köln: Hermann Böhlaus, 1966), 28.

27. See Gerhart B. Ladner, *The Idea of Reform: Its Impact on Christian Thought and Action in the Age of the Fathers* (New York: Harper and Row, 1967), 326 ff.; and Heiko Oberman, *The Harvest of Medieval Theology: Gabriel Biel and Late Medieval Nominalism* (Grand Rapids, Mich.: Eerdmans, 1967), 281.

28. Maccoby, *Sacred Executioner,* 147. See also the brief discussion in R. N. Swanson, *Religion and Devotion in Europe, c. 1215–c. 1515* (Cambridge: Cambridge University Press, 1995), 144–45.

29. Robert Hanning, "From *Eva* to *Ave* to Eglentyne and Alisoun: Chaucer's Insight into the Roles Women Play," *Signs* 2 (1977): 588.

30. See Jaroslav Pelikan, *The Growth of Medieval Theology* (Chicago: University of Chicago Press, 1978), 160–74.

31. See Gerhart B. Ladner, *"Ad Imaginem Dei": The Image of Man in Medieval Art* (Latrobe, Pa.: Archabbey Press, 1965), 11–12.

32. See M.-D. Chenu, *Nature, Man, and Society in the Twelfth Century,* trans. and ed. Jerome Taylor (Chicago: University of Chicago Press, 1968), 4–18.

33. See Guldan, *Eva und Maria,* 117 ff.

34. Numerous illustrations of the parallels appear in the *Bible Moralisee* and in the *Pauper's Bible*. See also the example provided from the twelfth-century Hildesheim Doors.

35. Leo Steinberg, *The Sexuality of Christ in Renaissance Art and in Modern Oblivion* (New York: Pantheon, 1984), 13–15.

36. See Charles Wood, "The Doctor's Dilemma: Sin, Salvation, and the Menstrual Cycle in Medieval Thought," *Speculum* 56 (1981): 710–27.

37. See Guldan, *Eva und Maria,* 130 ff.

38. See Joan Ferrante, *Woman as Image in Medieval Literature* (New York: Columbia University Press, 1975), 30.

39. George Rowley, *Ambrogio Lorenzetti* (Princeton: Princeton University Press, 1958), 57–66. Rowley has determined that Lorenzetti probably did not paint the fresco as it now exists but the present one is surely based on a Lorenzetti prototype.

40. Ferrante, *Woman as Image,* 129–52.

41. The Middle English version of the *Alma redemptoris* appears in Carleton Brown's discussion of the sources and analogues to the Prioress's tale, "The Prioress's Tale," in *Sources and Analogues of Chaucer's Canterbury Tales,* ed. W. F. Bryan and Germaine Dempster (New York: Humanities Press, 1958), 469.

42. For discussion of this point, see Fradenburg, "Criticism," 99–100.

43. See Robert Worth Frank, Jr., "Miracles of the Virgin, Medieval Anti-Semitism, and the Prioress's Tale," in *The Wisdom of Poetry: Essays in Early English Literature in Honor of Morton W. Bloomfield,* ed. Larry Benson and Siegfried Wenzel (Kalamazoo, Mich.: Medieval Institute Publications, 1982), 177–88.

44. See Sister Nicholas Maltman, O.P., "The Divine Granary, or the End of the Prioress's 'Greyn,'" *Chaucer Review* 17 (1981–82): 164.

45. Ibid., 165.

46. Frank Kermode, *The Genesis of Secrecy: On the Interpretation of Narrative* (Cambridge: Harvard University Press, 1979), 2.

47. Kermode, *Genesis of Secrecy,* 3.

48. Slavoj Žižek, *The Sublime Object of Ideology* (London: Verso, 1989), 56.

49. See Gordon Leff, *The Dissolution of the Medieval Outlook* (New York: New York University Press, 1976), 130–31.

50. See especially Sherry Reames, "The Cecilia Legend as Chaucer Inherited It and Retold It: The Disappearance of an Augustinian Ideal," *Speculum* 55 (1980): 38–57.

51. On this point, see Paul Olson, *The* Canterbury Tales *and the Good Society* (Princeton: Princeton University Press, 1986), 150.

52. For seeing and blindness in the Second Nun's tale, see Carolyn Collette, "A Closer Look at Seinte Cecile's Special Vision," *Chaucer Review* 10 (1976): 337–49.

53. See the sermon in *Mirk's Festial,* "On the Conversion of St. Paul," where Paul is described as learning the law of Christ during his three days of

blindness and is a prime example of God's desire that everyone be included in his conversion (cited in David Lyle Jeffrey, ed. and trans., *The Law of Love: English Spirituality in the Age of Wyclif* [Grand Rapids, Mich.: Eerdmans, 1988], 320–24).

54. In the *City of God* 11.28, Augustine speaks of love in terms of the specific weight of bodies: "For the specific weight of bodies is, in a manner, their love, whether bodies tend downward in virtue of their heaviness or strive upwards in virtue of their lightness. A material body is borne along by its weight in a particular direction, just as a soul is by its love" (cited in John M. Rist, *Augustine: Ancient Thought Baptized* [Cambridge: Cambridge University Press, 1994], 174).

55. See H. Marshall Leicester, *The Disenchanted Self: Representing the Subject in the* Canterbury Tales (Berkeley: University of California Press, 1990), 203–5.

56. See Paul Beichner, "Confrontation, Contempt of Court, and Chaucer's Cecilia," *Chaucer Review* 8 (1974): 198–204.

57. For further discussion, see L. Shannon Jung, "Ethics and the Image of the Self in the Theology of Story," in *Religious Sociology: Interfaces and Boundaries,* ed. William H. Swatos, Jr. (New York: Greenwood Press, 1987), 71.

58. The Second Nun relies heavily on Dante's text, but when she adds to it she brings even greater attention to the human elements in Christ. See, for example, the line "His Sone in blood and flessh to clothe and wynde" (8.42).

59. See Paul Ricoeur, "Mimesis and Representation," trans. David Pellauer, in *A Ricoeur Reader: Reflection and Imagination,* ed. Mario J. Valdés (Toronto: University of Toronto Press, 1991), 138.

60. For a discussion of *multiplication* and related terms, see Lee Patterson's excellent discussion, "Perpetual Motion: Alchemy and the Technology of the Self," *Studies in the Age of Chaucer* 15 (1993), 25–57. See also Joseph Grennen, "The Canon's Yeoman and the Cosmic Furnace: Language and Meaning in the *Canon's Yeoman's Tale*," *Criticism* 4 (1962): 225–40.

61. See Mircea Eliade, *The Forge and the Crucible: The Origins and Structures of Alchemy* (Chicago: University of Chicago Press, 1962), 169.

62. D. W. Robertson, Jr., *Chaucer's London* (New York: John Wiley, 1968), 217.

63. Robertson, *Chaucer's London,* 217. For further discussion of *pietas,* see D. W. Robertson, Jr., *A Preface to Chaucer: Studies in Medieval Perspectives* (Princeton: Princeton University Press, 1962), 163.

64. For a discussion of this point, see David Luscombe, "City and Politics before the Coming of the *Politics,* Some Illustrations," in *Church and City, 1000–1500: Essays in Honour of Christopher Brooke,* ed. David Abulafia,

Michael Franklin, and Miri Rubin (Cambridge: Cambridge University Press, 1992), 41–55. See also Joseph Canning, "A Fourteenth-Century Contribution to the Theory of Citizenship: Political Man and the Problem of Created Citizenship in the Thought of Baldus De Ubaldis," in *Authority and Power: Studies on Medieval Law and Government Presented to Walter Ullmann on His Seventieth Birthday,* ed. Brian Tierney and Peter Linehan (Cambridge: Cambridge University Press, 1980), 197–212.

65. See Ernst Kantorowicz, *The King's Two Bodies: A Study in Medieval Political Theology* (Princeton: Princeton University Press, 1957), 232–42.

66. I am indebted to Peter S. Hawkins for his illuminating discussion of this theme in relation to Dante, "Divide and Conquer: Augustine in the *Divine Comedy,*" *Proceedings of the Modern Language Association* 106 (1991): 471–82.

67. Russell Peck has suggested that Cecilia spiritually "marries" Tiburce ("The Ideas of 'Entente' and Translation in Chaucer's *Second Nun's Tale,*" *Annuale mediaevale* 8 [1967]: 31). For a discussion of marriage in the tale, see V. A. Kolve, "Chaucer's *Second Nun's Tale* and the Iconography of Saint Cecilia," in *New Perspectives in Chaucer Criticism,* ed. Donald M. Rose (Norman, Okla.: Pilgrim Books, 1981), 137–74. I have benefited greatly from Kolve's discussion.

68. For a discussion of this point, see Thomas J. Heffernan, *Sacred Biography: Saints and Their Biographers in the Middle Ages* (Oxford: Oxford University Press, 1988), 5.

69. See Jeffrey Schnapp, *The Transfiguration of History at the Center of Dante's Paradise* (Princeton: Princeton University Press, 1986), 203 and 216.

70. See Joseph Grennen, "Saint Cecilia's 'Chemical Wedding': The Unity of the *Canterbury Tales,* Fragment VIII," *Journal of English and Germanic Philology* 65 (1966): 466–81.

71. Although I do not see any direct connection between them, the words of the Yeoman are reminiscent of those of Mechthild of Magdeburg, a nun, who used alchemical imagery to explain how God reveals his secrets: "My daughter, more than one man has lost his precious gold / Through negligence, on the highway of the armies, / When his intention was to use it for higher studies. / Now, somebody must find this gold. / By nature I have withheld it so many days: / Whenever I decided to bestow extraordinary gifts, / Each time I have sought out the lowest place, / The humblest, the most hidden spot" (*The Flowing Light of the Godhead* 2.26, in Emilie Zum Brunn and Georgette Epiney-Burgard, *Women Mystics in Medieval Europe,* trans. Sheila Hughes [New York: Paragon House, 1989]).

72. The *coltes tooth* is an interesting term because it refers to a present or youthful desire that continues into old age. It is not a symptom of a desire but the inability or incapacity to act on that desire. See the Wife of Bath's acknowledgment of the same condition: "But yet I hadde alwey a coltes tooth" (3.602). For more on this point, see Olson, Canterbury Tales *and the Good Society, 7.*

73. See the discussion of the penitentials in regard to marital sex in James A. Brundage, *Law, Sex, and Christian Society in Medieval Europe* (Chicago: University of Chicago Press, 1987), 155–74. See especially the chart on page 162.

74. See 1 Corinthians 7.28; also the Wife of Bath's prologue, 3.156–57.

75. For a sampling of these views, see Paul A. Olson, "*The Reeve's Tale*: Chaucer's *Measure for Measure*," *Studies in Philology* 59 (1962): 1–17; M. Copland, "*The Reeve's Tale:* Harlotrie or Sermonyng?" *Medium Aevum* 31 (1962): 14–32; Alfred David, *The Strumpet Muse: Art and Morals in Chaucer's Poetry* (Bloomington: Indiana University Press, 1976), 90–118. Each of these studies has contributed to my understanding of the Reeve's tale but they have failed to take seriously the interest the Reeve has in the love question.

76. For a discussion of the way Joseph was depicted in the Middle Ages in general and in drama in particular, see V. A. Kolve, *The Play Called Corpus Christi* (Stanford: Stanford University Press, 1966), 247–53.

77. Rist, *Augustine,* 2

78. Ibid., 246.

79. See Hugh of St. Victor, *The Sacraments of the Christian Faith,* trans. Roy J. Deferrari (Cambridge, Mass.: Medieval Academy, 1951), 325–26.

80. We can assume that the Wife is not being coy when she employs a euphemism here, giving us instead a typical example of her supple word play. First of all, the word is a conjunction, undoubtedly her favorite part of speech. Second, her choice of Latin makes it a clerkly term, implying that clerks invent quaint terms for women and their bodily parts as a kind of rhetorical exercise in synecdoche. The Wife takes its Latin meaning, "therefore," and uses it as a sign of how she can close an argument.

81. See A. C. Spearing and J. E. Spearing, eds., *The Reeve's Prologue and Tale with the Cook's Prologue and the Fragment of His Tale* (Cambridge: Cambridge University Press, 1979), 30.

82. See Maurice Keen, *English Society in the Later Middle Ages 1348–1500* (London: Penguin Books, 1990), 593–601.

83. On this point, see D. W. Robertson, Jr., "Who Were 'the People'?" in *The Popular Literature of Medieval England,* ed. Thomas Heffernan (Knoxville: University of Tennessee Press, 1985), 10–11.

84. See Richard B. McDonald, "The Reve Was a Sclendre Colerik Man," in *Chaucer's Pilgrims: An Historical Guide to the Pilgrims in the* Canterbury Tales, ed. Laura Lambdin and Robert Lambdin (Westport, Conn.: Greenwood Press, 1996), 292.

85. The name of the Reeve's horse might suggest John the Scot, particularly his argument, to cite Chenu, "that God had not originally intended his creative power to descend as far down the scale as corruptible matter, and that the subsequent descent of that power followed upon a defeat or fall. Man had been intended to have a spiritual body only, without animal needs" (*Nature, Man, and Society,* 25). That would have resolved the Reeve's problem.

86. See Winthrop Wetherbee, *Geoffrey Chaucer: The* Canterbury Tales (Cambridge: Cambridge University Press, 1989), 60–62.

87. For comment on the sexual connotation of the unfettered stallion, see V. A. Kolve, *Chaucer and the Imagery of Narrative: The First Five* Canterbury Tales (Stanford: Stanford University Press, 1984), 237; also J. A. W. Bennett, *Chaucer at Oxford and Cambridge* (Toronto: University of Toronto Press, 1974), 87.

88. In his discussion of the Peasant's Revolt, Steven Justice takes up the matter of the goods of the church, citing Wyclif's use of the canon law maxim of "Bona ecclesiae sunt bona pauperum": "To canonists, this maxim meant that pastors and religious were to give relief where it was needed. But Wyclif made the phrase his own, giving it a literal inflection and the poor a literal claim on ecclesiastical *temporalia*. They rightly own the wealth unjustly appropriated by the church, he says, and the lords are bound to render it to them again" (*Writing and Rebellion: England in 1381* [Berkeley: University of California Press, 1994], 84).

89. For a discussion of this point, see Tamarah Kohanski, "In Search of Malyne," *Chaucer Review* 27 (1993): 228–38.

90. If it is difficult to believe that the wife does not realize that it is not her husband with whom she consorts in the dark, it is equally difficult to believe she would get into the wrong bed, especially since she does know the "estres" or contours of the room so well. It may be revealing that the Reeve does not see this inconsistency.

91. Eustache Deschamps, *Oeuvres complètes,* ed. Gaston Raynaud (Paris: SATF, 1901; reprint, New York: Johnson Reprint Corp., 1966), lines 10178–10200.

92. See Caroline Walker Bynum, *Holy Feast and Holy Fast: The Religious Significance of Food to Medieval Women* (Berkeley: University of California Press, 1987): 261–76 and 288–94.

93. Bakhtin, *Dialogic Imagination,* 206.

94. Ibid., 208.

95. Ibid., 217.

96. Lee Patterson, "'No man his reson herde': Peasant Consciousness, Chaucer's Miller, and the Structure of the *Canterbury Tales*," *South Atlantic Quarterly* 86 (1987): 482.

97. Salman Rushdie, "1,000 Days 'Trapped Inside a Metaphor,'" *New York Times,* 12 December 1991, B8, col. 5, excerpts from a speech delivered at Columbia University, 11 December 1991.

98. David Aers, *Chaucer* (Brighton: Harvester, 1986), 46.

99. Lee Patterson, *Chaucer and the Subject of History* (Madison: University of Wisconsin Press, 1991), 420–21.

100. The most complete and influential studies that have been conducted on the Pardoner and his tale are those of Patterson, *Chaucer,* 367–421; Leicester, *Disenchanted Self,* 35–64 and 161–77; and Carolyn Dinshaw, *Chaucer's Sexual Poetics* (Madison: University of Wisconsin Press, 1989), 156–84. I am greatly indebted to all three of these studies for helping me to form my own thoughts and views on both the Pardoner and his tale.

101. Here again, Patterson, *Chaucer,* Leicester, *Disenchanted Self,* and Dinshaw, *Chaucer's Sexual Poetics,* are informative, both in summarizing past assessments and in advancing substantially new and innovative readings.

102. James Joyce, *Ulysses* (New York: Vintage, 1986), 175.

103. Eamon Duffy, *The Stripping of the Altars: Traditional Religion in England 1400–1580* (New Haven: Yale University Press, 1992), 91.

104. Ibid., 91–94.

105. Ibid., 108 and 93.

106. See J. Bossy, "The Mass as a Social Institution, 1200–1700," *Past and Present* 100 (1983): 32.

107. Duffy, *Stripping of the Altars,* 92.

108. For a discussion of these points, see R. N. Swanson, *Catholic England: Faith, Religion and Observance before the Reformation* (Manchester: Manchester University Press, 1993), 80–87.

109. See, for example, the comprehensive discussion of the sacrament of penance in Thomas Tentler, *Sin and Confession on the Eve of the Reformation* (Princeton: Princeton University Press, 1977). See also Patterson's abbreviated but incisive discussion in *Chaucer,* 374–77; Patterson observes that scholastic theology taught that justification is fully accomplished only by the sacrament itself, that sincere renunciation was not adequate in itself, thus the church "firmly located the power of binding and loosing with the Church in its administration of the sacraments" (374). For Ockham's argument on the church as the totality of its believers rather than a hierarchy, see John J. Ryan, *The Nature, Structure,*

and Function of the Church in William of Ockham (Missoula, Mont.: Scholars Press, 1979), 30 and 55.

110. Swanson, *Religion and Devotion,* 66–68.

111. See the words of Valentius, "Jesus ate and drank but did not defecate." See also Saint Bernard: "A man is, first, fetid sperm, then a sack of excrement, then food for worms." Cited in "Holy Shit," a wonderful poem by Galway Kinnell, in *Imperfect Thirst* (New York: Houghton-Mifflin, 1994), 61–67.

112. Blumenberg, *The Legitimacy of the Modern Age,* trans. Robert M. Wallace (Cambridge: MIT Press, 1987), 171.

113. David Aers and Lynn Staley, *The Powers of the Holy: Religion, Politics, and Gender in Late Medieval English Culture* (University Park: Pennsylvania State University Press, 1996), 59. Aers goes on to point out that a proper imitation of Christ called for identification with Christ's attitude toward the poor and an internalization of his egalitarianism (65).

114. For the story of the *veronica* in the western church and in orthodox iconography, see Paul Perdrizet, "De la véronique et de Seinte Véronique," *Seminarium Kondakovianum* 5 (1932): 1–15. For a longer discussion of the Veronica story in relation to the Pardoner, see my article, "The Pardoner's *Vernycle* and His *Vera Icon,*" *Modern Language Studies* 12 (1982): 34–40.

115. See Gertrude Schiller, *Iconography of Christian Art,* trans. Janet Seligman, 3 vols. (Greenwich, Conn.: New York Graphic Society, 1972), 2:78. Perdrizet ("De la véronique," 2–4) speculates that the Franciscans were primarily responsible for introducing the Veronica legend into the passion while others believe that it entered as a consequence of the drama, particularly in the "Women of Jerusalem" scenes. See also Ernst von Dobschütz, *Christusbilder: Untersuchungen zur christlichen Legende,* 2 vols. (Leipzig: J. C. Hinrichs, 1899), 1:304.

116. See Christine Tischendorf, *Evangelica Apochrypha* (Leipzig: Avenarius et Mendelssohn, 1853), 432–35.

117. Chaucer's Parson proves a worthy example of a sincere imitation of Christ. No other pilgrim among those en route to Canterbury approaches the Parson's self-integration. He has no professional identity apart from his personal one. He *is* the Parson. He shows that Christ abides in the "lewed" and lowly as well as the exalted, for he was "a shepherde and noght a mercenarie."

118. Numerous scholars have pointed to the parallels between the Pardoner and the Wife of Bath. See especially Leicester, *Disenchanted Self,* 161–73; and Anne Kernan, "The Archwife and the Eunuch," *English Literary History* 41 (1974): 1–25. Kernan points to a series of parallels in oratorical style, audience manipulation, and sexual candor that make their respective confessions similar in aim and method. "The prologue and tales of the Wife of Bath and the

Pardoner," she says, "contain a similar irony which arises from the 'confessions' by which both *prechours* reveal that their *praktike* exemplifies the evils which they preach against" (8). See also my article, "Motivation in Chaucer's *Pardoner's Tale:* Winner Take Nothing," *Chaucer Review* 17 (1982): 40–61, especially 41–45.

119. Albert Camus, "Summer in Algiers," in *The Myth of Sisyphus and Other Essays,* trans. Justin O'Brien (New York: Vintage Books, 1955), 113.

120. Theodor Adorno, "Theses upon Art and Religion Today," in *Notes to Literature,* ed. Rolf Tiedemann, trans. Sherry Weber Nicholsen, 2 vols. (New York: Columbia University Press, 1992), 298.

Works Cited

Adorno, Theodor W. *Notes to Literature*. 2 vols. Edited by Rolf Tiedemann. Translated by Shierry Weber Nicholsen. New York: Columbia University Press, 1992.

———. "Theses upon Art and Religion Today." In *Notes to Literature,* edited by Rolf Tiedemann, translated by Sherry Weber Nicholsen. 2 vols. New York: Columbia University Press, 1992.

Aers, David. *Chaucer*. Brighton: Harvester, 1986.

———. "Christianity for Courtly Subjects: Reflections on the *Gawain*-Poet." In *A Companion to the* Gawain-*Poet,* edited by Derek Brewer and Jonathan Gibson, 91–101. Cambridge: D. S. Brewer, 1997.

———. "Faith, Ethics, and Community: Reflections on Reading Late Medieval English Writing." *Journal of Medieval and Early Modern Studies* 28 (1998): 341–69.

———. "The Humanity of Christ: Representations in Wycliffite Texts and *Piers Plowman*." In David Aers and Lynn Staley, *The Powers of the Holy: Religion, Politics, and Gender in Late Medieval English Culture,* 65–70. University Park: Pennsylvania State University Press, 1996.

———. Piers Plowman *and Christian Allegory*. London: Edward Arnold, 1975.

———. "The Self Mourning: Reflections on *Pearl*." *Speculum* 68 (1993): 54–73.

Aers, David, and Lynn Staley. *The Powers of the Holy: Religion, Politics, and Gender in Late Medieval English Culture*. University Park: Pennsylvania State University Press, 1996.

Agamben, Giorgio. *Infancy and History: Essays on the Destruction of Experience*. Translated by Liz Heron. New York: Verso, 1993.

———. *The Man without Content*. Translated by Georgia Albert. Stanford: Stanford University Press, 1999.

Alter, Robert. *The Art of Biblical Narrative*. New York: Basic Books, 1981.

Ames, Ruth. *God's Plenty: Chaucer's Christian Humanism*. Chicago: Loyola University Press, 1984.

Anderson, J. J., ed. *Patience*. New York: Barnes and Noble, 1969.

Andrew, Malcolm. "The Realizing Imagination in Late Medieval English Narrative." *English Studies* 76 (1995): 113–28.

Andrew, Malcolm, and Ronald Waldron, eds. *The Poems of the* Pearl *Manuscript:* Pearl, Cleanness, Patience, Sir Gawain and the Green Knight. Exeter: University Press of Exeter, 1987.

Anselm, Saint. *Why God Became Man*. In *Anselm of Canterbury: The Major Works*. Edited by Brian Davies and G. R. Evans. Oxford: Oxford University Press, 1998.

Aquinas, Saint Thomas. *Articles of Faith*. Article 3. In *An Aquinas Reader: Selections from the Writings of Thomas Aquinas*. Edited by Mary T. Clark. New York: Fordham University Press, 1988.

———. *Commentary on the Gospel of St. John*. Translated by James A. Weisheipel, O.P., S.T.M. Albany: Magi Books, 1980.

———. *On the Power of God (Quaestiones disputatae de potentia dei)*. Translated by the English Dominican Fathers. Westminster, Md.: Newman Press, 1952.

Aston, Margaret. *Lollards and Reformers: Images and Literacy in Late Medieval Religion*. London: Hambledon, 1984.

———. "Wyclif and the Vernacular." In *From Ockham to Wyclif,* edited by Anne Hudson and Michael Wilkes. Studies in Church History, Subsidia 5. Oxford: Blackwell, 1987.

Auerbach, Erich. *Dante: Poet of the Secular World*. Translated by Ralph Manheim. Chicago: University of Chicago Press, 1961.

———. *Literary Language and Its Public*. Translated by Ralph Manheim. Princeton: Princeton University Press, 1995.

Augustine. *Sermon 40*. In "Sermons on Selected Lessons of the Gospels." *The Nicene and Post-Nicene Fathers of the Christian Church,* edited by Philip Schaff, vol. 6. Grand Rapids, Mich.: Eerdmans, 1974.

Bakhtin, M. M. *The Dialogical Imagination: Four Essays*. Edited by Michael Holquist. Translated by Caryl Emerson and Michael Holquist. Austin: University of Texas Press, 1981.

———. *Problems of Dostoevsky's Poetics*. Translated by Caryl Emerson. Minneapolis: University of Minnesota Press, 1984.

Bal, Mieke. *Death and Dissymmetry: The Politics of Coherence in the Book of Judges*. Chicago: University of Chicago Press, 1988.

Barthes, Roland. "Authors and Writers." In *A Barthes Reader,* edited by Susan Sontag, 185–93. New York: Hill and Wang, 1982.

———. *Camera Lucida: Reflections on Photography*. Translated by Richard Howard. New York: Hill and Wang, 1981.

———. "The Death of the Author." In *Image—Music—Text,* translated by Stephen Heath, 142–48. New York: Hill and Wang, 1977.

———. From *The Pleasure of the Text.* In *A Barthes Reader,* edited by Susan Sontag, translated by Richard Miller, 404–14. New York: Hill and Wang, 1982.

Bataille, Georges. *Theory of Religion.* Translated by Robert Hurley. New York: Zone Books, 1989.

Beckwith, Sarah. *Christ's Body: Identity, Culture, and Society in Late Medieval Writings.* London: Routledge, 1993.

Beichner, Paul. "Confrontation, Contempt of Court, and Chaucer's Cecilia." *Chaucer Review* 8 (1974): 198–204.

Benjamin, Walter. "On Language as Such and on the Language of Man." In *Reflections: Essays, Aphorisms, Autobiographical Writings,* translated by Edmund Jephcott, edited by Peter Demetz, 314–32. New York: Schocken Books, 1978.

———. "Theses on the Philosophy of History." In *Illuminations,* translated by Harry Zohn, edited by Hannah Arendt, 253–64. New York: Shocken Books, 1968.

Bennett, J. A. W. *Chaucer at Oxford and Cambridge.* Toronto: University of Toronto Press, 1974.

Benson, C. David. "The Impatient Reader of *Patience.*" In *Form and Matter: New Critical Perspectives on the* Pearl-*Poet,* edited by Robert J. Blanch, Miriam Youngerman Miller, and Julian N. Wasserman, 147–61. Troy, N.Y.: Whitson Publishing, 1991.

Benson, C. David, and Elizabeth Robertson, eds. *Chaucer's Religious Tales.* Chaucer Studies 15. Cambridge: D. S. Brewer, 1990.

Bishop, Ian. Pearl *in Its Setting: A Critical Study of the Structure and Meaning of the Middle English Poem.* Oxford: Blackwell, 1968.

Black, Anthony. "The Individual and Society." In *The Cambridge History of Medieval Political Thought c. 350–c. 1450,* edited by J. H. Burns, 588–606. Cambridge: Cambridge University Press, 1988.

Blanch, Robert J., and Julian N. Wasserman. *From* Pearl *to* Gawain: *Forme and Fynisment.* Gainesville: University of Florida Press, 1995.

Blanch, Robert J., Miriam Youngerman Miller, and Julian N. Wasserman, eds. *Form and Matter: New Critical Perspectives on the* Pearl-*Poet.* Troy, N.Y.: Whitson Publishing, 1991.

Bloch, R. Howard. *Medieval Misogyny and the Invention of Western Romantic Love.* Chicago: University of Chicago Press, 1991.

Blumenberg, Hans. "An Anthropological Approach to the Contemporary Significance of Rhetoric." In *After Philosophy: End or Transformation?* edited by Kenneth Baynes, James Bohman, and Thomas McCarthy, 429–58. Cambridge: MIT Press, 1988.

———. *The Genesis of the Copernican World.* Translated by Robert M. Wallace. Cambridge: MIT Press, 1987.

———. *The Legitimacy of the Modern Age.* Translated by Robert M. Wallace, Cambridge: MIT Press, 1985.

Boccaccio, Giovanni. *Boccaccio on Poetry: Being the Preface and the Fourteenth and Fifteenth Books of Boccaccio's* Genealogia Deorum Gentilium. Edited by Charles B. Osgood. New York: Bobbs-Merrill, 1956.

———. *The Decameron.* Selected, translated, and edited by Mark Musa and Peter Bondanella. New York: W. W. Norton, 1977.

———. *Vita di Dante e difesa della poesia.* Edited by Carlo Muscetta. Roma: Edizioni dell'Ateneo, 1963.

Bogdanos, Theodore. Pearl: *Image of the Ineffable: A Study in Medieval Poetic Symbolism.* University Park: Pennsylvania State University Press, 1983.

Bossy, J. "The Mass as a Social Institution, 1200–1700." *Past and Present* 100 (1983): 29–61.

Bowie, Malcolm. *Freud, Proust, and Lacan: Theory as Fiction.* Cambridge: Cambridge University Press, 1988.

Breidecker, Volker. *Florenz oder "Die Rede, die zum Auge spricht": Kunst, Fest und Macht im Ambiente der Stadt.* München: Wilhelm Fink Verlag, 1990.

Brewer, Derek, and Jonathan Gibson, eds. *A Companion to the* Gawain-*Poet.* Cambridge: D. S. Brewer, 1997.

Brown, Carleton. "The Prioress's Tale." In *Sources and Analogues of Chaucer's* Canterbury Tales, ed. W. F. Bryan and Germaine Dempster. New York: Humanities Press, 1958.

Brundage, James A. *Law, Sex, and Christian Society in Medieval Europe.* Chicago: University of Chicago Press, 1987.

Bryan, W. F., and Germaine Dempster, eds. *Sources and Analogues of Chaucer's* Canterbury Tales. New York: Humanities Press, 1958.

Bultmann, Rudolf. *Jesus Christ and Mythology.* New York: Charles Scribner's and Sons, 1958.

Burrow, John A. *Langland's Fictions.* Oxford: Clarendon Press, 1993.

———. *Ricardian Poetry: Chaucer, Gower, Langland and the* Gawain-*Poet.* New Haven: Yale University Press, 1971.

Burrow, John A., and Thorlac Turville-Petre, eds. *A Book of Middle English.* 2d ed. Oxford: Blackwell, 1996.

———. *Patience.* In *A Book of Middle English.* 2d ed. Oxford: Blackwell, 1996.

———. *Saint Erkenwald.* In *A Book of Middle English.* 2d ed. Oxford: Blackwell, 1996.

Bynum, Caroline Walker. *Fragmentation and Redemption: Essays on Gender and the Human Body in Medieval Religion.* New York: Zone Books, 1991.

———. *Holy Feast and Holy Fast: The Religious Significance of Food to Medieval Women.* Berkeley: University of California Press, 1987.

———. *Jesus as Mother: Studies in the Spirituality of the High Middle Ages.* Berkeley: University of California Press, 1982.

———. *The Resurrection of the Body in Western Christianity, 200–1336.* New York: Columbia University Press, 1995.

Camus, Albert. "The Artist at Work." In *Exile and the Kingdom.* Translated by Justin O'Brien. New York: Random House, 1957.

———. "Summer in Algiers." In *The Myth of Sisyphus and Other Essays.* Translated by Justin O'Brien. New York: Vintage Books, 1955.

Canning, Joseph. "A Fourteenth-Century Contribution to the Theory of Citizenship: Political Man and the Problem of Created Citizenship in the Thought of Baldus De Ubaldis." In *Authority and Power: Studies on Medieval Law and Government Presented to Walter Ullmann on His Seventieth Birthday,* edited by Brian Tierney and Peter Linehan, 197–212. Cambridge: Cambridge University Press, 1980.

Carroll, Michael P. *The Cult of the Virgin Mary: Psychological Origins.* Princeton: Princeton University Press, 1986.

Caygill, Howard. "Benjamin, Heidegger, and the Destruction of Tradition." In *Walter Benjamin's Philosophy: Destruction and Experience,* edited by Andrew Benjamin and Peter Osborne, 1–31. London: Routledge, 1994.

Chaucer, Geoffrey. *The Riverside Chaucer.* Edited by Larry D. Benson. 3d ed. Boston: Houghton-Mifflin, 1987.

Chenu, M.-D. *Nature, Man, and Society in the Twelfth Century.* Translated and edited by Jerome Taylor. Chicago: University of Chicago Press, 1968.

Clanchy, M. T. *Abelard: A Medieval Life.* Oxford: Blackwell, 1999.

Coleman, Janet. *Ancient and Medieval Memories: Studies in the Reconstruction of the Past.* Cambridge: Cambridge University Press, 1992.

———. *Medieval Readers and Writers, 1350–1400.* New York: Columbia University Press, 1981.

———. Piers Plowman *and the "Moderni."* Roma: Edizioni di Storia e Letteratura, 1981.

Colish, Marcia. *The Mirror of Language: A Study in the Medieval Theory of Knowledge.* Lincoln: University of Nebraska Press, 1983.

———. "The Virtuous Pagan: Dante and the Christian Tradition." In *The Unbounded Community: Conversations across Times and Disciplines,* edited by Duncan Fisher and William Caferro, 1–66. New York: Garland Publishing, 1995.

Collette, Carolyn. "A Closer Look at Seinte Cecile's Special Vision." *Chaucer Review* 10 (1976): 337–49.

Cook, Albert. *History / Writing: The Theory and Practice of History in Antiquity and in Modern Times.* Cambridge: Cambridge University Press, 1988.

Copeland, Rita. *Rhetoric, Hermeneutics, and Translation in the Middle Ages: Academic Traditions and Vernacular Texts.* Cambridge: Cambridge University Press, 1991.

Copland, M. "*The Reeve's Tale:* Harlotrie or Sermonyng?" *Medium Aevum* 31 (1962): 14–32.

Courtenay, William. "*Antiqui* and *Moderni* in Late Medieval Thought." *Journal of the History of Ideas* 48 (1987): 3–10.

———. *Covenant and Causality in Medieval Thought.* London: Variorum Reprints, 1984.

———. "Covenant and Causality in Pierre D'Ailly." In *Covenant and Causality in Medieval Thought.* London: Variorum Reprints, 1984.

———. "Nature and the Natural in Twelfth-Century Thought." In *Covenant and Causality in Medieval Thought.* London: Variorum Reprints, 1984.

———. *Schools and Scholars in Fourteenth Century England.* Princeton: Princeton University Press, 1987.

Cranz, F. Edward. "Cusanus, Luther, and the Mystical Tradition." In *The Pursuit of Holiness in Late Medieval and Renaissance Religion,* edited by Charles Trinkaus and Heiko Oberman, 93–102. Leiden: E. J. Brill, 1974.

Dales, Richard C. *The Intellectual Life of Western Europe in the Middle Ages.* Leiden: Brill, 1992.

———. "Robert Grosseteste on the Soul's Care for the Body." In *Robert Grosseteste: New Perspectives on His Thought and Scholarship,* edited by James McEvoy, 313–19. Instrumenta Patristica 27. Steenbruges: Brepols, 1995.

Dante Alighieri. *The Divine Comedy.* Translated by Charles Singleton. 3 vols. in 6. Bollingen Series 80. Princeton: Princeton University Press, 1980, 1982.

———. *The Divine Comedy of Dante Alighieri: A Verse Translation.* Translated and edited by Allen Mandelbaum. 3 vols. New York: Bantam Books, 1980, 1982.

Davenport, W. A. *The Art of the* Gawain-*Poet.* London: Athlone Press, 1978.

David, Alfred. "An ABC to the Style of the Prioress." In *Acts of Interpretation: The Text in Its Contexts 700–1600: Essays on Medieval and Renaissance Literature in Honor of E. Talbot Donaldson,* edited by Mary J. Carruthers and Elizabeth Kirk, 147–57. Norman, Okla.: Pilgrim Books, 1982.

———. *The Strumpet Muse: Art and Morals in Chaucer's Poetry.* Bloomington: Indiana University Press, 1976.

Davidson, Arnold. "Mystery, Miracle, and Meaning in *St. Erkenwald.*" *Papers on Language and Literature* 16 (1980): 37–44.

Davis, Nick. "Narrative Form and Insight." In *A Companion to the* Gawain-*Poet,* edited by Derek Brewer and Jonathan Gibson, 329–49. Cambridge: D. S. Brewer, 1997.

Davis, Norman, Douglas Gray, Patricia Ingham, and Anne Wallace-Hadrill, eds. *A Chaucer Glossary.* Oxford: Clarendon Press, 1979.

Deschamps, Eustache. *Oeuvres complètes.* Edited by Gaston Raynaud. Paris: SATF, 1901. Reprint, New York: Johnson Reprint Corp., 1966.

Diekstra, F. N. M. "Jonah and *Patience*: The Psychology of a Prophet." *English Studies* 55 (1974): 205–17.

Dinshaw, Carolyn. *Chaucer's Sexual Poetics.* Madison: University of Wisconsin Press, 1989.

Dobschütz, Ernst von. *Christusbilder: Untersuchungen zur christlichen Legende.* 2 vols. Leipzig: J. C. Hinrichs, 1899.

Duffy, Eamon. *The Stripping of the Altars: Traditional Religion in England 1400–1580.* New Haven: Yale University Press, 1992.

Dunbabin, Jean. "The Reception and Interpretation of Aristotle's *Politics.*" In *The Cambridge History of Later Medieval Philosophy: From the Rediscovery of Aristotle to the Disintegration of Scholasticism 1100–1600,* edited by Norman Kretzmann, Anthony Kenny, and Jan Pinborg, 723– 37. Cambridge: Cambridge University Press, 1988.

Dupré, Louis. *Passage to Modernity: An Essay in the Hermeneutics of Nature and Culture.* New Haven: Yale University Press, 1993.

Dyer, Christopher. *Standards of Living in the Later Middle Ages: Social Change in England, c. 1200–1520.* Cambridge: Cambridge University Press, 1989.

Eagleton, Terry. "History, Narrative, and Marxism." In *Reading Narrative,* edited by James Phelan, 272–81. Columbus: Ohio State University Press, 1989.

———. "J. L. Austin and the Book of Jonah." In *The Book and the Text: The Bible and Literary History,* edited by Regina Schwartz, 231–36. Oxford: Blackwell, 1990.

Eldredge, Laurence. "Late Medieval Discussions of the Continuum and the *Point* of the Middle English *Patience.*" *Vivarium* 17 (1979): 114–15.

———. "Sheltering Space and Cosmic Space in the Middle English *Patience.*" *Annuale Mediaevale* 21 (1981): 121–33.

Eliade, Mircea. *The Forge and the Crucible: The Origins and Structures of Alchemy.* Chicago: University of Chicago Press, 1962.

Evans, Ruth. "An Afterword on the Prologue." In *The Idea of the Vernacular: An Anthology of Middle English Literary Criticism,* ed. Jocelyn Wogan-Browne, Nicholas Watson, Andrew Taylor, and Ruth Evans, 371–78. University Park: Pennsylvania State University Press, 1999.

———. "Historicizing Postcolonial Criticism: Cultural Difference and the Vernacular." In *The Idea of the Vernacular: An Anthology of Middle English Literary Criticism,* ed. Jocelyn Wogan-Browne, Nicholas Watson, Andrew Taylor, and Ruth Evans, 366–70. University Park: Pennsylvania State University Press, 1999.

Febvre, Lucien. *A New Kind of History: From the Writings of Febvre.* Translated by K. Folca. Edited by Peter Burke. New York: Harper, 1973.

Ferrante, Joan. *Woman as Image in Medieval Literature.* New York: Columbia University Press, 1975.

Foster, Kenelm, O.P. *The Two Dantes and Other Studies.* Berkeley: University of California Press, 1977.

Fradenburg, Louise. *City, Marriage, Tournament: Arts of Rule in Late Medieval Scotland.* Madison: University of Wisconsin Press, 1991.

———. "Criticism, Anti-Semitism, and the Prioress's Tale." *Exemplaria* 1 (1989): 69–115.

Frank, Robert Worth, Jr. "Miracles of the Virgin, Medieval Anti-Semitism, and the Prioress's Tale." In *The Wisdom of Poetry: Essays in Early English Literature in Honor of Morton W. Bloomfield,* edited by Larry Benson and Siegfried Wenzel, 177–88. Kalamazoo, Mich.: Medieval Institute Publications, 1982.

Frantzen, Allen J. "The Disclosure of Sodomy in *Cleanness.*" *Proceedings of the Modern Language Association* 111 (1996): 451–64.

Friedman, John B. "Figural Typology in *Patience.*" In *The Alliterative Tradition in the Fourteenth Century,* edited by Bernard Levy and Paul Szarmach, 99–129. Kent, Ohio: Kent State University Press, 1981.

Gallop, Jane. *Reading Lacan.* Ithaca: Cornell University Press, 1985.

Gewirth, Alan. "Philosophy and Political Thought in the Fourteenth Century." In *The Forward Movement of the Fourteenth Century,* edited by Francis Lee Utley, 125–64. Columbus: Ohio University Press, 1961.

Grady, Frank. "*Piers Plowman, St. Erkenwald,* and the Rule of Exceptional Salvations." *Yearbook of Langland Studies* 6 (1992): 61–86.

Graef, Hilda. *Mary: A History of Doctrine and Devotion.* Vol. 1. New York: Sheed and Ward, 1963.

Green, Richard Firth. *A Crisis of Truth: Literature and Law in Ricardian England.* Philadelphia: University of Pennsylvania Press, 1999.

Grennen, Joseph. "The Canon's Yeoman and the Cosmic Furnace: Language and Meaning in the *Canon's Yeoman's Tale*." *Criticism* 4 (1962): 225–40.

———. "The Canon's Yeoman's Alchemical Mass." *Studies in Philology* 62 (1965): 546–60.

———. "St. Cecilia's 'Chemical Wedding': The Unity of the *Canterbury Tales*, Fragment VIII." *Journal of English and Germanic Philology* 65 (1966): 466–81.

Grosseteste, Robert. *Le* Chateau d'amour *de Robert Grosseteste évêque de Lincoln*. Edited by J. Murray. Paris: Champion, 1918.

———. *Hexaemeron*. Edited by Richard C. Dales and Servus Gieben, O.F.M.Cap. Oxford: Oxford University Press, 1982.

———. *The Middle English Translations of Robert Grosseteste's* Chateau d'amour. Edited by Kari Sajavaara. Memoires de la Société Néophilologique de Helsinki 32. Helsinki: Société Néophilologique, 1967.

———. *On the Six Days of Creation*. Translated by C. F. J. Martin. Oxford: Oxford University Press, 1996.

Guardini, Romano. *The Death of Socrates: An Interpretation of the Platonic Dialogues:* Euthyphro, Apology, Crito, *and* Phaedo. Translated by Basil Wrighton. New York: World Publishing, 1969.

Guldan, Ernst. *Eva und Maria: Eine Antithese als Bildmotiv*. Köln: Hermann Böhlaus, 1966.

Gurevich, Aron. *Medieval Popular Culture: Problems of Belief and Perception*. Translated by Janos M. Bak and Paul A. Hollingsworth. Cambridge: Cambridge University Press, 1988.

Hahn, Tom. "Chaucer and Academic Theology." Paper presented at the Seventh International Congress of the New Chaucer Society, 6–11 August 1990, University of Kent, Canterbury.

Haidu, Peter. "Repetition: Modern Reflections on Medieval Aesthetics." *Modern Language Notes* 92 (1977): 875–87.

Haimo of Auxerre. *Commentary on the Book of Jonah*. Translated, with introduction and notes by Deborah Everhart. Kalamazoo, Mich.: Medieval Institute Publications, 1993.

Hanning, Robert. "From *Eva* to *Ave* to Eglentyne and Alisoun: Chaucer's Insight into the Roles Women Play." *Signs* 2 (1977): 580–99.

Hare, Douglas. *Interpretation: A Bible Commentary for Teaching and Preaching*. Louisville: John Knox Press, 1993.

Hawkins, Peter S. "Divide and Conquer: Augustine in the *Divine Comedy*." *Proceedings of the Modern Language Association* 106 (1991): 471–82.

Heffernan, Thomas J. *Sacred Biography: Saints and Their Biographers in the Middle Ages.* Oxford: Oxford University Press, 1988.

Hill, Thomas D. "Universal Salvation and Its Literary Context in *Piers Plowman* B. 18." *Yearbook of Langland Studies* 5 (1991): 65–76.

Holquist, Michael. *Dialogism: Bakhtin and His World.* London: Routledge, 1990.

Howard, Donald. *The Idea of the* Canterbury Tales. Berkeley: University of California Press, 1976.

Hudson, Anne, ed. *Selections from English Wycliffite Writings.* Cambridge: Cambridge University Press, 1978.

Hugh of St. Victor. *The Sacraments of the Christian Faith.* Translated by Roy J. Deferrari. Cambridge, Mass.: Medieval Academy, 1951.

Iser, Wolfgang. *The Act of Reading.* Baltimore: Johns Hopkins University Press, 1978.

———. "Feigning in Fiction." In *Identity of the Literary Text,* edited by Mario J. Valdés and Owen Miller, 204–28. Toronto: University of Toronto Press, 1985.

———. *The Fictive and the Imaginary: Charting Literary Anthropology.* Baltimore: Johns Hopkins University Press, 1993.

———. "The Play of the Text." In *Languages of the Unsayable: The Play of Negativity in Literature and Literary Theory,* edited by Sanford Budick and Wolfgang Iser, 325–39. Stanford: Stanford University Press, 1996.

Jacobus de Voragine. *The Golden Legend: Readings on the Saints.* Translated by William Granger Ryan. 2 vols. Princeton: Princeton University Press, 1993.

Jefferson, Bernard L. *Chaucer and the* Consolation of Philosophy *of Boethius* New York: Gordian Press, 1916.

Jeffrey, David Lyle. "Chaucer and Wyclif: Biblical Hermeneutics and Literary Theory in the XIVth Century." In *Chaucer and Scriptural Tradition,* edited by David Lyle Jeffrey, 109–40. Ottawa: University of Ottawa Press, 1984.

———. "John Wyclif and the Hermeneutics of Reader Response." *Interpretation* 39 (1985): 272–87.

———. "Postscript." In *By Things Seen: Reference and Recognition in Medieval Thought,* edited by David Lyle Jeffrey. Ottawa: University of Ottawa Press, 1979.

Jeffrey, David Lyle, trans. and ed. *The Law of Love: English Spirituality in the Age of Wyclif.* Grand Rapids, Mich.: Eerdmans, 1988.

Jennings, Michael. *Dialectical Images: Walter Benjamin's Theory of Literary Criticism.* Ithaca: Cornell University Press, 1987.

Johnson, Lynn Staley. "The *Pearl* Dreamer and the Eleventh Hour." In *Text and Matter: New Critical Perspectives on the* Pearl-*Poet,* edited by Robert

J. Blanch, Miriam Youngerman Miller, and Julian N. Wasserman, 3–15.
Troy, N.Y.: Whitson Publishing, 1991.

———. *The Voice of the* Gawain-*Poet*. Madison: University of Wisconsin Press, 1984.

Joyce, James. *Ulysses*. New York: Vintage, 1986.

Jung, L. Shannon. "Ethics and the Image of the Self in the Theology of Story." In *Religious Sociology: Interfaces and Boundaries,* edited by William H. Swatos, Jr., 69–83. New York: Greenwood Press, 1987.

Justice, Steven. *Writing and Rebellion: England in 1381*. Berkeley: University of California Press, 1994.

Kantorowicz, Ernst. *The King's Two Bodies: A Study in Medieval Political Theology*. Princeton: Princeton University Press, 1957.

Keen, Maurice. *English Society in the Later Middle Ages 1348–1500*. London: Penguin Books, 1990.

Keen, Patricia. *The* Pearl: *An Interpretation*. London: Routledge and Kegan Paul, 1967.

Keiser, Elizabeth. *Courtly Desire and Medieval Homophobia: The Legitimation of Sexual Pleasure in* Cleanness *and Its Contexts*. New Haven: Yale University Press, 1997.

Kermode, Frank. *The Genesis of Secrecy: On the Interpretation of Narrative*. Cambridge: Harvard University Press, 1979.

———. *The Sense of an Ending: Studies in the Theory of Fiction*. Oxford: Oxford University Press, 1967.

Kernan, Anne. "The Archwife and the Eunuch." *English Literary History* 41 (1974): 1–25.

Kerrigan, William. *The Sacred Complex: On the Psychogenesis of* Paradise Lost. Cambridge: Harvard University Press, 1983.

Kinnell, Galway. *Imperfect Thirst*. New York: Houghton-Mifflin, 1994.

Kiser, Lisa. *Truth and Textuality in Chaucer's Poetry*. Hanover, N.H.: University Press of New England, 1991.

Knapp, Steven. *Literary Interest: The Limits of Anti-Formalism*. Cambridge: Harvard University Press, 1993.

Kohanski, Tamara. "In Search of Malyne." *Chaucer Review* 27 (1993): 228–38.

Kolve, V. A. *Chaucer and the Imagery of Narrative: The First Five* Canterbury Tales. Stanford: Stanford University Press, 1984.

———. "Chaucer's *Second Nun's Tale* and the Iconography of Saint Cecilia." In *New Perspectives in Chaucer Criticism,* edited by Donald M. Rose, 137–74. Norman, Okla.: Pilgrim Books, 1981.

———. *The Play Called Corpus Christi*. Stanford: Standford University Press, 1966.

Kötting, Bernhard. *Peregrinatio Religiosa: Wallfahrten in der Antike und das Pilgerwesen in der alten Kirche.* Münster: Antiquriat Th. Stenderhoff, 1980.

Kristeva, Julia. *"Ego affectus est:* Bernard of Clairvaux: Affect, Desire, Love." In *Tales of Love,* translated by Leon S. Roudiez. New York: Columbia University Press, 1987.

Labande, Edmond-René. "Recherches sur les pèlerins dans l'europe des XIᵉ et XIIᵉ siecles." *Cahiers de civilisation médiévale* 1 (1958): 159–69.

Ladner, Gerhart B. *"Ad imaginem dei" : The Image of Man in Medieval Art.* Latrobe, Pa.: The Archabbey Press, 1965.

———. "Greatness in Medieval History." *Catholic Historical Review* 50 (1964): 1–26.

———. *"Homo viator*: Medieval Ideas on Alienation and Order." *Speculum* 42 (1967): 233–59.

———. *The Idea of Reform: Its Impact on Christian Thought and Action in the Age of the Fathers.* New York: Harper and Row, 1967.

———. "Terms and Ideas of Renewal." In *Renaissance and Renewal in the Twelfth Century,* edited by Robert L. Benson and Giles Constable, with Carol D. Lanham, 1–33. Toronto: University of Toronto Press, 1982.

Langland, William. Piers Plowman: *The B-Text.* Edited by George Kane and E. Talbot Donaldson. London: Athlone Press, 1975.

———. Piers Plowman *by William Langland: An Edition of the C-Text.* Edited by Derek Pearsall. Berkeley: University of California Press, 1978.

Lanham, Richard. "Game, Play, and High Seriousness in Chaucer's Poetry." *English Studies* 48 (1967): 1–24.

Leclerq, Jean. "The Renewal of Theology." In *Renaissance and Renewal in the Twelfth Century,* edited by Robert L. Benson and Giles Constable, with Carol D. Lanham, 68–87. Toronto: University of Toronto Press, 1991.

Leff, Gordon. *Bradwardine and the Pelagians: A Study of His* De causa dei *and Its Opponents.* Cambridge: Cambridge University Press, 1957.

———. *The Dissolution of the Medieval Outlook.* New York: New York University Press, 1976.

———. *William of Ockham: The Metamorphosis of Scholastic Discourse.* Manchester: University of Manchester Press, 1975.

LeGoff, Jacques. *The Birth of Purgatory.* Translated by Arthur Goldhammer. Chicago: University of Chicago Press, 1986.

———. *Time, Work, and Culture in the Middle Ages.* Translated by Arthur Goldhammer. Chicago: University of Chicago Press, 1980.

Leicester, H. Marshall. *The Disenchanted Self: Representing the Subject in the* Canterbury Tales. Berkeley: University of California Press, 1990.

Levy, Bernard, and George R. Adams. "Chauntecleer's Paradise Lost and Re-
gained." *Medieval Studies* 29 (1967): 178–92.

Lohr, C. H. "The Medieval Interpretation of Aristotle." In *The Cambridge His-
tory of Later Medieval Philosophy: From the Rediscovery of Aristotle to the
Disintegration of Scholasticism 1100–1600,* edited by Norman Kretzmann,
Anthony Kenny, and Jan Pinborg, 80–98. Cambridge: Cambridge Univer-
sity Press, 1988.

Lucretius, Carus Titus. *On the Nature of the Universe.* Translated by Ronald E.
Latham. Harmondsworth: Penguin Books, 1960.

Luscombe, David. "City and Politics before the Coming of the *Politics*: Some
Illustrations." In *Church and City, 1000–1500: Essays in Honour of Chris-
topher Brooke,* edited by David Abulafia, Michael Franklin, and Miri Rubin,
41–55. Cambridge: Cambridge University Press, 1992.

———. "Introduction: The Formation of Political Thought in the West." In
The Cambridge History of Medieval Political Thought c. 350–c. 1450, ed-
ited by J. H. Burns, 157–73. Cambridge: Cambridge University Press, 1988.

———. *Medieval Thought.* Oxford: Oxford University Press, 1997.

Luscombe, David, and G. R. Evans. "The Twelfth-Century Renaissance." In
The Cambridge History of Medieval Political Thought c. 350–c. 1450, ed-
ited by J. H. Burns, 306–38. Cambridge: Cambridge University Press, 1988.

Maccoby, Hyam. *The Sacred Executioner: Human Sacrifice and the Legacy of
Guilt.* New York: Thames and Hudson, 1982.

MacLean, Marie. *Narrative as Performance: The Baudelairean Experiment.*
London: Routledge, 1988.

Maltman, Sister Nicholas, O.P. "The Divine Granary, or the End of the Prioress's
'Greyn.'" *Chaucer Review* 17 (1981–82): 163–70.

Marx, C. W. *The Devil's Rights and the Redemption in the Literature of Medi-
eval England.* Cambridge: D. S. Brewer, 1995.

McAlindon, T. "Hagiography into Art: A Study on *St. Erkenwald.*" *Studies in
Philology* 67 (1970): 472–94.

McAlpine, Monica. "The Triumph of Fiction in the *Nun's Priest's Tale.*" In *Art
and Context in Late Medieval English Narrative,* edited by Robert R.
Edwards, 79–92. Woodbridge, Suffolk: D. S. Brewer, 1994.

McDonald, Richard B. "The Reve Was a Sclendre Colerik Man." In *Chaucer's
Pilgrims: An Historical Guide to the Pilgrims in the* Canterbury Tales, ed-
ited by Laura Lambdin and Robert Lambdin, 288–99. Westport, Conn.:
Greenwood Press, 1996.

McEvoy, James. "The Absolute Predestination of Christ in the Theology of
Robert Grosseteste." In *Sapientiae Doctrina: Mélanges de théologie et de
littérature médiévales offerts a Dom Hildebrand Bascour O.S.B.,* 212–30.

Recherches de théologie ancienne et médiévale 1. Leuven: Abbaye du Mont Cesar, 1980.

———. "Grosseteste on the Soul's Care for the Body: A New Text and a New Source for the Idea." In *Aspectus and Affectus: Essays and Editions in Grosseteste and Medieval Intellectual Life in Honor of Richard C. Dales,* edited by Gunar Freibergs, 37–56. New York: AMS Press, 1993.

———. *The Philosophy of Robert Grosseteste.* Oxford: Clarendon Press, 1982.

McGrade, A. S. "Enjoyment at Oxford after Ockham: Philosophy, Psychology and the Love of God." In *From Ockham to Wyclif,* edited by Anne Hudson and Michael Wilkes, 63–88. Oxford: Blackwell, 1987.

———. "Ockham on Enjoyment: Towards an Understanding of Fourteenth-Century Philosophy and Psychology." *Review of Metaphysics* 33 (1981): 706–28.

McGrath, Alister. *"Iustitia Dei" : A History of the Christian Doctrine of Justification.* Cambridge: Cambridge University Press, 1989.

———. *The Intellectual Origins of the European Reformation.* Oxford: Blackwell, 1993.

McKenna, J. W. "Popular Canonization as Political Propaganda: The Cult of Archbishop Scrope." *Speculum* 45 (1970): 608–23.

Middleton, Anne. "The Idea of Public Poetry in the Reign of Richard II." In *Medieval English Poetry,* edited by Stephanie Trigg, 24–46. London: Longman, 1993.

Migne, J.-P., ed. Patrologia Cursus Completus. Series Latina. 221 vols. Paris: Migne, 1844–91.

Milbank, John. *The Word Made Strange: Theology, Language, Culture.* Oxford: Blackwell, 1997.

Milton, John. *Samson Agonistes: A Dramatic Poem.* In *John Milton: Complete Poems and Major Prose,* edited by Merritt Y. Hughes. New York: Odyssey Press, 1957.

Moeller, Berndt. *Imperial Cities and the Reformation: Three Essays.* Translated and edited by H. C. Erik Midelfort and Mark U. Edwards, Jr. Durham, N.C.: Labyrinth Press, 1982.

Morse, Ruth, ed. *St. Erkenwald.* Cambridge: D. S. Brewer, 1975.

Muscatine, Charles. *Poetry and Crisis in the Age of Chaucer.* Notre Dame: University of Notre Dame Press, 1972.

Neuse, Richard. *Chaucer's Dante: Allegory and Epic Theatre in the* Canterbury Tales. Berkeley: University of California Press, 1991.

Newhauser, Richard. "Sources II: Scriptural and Devotional Sources." In *A Companion to the* Gawain-*Poet,* edited by Derek Brewer and Jonathan Gibson, 257–75. Cambridge: D. S. Brewer, 1997.

Nicholas, David. *The Later Medieval City: 1300–1500*. New York: Longman, 1997.

Nicholls, Jonathan. *The Matter of Courtesy: Medieval Courtesy Books and the Gawain-Poet*. Woodbridge, Suffolk: D. S. Brewer, 1985.

Nussbaum, Martha. "Beyond Obsession and Disgust: Lucretius' Genealogy of Love." *Apeiron* 22 (1989): 1–59.

Oakeshott, Michael. "The Voice of Poetry in the Conversation of Mankind." In *Rationalism in Politics and Other Essays*. New York: Basic Books, 1962.

Oakley, Francis. *The Western Church in the Later Middle Ages*. Ithaca: Cornell University Press, 1979.

Oberman, Heiko. *The Harvest of Medieval Theology: Gabriel Biel and Late Medieval Nominalism*. Grand Rapids, Mich.: Eerdmans, 1967.

———. "The Shape of Late Medieval Thought: The Birthpangs of the Modern Era." In *The Pursuit of Holiness in Later Medieval and Renaissance Religion,* edited by Charles Trinkaus and Heiko Oberman, 3–25. Leiden: E. J. Brill, 1974.

———. "Some Notes on the Theology of Nominalism with Attention to Its Relation to the Renaissance." *Harvard Theological Review* 53 (1960): 47–76.

Olson, Paul. *The* Canterbury Tales *and the Good Society*. Princeton: Princeton University Press, 1986.

———. "*The Reeve's Tale:* Chaucer's *Measure for Measure*." *Studies in Philology* 59 (1962): 1–17.

"Our Daily Work: A Mirror of Discipline." In *The Law of Love: English Spirituality in the Age of Wyclif,* edited by David Lyle Jeffrey, 236–64. Grand Rapids, Mich.: Eerdmans, 1988.

Owen, Charles A. *Pilgrimage and Storytelling in the* Canterbury Tales: *The Dialectic of "Ernest" and "Game."* Norman: University of Oklahoma Press, 1977.

Ozment, Steven. *The Age of Reform 1250–1550: An Intellectual and Religious History of Late Medieval and Reformation Europe*. New Haven: Yale University Press, 1980.

———. *Protestants: The Birth of a Revolution*. New York: Doubleday, 1993.

———. *The Reformation in the Cities: The Appeal of Protestantism to Sixteenth-Century Germany and Switzerland*. New Haven: Yale University Press, 1975.

Pagels, Elaine. *Adam, Eve, and the Serpent*. New York: Random House, 1988.

Panofsky, Erwin. *Gothic Architecture and Scholasticism*. New York: New American Library, 1957.

Patience. See under John A. Burrow and Thorlac Turville-Petre, eds.

Patterson, Lee. *Chaucer and the Subject of History*. Madison: University of Wisconsin Press, 1991.

———. "Court Politics and the Invention of Literature: The Case of Sir John Clanvowe." In *Culture and History 1350–1600: Essays of English Communities, Identities, and Writing,* edited by David Aers, 7–41. Detroit: Wayne State University Press, 1992.

———. "'No man his reson herde': Peasant Consciousness, Chaucer's Miller, and the Structure of the *Canterbury Tales*." *South Atlantic Quarterly* 86 (1987): 457–95.

———. "The *Parson's Tale* and the Quitting of the *Canterbury Tales*." *Traditio* 34 (1978): 331–80.

———. "Perpetual Motion: Alchemy and the Technology of the Self." *Studies in the Age of Chaucer* 15 (1993): 25–57.

———. "'What man artow?': Authorial Self-Definition in the *Tale of Sir Thopas* and the *Tale of Melibee*." *Studies in the Age of Chaucer* 11 (1989): 117–76.

Payne, Robert O. "Chaucer and the Art of Rhetoric." In *Companion to Chaucer Studies,* edited by Beryl Rowland, 42–64. Rev. ed. New York: Oxford University Press, 1979.

Peck, Russell. "The Ideas of 'Entente' and Translation in Chaucer's *Second Nun's Tale*." *Annuale mediaevale* 8 (1967): 17–37.

Pelikan, Jaroslav. *The Growth of Medieval Theology*. Chicago: University of Chicago Press, 1978.

Perdrizet, Paul. "De la véronique et de Seinte Véronique." *Seminarium Kondakovianum* 5 (1932): 1–15.

Peterson, Clifford, ed. *Saint Erkenwald*. Philadelphia: University of Pennsylvania Press, 1977.

Petroff, Elizabeth. "Landscape in *Pearl:* The Transformation of Nature." *Chaucer Review* 16 (1981): 181–93.

Piehler, Paul. *The Visionary Landscape: A Study in Medieval Allegory*. London: Edward Arnold, 1971.

Pieper, Josef. *Guide to Thomas Aquinas*. Translated by Richard and Clara Winston. New York: New American Library, 1964.

Potkay, Monica Brzezenski. "*Cleanness*'s Fecund and Barren Speech Acts." *Studies in the Age of Chaucer* 17 (1995): 99–110.

Price, B. B. *Medieval Thought: An Introduction*. Cambridge: Blackwell, 1992.

Prior, Sandra Pierson. *The* Pearl-*Poet Revisited*. New York: Twayne Publishers, 1994.

Putter, Ad. *An Introduction to the* Gawain-*Poet*. London: Longman, 1996.

Quillet, Jeanne. "Community, Counsel, and Representation." In *The Cambridge History of Medieval Political Thought c. 350–c. 1450,* edited by J. H. Burns, 520–72. Cambridge: Cambridge University Press, 1988.

Rahner, Karl. *Foundations of Christian Faith: An Introduction to the Idea of Christianity.* Translated by William V. Dych. New York: Seabury Press, 1978.

Raw, Barbara. "Piers and the Image of God in Man." In *Piers Plowman: Critical Approaches,* edited by S. S. Hussey, 143–79. London: Methuen, 1969.

Reames, Sherry. "The Cecilia Legend as Chaucer Inherited It and Retold It: The Disappearance of an Augustinian Ideal." *Speculum* 55 (1980): 38–57.

Reiss, Edmund. "The Pilgrimage Narrative and the *Canterbury Tales.*" *Studies in Philology* 67 (1970): 295–305.

Rex, Richard. *"The Sins of Madame Eglentyne" and Other Essays on Chaucer.* Newark: University of Delaware Press, 1995.

Reynolds, Susan. *Fiefs and Vassals: The Medieval Evidence Reinterpreted.* Oxford: Oxford University Press, 1994.

Rhodes, Jim. "Motivation in Chaucer's *Pardoner's Tale:* Winner Take Nothing." *Chaucer Review* 17 (1982): 40–61.

———. "The Pardoner's *Vernycle* and His *Vera Icon.*" *Modern Language Studies* 12 (1982): 34–40.

Ricoeur, Paul. "Interpretative Narrative." In *The Book and the Text,* translated by David Pellauer, edited by Regina Schwartz, 23–57. London: Blackwell, 1990.

———. "Mimesis and Representation." Translated by David Pellauer. In *A Ricoeur Reader: Reflection and Imagination,* edited by Mario J. Valdés, 137–55. Toronto: University of Toronto Press, 1991.

———. "Poetry and Possibility." In *A Ricoeur Reader: Reflection and Imagination,* edited by Mario J. Valdés, 448–62. Toronto: University of Toronto Press, 1991.

———. *The Symbolism of Evil.* Translated by Emerson Buchanan. Boston: Beacon Press, 1969.

Riesenberg, Peter. *Citizenship in the Western Tradition.* Chapel Hill: University of North Carolina Press, 1992.

Rist, John M. *Augustine: Ancient Thought Baptized.* Cambridge: Cambridge University Press, 1994.

Robertson, D. W., Jr. *Chaucer's London.* New York: John Wiley, 1968.

———. *A Preface to Chaucer: Studies in Medieval Perspectives.* Princeton: Princeton University Press, 1962.

———. "Who Were 'the People'?" In *The Popular Literature of Medieval England,* edited by Thomas Heffernan, 3–29. Knoxville: University of Tennessee Press, 1985.

Rorty, Richard. *Contingency, Irony, Solidarity.* Cambridge: Cambridge University Press, 1989.

Rosser, Gervase, and Richard Holt, eds. *The English Medieval Town: A Reader in English Urban History.* New York: Longman, 1990.

Rowley, George. *Ambrogio Lorenzetti.* Princeton: Princeton University Press, 1958.

Rubenstein, Nicolai. "Political Ideas in Sienese Art: The Frescoes of Ambrogio Lorenzetti and Taddeo di Bartolo in the Palazzo Pubblico." *Journal of the Warburg and Courtauld Institutes* 21 (1958): 179–207.

Rubin, Miri. *Charity and Community in Medieval Cambridge.* Cambridge: Cambridge University Press, 1987.

———. *Corpus Christi: The Eucharist in Late Medieval Culture.* Cambridge: Cambridge University Press, 1991.

Rushdie, Salman. "1,000 Days 'Trapped inside a Metaphor.'" *New York Times,* 12 December 1991, B8, col. 5. Excerpts from a speech delivered at Columbia University, 11 December 1991.

Ryan, John J. *The Nature, Structure, and Function of the Church in William of Ockham.* Missoula, Mont.: Scholars Press, 1979.

Saint Erkenwald. See Clifford Peterson, ed.

Scanlon, Larry. *Narrative, Authority, and Power: The Medieval Exemplum and the Chaucerian Tradition.* Cambridge: Cambridge University Press, 1994.

Schiller, Gertrude. *Iconography of Christian Art.* Translated by Janet Seligman. 3 vols. Greenwich, Conn.: New York Graphic Society, Ltd., 1972.

Schleusner, Jay. "History and Action in *Patience.*" *Proceedings of the Modern Language Association* 86 (1971): 959–65.

Schnapp, Jeffrey. *The Transfiguration of History at the Center of Dante's Paradise.* Princeton: Princeton University Press, 1986.

Schneiderman, Stuart. *Jacques Lacan: The Death of an Intellectual Hero.* Cambridge: Harvard University Press, 1983.

Schwartz, Regina. *The Curse of Cain: The Violent Legacy of Monotheism.* Chicago: University of Chicago Press, 1997.

Shoaf, R. A. "God's 'malyse' Metaphor and Conversion in *Patience.*" *Journal of Medieval and Renaissance Studies* 11 (1982): 261–79.

———. "'Noon Englissh Digne': Dante in Late Medieval England." In *Dante Now: Current Trends in Dante Studies,* edited by Theodore J. Cachey, Jr., 189–203. William and Katherine Devers Series in Dante Studies 1. Notre Dame: University of Notre Dame Press, 1995.

———. "*Purgatorio* and *Pearl:* Transgression and Transcendence." *Texas Studies in Literature and Language* 32 (1990): 152–68.

Simpson, James. Piers Plowman: *An Introduction to the B-Text.* New York and London: Longman, 1990.

———. *Sciences and the Self in Medieval Poetry: Alan of Lille's* Anticlaudianus *and John Gower's* Confessio amantis. Cambridge: Cambridge University Press, 1995.

Southern, R. W. *Medieval Humanism and Other Studies.* Oxford: Blackwell, 1970.

———. *Robert Grosseteste: The Growth of an English Mind in Medieval Europe.* Oxford: Clarendon Press, 1988.

———. *Scholastic Humanism and the Unification of Europe.* Vol. 1. Oxford: Blackwell, 1995.

Spearing, A. C. *The* Gawain-*Poet: A Critical Study.* Cambridge: Cambridge University Press, 1970.

———. *Readings in Medieval Poetry.* Cambridge: Cambridge University Press, 1987.

———. "The Subtext of *Patience:* God as Mother and the Whale's Belly." *Journal of Medieval and Early Modern Studies* 29 (1999): 293–323.

Spearing, A. C., and J. E. Spearing, eds. *The Reeve's Prologue and Tale with the Cook's Prologue and the Fragment of His Tale.* Cambridge: Cambridge University Press, 1979.

Stanbury, Sarah. *Seeing the* Gawain-*Poet: Description and the Art of Perception.* Philadelphia: University of Pennsylvania Press, 1991.

Steinberg, Leo. *The Sexuality of Christ in Renaissance Art and in Modern Oblivion.* New York: Pantheon, 1984.

Sternberg, Meir. *The Poetics of Biblical Narrative: Ideological Literature and the Drama of Reading.* Bloomington: Indiana University Press, 1987.

Stock, Brian. *Listening for the Text: On the Uses of the Past.* Philadelphia: University of Pennsylvania Press, 1996.

Stock, Lorraine Kochanske. "The 'Poynt' of *Patience.*" In *Form and Matter: New Critical Perspectives on the* Pearl-*Poet,* edited by Robert J. Blanch, Miriam Youngerman Miller, and Julian N. Wasserman, 163–75. Troy, N.Y.: Whitson Publishing, 1991.

Stokes, Myra. "'Suffering' in *Patience.*" *Chaucer Review* 18 (1984): 354–63.

Struever, Nancy. *The Language of History in the Renaissance: Rhetoric and Historical Consciousness in Florentine Humanism.* Princeton: Princeton University Press, 1970.

Swanson, R. N. *Catholic England: Faith, Religion and Observance before the Reformation.* Manchester: Manchester University Press, 1993.

———. *Church and Society in Late Medieval England.* London: Blackwell, 1993.

———. *Religion and Devotion in Europe, c. 1215–c. 1515.* Cambridge: Cambridge University Press, 1995.

Swinburne, Richard. "Could God Become Man?" In *The Philosophy in Christianity*, edited by Godfrey Vesey, 53–70. Cambridge: Cambridge University Press, 1989.

Tentler, Thomas. *Sin and Confession on the Eve of the Reformation.* Princeton: Princeton University Press, 1977.

Tertullian. *Treatise on the Resurrection.* Edited with an introduction, translation, and commentary by Ernest Evans. London: SPCK, 1960.

Thomas, Brook. *The New Historicism and Other Old-Fashioned Topics.* Princeton: Princeton University Press, 1991.

Thrupp, Sylvia L. "The City as the Idea of Social Order." In *Society and History: Essays by Sylvia L. Thrupp,* edited by Raymond Grew and Nicholas Stenech, 89–100. Ann Arbor: University of Michigan Press, 1977.

Tischendorf, Christine. *Evangelica Apochrypha.* Leipzig: Avenarius et Mendelssohn, 1853.

Traver, Hope. "The Four Daughters of God: A Study of the Versions of the Allegory with Special Reference to Those in Latin, French, and English." Ph.D. diss., Bryn Mawr, 1907.

Travis, Peter. "Deconstructing Chaucer's Retraction." *Exemplaria* 3 (1991): 135–58.

———. "The Semiotics of Christ's Body in the English Cycles." In *Approaches to Teaching Medieval English Drama,* edited by Richard Emmerson, 67–78. New York: MLA Publications, 1990.

———. "The Social Body of the Dramatic Christ in Medieval England." *Acta* 13 (1985): 17–36.

Trinkaus, Charles. "The Religious Thought of the Italian Humanists, and the Reformers: Anticipation or Autonomy." In *The Pursuit of Holiness in Later Medieval and Renaissance Religion,* edited by Charles Trinkaus and Heiko Oberman, 339–66. Leiden: E. J. Brill, 1974.

Turville-Petre, Thorlac. *England the Nation: Language, Literature, and National Identity, 1290–1340.* Oxford: Clarendon Press, 1996.

Ullmann, Walter. *The Individual and Society in the Middle Ages.* Baltimore: Johns Hopkins University Press, 1966.

———. *The Medieval Foundations of Renaissance Humanism.* Ithaca: Cornell University Press, 1977.

———. *Principles of Government and Politics in the Middle Ages.* London: Methuen, 1974.

Unger, D. J., O.F.M.Cap. "Robert Grosseteste, Bishop of Lincoln (1235–1253), on the Reasons for the Incarnation." *Franciscan Studies* 16 (1956): 1–36.

Vantuono, William., ed. *The* Pearl *Poems: An Omnibus Edition.* 2 vols. New York: Garland Publishing, 1984.

Vauchez, André. *The Laity in the Middle Ages: Religious Beliefs and Devotional Practices.* Translated by Margery Schneider. Edited by Daniel Bornstein. Notre Dame: University of Notre Dame Press, 1993.

Vitto, Cindy L. *The Virtuous Pagan in Middle English Literature.* Transactions of the American Philosophical Society 79:5. Philadelphia: American Philosophical Society, 1989.

Waldron, Ronald. "Langland's Originality: The Christ-Knight and the Harrowing of Hell." In *Medieval English Religious and Ethical Literature,* edited by Gregory Kratzmann and James Simpson, 66–81. Cambridge: Boydell and Brewer, 1986.

Wallace, David. *Chaucerian Polity: Absolutist Lineages and Associational Forms in England and Italy.* Stanford: Stanford University Press, 1997.

Walsh, Gerald Groveland. "Dante's Philosophy of History." *Catholic Historical Review* 20 (1934): 117–34.

Warner, Marina. *Alone of All Her Sex: The Myth and the Cult of the Virgin Mary.* New York: Alfred Knopf, 1976.

Watson, Nicholas. "Censorship and Cultural Change in Late-Medieval England: Vernacular Theology, the Oxford Translation Debate, and Arundel's Constitutions of 1409." *Speculum* 70 (1995): 822–65.

———. "Conceptions of the Word: The Mother Tongue and the Incarnation of God." In *New Medieval Literatures,* vol. 1, edited by Wendy Scase, Rita Copeland, and David Lawton, 85–124. Oxford: Clarendon Press, 1997.

———. "The *Gawain*-Poet as a Vernacular Theologian." In *A Companion to the* Gawain-*Poet,* edited by Derek Brewer and Jonathan Gibson, 293–313. Cambridge: D. S. Brewer, 1997.

———. "The Politics of Middle English Writing." In *The Idea of the Vernacular: An Anthology of Middle English Literary Theory, 1280–1520,* edited by Jocelyn Wogan-Browne, Nicholas Watson, Andrew Taylor, and Ruth Evans, 331–52. University Park: Pennsylvania State University Press, 1999.

———. *Richard Rolle and the Invention of Authority.* Cambridge: Cambridge University Press, 1991.

———. "Visions of Inclusion: Salvation and Vernacular Theology in Pre-Reformation England." *Journal of Medieval and Early Modern Studies* 27 (1997): 145–87.

Weatherby, H. L. "Dame Nature and the Nymph." *English Literary Renaissance* 26 (1996): 243–58.

313

Weisheipl, James, O.P. "Aristotle's Concept of Nature: Avicenna and Aquinas." In *Approaches to Nature in the Middle Ages,* edited by Lawrence Roberts, 137–60. Binghamton: MRTS, 1982.

Wetherbee, Winthrop. *Geoffrey Chaucer: The* Canterbury Tales. Cambridge: Cambridge University Press, 1989.

Whatley, E. Gordon. "Heathens and Saints: *St. Erkenwald* in Its Legendary Context." *Speculum* 61 (1986): 330–63.

———. "The Uses of Hagiography: The Legend of Pope Gregory and the Emperor Trajan in the Middle Ages." *Viator* 15 (1984): 25–63.

Whatley, E. Gordon, ed. and trans. *The Saint of London: The Life and Miracles of St. Erkenwald.* Binghamton: MRTS, 1989.

"The White Man Will Never Be Alone." In *Literature of the American Indian.* Edited by Thomas Sanders and Walter W. Peck. Beverly Hills, Ca.: Glencoe Press, 1973.

Williams, David. *The* Canterbury Tales: *A Literary Pilgrimage.* Boston: Twayne, 1987.

———. "The Point of *Patience.*" *Modern Philology* 68 (1970): 127–36.

Wogan-Browne, Jocelyn, Nicholas Watson, Andrew Taylor, and Ruth Evans, eds. *The Idea of the Vernacular: An Anthology of Middle English Literary Theory, 1280–1520.* University Park: Pennsylvania State University Press, 1999.

Wolin, Richard. *Walter Benjamin: An Aesthetic of Redemption.* New York: Columbia University Press, 1982.

Wolter, Allen. "John Duns Scotus on the Primacy and Personality of Christ." In *Franciscan Christology: Selected Texts, Translations, and Introductory Essays,* edited by Daniel McElrath, 139–82. St. Bonaventure, N.Y.: Franciscan Institute, 1980.

Wood, Charles. "The Doctor's Dilemma: Sin, Salvation, and the Menstrual Cycle in Medieval Thought." *Speculum* 56 (1981): 710–27.

Workman, Herbert. *John Wyclif: A Study of the English Medieval Church.* 2 vols. Hamden, Conn.: Archon Books, 1966.

Zander, Léon. "Le pèlerinage." *Irenikon,* issue *L'Église et les églises* (1955): 469–86.

Žižek, Slavoj. *The Sublime Object of Ideology.* London: Verso, 1989.

Zum Brunn, Emilie, and Georgette Epiney-Burgard. *Women Mystics in Medieval Europe.* Translated by Sheila Hughes. New York: Paragon House, 1989.

Zumthor, Paul. *Speaking of the Middle Ages.* Translated by Sarah White. Lincoln: University of Nebraska Press, 1986.

Index

315

Index